T0327316

GOODBYE GLOBALIZATION

'The idea of mutual dependency between liberal democracies and authoritarian states brought money to some, but war and misery to many. Elisabeth Braw brilliantly analyses the causes behind the current global turmoil. Unfortunately more are set to come due to these misjudgements. Read this book and buckle up.'
Artis Pabriks, former Deputy Prime Minister of Latvia

'Elisabeth Braw has carved a well-deserved and eminent role as a global advisor of security and defence. It is no accident that she provides expert analytic and practical testimony to governments and other key decision-makers. I think she has now achieved the impossible – a page-turner account of the rise and decline of globalization, the miscalculations of China's leadership and our own stumbling responses. Who could have imagined this could be made so readable and so timely.'
The Rt Hon Lord David Triesman, former UK Foreign Office Minister

'An enthralling and in-depth analysis of the rise and collapse of globalization. A text necessary to understand the reasons and opportunisms that have led to the dramatic geopolitical tensions we are experiencing today.'
Deborah Bergamini, journalist and Member of the Italian Parliament

'A thought-provoking analysis that helps us to understand the emergence and failure of globalization through the lens of individual biographies. Definitely a must-read.'
Gabriele Woidelko, Head of the History Forum, Körber-Stiftung

GOODBYE GLOBALIZATION

THE RETURN OF A DIVIDED WORLD

ELISABETH BRAW

YALE UNIVERSITY PRESS
NEW HAVEN AND LONDON

For information about this and other Yale University Press publications, please contact:
U.S. Office: sales.press@yale.edu yalebooks.com
Europe Office: sales@yaleup.co.uk yalebooks.co.uk

Set in Adobe Garamond Pro by IDSUK (DataConnection) Ltd
Printed in Great Britain by TJ Books Limited, Padstow, Cornwall

Library of Congress Control Number: 2023949837

ISBN 978-0-300-27227-7

A catalogue record for this book is available from the British Library.

10 9 8 7 6 5 4 3 2 1

For Karin and Christian Braw

The glove has been thrown from the highest position.

Anatoly Chernyaev[1]

CONTENTS

ILLUSTRATIONS

INTRODUCTION

On 27 September 2022, Solveig Artsman, a pensioner on the Swedish island of Gotland, woke up to terrible news. Nord Stream 1 and Nord Stream 2, the two pipelines built to bring Russian natural gas to Germany, had suddenly begun leaking in three places. Because both pipelines were filled with gas, large volumes of methane – a greenhouse gas far more harmful than carbon dioxide – were spreading into the sea and the atmosphere. A few hours later, Swedish authorities announced that a fourth leak had been detected.

'It made me want to cry, seeing this happen to our beautiful Baltic Sea,' Artsman told me a few days later. 'I thought about the fish that would be harmed by the leaks, and I thought about the fact that gas rises and how the leaks would damage the atmosphere. I thought about all the coastguard employees and other experts having to put themselves at risk to investigate the situation.' A short while later, Sweden, Denmark, the European Commission and the US government announced the leaks were the result of sabotage. Whoever the culprit, the sabotage meant the dramatic end of the two pipelines, conceived at the height of globalization to supply Germany and other European countries with natural gas from Russia.

Since retiring from her job as a government administrator a few years ago, Artsman has been pursuing her interest in photography. But she wasn't just any citizen waking up to the terrible news. 'I took out all the documents I've kept regarding Nord Stream,' she told me. 'Things turning out this way – well, that's what so many told me was impossible.' Artsman was one of only a few people in Sweden who had objected to the construction of Nord Stream 1, the first of the two pipelines to be built. That was in mid-2007, and Artsman was a member of Gotland's municipal council for the centre-right Moderate Party. At that time, the Moderates also led Sweden's centre-right government coalition, a staunchly pro-business group of ministers who firmly believed in globalization. Then again, most people, regardless of ideology, seemed to believe in the virtue of closer commercial links between countries. And all over the world, trade was booming.

One day, Artsman was summoned to an unexpected meeting involving her party's municipal politicians, regarding a potential contract with Nord Stream. The company, majority-owned by Russia's state-owned energy giant Gazprom, was planning a new pipeline that would transport gas from Russia to Germany through the Baltic Sea. And Gotland, located in the middle of the Baltic Sea, was crucial to the construction.

The proposed project would give Nord Stream sole access to the island's Slite harbour for the duration of Nord Stream 1's construction needs. In Stockholm, the government had already indicated that it was content for the project to go ahead. And what was not to like? It was a commercial project involving companies from several different countries that would build crucial energy infrastructure – and bring revenue to Gotland in the process. But the more research Artsman did, the more her reservations grew. She worried about harm to the seabed. She thought about unexploded ordnance from two world wars that might injure the construction crews. And she wasn't willing to bet on Russia. 'It doesn't matter how many million krona they're willing to "give" us. I'd never sell Gotland out in this way. Considering Nord Stream's ownership, with Russian interests, it would jeopardize the island's security,'[1] she told the local newspaper.

Now, in September 2022, with Nord Stream 1 and Nord Stream 2 haemorrhaging gas into the Baltic Sea and the atmosphere, with the world's attention on the waters surrounding Gotland and with public opinion concluding that Western energy infrastructure wasn't safe from attacks, Artsman felt herself reliving those strange events. After the initial meeting with her party colleagues in 2007, 'they gave me a couple of weeks to do my research, and I began looking into the project. And the more I read, the more I doubted that this was a good idea,' she told me.

When the municipal council voted to approve the Nord Stream project in March 2008, only Artsman and a scattering of other members objected, while three-quarters voted in favour. Artsman logged an official reservation, noting that 'the pipeline project brings risk to the security of Sweden. It is every citizen's duty to defend the security of our country.'[2] Her public opposition came at great personal cost. 'After the Nord Stream decision, my spare time was essentially consumed by having to defend myself,' she told me. 'And other council members crossed the street when they saw me.'

Now the pipelines were unusable and the optimistic thinking behind their creation discredited as misplaced hope in globalization. I asked Artsman whether the explosions felt like a vindication. 'No,' she said. 'But I've thought to myself, "This Nord Stream project, it was part of Russia's power plan all along." I just didn't manage to convince anyone of it.'

All decisions involve people: the people who make the decisions and the people affected by them. Virtually no decision carried out over the past three and a half decades, though, has influenced as many people's lives as globalization. But globalization was far more than a decision: it was an effort by all manner of politicians and business leaders to create an interconnected world that would create a better life for (almost) everyone. Better yet, such an interconnected world would dramatically reduce the risk of war. A country whose prosperity depends on well-functioning relations with other countries will have no interest in harming those relations, the thinking went. Even to its detractors, globalization felt unstoppable. Indeed, political leaders and business-people didn't create globalization as a united effort, let alone to spite ordinary citizens: for often very different reasons, they simply contributed to the blend that was to become known as globalization. And they did so not because they wanted to impose an idea known as globalization on the world, but because suddenly opportunities arose that were so attractive that not seizing them would have been foolish.

In the late eighties and early nineties, the Western countries that had been perfecting market economies thus went about exporting them to closed countries all over the world that had begun opening themselves up. It was an exhilarating time, with limitless opportunities for companies, cheaper products for consumers and better relations between countries. Western policymakers even hoped that Western-style free markets would bring Western-style liberal democracy to the many countries now embracing capitalism. This revolution of combined hope and commerce touched almost every part of society: ordinary citizens could buy consumer products at much lower prices, while workers found themselves part of global supply chains or had to find new jobs as their employers offshored. A whole generation has grown up knowing no world other than this globalized one. The cheerful 2008 Beijing Olympics, conducted under the motto 'One World, One Dream', perfectly symbolized this harmonious state of global affairs. Countries seemed to get along, and if there was any ill will, it was towards the bankers who'd caused the financial crisis then ripping through the world.

Yet in 2023 Russia is fighting a war in Ukraine, the United States and China are squabbling over the very nature of their coexistence, and there's fear of war involving China. Two new blocs are emerging, and unlike the Cold War's two blocs, they're based less on military allegiance than on commercial fealty. Scores of Western companies, for their part, are swiftly trying to withdraw, at least partially, from the new front line. Even at the beginning of this decade, decision-makers were holding out hope that globalization would recover after it, too, was laid low by Covid-19. Instead, things got worse.

This is the story of globalization's rise since the late eighties, its peak and accelerating demise – and why the demise may eventually bring about a better world. Globalization seemed destined to not just increase global prosperity but also to minimize cracks and frictions. But instead of fading away, the cracks grew: citizens remained unhappy (despite access to cheaper goods), unfair business competition prevailed, key joiners Russia and China became more authoritarian and aggressive rather than more democratic and peaceful. And on top of it all, climate change accelerated. Not even in tackling this existential, global task did the globalized world succeed. Now globalization is retreating. The slow-motion separation will lead to turbulence in the short term, but it will also give countries – Western and non-Western alike – the opportunity to devise a better way of organizing our coexistence on this planet. And it will give Generation Z a couple of decades to come up with a better plan, too. The fracturing globalization is an opportunity to fix the things that were forgotten or neglected last time.

Because globalization involves people from all walks of life, this is the story seen through the lives of some of those who helped shape globalization – and some of those whose lives have been affected by it. We follow Michael Treschow, whose international business career began in the sixties and rose along with the globalized economy, which he eventually surveyed as the powerful chairman, first of Ericsson, then of Unilever. We follow Gintarė Skaistė, who experienced the command economy as a young child in Soviet Lithuania and, as Lithuania's current minister of finance, has had to battle China's commercial pressure on her country. We follow Mo Ibrahim, who brought globalization's transforming technological innovation – the mobile phone – to large parts of Africa. We follow Russian economist Sergei Guriev, footwear executive Antony Perillo and John Spellar, a British member of parliament representing a constituency that has been struggling since losing many of its factories. We follow Mike Turner, the chair of the House Permanent Select Committee on Intelligence (and a former mayor in America's manufacturing heartland) and Michael Cole-Fontayn, an executive who helped bring investment banking to China. We follow Maria Ohisalo, Finland's Green Party leader and environment minister. We follow other politicians, business leaders and ordinary citizens, too – and we meet members of Generation Z, which has only known this globalized world. We follow the battle over Huawei. We experience the birth and sudden death of Nord Stream through the eyes of local residents. Yes, large volumes of goods still go back and forth between China and the West, but the belief in globalization is evaporating – and globalization is as much about faith as it is about money.

There will be many future books about globalization's demise written from a Chinese or Russian perspective. I write from a Western perspective. Western politicians and business leaders were globalization's foremost champions as they set out to bring their free-market system to newly opening countries. That makes following the experiences of some of the people on the front lines of globalization an exhilarating and instructive ride. I'm enormously grateful to the many people who have generously shared their time, recollections and insights with me. I'm also very grateful to my editor, Joanna Godfrey, and to the people who read early versions of different chapters: Chris Brannigan, David Manero, Ilkka Salonen and Derek Scissors, and most especially Gerhard Wheeler, Sebastian Braw-Smith and Timothy Dowse. Any errors are, of course, mine. Very special thanks, too, to Daniela Braw-Smith and Jeffrey Smith for their patience and unfailingly cheerful support.

1
THE BIG BANG

When Gintarė Skaistė was growing up in the eighties, her world was grey. 'People like me obviously didn't know much about the world outside our town or our country,' she told me. 'But you could tell when someone had contacts in the outside world. We had relatives in the US and they'd bring gifts for our family. It was always very colourful toys and clothes. You'd never see such colourful clothes in the Soviet Union.' The outside world was everything outside the Soviet Union, where Skaistė was born in 1981. Her parents insisted that the country the family lived in was called Lithuania, but officially it was the Lithuanian Soviet Socialist Republic, one of the Soviet Union's fifteen member republics. Skaistė and her parents had visited Lithuania's neighbours, the Estonian Soviet Socialist Republic and the Latvian Soviet Socialist Republic, and Skaistė's family had even been to Moscow once. Apart from that, most of the world was closed to her. But thanks to the colourful toys and clothes American relatives brought, young Gintarė knew the world was different outside the Soviet Union.

Across the border, in the Latvian SSR, another girl was growing up in the same ocean of grey. 'One of my earliest memories is going to a grocery store with my parents and that most of the shelves were empty,' Ivita Burmistre told me. 'Every day at a certain time products were delivered to the store, and you had to stand in a very long queue to try to get them. Sometimes you were successful, but not always.' Young Ivita's grandmother, who lived with the family, kept pointing out that

Latvia was once the world's leading exporter of butter and bacon, but such stories seemed to be from a different world.

Ivita couldn't know that Soviet leader Mikhail Gorbachev was trying to reform his enormous country's economy. In 1987, the Politburo and the Supreme Soviet passed a new law that allowed international companies to do business in the Soviet Union. Few arrived, which was hardly surprising, since Soviet state enterprises had to be majority-owners and the Soviet bureaucracy seemed insurmountable. But by the summer of 1988, the first private banks were appearing, and by early 1989 the country was home to 150 private banks.[1] A few months later, Gorbachev even invited the chairman of the New York Stock Exchange to come to the Soviet Union with a delegation of bankers interested in teaching the Soviets how to establish capital markets.[2]

Not long afterwards, Gorbachev made another attempt to attract Western firms, this time without the Soviet majority-ownership requirement, and now companies responded in force. On 31 January 1990, McDonald's triumphantly opened its first restaurant in the Soviet Union. By the beginning of 1991, a staggering 400 foreign-owned companies had registered themselves in the small Estonian Soviet Socialist Republic and many others in the Latvian and Lithuanian Soviet Socialist Republics.

In Moscow, a nineteen-year-old mathematics student named Sergei Guriev was plugging away at economic models. After graduating from secondary school in 1988, he'd opted for mathematics, since mathematics students were less at risk of being conscripted for service in Afghanistan.

Guriev needn't have worried about serving in Afghanistan. When the young Sergei reached conscription age, Gorbachev was beginning to withdraw Soviet forces from that disastrous war, and by the beginning of 1989 there were no Soviet troops left in the country. Gorbachev's reform of the Soviet Union, though, was not going according to plan. By the summer of 1990, all three Baltic republics had declared themselves independent. In October 1990, East Germany joined West Germany in the capitalist world. Poland, Czechoslovakia, Hungary and other Warsaw Pact states held democratic elections and began transforming themselves into market economies. By September 1991, the weakened Gorbachev had granted the Baltic states their independence.

Now things began accelerating even faster. By October, more than 1,100 Western companies had, for example, set up operations in Estonia and nearly 200 others were registering in the new republic each month.[3] Michael Treschow, a rising executive with the Swedish mining-equipment maker Atlas Copco, was watching closely. 'There were unlimited countries to expand to,' he said. 'If a country was too isolationist, you didn't need to bother with it because there were so many other ones.' That December, the Soviet Union itself ceased to exist and Gorbachev's position with it. Now Russia and its newly elected president, Boris Yeltsin, represented what was left of the superpower.

Across the Baltic Sea, a young executive had just returned from his first overseas posting. Immediately after graduating from Sweden's Uppsala University in the mid-eighties, Karl-Henrik Sundström had been hired by telecoms giant LM Ericsson. He was swiftly given the chance to work in Australia for a few months, and two years later the firm had dispatched him to Argentina as the chief financial officer at its subsidiary there. 'There were a lot of us young people who made careers very, very fast,' Sundström observed. 'You started as a low-end manager and suddenly you started to rise because we were growing so much. Young people were able to get very good positions very, very fast. I became a director of one of Ericsson's largest practice areas at age twenty-nine. Today you have to wait until your late forties before you get a position like that. But there was huge demand for managers because companies were growing so quickly.'

When Treschow began his career in the sixties, globalized business mostly meant precisely what Atlas Copco had been doing at home and in a few countries like the United States: Western companies importing and exporting between each other, including countries like Japan and Australia located outside the geographical West. In his first job, Treschow had been dispatched for a while to France. Internationally ambitious companies like Atlas Copco sometimes went beyond those easily accessible countries, but that usually meant creating a local version of the home company in each country.

Some Western firms even had contracts with Warsaw Pact states. In the 1920s, revolutionary leaders turned national leaders Vladimir Lenin and Leon Trotsky were so enamoured with Ford that they imported Ford engineers and production techniques. The decade after, Ford produced more than a million Ford AA trucks under contract with the Soviet government.[4] In the late sixties, Renault began making cars in Romania, and soon thereafter Fiat launched production in Poland and the Soviet Union.[5] So excited was Soviet leader Leonid Brezhnev about his country's massive new commercial arrangement with the Italian automotive giant in the 1960s that he arranged for the town housing Fiat's new plant to be massively expanded and renamed in honour of the long-time leader of Italy's Communist Party, Palmiro Togliatti.[6] Some years later, PepsiCo struck a pioneering deal allowing the fizzy drink to be manufactured and sold in the Soviet Union; in return, PepsiCo agreed to sell Stolichnaya and other Soviet alcoholic drinks in the West. Around the same time, PepsiCo's arch-rival Coca-Cola was allowed to launch production and sale in Poland. PepsiCo soon followed.[7]

But these were not traditional business arrangements: they were arrangements between Western companies and Warsaw Pact governments. By the eighties, a few Warsaw Pact countries were also manufacturing goods for export to the West to earn hard currency. East Germany's government-owned Deutrans hauling firm brilliantly captured the cargo market for exports going through the Iron Curtain.[8] Still, the trade between East and West was modest. 'If you manufactured anything in those countries, you sold it there,' Treschow said. 'We were a global company that operated a number of islands, you might say. Every now and then you might be allowed to import some components, but that was it.'

But gas seeped through. In the early seventies, West German chancellor Willy Brandt included Soviet gas in his policy of improving relations with the Soviet bloc; indeed, it was part of West Germany's efforts to create some manner of coexistence with the Soviet Union by trading with it. The Soviets needed pipeline parts while West Germany wanted more gas imports. From 1973, West Germany received Soviet gas even as NATO prepared for war with the Warsaw Pact, and it kept receiving Soviet gas even when the United States placed nuclear weapons on its soil in response to Soviet ones in East Germany.[9] In 1981, the Soviet Union signed an agreement to supply gas to West Germany, France,

Belgium, Austria, Italy and the Netherlands. West German, French, Italian and Dutch companies were given contracts to build the 3,500-mile pipeline. Ronald Reagan was so furious that he authorized the CIA to sabotage the pipeline.[10]

Deng Xiaoping, though, had beaten his comrades in Moscow to a strategic decision: to open his country to not just a little bit of licence production but to a market economy.[11] In 1979, the chairman of the Chinese Communist Party had sent China's first-ever delegation to the World Economic Forum in Davos, and a short time later Davos titans arranged for a group of European CEOs to visit China.[12] Deng had decided that his country needed economic reform, and he proceeded with small but determined steps. Peasants were given some freedom over their crops and harvests, and a while later Western companies were granted opportunities to invest in Chinese firms. For that, they needed to be able to get to the country. Until 1980, the most convenient way of getting to Beijing involved lengthy flights on Iran Air or Pakistan International Airlines with a corresponding stopover in Iran or Pakistan. That year, Lufthansa, British Airways and Air France launched their first direct flights between Beijing and Frankfurt, Berlin, London and Paris, respectively.[13] It was a revolutionary shift for a country that had in the past sealed itself off from capitalism and global markets.

In 1985 Volkswagen began manufacturing in China. Coca-Cola had arrived too, as had IBM and even the French fashion brand Pierre Cardin.[14] Treschow was about to launch his company's first-ever operations there. As was the case with every other company setting itself up in China, Atlas Copco's operations were dictated by the government: 'Our office was in a hotel, and the manufacturing was done by a local licensee or joint-venture partner,' Treschow said. 'We didn't control our operations there, nor did any other Western companies control theirs.' But compared with China's enormous potential for low-cost manufacturing and its massive consumer base, that was a minor headache.

Before China did so in its own way, Japan and South Korea had joined the globalized economy, and they had done so with such phenomenal success that brands from both countries had become household names. That led a Harvard Business School professor to prophesy a global consumer-product era. 'A powerful force drives the world toward a converging commonality, and that force is technology. It has proletarianized communication, transport, and travel. It has made isolated places and impoverished peoples eager for modernity's allurements. Almost everyone everywhere wants all the things they have heard about, seen, or experienced via the new technologies. The result is a new commercial reality – the emergence of global markets for standardized consumer products on a previously unimagined scale of magnitude,' Theodore Levitt – a German Jew whose family had fled to America and settled in the Ohio city of Dayton – wrote. He concluded that 'the globalization of markets is at hand'. And with that, he popularized the term globalization.[15] In the late eighties, consumers in the West loved the fact that all manner of goods were becoming more affordable. And they hadn't even experienced real globalization yet.

A New York real-estate developer named Donald Trump viewed matters very differently. 'Japan and other nations have been taking advantage of the United States,' he complained in open letters addressed 'To The American People', which he published in the *New York Times*, the *Washington Post* and the *Boston Globe* in 1987, adding that 'the Japanese, unimpeded by the huge costs of defending themselves (as long as the United States will do it for free), have built a strong and vibrant economy with unprecedented surpluses'.[16] But many of Trump's fellow executives, men (and some women) involved in the manufacturing of goods and the generation of new wealth, were now occupying themselves not with competition from Japan but opportunities in China. 'From the late eighties, things went very quickly in China,' Treschow said. 'That's when Deng Xiaoping's opening up of the country really took off.' It did so until June 1989, when the authorities cracked down on student protests in Tiananmen Square with extreme brutality. The United States imposed an unofficial moratorium on investment in China, and other Western governments, too, ensured their companies kept their distance.

The United States, Canada and Western European countries were continuing to let Japanese and South Korean consumer products into their countries, even though this eliminated jobs at home, because they believed in specialization and efficiency. And the more Europe, North America and their Far East friends-cum-rivals demonstrated the benefits of free trade and efficiencies, the more other countries realized that they ought to try too. By the late eighties, many countries that had tried autarky – economic self-sufficiency – had concluded that it was never going to work and that they needed to attract foreign businesses. Mineral-rich African countries led by Ghana opened up their mining to foreign companies,[17] and, eventually, by reducing their stakes or selling them altogether, Brazil, Argentina and India became potential locations for serious manufacturing and sales.

That's why Sundström, who had envisaged a career in Western Europe and North America, had been made chief financial officer of Ericsson's subsidiary in Argentina. After emerging from a near-decade under military rule, the country had returned to democracy and was trying to reform its economy. That made it one of the countries outside Europe, North America, Japan, South Korea, Australia and New Zealand to which Western companies were able to expand, albeit in a limited way. 'These were totally separate operations, self-sufficient and with just a few imported components,' Treschow said. 'That way you had a foot in the door in these markets. But these were not completely free markets and such countries also had high tariffs. That meant you had to manufacture as much as possible locally.' That, though, was a whole lot better than not doing business there at all.

By the late eighties, banking was conquering new markets too. After getting a job with the London office of the Bank of New York in the early eighties, Michael Cole-Fontayn had been looking forward to a career that he thought might take him to New York or perhaps Frankfurt. But now, being a British banker was suddenly becoming extremely attractive. In 1986, Prime Minister Margaret Thatcher had introduced banking reforms so radical that they became known as the Big Bang. Only a short while after being hired as an analyst, Cole-Fontayn was promoted to looking after clients in the telecoms and oil and gas sectors. These were fast-paced days.

The Big Bang generated investment from all over the world, which travelled to London's energized financial markets. West German banks, US banks, French banks, even some Japanese banks invested in London. And they sent bankers along to learn. 'In effect, the world capital market, for quite a long period of time, came to London to grow expertise,' Cole-Fontayn said. Large volumes of capital started flowing, not just into London but out of it too. London bankers, now equipped with consummate expertise in unchained financial markets, began their march to new cities, where they would make even more money for their banks by putting capital to work as countries opened themselves up to all manner of foreign companies, foreign capital and foreign expertise.

Three short years after the Big Bang, citizens behind the Iron Curtain delivered a different Big Bang and brought down their communist rulers. Deng not only managed to avoid such a fate but also delivered a smooth handover to his successor, Jiang Zemin. But China's opening economy was accelerating quickly without its communist regime being discarded. 'Among the U.S. companies that have struck deals with China this year are such giants as IBM, Avon, Coca-Cola, KPMG Peat Marwick and Polaroid. Some, lured by China's inexpensive labor costs, look to manufacture goods in that country for export elsewhere. Others see major market potential in China's huge population,' the *Los Angeles Times* reported.[18] The post-Tiananmen rift in China's relations with the West hadn't lasted long. China's governing Communist Party had prevailed, while its long-time mentor and rival, the Communist Party of the Soviet Union, had seen its creation pulverized.

As the eventful eighties handed over the baton to the nimble nineties, the political and geopolitical transformations were converging with another revolution: mobile telecommunications. In the late eighties, a group of Western European countries had agreed on a new mobile communications standard, GSM (Global System for Mobile Communications), which allowed mobile telephones to call any other phone inside these countries. It was a massive step up from the first-generation mobile technology that had existed until then. Ericsson and its Finnish rival Nokia were now reaping the benefits of their years of experimental work on mobile telephony.[19] The United States was setting up a similar standard, and so were Japan and some other countries – but a mobile phone is of little use if it can't communicate with phones that use other standards. 'And with GSM, you got phones down to around $50 to $70 per handset, and then things started to happen,' Sundström said. In 1991, the world's first-ever mobile GSM call was made using Nokia equipment. Mobile telephones were on the cusp of becoming a product for ordinary people.

Mo Ibrahim's expertise was made for this moment. Young Mohamed was born in Anglo-Egyptian Sudan just after World War II. As a young boy, he moved with his family to Egypt, where Mohamed's father found work with a cotton company. But Mohamed's mother didn't want her five sons to work in the cotton industry and pushed them to focus on their studies. Mo earned a degree from Alexandria University's electrical engineering programme, and he kept going, earning a master's degree in the subject from Bradford University in Britain, and then, in 1981, a PhD in mobile communications from the University of Birmingham in the English Midlands. In 1983, he received the best offer an engineer with a PhD in the UK could dream of: an invitation to join the team designing the first cellular network for British Telecom, Britain's mighty telephony.

By the early nineties, Ibrahim was running his own company, designing mobile networks in European countries, in the United States, in Singapore, even in China. 'The great manufacturers, Nokia in Finland, Ericsson in Sweden, AT&T in the US, Siemens in Germany: they all worked along the same lines and there was a great sense of global belonging,' he told me. 'We thought of ourselves as citizens of the world. We worked in Hong Kong the same way we worked in Singapore, the US, the same technology, same groups of people, full cooperation, publishing papers, sharing information. It was a great time.'

And phone calls from mobile devices heralded the arrival of a new lifestyle.

For mobile-phone companies, the timing was impeccable. GSM and other standards had paved the way for mobile telecommunications in wealthy countries, and now, in the early nineties, lots of new countries decided they wanted to join the trend. 'We suddenly realized that the communications market would expand into Central and Eastern Europe, and then it went very fast,' Sundström said. 'One of the first countries out was Hungary, then came Poland, then other countries. So everybody rushed in and started to sell in these markets.'

The companies now rushing in to sell mobile phones and other consumer products had mishaps too. Some were cheated by dishonest business partners; others just couldn't figure out how to do business in these wobbly economies, especially in Russia.[20]

But these were also spectacular times for consumer-product companies. And investment banks. And retail banks. And engineering firms. Even mining companies found new business, despite Russia long having mined its mountains. Treschow was astonished to see the developments around him. 'Countries of all kinds were finally realizing that removing trade barriers is a smart thing to do because trade barriers don't protect your citizens – they force your citizens to pay more for the products they buy,' he told me. 'And it wasn't a process where you thought, "Now the world is about to become global." You just realized, "Now the world is global."' The Atlas Copco subsidiaries he established in the early nineties illustrated the suddenly open doors around the world: Hungary, Ghana, Poland, Slovakia and Thailand.[21]

In Costa Rica's capital, San José, a young law student named Kevin Casas-Zamora shared Treschow's sentiment without having heard of him. In the sixties and seventies, the Central American country of 5 million people had tried to strengthen its economy by becoming more self-reliant. That meant protectionism. The experiment ended badly, with massive debts, currency devaluation, skyrocketing inflation and poverty.[22] A new government, elected in 1986 and led by Oscar Arias, a social democrat, set about reforming his country's bananas-and-coffee-based economy. Despite opposition from within his own party, Arias began opening Costa Rica to trade and even established free-trade zones, designated regions where companies were allowed to operate tax-free as long as their production was solely intended for export.[23]

The change to ordinary citizens' lives was dramatic. 'The availability of goods, the availability of choices, the opportunities to consume goods and services expanded almost overnight,' Casas-Zamora recalled. That availability was a trademark study in what happens when a country fully joins the globalized economy: it gets access to all manner of goods and services at low prices, and simply has to accept that this will affect its own companies. But as Costa Rica had discovered, keeping up protectionist walls was simply unsustainable. Arias tackled intractable problems in other areas too: for his successful efforts to help solve the civil wars in El Salvador, Guatemala and Nicaragua, he was awarded the Nobel Peace Prize.

In the early nineties, Casas-Zamora had decided to continue his studies abroad, and he already knew that this opportunity made him one of globalization's winners. But he did wonder what effect the emerging economic stratification he was observing would eventually have on his traditionally egalitarian country. Many Hong Kongers were even less sure about the trajectory of their unique city. 'The city is gloomy about being handed over to Chinese sovereignty,' the *Harvard Business Review* reported, and continued, 'Already, China's business-people are moving in – into business, trade, and politics – and treading so clumsily that the best of the local population are fleeing, distrustful of Beijing's promises about the autonomous capitalist existence that the colony will supposedly enjoy.'[24] But whatever their fears, Hong Kongers didn't have a voice: Beijing and London had already decided that the British crown colony would be returned to China in 1997.

In the three Baltic republics, meanwhile, not a week went by without a new company announcing its arrival. 'Suddenly you could go to the shop and you'd see things you'd never seen before,' Burmistre told me. Young Ivita and her family had already visited the former East Germany, which was now part of reunited Germany and whose shops looked nothing like the ones she was used to. 'That was the first time I saw that you could have full shelves in the grocery and that people could wear colourful clothes,' she said. 'During Soviet times, if you saw a girl in the street wearing a pink dress, you knew that she had relatives in the West.'

That said, it was a shaky ride. In 1992, Latvia's GDP made a terrifying plunge of nearly one-third.[25] By declaring independence, the country had in effect forfeited its massive, previously guaranteed, exports to Russia.[26] Around the same time, the three Baltic states were crippled by hyperinflation.[27] Despite such misery, and despite the shady dealings some of their compatriots engaged in, Estonians, Latvians and Lithuanians kept supporting their governments' course of rapid transition.[28] 'We knew that our previous economy didn't work,' Burmistre said. 'If you can't buy simple things like soap, or if you have to stand in a long queue to buy bread or sausage, something is not right. Even during those really bad months, I felt that whatever is coming is bound to be better than what we had in the Soviet Union.' At university, she knew she had a shot at being part of Latvia's insertion into the big world outside the Soviet Union.

In China, the governments pushed ahead with market reforms without asking people what they wanted. But Chinese citizens certainly seemed to be enjoying the products now available to them. In 1992, Coca-Cola sold 75 million cases – each case containing twenty-four bottles – in the country; between January and September the following year, it sold 100 million cases.[29]

That year, Deng conducted a tour of Shenzhen, Guangzhou and other southern cities to make the case for his economic reforms. 'The reason some people hesitate to carry out the reform and the open policy and dare not break new ground is, in essence, that they're afraid it would mean introducing too many elements of capitalism and, indeed, taking the capitalist road,' he declared, and continued: 'Are securities and the stock market good or bad? Do they entail any dangers? Are they peculiar to capitalism? Can socialism make use of them? We allow people to reserve their judgement, but we must try these things out.'[30] By now, Chinese officials knew the chairman's mantra: 'It doesn't matter whether a cat is black or white as long as it catches mice.'[31]

Investment banks realized that they were now welcome in a country they'd been coveting. 'Deng created a new form of state capitalism where the state had majority control, but foreigners were allowed to purchase stakes in Chinese enterprises through various special classes of share that conferred conditional rights,' Cole-Fontayn said. 'All of this was taking place whilst China was seeking to control its capital accounts. It was not subject to the faults of free markets. This all meant that China could try to control its internal economy whilst enabling it to open up and trade with the rest of the world.' The Shanghai Stock Exchange – which had been closed after China's communist takeover – was once again operating and had been joined by the Shenzhen Stock Exchange.

For young university graduates and early-career employees, the opening markets and their need for everything from consumer goods to capital meant unfathomable opportunities. After returning from Argentina, Sundström opted to stay with Ericsson because he enjoyed working for the company, but he could have had pretty much any job he wanted. 'Everything was moving so quickly,' he told me. 'It was super-easy to get a job. Companies couldn't find enough people for all the posts they needed to fill as they expanded. If you wanted to work in business, the sky was the limit.'

Countries now turning themselves into market economies needed everything from colourful clothes to retail banks and the rapidly advancing mobile telephony. The World Economic Forum's annual gatherings in the Swiss skiing resort of Davos evolved from high-octane affairs for the political and business elite from wealthy countries to also include the new elites from countries liberalizing their economies. And who could object to an organization that argues, 'Progress happens by bringing together people from all walks of life who have the drive and the influence to make positive change'?[32] There was an enormous portfolio of issues, ranging from investments to environmental protection, that needed to be discussed.

Western commercial links to newly opening markets offered enormous benefits for the Western countries now exporting their market economies and for the ones adopting them too: new consumers, new markets, new opportunities for economies of scale. But the commercial links now presenting themselves brought the promise of something even better: a world without war. The French economist Frédéric Bastiat is thought to have coined the maxim that 'when goods don't cross borders, soldiers will', and on his own war-torn continent he'd been proven right.[33] The European Coal and Steel Community, known during these years as the European Community, now linked former enemies in a commercial embrace that had made them astonishingly prosperous. No country had been a bigger believer in Bastiat's maxim than West Germany, whose identity rested on economic integration with other countries its identity. Now the rapprochement-cum-trade Bonn had been practising with Moscow was there, ready to be expanded not just within the Soviet Union but with lots of different countries. Suddenly there was much talk of *Wandel durch Handel* – change through trade.[34]

In executive suites, people like Treschow became convinced that the time of islands dotting the world was over. Now businesses would be based in one country and have operational hubs in others, and parts would travel seamlessly between different locations until they became finished products that could be sold in other countries still. And each company's own manufacturing would be supported by globe-spanning supply chains. 'There really were unlimited opportunities,' Treschow said. 'There were so many countries at the same time. The balance you had to strike was that the countries where you had operations also had to be countries where you could sell your goods. It was rare to find a country that had perfect manufacturing conditions but no market to speak of.' How to choose among this embarrassment of riches? 'Mostly you started by selling and then you learnt whether the country had a promising basis for production,' Treschow said. 'The idea was that we'd try to connect these countries to our operations in Western Europe and North America and create global systems. In the new countries you needed to find qualified staff and good production ethics. That meant that in the process we had to disqualify some countries because they just didn't have those things, or because we couldn't find structures and people we could trust. You had to do the legwork by travelling to the countries and talking to government officials and local businesspeople, so I spent an enormous amount of time travelling to all these countries. We usually also put sales teams in place early on, so we could ask them.' Treschow's formation of global manufacturing networks yielded enormous efficiencies and pleased old and new clients. So successful had his tenure been that he was now Atlas Copco's CEO.

In some cases, Western companies decided that the best strategy in a new country was to buy a local manufacturer, usually a government-owned enterprise. In March 1991, for example, Germany's Volkswagen acquired Czechoslovakia's state-owned carmaker, Skoda.[35] But many state-owned companies, including East Germany's Trabant and Wartburg, waited in vain for Western suitors. In Germany, the government had set up the Treuhand, an agency tasked with finding commercial buyers for as many companies as possible and liquidating the remaining ones. In their heads, many locals knew that was what needed to be done, but the experience was traumatic for the many workers who were laid off, not to mention for the towns and cities where the largest employer received a death warrant.

Consider the VE Kombinat Kernkraftwerke 'Bruno Leuschner' Greifswald in the small seaside town of Lubmin, some thirty minutes from Greifswald on the Baltic Sea coast. Of East Germany's two nuclear power plants, this one – the KKW Greifswald, as people called it – was the larger. In fact, it was among Europe's largest. When, in the 1960s, the East German government decided to build the plant, it chose Lubmin, where access to the Baltic Sea provided the large volumes of water nuclear reactors need for cooling. The plant was the dominating employer in Lubmin and its surroundings; some 15,000 people worked there, including Jana Burow, a young woman employed in the administration office, and her brother, a reactor technician.[36] 'Then came the Wende [East Germany's collapse] and we were told that everything we had been doing was bad,' she recounted. 'We got new equipment from Siemens with small buttons even though the Russian equipment we had, with large buttons, worked perfectly fine.' Not long after Germany's reunification, KKW Greifswald was shut down and Burow and her colleagues lost their jobs. The authorities had documented numerous safety risks, though Burow and other locals suspected it was because West German energy firms wanted the business.

Aged twenty-three, Burow started a family while considering what to do next. Many other now-unemployed workers, though, left the area to find work in western Germany. Those who remained often found work in tourism, as Burow eventually did. 'It was the only thing we had here,' she explained to me. Others got jobs in the dismantlement of the nuclear plant, which is still under way and will continue for many years to come.

Like other East Germans laid off from unsustainable enterprises, Burow received financial support from the government. Less generously, so did her fellow newly unemployed workers in other former Warsaw Pact countries which didn't have the benefit of having joined a Western twin. But unemployment benefits didn't make up for the pain of workers having lost their jobs and much of their identity. This was the human price countries had to pay to become market economies. Even so, the countries persisted, and soon their economies were on a much better footing, with new jobs to boot. Bastiat's maxim had been proven right once again – and so had the Germans' *Wandel durch Handel*.

Around the same time that Burow was laid off, Michael Cole-Fontayn got married. For their honeymoon, he and his new wife travelled to Hong Kong, from where Cole-Fontayn, still in his early thirties, would look after all of Asia (bar Japan) for his bank. And because Deng had now opened the door to Western banks, Cole-Fontayn's brief included China too. Where should he spend most of his time? Which countries held the most promise in the immediate future and the long term? He had to improvise. 'Of course you had to focus on those markets that were already open or opening and had strong global trade practices, for example Korea and Taiwan but also Singapore and Malaysia and Indonesia and Thailand,' Cole-Fontayn explained to me in the elegant salon of the London members' club many bankers frequent. 'And then of course the two great markets that were beginning to open up: China under Deng Xiaoping, and India.'

Ordinary citizens in newly opening markets were beginning to see not only desirable consumer goods but job opportunities too. As for the ordinary citizens in the countries now exporting capitalism and jobs, they hadn't been given a say. But a rising tide lifts all boats, they were told. They'd get cheaper consumer goods, and surely good jobs would replace the evaporating ones.

2
COMPANIES WITHOUT BORDERS

Nokia began its life in the 1860s as a single paper mill in the town of Nokia some two hours north of Helsinki. It later expanded to manufacturing rubber products and telephone cables, and then it expanded further, making all manner of consumer electronics. Building on its electronics focus, since the 1960s the company had also been developing portable telephones.

Across the border in Sweden, pioneering engineers at Ericsson had spent decades building switches and other infrastructure that could transmit mobile-phone calls. In the United States, Chicago-based Motorola had, like Nokia, been developing phones that needed neither a jack in the wall nor a landline. Mo Ibrahim told me how he got to test one of these revolutionary phones at an experimental stage. 'The Motorola lab director said to me, "Will there be a market for this?"' he recalled. 'And I said, "Let's try!" And I spent a week testing it. When I got back to BT, I told my colleagues, "This phone has enormous potential."' Motorola's next phone, which entered the market in 1984 with a price tag of nearly $9,000, was precisely such a phone.[1] 'That really changed everything, because you were not calling a car or a house or an office,' Ibrahim said. 'You were calling a person!'

In 1986, Nokia's Mobira Cityman made its debut. Like the Motorola 8000X, it came with a hefty price tag and took hours to charge for only one hour's usage.[2] In 1989, Motorola launched the world's first flip phone, and two years later it released the world's first phone for the

GSM system, the second-generation mobile telephony about to replace the rudimentary 1G.[3]

By the early nineties, the pioneers' bet was paying off. Mobile telephony stood to benefit from globalization. Indeed, the technology was made for it. Nokia had the booming world of mobile telephony in its grip thanks to its 1011 handset, which had become the world's first mass-produced mobile phone.[4] The small 1011 – and its growing number of rivals – was a gigantic step forward from the bulky and expensive phones of the eighties. Scientists' years-long efforts to create lithium batteries, which were smaller and lasted longer, had borne fruit. And China was now the place to manufacture not just parts for the phones but most kinds of consumer products. 'China has been attracting increasing amounts of investment money, with foreign investment jumping 76.9 percent in the first 10 months of last year, to $4.96 billion. A further rise is expected this year,' the Associated Press reported in March 1992.[5]

On the first day of 1993, the European Single Market came into force; it made travel for people, goods, services and capitals virtually indistinguishable from movement within a member country.

But Gerard Coyne was seeing a different world. A trade unionist primarily representing manufacturing workers in Britain's Midlands, he had been prepared for the Single Market. He hadn't been prepared, though, for the manufacturing exodus it, and globalization, triggered in this heartland of British manufacturing. 'We began seeing a process of companies closing manufacturing here and moving it to continental Europe and later to China,' he told me. 'In the past, it had been extremely easy to get jobs here, and it was well-paid jobs with good hours. But in the early nineties barely a week went by without a factory closing.' Coyne was astounded to see laid-off workers seemingly just accepting this turn of events. 'They were quite happy to get their redundancy payment because it meant they'd be able to pay down their mortgage,' he recalled. 'And they assumed they'd be able to get jobs in the service sector.' Manufacturing-wise, Coyne mostly heard about the bright future that cheap electronics made abroad would bring.

In Theodore Levitt's hometown of Dayton, Ohio, newly elected mayor Mike Turner was seeing a similar picture. Dayton was once a formidable hub of American manufacturing, bustling with production by companies like the National Cash Register, which in the mid-1960s had 18,000 employees in the city.[6] General Motors had more employees in Dayton than anywhere else outside Michigan.[7] 'In the seventies going into the eighties, Ohio was a manufacturing powerhouse,' Turner recalled. 'We had thousands of thousands of manufacturing jobs and obviously many factories. And because of that, Ohio was a breeding ground for innovation, because all of these manufacturing lines were together and companies thrived off each other's unique operations.' Then came automation, globalization and the exodus of jobs. 'We saw the manufacturing base in Ohio and Michigan, which really operated as one ecosystem, being decimated,' Turner told me. 'That had a big impact on the unskilled workforce and the part of the workforce without college education. A lot of people retired, but you didn't see opportunities coming up for the next generation.' Fortunately Dayton's largest employer – the Wright-Patterson Air Force Base – was going nowhere.[8]

In the Midlands, Gerard Coyne thought he had a trump card to reverse the job exodus: the environment. It was already common knowledge that greenhouse gas emissions were harming the atmosphere, and the new Intergovernmental Panel on Climate Change had reported that the world was on track to double its carbon-dioxide emissions compared to pre-industrial levels.[9] Since lorries, aeroplanes and ships emit a great deal of carbon dioxide, Coyne thought he could convince manufacturers that it was a bad idea to transport components to other countries and then transport the finished product back to Britain. But he was too optimistic. In these heady days of globalization, long-term harm like climate change and dependence on China seemed abstract considerations.

There was, however, some good news in the Midlands' Smethwick area: a local company decided to invest in brownfield – abandoned industrial sites. On the site of a former steelworks that once employed some 13,000, Richardsons Ltd eventually built a shopping centre that generated thousands of jobs in construction and retail.[10] In Dayton, Mike Turner, too, decided to focus on getting new investment to brownfield.

But by and large, getting new investors to brownfield in Ohio, the Midlands and other former manufacturing powerhouses was a struggle: hardly a surprise given the abundance of opportunities behind the former Iron Curtain, in Latin America, in China, even in places like Costa Rica. In China, pioneers like Volkswagen who'd invested in the eighties were being joined by other manufacturers who, with the obligatory local partners, set up factories making everything from shoes to telecoms equipment. Ericsson, too, was a determined participant. And because this was capitalism the Chinese way, the Chinese authorities informed the Swedish telecoms giant that it had to share its technologies with a Chinese telecoms firm. That company was a young firm called Huawei, and its technology was so rudimentary that the company was barely on Ericsson's radar. 'The Chinese authorities said we had to cross-license with Huawei,' Sundström recalled. 'Huawei had nothing we needed, so cross-licensing just meant us giving to them . . . but what could we do? Signing the cross-licensing deal was the price you had to pay to be on the Chinese market.' The Chinese telecoms market was growing rapidly, both in fixed and mobile telephony, and Huawei was hardly a competitor. Indeed, it owned no intellectual property.[11]

Chinese authorities, in fact, were not minded to protect the intellectual property of Western firms entering the country. 'Just as policy makers in the United States in the eighteenth century who wanted to import British technology without high licensing fees and German policy makers in the nineteenth who wanted to catch up with Britain, Chinese policy makers initially had very few incentives to protect and enforce intellectual property because most of it was owned by foreign firms,' three management scholars subsequently explained.[12] IP loss has indeed blighted innovative companies for as long as innovation-based commerce has existed. In 1791, US Treasury Secretary Alexander Hamilton declared that his country needed 'to procure all such machines as are known in any part of Europe', and he asked his department to pay $48 'to subsidize the living expenses of an English weaver who pledged to deliver to the U.S. a copycat version of a British spinning machine'.[13] And Sundström pointed out that Ericsson owed part of its early success to another company's IP: 'In the late 18th century, we copied a telephone from Graham Bell. He held the patent in the United States but not in Sweden, so we could do it.' But now such countries had created more IP order amongst themselves, with laws and regulations to ensure companies could reap international benefits from the hard work they'd put into their research. But, the scholars explained, when China opened up to global commerce, 'Chinese companies similar to German firms in the early period of German industrialization did not have the capabilities to create innovations to compete with leading foreign firms. For this reason, protecting IP would favor foreign firms at the expense of local firms which were in imitative mode.'[14] So the country didn't. Ericsson would have to make sure it constantly remained far ahead of Huawei.

Sitting in his office at the US Embassy in Beijing, a diplomat named William Monroe witnessed American firms signing countless such deals. 'Technology transfer was a concern for companies coming to China,' he later recalled. 'If a company wanted to invest and build a factory in China, it would often have to form a joint venture, and the Chinese partner would then have access to the invested technology. The fear was that in time the Chinese would copy the technology, then produce their own version of the product, and start exporting back to the US.'[15] But, like Ericsson, the American companies invested anyway. It seemed unlikely that Chinese firms would ever be able to perform the quantum leap that would take them from poor cousins to neck-and-neck rivals of the West's most sophisticated firms.[16]

Western companies were arriving in quick succession in Russia, too, but with more limited goals. Rather than planning to set up global manufacturing hubs, most just wanted to tap into raw materials like oil and gas or sell their wares to the Russian public. They were arriving in a country of massive potential but fast-spreading turmoil. Ever since the final months of the Soviet Union, a steady stream of Western academics and advisors had been arriving in Moscow, encouraging the Kremlin to embark on radical reforms that, the idea went, would help the country to morph from planned economy to a market economy in one quick painful swoop, just as other former Warsaw Pact states had done. 'Nobody understood the initial conditions of this transformation, because a lot of the information regarding the state of the Russian economy was still classified,' Guriev told me. 'And the whole reform was also unprecedented.' But the Western economic experts considered it inevitable. 'The Russian economy was facing complete collapse,' said Anders Åslund, an economist who in the early nineties was a professor at the Stockholm School of Economics. 'The currency reserves were almost entirely depleted. GDP was plummeting, inflation was skyrocketing and the shops were almost completely empty. It was a free-fall, with obvious hyperinflation coming. The regime hadn't a clue what to do and it also didn't understand how bad the situation was.' The man assigned the task of leading the Russian economy was Yegor Gaidar, an economist whom Yeltsin had initially appointed as an advisor.

A short time later, Åslund arrived in Moscow to visit colleagues, 'and I bumped into my friend Aleksandr Shokhin, who had just become minister of labour. That's how quickly things were happening at that point. Shokhin told me that he and Gaidar were putting together an economic programme, and I said that Sachs, Lipton and I would be happy to help if they needed us.' Jeffrey Sachs, an economics professor at Harvard, had already advised the Polish government on its transition to market economy, and his former PhD student David Lipton had also established himself as an economist of note.

That November, Yeltsin appointed Gaidar as finance minister, though in reality Gaidar's brief was much more expansive: he was now the economic reform czar in a country facing economic collapse. The following month, Sachs, Åslund and Lipton began advising the government. Åslund took possession of an office in Moscow's old Central Committee building.

The reforms had to happen quickly. Around the time of Åslund and Lipton's arrival, Gaidar issued a decree lifting price controls on all but the most essential items that came into force a few weeks later, in January 1992. Desperate Russians immediately began selling their belongings in improvised street markets. Petty crime proliferated. The problem, as Åslund sees it, is that Gaidar's team was simply too small: 'The Gaidar people were perhaps a total of one hundred. They were sitting on top of an old communist government, people who hated the guts of the reformers. Gaidar's people were not skilled in administration and they were in a completely hostile environment.' Elsewhere around Moscow and the rest of the country, an army of alternately well-meaning, competent, clueless, unscrupulous and misguided advisors and businesspeople from various Western countries were peddling their services to the transitioning country.

Ordinary Russians saw their savings wiped out and trained their verbal guns on Gaidar, but the reformer forged ahead. The Russian government began issuing certificates of ownership in state enterprises to all Russian citizens. By the end of the following year, some 11,000 companies had been privatized, with shares in them given to each citizen in the form of a voucher.[17] What happened next has become a cautionary tale for socialist economies trying to become market economies: cash-strapped Russians sold their vouchers to wealthy ones, soon-to-be-called oligarchs, who thus managed to buy extremely lucrative companies for a song.

Guriev, who had just graduated from the Moscow Institute of Physics and Technology, watched his discipline suddenly become extremely useful and extremely maddening at the same time. 'The reforms were an experiment without precedent: massive institutional change that had never happened before,' he recalled. 'The government did have qualified economists who wanted to listen. Some of the decision-makers were very smart and wanted good advice. But in some cases, they didn't want to listen. I won't say that you can't model economics, but the whole economy was just so turbulent.'

Things were so turbulent that in late 1993, civil war nearly erupted when President Boris Yeltsin and the Russian parliament, the Duma, clashed and the military intervened. But the conflict subsided, companies stayed and more arrived.

Despite the constant disruption, not to mention the debilitating uncertainty facing his country, Guriev had managed to graduate with top grades. Nobody had told him there was such a thing as an international academic circuit that allows young academics to earn a degree in another country, or simply to spend a year at a foreign university. At any rate, Guriev was off to a good career at the Russian Academy of Science, where a group of mathematicians were using mathematical models to analyse economic processes. A country convulsing as it tried to transform itself from a planned economy to a functioning capitalist system offered a spectacular case study.

As the summer of 1994 turned to autumn, Russia pulled itself back from the brink. For Western businesses, some normality materialized: Ericsson received a contract for a phone network for a city in Siberia and another assignment in Moscow.[18] The manufacturers setting up shop in China and Central and Eastern Europe were hitting their stride. The economic downturn that had plagued large parts of the West had been excised. Then post-Cold War globalization's first disaster struck. A change in the United States' federal interest rates knocked some $600 billion off the trade value of US bonds, and that in turn caused a $1.5 trillion loss of traded value in government bonds around the world.[19] The calamity became known as the Bond Massacre, and markets had barely recovered from the shock when misfortune struck again. Mexico, a star performer among opening-up countries, devalued the peso, spooking the country's many foreign investors and its regional neighbours alike.

But the expanding companies setting themselves up in China were facing more practical challenges. How does one set up manufacturing operations in a vast and economically transitioning country for the first time? They had to work out what sort of permits one needs to launch manufacturing in a quickly changing economy that's somehow still socialist. They had to find staff and suppliers and figure out where to house the expats dispatched to run the operations.

Such were the questions that Antony Perillo asked himself when he, in the mid-nineties and after several visits to China, arrived in Guangdong Province to set up a factory. Perillo, a New Zealand-born executive with a British shoe manufacturer, and his company had joined the large number of other footwear firms and furniture-makers now setting themselves up in eastern China. The expat managers had landed in Guangdong because the Chinese authorities had directed them there, part of Beijing's strategy to turn different parts of the country into manufacturing hubs for specific sectors. 'It felt very foreign, but we expats felt very comfortable with it, because within a few hours' drive you could be in downtown Hong Kong,' Perillo said. 'Admittedly, that was more of a theoretical advantage, since we foreigners all had to travel by ferry.'

Still, the expats and their firms felt welcome. 'By the mid-nineties, there were no obstacles,' Perillo told me. 'The central government had said, "This is happening, this is how it will work. And this is how you do it." And it worked incredibly well.' Guangdong had a massive local labour force, including people who'd arrived from the surrounding regions, and it was willing and available to be trained. While Western companies were not allowed to fully own their operations in China, they could set up cooperation with domestic firms or, in some cases, with Taiwan-based ones. Lacking a handbook of how to set up operations in this massive market, the managers improvised. 'When I look back on it now, I realize that nobody really knew what to do, neither on the government side nor among the corporates,' Perillo said. 'We literally went in and found a Taiwanese partner, and we built a factory with them. And then we bought machinery from Europe and sent it there.'

But after a while, Perillo and his colleagues began noticing that the shoe-machine deliveries arrived later than scheduled. When they looked into the matter, they discovered that local Chinese machine manufacturers were copying the equipment. 'The same thing was happening with the styles for the shoes and the tooling for the shoe moulds,' he told me. 'Everything was being replicated by local companies. But the shoe manufacturers didn't really have a problem with it, because what it meant for us was that quite often the machine was improved over the original, and it was also a lot cheaper. I would call it naïvety or a little bit of entrepreneurialism, but that's what was happening.' The shoe manufacturers soon discovered that their style designs, too, were being copied by Chinese competitors – and, once again, they decided it was not worth trying to do anything about it. Besides, manufacturing in Guangdong was cheap, the transportation infrastructure was reliable and shipping firms assisted the growing manufacturing hub by increasing their calls to the Port of Hong Kong. 'Of the total foreign investment in China, over one-third of the realized amount has flowed into Guangdong, more than the combined total received by Beijing and Shanghai,' two scholars reported.[20] Only a couple of hours away, Shenzhen was being turned into a hub for higher-tech companies. One company based in the city was, for example, already making good progress on mobile-telephony infrastructure: Huawei.

As cities in Guangdong industrialized, they became more like Hong Kong: hubs for expats and local managers of the kind that could by now be found in any globalizing city. After completing a stint in Dongguan or Shenzhen, expats often packed up and left for new assignments in a hub elsewhere in the world. And despite its machinery having been held up and apparently copied, Perillo's firm was now on firm footing in Dongguan. Production was proceeding smoothly, conducted by workers who had quickly learnt to operate the machinery. One day, Perillo found to his astonishment that the factory staff had closed the plant to go and watch a procession of prisoners being transported on a nearby highway. They were going to their executions, a staff member helpfully informed him. But like the other expat managing operations in China, Perillo was used to experiencing new local customs.

He didn't know that in another region of China, the human rights of the locals were now increasingly being violated too. When the Soviet Union collapsed, its Central Asian republics gained independence along with the Baltic states, Ukraine and the other Soviet states. Such departures fed a feeling among the people of Xinjiang, a Chinese Central Asian province whose majority Uyghur inhabitants are closely related to fellow Central Asians, that they too ought to become independent. Beijing, though, responded not by granting these wishes but by punishing them with bans on Uyghur gatherings and even with executions.[21] Perhaps that desire to keep Xinjiang in the Chinese fold was linked to the province's perfect conditions for cotton production. Between 1990 and 1997, authorities more than doubled Xinjiang's cotton-growing acreage – and Western clothing manufacturers loved the excellent fibre.[22]

In Britain's Midlands, a member of parliament was watching the global transformation and worrying about its effect on workers in his community. John Spellar is a Labour politician of the traditional mould, and before being elected to parliament, he worked for the trade union representing electricians and plumbers. 'The original James Watt Matthew Boulton steam engine was built by Soho Foundry, which stood in my constituency,' he pointed out as we discussed his region's contributions to the global economy. The two engineers' pioneering steam engine came to power the Industrial Revolution and make the UK the world's leading manufacturing power, and the Midlands area was the centre of that superpowerdom. Adjacent to Spellar's constituency is Birmingham, which became known as the world's first manufacturing city.

Spellar's constituency includes many smaller Birminghams. Most of the factories that once dotted the constituency were located in Smethwick, a town that today has some 50,000 residents. Smethwick's glory days peaked in the early 1900s, when the town produced staggering volumes of steel sheets, screws, tubing, bicycles, glass and railway cars destined for countries around the world. In the early eighties, the area was still a manufacturing hub: more than 42 per cent of its working-age residents worked in factories, compared with 28 per cent in the rest of the UK.[23] Residents sent Spellar to represent them in London just as jobs had begun to be lost in large numbers to China and Eastern Europe – and at that point, many were hopeful that globalization would ultimately replace the region's high-skilled jobs with other decent ones. The future was, after all, not in the manufacturing economy but in the service economy.

Spellar takes a pragmatic view of globalization. 'There's simply no point producing socks and underwear in the UK, because they're easy to make and easy to transport,' he told me in his Smethwick constituency office. In the early nineties, as he saw companies slash jobs in his constituency and the rest of the Midlands, Spellar worried about the long-term consequences for those laid off, their family members and the community. He knew that the countries opening up their economies presented an unparalleled opportunity for Western companies to sell more products, and that some of this income was going to come back to their home countries as taxes. And he knew that automation had at any rate been causing jobs to disappear. One former screw-factory worker in Smethwick told me that his factory used to employ 7,000 workers making some 90 million screws per week. When he left in 1986, the factory was still making the same number of screws but employing 300 people. Then the company began making the same screws in cheaper countries, and eventually the headquarters moved too.

In those turbulent years, Gerard Coyne kept driving around Midlands towns to support factory workers facing job loss. But the workers were still in no mood to protest. 'There was a feeling of, "Well, we'll be next, anyway,"' Coyne told me. 'I was shocked at how easy it was to sell off the next generation's jobs. We stripped our communities of high-skilled work.' Yes, service-sector jobs were cropping up, but they were of a more fleeting nature, and often with lower pay. For the time being, though, those jobs would have to suffice. In theory, those laid off could move to other parts of the country or even abroad. But they'd lived in the region for generations. Besides, what sort of work would they find elsewhere?

Another fundamental change was also afoot: the growth of personal computers and the internet. By 1993, some 2 million computers around the world were connected to the internet.[24] PCs would need to be manufactured in large numbers, but despite the manufacturing skills of Midlands workers, Spellar knew the chances were low that his region would be able to capture this highest end of manufacturing.

A world away, Michael Cole-Fontayn was making regular trips around the countries in his portfolio. He examined opportunities and set up new operations. His home base of Hong Kong was quickly becoming one of globalization's new epicentres, the hub from which retail banks, investment banks and other conglomerates directed their growing activities in the region's transforming economies. And across the border in China, the march of Western manufacturers was growing. 'It was just non-stop with delegations of high level business groups, business signings. I can't tell you how many banquets and signing ceremonies I attended for new deals or factories,' Monroe reported.[25]

Giorgio La Malfa was equally thrilled to see unimpeded global trade finally beginning to take shape. The Italian professor, who has degrees from Cambridge and MIT, is an expert on the economic theory of John Maynard Keynes and a noted economist in his own right. He also belongs to Italy's political royalty; his father, Ugo La Malfa, for years led the powerful centrist Partito Repubblicano Italiano and was a central figure in Italy's post-war reconstruction. In the early seventies the younger La Malfa was elected to the Italian parliament on the PRI ticket: the beginning of a long career in Italian and European politics. The early nineties 'truly was a sense of elation,' he told me. 'People like me felt that finally those countries that have had authoritarian regimes are opening up in economic terms but even more importantly in political terms. The perhaps naïve idea was that opening up the economies would bring both economic advantages and political change.'

But just as the elation was beginning to produce financial results, an old menace reappeared: genocide. Following the path beaten by many other republics in Yugoslavia and the Soviet Union, Bosnia-Herzegovina had declared independence, only to see things turn bloody when fighting broke out between its Serb, Croat and Bosniak factions. By 1995, the war had claimed nearly 100,000 lives and unleashed a refugee wave of more than 2 million Bosnians who had made their way to Germany, Sweden and other Western European countries.[26]

Europe's largest countries and the United States quarrelled about what needed to be done to end the war. 'Germany and the United States felt that France and the UK ought to be doing a bloody bit more than they were,' said Pauline Neville-Jones, a veteran British diplomat who led her country's efforts to halt the fighting. 'Germany saw Croatia as an early prize where their newfound sovereignty could exert a lot of influence and establish a profitable market.' Croatia unsurprisingly supported Bosnia's Croats, while Serbia massively supported its Serbs, and in this effort Serbia was in turn backed by Russia. By the summer of 1995, the conflict was claiming so many lives that in an extraordinary turn of events, NATO leaders agreed to take action – even though Bosnia was not a member of the alliance and even though Russia was guaranteed to be displeased. That August, in the alliance's first-ever active combat, NATO fighter jets began bombing the Bosnian Serbs' military installations.

The intervention worked. Within three weeks, the Bosnian Serbs were willing to negotiate.[27] That November, the United States, Britain, France, Germany, Italy, Russia, the European Union and Bosnia's three warring parties convened at Dayton's Wright-Patterson Air Force Base – and they managed to reach an agreement. During the negotiations, though, Neville-Jones noticed something that worried her: even though Russian negotiators were present and Moscow had affiliated itself with the Serbs, the negotiators didn't say a great deal. In fact, they seemed to have received no instructions from Moscow. 'Their name was appended to the agreement, but the Russians were not in any real sense signed up,' Neville-Jones said. NATO's bombing of a Russian ally was unlikely to endear Moscow to the Dayton Accords, but the weakened former superpower was hardly in a position to block the agreement.

Mayor Mike Turner had never expected his town to play a role in global politics. Now he was suddenly thrust into that world, too, when the Clinton administration asked him to join peace-building efforts in Bosnia-Herzegovina and outreach with Croatia, and in this new and unexpected role made his first trip to the troubled region. 'Our Dayton homicide detectives trained the Sarajevo police, our hospitals twinned, our chambers of commerce twinned,' Turner told me. 'I'm proud that my community rose to the occasion and participated in these efforts, but through that we saw and followed the unbelievable atrocities in this place.' Those memories stayed with him.

Other former communist countries were faring decidedly better. The South Korean carmaker Daewoo outbid rivals to buy Avia, a Czech lorry manufacturer, and also acquired another eighty companies formerly behind the Iron Curtain.[28] Sony built a factory in Hungary. (The factory would later be moved to Malaysia.)[29] Goodyear bought the Polish tyre-maker TC Debica.[30] In Russia, BP launched a chain of petrol stations and paid more than $0.5 billion for a 10 per cent share of Sidanco, an oil producer owned by one of the country's new oligarchs.[31]

But in China, expat executives were increasingly irked by a price of entry that they hadn't fully anticipated. It wasn't China's unorthodox interpretation of capitalism that bothered them, or the enigmatic government bureaucracy whose decisions were virtually impossible to predict. Nor was it the occasional chaos, bribery requests or other hiccups companies expanding to new markets habitually encounter. It was the unfair business play by the government and Chinese companies, but most of all it was IP loss. Stories about the problem popped up on a daily basis, at staff meetings and, gradually, when expat managers got together for a drink. The official loss was the intellectual property handed over through cross-licensing agreements and to Chinese joint-venture partners. And there was a great deal of unofficial loss, too: local competitors and officials copying machinery or blueprints.

Western executives weren't naïve; they'd done business in other countries where the government, competitors or both stole their companies' commercial secrets. A previous generation of executives had lost IP to the Soviets this way, and back then the loss wasn't even offset by the access to a country of manufacturing and consumption potential. They were also used to emerging economies' habit of demanding cross-licensing agreements. But the scale of lost IP in China bothered the managers and their bosses at home. Even so, they didn't try to prevent it. 'Everybody was extremely well behaved in order to make the relationship work,' Perillo said. They had seen the success of Volkswagen, which by 1996 was selling a staggering 55 per cent of its passenger cars in China, compared with only 17 per cent in Western Europe.[32] And for Ericsson, China (with Hong Kong) was already the second-largest market, after the United States.[33]

So massive were the opportunities that, IP loss notwithstanding, US carmakers were furiously fighting to copy VW's success in China. 'The Chinese went down a very clear path: "I want one European and I want one American",' an automotive executive who worked for GM during this period told me. 'The European one was Volkswagen and for the American slot there was a dogfight between General Motors and Ford. And the two firms literally tripped over each other, bent over backwards, did whatever they could to please the Chinese in order to emerge the "winning" candidate.' Winning the coveted slot required making concessions far beyond joint ventures and cross-licensing. 'China had already identified universities, including Tsinghua University, which they called their MIT,' the former GM executive observed. 'They said, "You have to bring in technology." It reached a point where GM's advanced technology centre offloaded valuable automotive technology, including cutting-edge areas like safety engineering, into China to essentially say, "Look how committed we are."' Keith Krach, a young vice president at GM, watched the development from the carmaker's headquarters in Detroit. 'When you build a plant in China, you're not just giving them the blueprints. You're giving them process engineering,' he concluded.

But the rewards were irresistible and, besides, everyone else was China-bound. There was also a great deal of arrogance – the belief that the strategy would still make sense however much IP Chinese authorities and competitors appropriated, because the Western firms would keep innovating and always be ahead. 'We went into China after the Germans, and we said to the Chinese, "Oh, you guys don't know how to make things",' the former GM executive told me. 'And, step by step, we started saying, "Oh, you make such lousy cars; you'll never get as competitive as us."' He was paraphrasing a *Washington Post* column from 1981 about Japanese car manufacturing. In the *Post* column, by the humorist Art Buchwald, an advisor to World War II General Douglas MacArthur magnanimously advises a defeated Japanese former admiral that Japan might like to build cars.

'How do you build an automobile?' the admiral asks.

The American tells him how.

'Can I keep the book?'

'Why not? Now that you are a poor defeated country we have no secrets.'

Years later, the American turns up in Tokyo.

'And what brings you to Tokyo, my good friend?' the ex-admiral asks.

'I've been sent by the president of the United States. He knows we go way back, and felt I should bring his message personally,' the American says.

'What message?'

'He wants you to stop making so many damn Japanese cars.'[34]

But for Chinese industry, such a future was far off. Ford had already formed a partnership with the Chinese automaker Jiangling Motors Corporation,[35] and soon GM formed one with SAIC General Motors Corporation. Motorola was mass-manufacturing mobile phones at its factory in Tianjin.

In 1997, British voters elected Tony Blair and his New Labour to form their new government. Where his party colleague John Spellar worried about lost factory jobs and seemed to embody a vanishing world, Blair believed in the opportunities beyond Britain's borders, and it seemed to be a world of unlimited potential. 'We are intensely relaxed about people getting filthy rich as long as they pay their taxes,' declared Peter Mandelson, the new prime minister's chief strategist.[36] Mandelson seemed unaware that many wealthy people were already moving their money to tax havens.

Michael Treschow illustrated globalization's upside. At Atlas Copco, he'd revamped the machinery giant's foreign presence from its previous collection of island-style operations into several regional hubs. Even though the process was not yet complete, the hubs now each looked after customers in several neighbouring countries and efficiently manufactured using supplies from these and elsewhere. 'In the business world, people began thinking more in terms of regions,' he explained. 'It didn't really matter whether a country was Uruguay or Paraguay, or Argentina or Brazil, it was the same region. Companies combined countries into regions that made sense for them as companies.' Treschow himself was now travelling so much that even though he was living in Sweden with his family, he had become the quintessential Davos Man, a business executive so at home in all corners of the world that nationalities no longer seemed to matter. Although he has proudly maintained his southern Swedish dialect when speaking in his native tongue, by now he mostly spoke English. 'Companies built a cadre of international executives, and just like you didn't think about yourself as being Swedish or whatever your nationality might be, you didn't really think about what others' nationalities were either,' he observed. 'They moved around the world and formed this community of expats which really became a global cadre, and I was a member of this cadre myself. Countries became less important and their borders basically disappeared.' The borderless executive was an indispensable part of the borderless company.

In 1997, with the Dayton Accords having consigned war in Europe to history, the world received confirmation that matters were heading in an exhilarating direction when Russia was invited to join the G7 club of leading economies. Even though the country didn't qualify on purely economic terms, it certainly was a boon to have the heir to the former Soviet Union as part of the Western group.

Treschow, too, received a prestigious invitation: he was appointed CEO of Electrolux. The venerable Swedish white-goods company enjoyed an excellent reputation for products like refrigerators and washing machines, and with families in formerly socialist economies still updating their households, one could sell a great deal of these appliances.[37] Before long, Treschow had gone on a global acquisition tour, and he'd also formed a joint venture with a leading white-goods firm in India.[38] He was also familiar with a growing Chinese white-goods firm called Haier – it had begun life in the mid-eighties as a maker of simple refrigerators, and was now making refrigerators through a joint venture with Germany's prestigious Liebherr – but decided its standard wasn't high enough for him to consider an acquisition or joint venture.

Paradoxically, though, expanding when much of the world had suddenly opened was much harder than when only one or two countries had done so. 'It wasn't really predictable where you would succeed,' Treschow recalled. 'In Hungary, for example, we did extremely well, not least because we bought a local company that was very solid. I recall that acquisition well, because it came with a zoo. That was part of the wild nature of those days – if you bought a white-goods company you might have to accept becoming the owner of a zoo as well.' Treschow was being modest: Electrolux's acquisition of Hungary's state-owned refrigerator factory Lehel (which just happened to own a zoo) became one of the nineties' most celebrated turnarounds of a communist state-owned company. Lehel went from making some 600,000 fridges per year to anually producing some 6 million fridges, hoovers and fridge-freezers.[39] In India, Electrolux set up manufacturing hubs in different parts of the country, only to realize that transportation between the different parts was a major hurdle. Globalization wasn't only unadulterated market success. But in the nineties, the opportunities were so plentiful that everyone seemed to benefit.

3
BANKERS CONQUER NEW TERRITORY

Just as past generations' iterations of globalization have always been accompanied by financing, in the late eighties and early nineties investment banks spotted the same growth opportunities as their professional forefathers once had. But how does one set up investment banking, or indeed any kind of commercial banking, in countries that have until recently been planned or closed economies? Investment bankers are often among the first to arrive when such countries decide to join the capitalist world. For bankers like Michael Cole-Fontayn who were being sent on a mission to establish operations in China and other countries in the region, the first step was Hong Kong. There they joined experienced Hong Kong bankers, and the crown colony was the lily pad from which they could travel around the region, teach investment banking and hire new local staff.

Chinese officials and budding business leaders were particularly numerous. 'The Chinese were very active in exploring each of these different business models, and they also sent some of their brightest and best policymakers out into the world to take business trips, often for the first time, to the United States, to the UK, to European markets, to understand what the market economy really looked like and understand what were the standards and rules under which it operates and how these could be adapted appropriately for Chinese purposes,' Cole-Fontayn recalled. 'In particular, they were very keen to study the UK privatization model, where the state held either a golden share or a strong minority and had incorporated into the articles of association of the company conditionality. Whether it was around voting rights, control rights, or any other aspect of ownership: the Chinese absolutely cherry-picked everything that worked for them and ended up with a model that was market-based but with "Chinese characteristics" or "socialist characteristics".' (A golden share, typically held by a government entity, gives the shareholder the right to veto the other shareholders on key issues.) Even though it was becoming clear that the Chinese market economy would look rather different from what Western economic experts would have proposed, it seemed an efficient model.

In Moscow, meanwhile, a Wisconsin-born investment banker named Michael Calvey was setting himself up for the long haul. In the early nineties, the Salomon Brothers alumnus had regularly been sent to Russia by the London-based European Bank of Reconstruction and Development, an outfit founded by Western governments to help former Warsaw Pact states transition to market economies and assist them through the financing of marquee projects. After representing the EBRD on a number of oil and gas projects, Calvey decided that Russia was a country in which one could do business. He decided to remain there and, in 1994, he launched Baring Vostok, one of the country's first private-equity firms.[1]

That meant meeting a motley crew of entrepreneurs, emerging oligarchs and government officials. As he later explained in an interview, 'The private sector was growing rapidly, but from a small base, so there were not many private companies of size in which to invest. So we invested about two-thirds of our first fund in former Soviet businesses that had been privatized, and about one-third in new private companies.' Some of those companies went on to great success, among them a leading mobile-telephony provider. But 'we also made a lot of money from investing in privatized businesses, which was a different type of opportunity requiring different skill sets. For most of these formerly state-owned businesses, there were huge assets that could be acquired very cheaply, but they needed to be restructured, cleaned up and repositioned to be profitable over the long term. This opportunity existed only briefly, but we took advantage of it,' Calvey explained in the interview.[2]

Investment bankers, too, spotted enormous opportunities. Credit Suisse First Boston arrived. Goldman Sachs arrived. Ordinary Russians, meanwhile, continued to suffer as the economy convulsed. From his new outpost at a research institute in Moscow, Sergei Guriev observed the misery around him, and he was convinced that the radical overhaul of his country's economy was necessary. 'Privatization, the way it happened, was not what Western advisors advised,' he told me. 'There were a number of political compromises that turned out to be really bad. But the turbulence was completely of Russians' own making.' Russia's chaotic privatization was simply the most aggressive outgrowth of the Western exuberance, missionary zeal and often opportunism that arrived in newly opening countries in the form of businesspeople and advisors. Local officials naturally lacked confidence and experience running a capitalist system. The power imbalance was undeniable.

Seeing the turbulence in Russia, Cole-Fontayn concluded that he'd made the right choice by opting for a position in Hong Kong. Now, after attending to logistics, he had to figure out how to turn his bank's presence into business deals. How does one get deals flowing in economies where people have no experience with investment banking? 'When I arrived, we had no one at all in China,' he said. 'But a couple of colleagues had already made trips to China, and they had made some assessments.' The bank hired the translator on these trips as its first employee in mainland China. Executives then located a Chinese citizen who'd been working for the bank in New York; he became the bank's second employee in China. 'And then,' Cole-Fontayn told me, 'it was a case of getting a good level of understanding from our Hong Kong colleagues, and from our Taiwanese colleagues, to build a picture of the opportunity.'

The Asian picture was rapidly becoming clear. Because China offered by far the biggest opportunity, it became Cole-Fontayn's focus. The investment-banking opportunities, of course, went hand in hand with China's rapid advance in other sectors. Shenzhen, the technology hub thought up by Beijing, was booming as Western companies were steered there and domestic ones grew thanks to government support and access to Western companies' technology. In 1980, when Deng Xiaoping declared the town China's first 'special economic zone', it only had a few roads and a population of some 30,000.[3] Now it was becoming a metropolis.

But before the Western banks could hire local staff to execute deals or trade financial instruments, they had to educate not just businesspeople and prospective employees but officials too, in ways that went beyond study trips to Western capitals. Inevitably, the need for such education was particularly widespread in China. Far from perceiving it as patronizing, Chinese officials and budding business leaders eagerly sought it because they wanted to swiftly benefit from it. The education also delivered some learning benefit for the Western money experts, since it helped them better understand the alternative iterations of capitalism emerging outside Europe.

That, Cole-Fontayn told me, 'was the beginning of China's embrace of the power of markets. But what China wanted to do was to have a level of control over the type of markets that it invited and embraced on its terms.' Such state-steered discipline was the opposite of Russia's very-free-market reforms. Indeed, even as the authorities invited manufacturers and investment banks to set up shop, the country remained a partially closed economy whose capital markets were closely regulated by the government, and not just through mandatory cross-licensing and co-ownership with Chinese partners. 'You constantly needed regulatory approval,' Cole-Fontayn observed. 'Understanding and navigating that meant a number of conversations with Chinese ministries and government agencies and bodies to help us understand what the substance was, and at the same time it meant meeting as many state-owned enterprises as possible.'

The Western executives working in China gradually learnt how the country worked and what to expect from this unique form of capitalism. By now, Antony Perillo was such a veteran of manufacturing in China that he was often asked to serve as an expert guide to financial-services managers visiting the country. 'The vast majority of them had never been to China, and many were quite young,' he noted. 'They'd come to China, and they were just in awe of its scale and potential. You'd have seminars with them, discuss various issues, have a meal afterwards, and you'd have to tell them, "Yes, but you have to be careful. Things are not always the way you see them. You can't just come here and invest. It's not a free market."' His interlocutors, though, seemed to think he was exaggerating the risks. When he heard politicians speak about China, he got the feeling that they, too, didn't grasp how capricious the Chinese market could be. Perillo wished Western politicians would come and spend a week in a factory to properly comprehend the situation on the ground, but they seemed content to only pay brief delegation visits to the country, if they visited at all.

Cole-Fontayn is not what one might call a finance bro; instead he's unfailingly polite and respectful of non-bankers' imperfect grasp of the profession's details. Whenever I kept asking for more details about how one builds investment banking in a country that has had none, I felt a certain affinity with the Chinese officials in the early nineties who were trying to learn investment banking by word of mouth. But Cole-Fontayn answered patiently, as I imagined he must have done many times in the early nineties. 'No question was too small,' he said of those years. 'We would take endless amounts of time, we would travel around in China, hosting events, arranging events. And none of this was hosted alone. It was always co-hosted, with law firms, banks, other professional-services firms, the accountancy profession, because we wanted to present a united approach.' An all-embracing capitalist hug, as it were, and an unprecedented opportunity for companies to make more money – but beyond that, to shape the new markets. 'The opportunities were limitless,' Cole-Fontayn said. 'For many business leaders and provincial officials, it was their first exposure to foreigners. It was a privilege to be able to work with them, talk with them about life in Britain and America, to explore their thirst for knowledge, point out risks, encourage them to explore.'

It worked. In 1994, Cole-Fontayn's bank – the Bank of New York – opened its first office in mainland China. Goldman had opened offices in Beijing and Shanghai.[4] JP Morgan arrived, Bank of America, Barclays, Citi, UBS. Many banks had also opened offices in Hong Kong before trying to enter China, and now there were suddenly a lot of Westerners – especially Britons with Thatcherite Big Bang expertise – in the crown colony. 'As finance ministries and industrial ministries began to understand the power of the techniques of opening up markets, this enabled ideas to spread,' Cole-Fontayn reflected. 'And it allowed people to move to different countries, and very simply, live, love and work around the world.' The yuppie generation had arrived, and borders didn't matter to its members. Cole-Fontayn wondered, though, what would happen in Hong Kong when his and his colleagues' head start began dissipating.

Bankers were ambitious not just in geographic expansion but in finding new ways of making money too, so-called financial instruments with exotic-sounding names like collateralized debt obligations. It didn't matter that most people had no idea what such terms meant: collateralized debt obligations – a package through which lenders resell assets like mortgages – were not intended for them. But bankers loved the CDOs. Indeed, they were moving away from trading concrete assets to trading instruments of the assets. It was lucrative because through this abstraction, the asset – whether that be a mortgage, a car loan or anything else – could be sliced and repackaged in countless ways. And like processed cheese, the item being traded had lost most links to its original state. Now banks were filling their books with such creative financial instruments. 'Over the last five years, banks have substituted securities for loans. In addition, they have continued to securitize many of their loans in order to move them off the balance sheet,' the Federal Reserve Bank of Chicago noted.[5] But the markets didn't seem concerned.

In 1996, Cole-Fontayn and his wife welcomed their second child, who seamlessly joined the Hong Kong expat set, just as their now-two-year-old had done. If the Cole-Fontayns wanted to stay in the city, or perhaps move to Shanghai or Beijing, they'd be able to choose from a growing number of international schools now setting themselves up.

Life in other major cities was booming too, but in former manufacturing centres like John Spellar's environs, life felt uncertain. By 1996, manufacturing in the troubled western part of the Midlands had declined by more than a third compared to fifteen years earlier, and while somewhat well-paying new jobs were arriving, they were of the professional or managerial variety.[6] These weren't jobs for former factory workers. The region had 'a mountain to climb' in the globalized economy, a newspaper column concluded.[7] 'Your factory is part of your social life and may also be a workplace where your children will follow you,' Spellar told me as we drove past a former factory in Smethwick. 'When that closes because of so-called international rules, then you feel that very acutely. It's no good to say, "You can get another job, which is less secure and may have less other compensation." Yes, in the early nineties we began receiving a lot of cheap imports, and people were being told that was for everyone's good, but they didn't see it that way.'

The 'it's-all-about-economics' school had no solutions to such sociological dilemmas. But everyone in charge, from prime ministers to CEOs of multinationals to local politicians and factory managers, seemed enthusiastic about the new globe-spanning way of conducting commerce, or they considered it inevitable. Gerard Coyne, with his calls for an end to the high-skill job loss in old manufacturing towns, was beginning to feel as though he was in the wrong movie.

Western-style finance was expanding as quickly as Western manufacturing. By the mid-nineties, Russia had more than 2,500 credit outfits that lent money to pretty much any business needing a loan. Investment banks, and now Russian investment banks and private-equity firms with names like Renaissance Capital and Troika Dialog were setting up shop. Unsurprisingly, that resulted in an extraordinary volume of financial transactions compared to what was being produced in the country – and there was little banking for ordinary Russians. Many of Guriev's compatriots had already concluded that their misery was the West's making.

In Hong Kong, the mood was sombre. The crown colony was approaching the date on which it would leave Britain and become part of China, and even though Beijing had promised that nothing would change for local Hong Kongers and expats living there, Cole-Fontayn and other residents were apprehensive. Hong Kong was, after all, operating according to Western rules, while Beijing was intent on developing capitalism in a Chinese way. On 1 July 1997, Hong Kongers woke up, prepared for disruption or worse as their patch of the world changed hands from one country to another. Financiers were understandably anxious about how a messy handover – not to mention permanent change towards authoritarian rule – would play out on financial markets. 'But nothing changed,' Cole-Fontayn said. 'China was absolutely true to its word. Yes, British officials and troops moved out, and the Chinese military moved in and took control of the military bases, the naval base, and so on. And they were invisible to the population. Otherwise, things were the same as they'd been the day before.'

Perillo, too, was surprised by how smoothly the British crown colony became the Hong Kong Special Administrative Region. 'They really made a very big effort to make it work,' he concluded. 'I think the Chinese authorities were still on that stage of trying to be slightly more liberal, open up, see what was going to happen, give more freedoms. By that time things were quite open. You could go for a meal. People would always be a little careful, but they were very happy to chat about things like the pros and cons of central control and Beijing.'

But the day after the handover, matters took a nasty turn of a different kind. Thailand had lost its ability to peg its currency to the dollar, and on 2 July the government floated the baht, which immediately lost value. Soon Malaysia, Indonesia, South Korea and the Philippines were in trouble too. The continent's first globalization-age financial crisis had arrived. 'The result was contagion, with foreign creditors pulling back from other countries in the region seen as having similar vulnerabilities,' the US Federal Reserve later summarized.[8] The IMF, the United States, and European and Asian governments had to swiftly marshal $118 billion for the worst-affected countries. But remarkably, China didn't catch the bug. Unlike Thailand and the other countries, who were harmed because their governments and companies had borrowed extensively in dollars, China and India had maintained control of their accounts. In 1998, Thailand's economy shrank while that of China grew.[9] Chinese officials took note.

That year, the Cole-Fontayns welcomed their third child, their first born under Chinese rule, and were relieved to find the British citizenship registration as smooth as it had been for their two older children. The constantly growing Hong Kong expat set now included a few Finns from Nokia, sent there to manage the Finnish super-brand's operations in China. By the end of the century, the Finnish master of handsets had an enviable share in China. Indeed, it was the world's largest maker of mobile phones.[10] In 2001, the former paper mill would account for an astonishing 4 per cent of Finland's GDP and 21 per cent of its exports.[11] Globalization had allowed it to specialize, and it was excelling. In Finland, too, almost everyone used a Nokia phone. A young girl, Maria Ohisalo, was growing up in Helsinki with her mother and stepfather, who were studying, working part-time jobs, and sometimes received welfare benefits. Even so, they were able to get Maria her first mobile phone – a used Nokia. 'After a while, even children from disadvantaged backgrounds could afford a Nokia phone, and you could always keep buying new models when they came out,' Ohisalo reflected. 'It was a success story for the whole country.'

But in Russia, the economy was teetering on the brink once again. Goldman Sachs could assist, the *New York Times* reported: 'The Government's bank accounts were almost empty and even the postal system was near collapse. Now was the time to prove that Goldman could come through with money in a crisis.'[12] Goldman helped the Kremlin quickly raise more than $1 billion. But the ambitious bankers were no match for Russia's complex economy. That August, the Russian government stopped paying its debt.

At home in London, Mo Ibrahim was reflecting on another part of the world where globalized business could be deployed to raise ordinary people's living standards. But he wasn't thinking of manufacturing or investment banking. He was thinking of mobile telephony for Africa, and he was painfully aware that the constant problems African countries had with corruption and poor governance, not to mention poverty, meant that the continent was constantly left behind. Only a quarter of the population had access to electricity, and not even three people out of every hundred had access to a landline. But precisely this perennial lack of infrastructure convinced Ibrahim that mobile telephones presented a unique opportunity. The technology could, he knew, allow less-developed countries to establish communications networks without going through the painstaking and expensive process of setting up landline infrastructure. Indeed, Ibrahim was convinced that mobile telephony could also transform ordinary Africans' lives by connecting them with information and services.

'There was an explosion of development in Europe and the United States, but nothing much was happening in Africa, which really needed mobile communication,' he told me. 'It needed mobile telephony because the fixed networks in Africa are hopeless. Because the African continent is so huge, it's not easy to build a fixed network, but you can develop mobile to meet demand where there's a concentration of population. Mobile telephony really was designed for Africa.' But who was going to do it? 'We talked to everybody. They were very reluctant to go to Africa. This was a time when everyone thought that Africa was a very corrupt place with dictators and military coups. "*Oh la la.* It's not safe. Nobody wants to raise money there."' The veteran mobile-telecommunications pioneer decided that he should do it himself.

4
9/11, ENRON AND OTHER DISRUPTIONS

On 11 September 2001, just before nine o'clock in the morning, Michael Chertoff was on his way to his office in central Washington, DC. The career prosecutor had made his name tackling the mob in eighties New York, where he served as an assistant prosecutor under US Attorney for the Southern District of New York Rudolph Giuliani. At one high-profile trial in 1986, Chertoff managed to secure convictions for leaders of all the five mafia syndicates that had been blighting the city for decades.[1] The families represented the 'largest and most vicious criminal business in the history of the United States,' Chertoff told the court.[2] In the nineties, when he was New Jersey's top prosecutor, his clean-up efforts in the worlds of white-collar and blue-collar crime landed both an electronics tycoon and the mayor of Jersey City in prison.[3] Now, in 2001, he had recently been appointed head of the Department of Justice's enormous criminal division and was envisaging further years battling organized crime and corruption.

But on this day, as Chertoff was travelling in his official car, a staff member unexpectedly called him. 'This person told me that a plane had hit the World Trade Center, but at first I wasn't too alarmed, because I thought it was a small plane whose pilot had gotten confused,' Chertoff recalled. 'But while we were on the phone, he saw on the television how another plane hit the second tower. We realized it was not an accident.'

Chertoff made his way to the FBI headquarters, which functioned as the US government's command central for terrorist-related activities, and met with the Bureau's newly appointed director, Robert Mueller, a fellow prosecutor whom Chertoff had known for years. President George W. Bush and the military had already been alerted. At 9.37 a.m., a third plane crashed into the Pentagon. Five minutes later, the US government grounded all travel in its airspace. A fourth hijacked plane, United Flight 93, was still in the air, but just after 10 a.m. it crashed into a field in Pennsylvania.

In the same manner as the business set moving from one country to the next, Mohammed Atta and some of the other hijackers piloting the four airliners had trained in the United States and lived in other Western countries. But unlike the business expats, the hijackers saw no benefits in such a connected world. 'The terrorists turned what we viewed as a strength – globalization – into a weapon against us,' Chertoff said. 'Globalization was the vehicle through which the terrorists were able to get into the United States to perpetrate these acts, and they chose as their main target the World Trade Center, which was the world's pre-eminent symbol of globalization.'

As Chertoff and other top US officials took stock of the situation that 11 September, it wasn't clear what they should do apart from sending fighter jets to make sure the US skies were completely clear of civilian aircraft. 'There were rumours about taxicabs with bombs in the trunk that were going to be detonated all over Washington, and a fire alarm went off in the State Department, which raised fears that there might be a bomb there,' Chertoff recalled. 'It was impossible to know what else the terrorists might have planned. So immediately, and over the weeks and months, we set up an architecture to detect any next wave of 9/11-style attacks that might be in the works.' The son of a rabbi father, Gershon Baruch Chertoff, who had been born in the United States to immigrant parents, and an Israeli-born mother, Livia, Chertoff is himself the beneficiary of open borders. Livia was, in fact, the Israeli airline El Al's first flight attendant. But terrorists had exploited those open borders, and Chertoff threw himself into the US government's efforts to keep the country as safe as possible.

That meant collecting large amounts of personal data about airline passengers and other travellers. The aviation industry went into a tailspin as tourists stayed home and businesses cancelled all but essential travel for their staff. But as far as aviation was concerned, the hijackers' efforts were in vain: soon air travel returned to normal, albeit with stricter airport security screening, and so did global business activities.[4] Treschow decided that it would take more than terrorism to halt the momentum of global trade. Not even the jihadist 'shoe bomber', who tried to cause another aviation disaster a few months later, managed to leave any permanent marks.[5]

In the Lithuanian city of Kaunas, Gintarė Skaistė was close to finishing her economics degree, and she was also trying to make sense of her country's journey towards a well-functioning market economy – and of the novelties like collateralized debt obligations, the internet and the mobile revolution that were changing countries' economies. Financially speaking, the nineties had been very bumpy for Lithuania. 'Many "single enterprise" towns ended up becoming towns "without a single enterprise",' one academic summarized.[6]

But Skaistė felt the bumps were a bearable price to pay for the prospect of her country becoming as prosperous as nearby Sweden and Finland: 'For us, for Lithuanians, you just understood that the transition would be difficult but that the end goal was a free market like the Western part of Europe and also the United States. And you wanted to be like them.'

Guriev, a decade older than Skaistė, had made the same discovery and realized that not only could Russia connect itself to the Western-led globalized economy, but Guriev could personally connect with it too. 'People in other countries encouraged me to somehow understand what was going on in the West,' he told me. After defending his PhD thesis at the Russian Academy of Science, Guriev spent a year at the Massachusetts Institute of Technology's economics department. 'And that really taught me how economics works,' he said. 'That's how I became a real economist.' A short while after Guriev returned from MIT, Boris Yeltsin resigned. That made the recently installed prime minister, a little-known official named Vladimir Putin, acting president. Yeltsin's resignation meant that Putin would have time to establish his credentials in the run-up to the presidential elections, and establish them he did. Russia was already in the midst of a brutal war against the independence-seeking Russian republic of Chechnya, and

Putin took swift action that further increased the brutality. But Russia gained the upper hand. When presidential elections were held a few months later, in March 2000, Putin won, thanks to his decisive performance in the war but also to the spin doctor Gleb Pavlovsky, who had found in him the perfect leader for what he called the 'Putin majority': the people who'd missed out on the previous decade's financial feast.[7] But at the same time, *Wandel durch Handel* seemed to be materializing in Russia: there were lots of Sergei Gurievs, lots of Mike Calveys, lots of NGOs, lots of newly founded news organizations.

Two months later, the new president declared direct rule over the previously semi-autonomous Chechnya.[8] By then, Europe had endured another war – in Kosovo, a Yugoslav republic whose independence Serbia had sought to stop with military means, which once again prompted NATO to intervene. Serbia was humbled – and so was its patron Russia. 'When the Western powers took a pretty unilateral path on Kosovo, that's when I think the souring of relations really began,' Pauline Neville-Jones, the Dayton Accords negotiator, told me. But Putin was not in a position to take action. Not yet.

At any rate, the Russian president's most urgent task wasn't Kosovo or any other foreign hotspot: it was Russia's economy. Watching Putin tackle Russia's chaotic government apparatus and equally chaotic economy, Guriev was impressed. And now Russians were regular participants in the world economy's corridors of power. A few months into Putin's tenure, in January 2001, Guriev attended his first World Economic Forum meeting at Davos with his wife, fellow economist Ekaterina Zhuravskaya, whom the Forum had just named one of its Global Leaders for Tomorrow.[9] 'People felt that Davos was creating opportunities,' he recalled. 'In my wife's class of Global Leaders for Tomorrow, there was for example a young Chinese entrepreneur named Jack Ma. He was optimistic too, and he was right.' Ma had every reason to be optimistic: his e-commerce platform, Alibaba, already counted among its investors Goldman Sachs, Japan's SoftBank and Sweden's mighty Investor AB (a part-owner of companies including ABB, Saab, Electrolux and AstraZeneca).[10] Among the other leaders of tomorrow selected that year were the British Labour politician Yvette Cooper, the German media executive Mathias Döpfner, the American broadcaster

Fareed Zakaria and the Polish pharmaceutical executive Jacek Szwajcowski.[11] It was a merry round in the Swiss Alps. Yes, there was talk about losers of globalization and the digital divide between those who had access to computers and mobile phones and those who didn't, but by and large the Davos crowd was upbeat. And when a financial dip arrived a couple of months later, politicians and business leaders managed to contain it. 'It was almost a crisis,' Guriev observed. 'And later, many who were involved thought, "We had a small financial crisis but no recession, and that was because we know how to manage financial markets." They became too confident.'

Such was the world when al-Qaida struck the World Trade Center and the Pentagon. Indeed, so upbeat was the mood until that September day that Putin put aside whatever resentment of the West he'd been harbouring. He was the first foreign leader to call President George W. Bush after the attacks, and he pledged Russia's support in America's fight against the terrorist scourge.[12]

Three months after the 9/11 attacks, the World Trade Organization's members welcomed China into their fold. 'China's accession to the WTO is a milestone in China's reform and opening up, bringing us into a new era to further open up. To join the WTO was a major strategic decision based on our comprehensive analysis of the situation at home and abroad in order to push forward China's reform and opening-up and socialist modernization drive,' Vice President Hu Jintao – soon to become his country's leader – declared.[13] Al-Qaida remained a global threat, for sure, but on the political front things were proceeding well, with the Peso Crisis, the Bond Massacre, the Asian Financial Crisis and the Balkan wars jointly tackled by governments striving for a more prosperous world for all.

As a WTO member, China stood to become even more integrated with global trade, but like all the organization's members it had to follow its rules governing fair play in the trade of goods, services and intellectual property. Of course, as a WTO member China – including its companies and the Western companies operating there – would also have easier access to other member states' markets, but that was not a bad thing. This, too, would reduce costs and make consumer goods cheaper for everyone. It was hardly surprising that WTO members were keen to add

China to their fold. But John Spellar was sceptical. 'We allowed China to join the international trading community without it actually paying the entrance fee, which is to behave properly,' he told me. 'A lot of this was down to the greed of company managers and owners.'

The day after China's accession to the community of countries committed to free and fair global trade, a firm in Houston delivered a reminder of the risks inherent in capitalism. The energy company Enron, whose shares had only a few months earlier been trading at over $90, declared bankruptcy. Its shares had lost nearly all their value, and now the company was being sued by its shareholders and investigated by the government. Another rapidly growing company, WorldCom, had recently been found to have committed similarly massive fraud: $11 billion in corporate assets simply did not exist. Even though both giants operated in the United States, their demise alarmed Cole-Fontayn and his colleagues in Asia. 'The governance scandals of WorldCom and Enron really undermined the trust and faith in the US-led business model and the US regulatory and accounting environment, which had been seen as the strongest in the world,' he said. 'When such things happen, you can have a breakdown in people's trust in markets, and that was very bruising.' The global markets seemed to stomach the collapse of Enron and WorldCom just as they'd stomached the Bond Massacre, the Peso Crisis and the Asian Financial Crisis, but Cole-Fontayn worried about what would happen next time.

In Washington, Chertoff was leading the investigations into the high-profile fraud cases. 'Enron was obviously not the world's first white-collar scandal, but it became very prominent because it was a company in Texas and because it had also had some interaction with President Bush,' he told me. 'And the president was 100 per cent in support of what I needed to do in order to bring these people to justice.' Chertoff established an Enron Task Force to investigate the perpetrators. Prosecuting mighty former executives would cause embarrassment to the US business community and perhaps even to capitalism. But, Chertoff said, 'what would have been even more harmful to the US economy would have been the idea that you can get away with fraud. I believed then, and still do, that confidence in our system requires trust in the law being applied equally.'

As the months went on, another kind of harm began to manifest itself: the surprising pain of China's WTO membership. 'China's accession to the WTO was beginning to create an import shock,' Guriev said. 'Imports from China displaced many, many workers, especially in the United States, especially in manufacturing. This is something nobody had expected. People thought, "China is joining the WTO, so what?" They obviously knew there would be an increase in imports from China, but they didn't realize how stratospheric it would be.' In 2001, the United States had imported goods worth slightly more than $19 billion from China. By 2003, that figure would grow to nearly $28.5 billion, and by 2015 to nearly $116 billion.[14] With so much being imported from China, it was no surprise that US jobs suffered. 'Offshoring has different effects on different groups. Typically, low-skill workers are harmed by offshoring, while high-skill workers benefit,' the US International Trade Commission summarized.[15]

Michael Treschow had spent the past five years conducting global acquisitions and expansion as CEO of Electrolux; the white-goods firm's globe-spanning presence now included its former American rival Westinghouse and European competitors AEG and Zanussi. And Treschow had promoted R&D and innovation as a strategy to stay ahead of lower-cost rivals – an important step now that China was part of the WTO. Under Treschow's leadership, Electrolux had pioneered gadgets like robot hoovers and smart fridges that indicated when they were running low on particular items. Even though Treschow's technology-wizardry vision was in some cases ahead of its time and failed to generate the hoped-for sales leaps, he'd steered the company towards a lucrative future.[16] So big, in fact, had Electrolux become that sometime after Treschow's departure, the US government nixed the firm's acquisition of General Electric's household division on competition grounds.

Despite such annoyances, these were indisputably good times for companies and for globalization. Still, Treschow and some other executives began worrying about not just the job losses among factory workers but also about the wider disparities globalization was causing. 'When I was living in the US Midwest in the eighties, lots of jobs in the auto industry went to Mexico, and now the same process was taking place in lots of other places,' Treschow told me. 'And as a result of globalization, some people were becoming extremely rich while others felt left behind. Imagine being someone who lived in a small town during these years. What would you make of the way the world was developing?' Spellar didn't have to imagine: 'Yes, people adjusted, but they still felt as though everyone was benefiting while they were particularly not benefiting.'

Concerns of that nature didn't elicit much action. The pain of 9/11 was fading, subsequent terrorist attacks had been painful but less severe, financial blips had been contained. Globalization's only malcontents seemed to be people like Spellar's constituents. For the winners of the globalizing economy, meanwhile, digital technology was creating exciting new sectors. India had become the hub of one of them: offshored call centres. Like so many other aspects of globalization, it was a corporate win-win that allowed countries to specialize in what they were good at. But as with other offshoring, it was certainly not a human victory, because it meant workers in the companies' home countries lost their jobs. 'I wouldn't say in all cases the performance of the UK is inferior. However, the quality of work overseas is exceptionally high,' HSBC's CEO Keith Whitson told the *Financial Times*.[17]

That month, the Department of Justice announced that Michael Kopper, Enron's managing director, had struck a plea deal and would cooperate with prosecutors.[18]

Chertoff returned to his office in the Department of Justice to continue pulling at threads in Enron's complex web of fraudulent transactions. He'd prosecuted plenty of powerful white-collar criminals before. In one such case, he'd managed to get consumer-electronics mogul Eddie Antar, known as Crazy Eddie, extradited from Israel to stand trial in a New York court. Antar was convicted on all counts and sentenced to twelve years in prison.[19] Chertoff had also secured a fifteen-month prison sentence for the New York Court of Appeal's Chief Judge Sol Wachtler, who was found guilty of threatening to kidnap his ex-mistress's daughter. 'Prosecuting the most powerful judge in New York wasn't an easy choice,' Chertoff told me. 'But you've got to apply the law equally, which means that when wealthy people commit crimes they have to be held accountable in the same way as the poorest thug is held accountable. The rich should get no breaks. In fact, they're privileged, and if they abuse that privilege, they should not have the expectation that they can escape justice. If we don't hold white-collar criminals to account, people will lose faith in the system.'

But Enron was more complex than Crazy Eddie and Judge Wachtler. It was a financial scandal with repercussions across the United States and even internationally. Still, 'I felt it was essential that the fraud be subjected to the legal process and that anyone who was found guilty should be punished with jail, so that they don't get a lesser punishment than somebody who picks your pocket on the street or robs a bank,' Chertoff told me.

That November, voters in Dayton and its surrounding communities elected Mike Turner to represent them in Congress. The son of a trade-union representative had campaigned on job creation for the area. But, partly as a result of the Bosnian peace negotiations conducted in his town and Dayton's role in helping Bosnian towns restore their services, he'd also developed a strong interest in national security. Seeing the aftermath of atrocities there had convinced Turner that history was in no way over.

Despite relations between the world's major countries being mostly harmonious, Turner even worried that what he'd seen in Bosnia could resurface elsewhere in Europe. Something involving Russia, say. With the United States and its allies at war in Afghanistan, international security was, in fact, returning to the top of the political agenda in Washington. But how many decision-makers would be interested in tackling Turner's other key concern, America's lost manufacturing jobs?

Russia under President Putin, meanwhile, was not only willing to assist the United States in fighting terrorism; it was becoming more stable too. Despite not having had a career as an elected politician before capturing the highest office in the country, Putin had emerged as an adept handler of the country's inefficient institutions and turbulent economy. 'Putin's first term was actually quite an optimistic period,' Guriev recalled. 'There were reforms, and we economists saw the impact of those reforms. There was deregulation, reform of the tax code, introduction of property rights for land. Ukraine just introduced property rights for land a few years ago, while Russia did it in 2002. The banking system was reformed and a normal deposit insurance system was introduced.' The effects of these reforms mattered far beyond the financial and legal community. 'Without macroeconomic stabilization, you cannot have economic growth,' Guriev pointed out. 'Once Russia defaulted, depreciated and then began growing and paying off its debt, suddenly the Russian economy looked like it was starting to move in the right direction.' When in early 2003 the United States assembled some of the countries that had joined capitalism and liberal democracy since the end of the Cold War and invaded Iraq, a string of Western European capitals joined Moscow in sharply criticizing the undertaking. Russia almost seemed like a normal country.

But just as things were starting to look really promising for the Russian economy, Mikhail Khodorkovsky, a tycoon who had accumulated a vast fortune as the owner of the oil giant Yukos, was arrested by Russian police in a dramatic fashion. The arrest seemed to many to be linked to the fact that Khodorkovsky wasn't just Russia's richest man and the head of Yukos; he was also a budding civil-society leader with a reform-oriented organization, Open Russia, to his name. 'From jail, Khodorkovsky told a Russian news agency that "somebody wants to demonstrate that even the most honest large-scale business cannot be secure".'[20]

Guriev followed the drama from a new perch at Princeton University. Later he would conclude that Khodorkovsky's arrest was a fork in the road and that his country had chosen the wrong direction. But in 2003, he hoped the oligarch's misfortune would turn out to be merely a hiccup. The following year he returned to Moscow, where he'd been appointed director of the prestigious New Economic School.

In China, the Western companies just kept arriving, and they just kept manufacturing. 'President Bush is on an eight-day tour of Asia. He's visiting American jobs,' David Letterman quipped.[21] Since November 1999, Ohio had lost nearly 200,000 high-paying manufacturing jobs.[22] To be sure, some of those jobs had been lost to automation, and state-wide unemployment was low.[23] But there, as in the English Midlands and other former manufacturing hubs, many residents resented not having been consulted about the fundamental shift in their lives. A collision could be seen on the horizon: while business leaders and many policymakers saw globalization as being about economics, many ordinary people saw it as being about their way of life.

At General Motors, meanwhile, executives were receiving alarming reports. The QQ minicar, a new car developed by the SAIC-Chery Automobile Company and about to go into production, had turned out to look rather a lot like GM's own Chevrolet Spark.[24] Even the name, Chery, was suspiciously close to Chevrolet's nickname, Chevy. GM sued,[25] but it was an uncomfortable situation, since SAIC was GM's Chinese partner, the company for whose attention it had fought so hard in that early competition with Ford.

In Rome, Giorgio La Malfa was about to relinquish his post as chairman of the lower house's Finance Committee to join Silvio Berlusconi's government as minister of European Union affairs. Since assuming the chairmanship, he'd been watching trade and finance even more closely than usual, and now he'd arrived at a paradoxical conclusion: even though globalization seemed to be proceeding mostly fine and allowed ordinary citizens to buy more consumer goods, citizens were not fully on board. '*The* problem with globalization is the loss of jobs in our countries, and that's what was becoming obvious in the early years of this century,' La Malfa told me. If voters had been asked whether they wanted lower consumer prices and a more convenient lifestyle and were willing to pay for it with the loss of some people's jobs, a majority may have said yes. But that choice had not been put to them. Indeed, starting in the early nineties globalization had seemed so inevitable that politicians and businesspeople didn't really view it as a choice. After the Warsaw Pact's demise and the opening of China and other formerly closed economies, there was no single globalization *fiat lux*. Not even the most ambitious G7 summit could have declared that globalization was to be created, because its execution involved countless people outside Western governments. Globalization happened because so many opportunities presented themselves – in the capitalist world and in the countries wanting to become like the capitalist world. Germany's capstone concept of *Wandel durch Handel* had triumphed.

It was to lead to resentment in some of the countries now implementing capitalism, but the velocity of this worldwide transformation created problems all its own. Had companies been more gradual in moving production and supply chains to other countries, the effect on jobs and sentiments at home may have been more gradual too. But in a free-market economy, governments can't command companies to keep jobs at home.

Then there was the issue of low wages based on iffy workplace practices in emerging economies. 'We didn't realize when globalization took off in the nineties that some countries would have extremely high advantages because they were not respecting certain standards like labour conditions and minimum wage,' La Malfa pointed out. 'That meant that in a sense we've had unfair competition between countries. We should not accept full competition from countries that don't respect certain fundamental rules of labour conditions and minimum wage. This issue should have been settled early on, but it wasn't.' To be sure, the International Labour Organization was created by the League of Nations' member states in 1919 with the task of setting and monitoring international labour standards. It has done so by adopting conventions, but the organization is so toothless that such rules have had minimal effect.

Many political leaders saw the stumbling labour market as an opportunity for much-needed reform. In Germany, Gerhard Schröder – the only child of a working-class mother widowed in the war who had risen to become chancellor and leader of the Social Democrats, the SPD – introduced Agenda 2010. The massive programme was designed to make the country's economy more flexible, and with unemployment at 11.6 per cent, reform was desperately needed. Agenda 2010 slashed unemployment benefits and combined them with social benefits in one category, known as Hartz IV.[26] By 2005, the labour cure was already beginning to make the German economy more agile and competitive – but globalization's losers felt marginalized once again.

On Gotland, residents were saying farewell to another Cold War legacy: the armed forces. During the Cold War, the exposed Baltic Sea island had unsurprisingly had a large military presence. Now 300 officers and as many civilian employees were still based there, along with hundreds of conscripts, but with peace having arrived, the Swedish government had decided to shut the island's regiment as well as numerous other regiments around the country.[27] Gotland was losing its most crucial employer, and the civilians – mostly local residents – would struggle to find new jobs. 'People kept saying that with globalization everyone benefits, that you can move to where the jobs are,' Solveig Artsman recalled.

'But there are a lot of people who can't move somewhere else to get a job. You have your home, you have your family. People are not just creatures that can switch places like chess pieces. But that world didn't seem to be worth much in the eyes of political and business leaders. They were almost contemptuous of "little people".' Skaistė, though, liked what global trade was doing for her country. 'Pretty much everyone in Lithuania felt that we were being invited into the globalized economy, and that that was a good thing,' she told me. 'We felt that if you're not a part of the global supply chain, you will not survive. Looking from today's perspective, you realize that things are not that straightforward. But at that time, it looked like economics was everything.'

La Malfa is an ardent believer in companies expanding globally, competing with rivals and letting the best ones win, and in governments helping their economies become as efficient as possible. By the middle of the noughties, Italian companies had lowered costs by moving some manufacturing abroad, mostly to Eastern European countries like Romania. But the Italian private sector, dominated as it is by small and medium-sized enterprises, hadn't been able to expand to China as much as mighty corporations from the United States and Germany.

That made the Italian economy feel a bit provincial. But La Malfa concluded that America's much more dynamic expansion had a price. 'When I started hearing Americans complaining about job losses, I realized that globalization was not working, at the very least not in political terms,' he told me. 'American companies had just been too quick to relocate manufacturing and supply chains to China, which created resentment among ordinary Americans. And already then it was becoming clear that the Chinese regime was not going to fundamentally change, which meant there was never going to be a level playing field.' But while this or that part of globalization was causing consternation, by and large the interconnected world was functioning, and no government saw reasons to collectively try to return to the drawing board. At any rate, what would globalization reform conducted by one country alone have looked like?

At least the Enron Task Force had kept Chertoff's word and was holding white-collar criminals to account. In 2006, a court in Houston sentenced former CEO Jeff Skilling to fourteen years in prison, while another former CEO, Kenneth Lay, died before his sentencing.[28] Chertoff himself was now serving as US secretary of homeland security, in charge of keeping the country safe from all manner of threats.

A few countries were left out of the international merriment. Outside its borders, Iran – under sanctions over its nuclear programme – functioned almost like a shadow economy. Bonyad Mostazafan, an NGO overseen by the supreme leader, operated hundreds of subsidiaries and affiliated companies specializing in railway construction to livestock and everything between. Though the companies did business in most parts of the world, clients often didn't realize they were dealing with an extended part of the Iranian state.[29]

And as Mike Turner had predicted, war was to return once again – though not in Bosnia. On 20 March 2003, the United States invaded Iraq to, as it saw it, rid the world of another prospective nuclear power. Not only did America's G7 and NATO friends Germany and France join Russia and China in opposing the invasion, so too did more than four in five Europeans.[30] Indeed, a whole world used to increasing peace was stunned by America's actions.

5
THE RACE FOR MOBILE-TELEPHONY SUPREMACY

Mobile-phone makers knew that handsets that could access the internet were the next frontier. But from his corner office at Electrolux, Michael Treschow had watched Ericsson fail to catch on to the defining consumer product of the post-Cold War age. 'Developing the mobile infrastructure suited Ericsson perfectly, since it was an engineering-focused company rather than a consumer-product one,' he told me. 'But Ericsson didn't really grasp how the mobile telephone had become a consumer product and instead kept treating the handset like a technical product.' In 2002, Ericsson decided that it needed a new chairman to help turn the ship around. It offered the post to a man who by now enjoyed a worldwide reputation as a 'company doctor': Treschow. He had to make gains on Nokia, the leader of the handset pack. The Finnish firm had, Treschow told me, emerged 'from a completely different world, a world of wellies and car tyres, and they understood that the mobile phone was becoming a consumer product and that it should look good and be comfortable to use. Nokia had consumer-product experts, which Ericsson didn't.'

A short time later, Karl-Henrik Sundström was promoted to Ericsson's CFO and executive vice president, which meant that he too was now part of the team trying to make the company a global leader in handsets. Being the master of the infrastructure was simply not enough when seemingly everyone was in the market for a mobile phone, and not just in the Western world. 'Even though we'd been a pioneer in building handsets we'd become a bit too focused on the infrastructure,' Sundström conceded. In true globalization style, the Swedish firm teamed up with Sony to form Sony Ericsson. Motorola's handset business, meanwhile, was struggling to close in on Nokia's momentum, while Canada's Nortel Networks focused on infrastructure, not handsets.

But seeing off Western competitors was only one of the tasks facing Treschow and Sundström. In China, Huawei had recorded sales of $3.8 billion by the end of 2003, and now it was beginning to file patents too: it was developing its own intellectual property.[1] Managers from companies like Ericsson and Cisco often recognized their companies' features in Huawei products, and Cisco had already sued the Chinese firm for IP theft.[2] The theft involved 'direct, verbatim copying of our source code, to say nothing of our command line interface, our help screens, our copyrighted manuals and other elements of our product', Cisco's executive vice president later wrote.[3] But mostly, Western company bosses decided the IP loss was something they had to live with. 'When you look at their equipment, it's either an Ericsson copy, or a Cisco copy, or copied from somebody else,' Sundström said. 'Everything we ever had in our product portfolio, Huawei did too. That was part of the game. Probably we were a bit innocent and didn't understand how big they would become.' Huawei was still mostly selling its mobile infrastructure to Chinese clients, but it was also beginning to win some clients in developing countries. But all in all, Ericsson still ruled the mobile infrastructure market. And then there was the fourth-generation mobile telephony Ericsson was developing.

IP loss didn't just bedevil Western companies' operations inside China. Ottawa-based Nortel Networks was a stunning globalization success story; the firm had risen to dominate the market for fibre-optic data transmission systems and had invented the Orbitor, a pioneering smartphone. Engineers came from all over the world to work on the company's glittering campus in Ottawa. But for years, the Canadian Security Intelligence Service had been warning the company that China was stealing its data and documents. 'We told the executives, "They're sucking your intellectual property out,"' Michel Juneau-Katsuya, the head of the CSIS's Asia-Pacific unit, later explained in a media interview. 'They didn't do anything.' In 2004, someone using the login of Nortel's CEO sent hundreds of internal documents to China.[4] (Huawei has repeatedly denied having anything to do with the theft.)[5]

All executives know that a bit of IP loss is unpreventable: when employees leave a firm, for example, they can take their knowledge with them to a new employer, and it's hard to determine when that sharing crosses a red line. There was no doubt, though, that someone was causing Nortel to haemorrhage commercial secrets. Shocked telecoms executives around the world followed the story of how mysterious hackers traced to China had stolen technical papers, research-and-development reports, business plans and other documents from Nortel.[6]

In Stockholm, Ericsson had decided to leave the handset business and focus even more on mobile infrastructure. Treschow, Ericsson's chairman, would not have been pleased had he known what was transpiring in Amsterdam at the same time: the Dutch mobile operator Telfort was about to pick Huawei to supply its infrastructure. It didn't seem to bother Telfort's CEO, a former Netherlands chief at Ericsson named Ton aan de Stegge, that he'd never heard of the Chinese firm until it pitched to him a few months earlier. And with his decision, Huawei had broken into the prestigious European market. 'I'm absolutely convinced that . . . three years from now Huawei will be one of the largest infrastructure suppliers in the telecoms area,' aan de Stegge told the *Financial Times*.[7]

The biggest mobile revolution, though, was happening in Africa. After deciding that the continent presented a massive business opportunity that he was going to pursue, Mo Ibrahim had to pick a place to start. He decided sub-Saharan countries should be his focus, and that Uganda would be first. The main selection criterion would be that countries had a high degree of rule of law. Aware that companies doing business in African countries frequently succumb to bribery, Ibrahim also knew that he'd need to proof his company against such temptations. 'At the first board meeting, we adopted the anti-bribery policy. And then we said, "Okay, how are we going to implement this?" Late at night, if the chief of police were to come to visit the local CEO at home and say, "Look, we have an election going on here, and you guys support the government, so we need some help," what will the CEO do? That's what we discussed at that first board meeting. Most of us, in the group leadership, would be sitting here in Europe, safe. This guy is over there. What does he do in such a situation? We came up with a very simple solution. Any chief executive would not have any authority to spend more than $30,000 without prior board approval.' Celtel, as his company was eventually known, first expanded to Kenya and Tanzania, then to Nigeria, the DRC, Sudan, Zambia, Gabon, Chad, Sierra Leone, Burkina Faso, Malawi, Madagascar and Congo-Brazzaville, and covered Egypt in cooperation with the British firm Vodafone. None of the countries had perfect rule of law, but they did have a promising combination of some rule of law and massive demand for mobile telephony. Around the same time, other companies, including France Telecom, Luxembourg-based Millicom, Vodafone and MTN of South Africa also launched mobile networks in various African countries.

The impact was immediate. Mobile use in Africa grew several times faster than in Europe.[8] 'Across urban–rural and rich–poor divides, mobile phones connect individuals to individuals, information, markets, and services. In Mali, residents of Timbuktu can call relatives living in the capital city of Bamako – or relatives in France. In Ghana, farmers in Tamale are able to send a text message to learn corn and tomato prices in Accra, over 400 kilometers away. In Niger, day laborers are able to call acquaintances in Benin to find out about job opportunities without making the US$40 trip,' two academics reported.[9]

'It was an incredible change,' Robert Okine told me. In the early 2000s, he was a mathematics student at the Kwame Nkrumah University of Science and Technology in Kumasi, Ghana's second-largest city. 'Before the mobile phones arrived, you made phone calls by going to a phone booth and putting some coins in, but that obviously meant that everyone around you could hear what you were saying,' he recalled. 'The first thing I remember about mobile phones is that they brought privacy. And they lead to financial inclusion, because everyone with a phone could receive money. You didn't have to open a bank account any more.'

Africans bought mobile phones despite even budget-range handsets being extremely expensive relative to their income.[10] 'When I left the store with the phone and the SIM card, I was so excited. It was something like buying a Tesla today,' Okine said. It was a Nokia, of course. 'Mobile telephony fuelled globalization,' Treschow reflected. 'And gradually the different mobile standards disappeared: the American one, the Japanese one and eventually the Chinese one. The European one remained. And generally, things were getting cheaper and cheaper and better and better.' Today most mobile systems operate using the standard originally created in Europe.

Just as he'd hit his stride building mobile telephony across sub-Saharan Africa, in 2005 Ibrahim sold Celtel to a Kuwaiti telecoms firm for a hefty $3.4 billion.[11] Despite eventually having 55 million mobile customers in fourteen African countries, he wasn't altogether happy with how his company had fared. 'I really struggled to raise money from international lenders,' he said. 'Globalization didn't really reach Africa. Only some aspects of it did, which was the extractive industry.' Since the eighties, Western companies had invested billions of dollars in African mining, which were feeding the world's (especially China's) increasing need for metals.[12] In 2005, Africa would see record foreign direct investments of $31 billion.[13] Mining companies, of course, operated in a sector that was well established and lucrative. But in other sectors requiring significant infrastructure, companies were much more dependent on loans. Western governments' export–import agencies were helping provide such loans – and by now, so was the Chinese government, and it was also willing to offer easily accessible loans to African governments. After starting out modestly in 2000, in 2005 it lent $2.2 billion to sub-Saharan African countries, including $552 million to the Democratic Republic of the Congo, whose natural resources Chinese companies were eager to tap into.[14]

By now Huawei and ZTE, a smaller, partly state-owned Chinese rival, had a steady sales presence in African countries.[15] So what if their gear was not as sophisticated as that of Ericsson? The Chinese firms were cheaper than the competition: Huawei up to 15 per cent cheaper than Ericsson and Nokia, which was now also focusing heavily on mobile infrastructure; ZTE up to 40 per cent cheaper.[16] Or so the price tag said. Ibrahim, too, had been regularly approached by Huawei about having Celtel buy Huawei equipment. Top executives made appointments with him; the chairman came to see him. They offered significant discounts.

But Ibrahim declined the offers. The chairman was most definitely not pleased. Ibrahim described what happened next: '"You're pro-Western,"' he told me. I said, "No, I'm not. Just look at the price."' Ibrahim had read the proposed deal's terms and conditions, and 'the equipment was cheap upfront, but it was going to become very expensive over time because software updates, maintenance and upgrades were not included. With those updates, Ericsson was cheaper.' Many other companies in developing countries, though, went with Huawei.

Huawei and ZTE's march continued, and Huawei especially was filing more and more patents. In foreign markets, Chinese authorities were standing by to sweeten prospective buyers' deals. Government-owned banks in China, for example, offered advantageous loans, while China's Export-Import Bank presented developing countries with so-called Angola-mode deals that allowed the lender to repay infrastructure loans with natural resources.[17]

Companies everywhere occasionally offer prospective clients financing packages, but not in these numbers. Watching the plethora of financing assistance Beijing was offering countries deciding on new telephony infrastructure, executives at Western firms were convinced that it was no longer a matter of the usual sweeteners but that the Chinese government was violating WTO rules. But what could they do? It was the same story as with the IP loss, that constant killjoy. In California, a Chinese citizen had recently pleaded guilty to illegally downloading source code belonging to the imaging company 3DGeo.[18] Still, companies were making good money, and since their fortunes depended on the Chinese market, manufacturing in China or both, they were hardly in a position to complain.

In Costa Rica, Oscar Arias was once again elected president in May 2006, and this time he wanted to fully bring his country into the globalized economy. Kevin Casas-Zamora had recently completed a doctorate in political science at Oxford, focusing on the study of democracy, and run for election as one of Arias's two vice-presidential candidates. He duly became second vice president, with Arias also appointing the young academic minister of planning and economic policy, which put Casas-Zamora in charge of mapping the government's strategy across all sectors. 'When we were elected, the big issue was building on the previous thirty years of economic policy,' Casas-Zamora told me. 'We wanted to open up the Costa Rican economy even more, and the culmination of that was the planned free-trade agreement with the US.'

The planned free-trade agreement was not only huge: as Arias's government saw it, it was also overwhelmingly positive. 'Our approach was, "Look, there's nothing inherently damaging in the free-trade agreement with the US, and public policy can compensate for some of the effects on specific sectors. If we are so incapable of putting in place public policies to mitigate those effects, then we deserve all the bad things that can come out of that agreement. But it's up to us," ' Casas-Zamora said. 'And I have to say, it's tricky. I'll give you one example: the telecoms sector.'

In 2006, Costa Rica's telecoms sector was still a government monopoly; even getting a mobile-phone contract was a highly time-consuming process. It was hardly a surprise that a mere thirty-three of every hundred Costa Ricans had a mobile phone.[19] Market liberalization quickly revolutionized this state of affairs. Mobile-telephony operators, infrastructure and handsets quickly materialized. Customers found themselves able to walk into a store and leave a short time later, phone and contract in hand. (Casas-Zamora had bought his first mobile phone a couple of years earlier. A Nokia, of course.)

Around the same time, Huawei opened an office in neighbouring Panama, from which it set about winning business in Central and Latin America. Costa Rica later awarded a five-year 3G contract to the Chinese firm. When Brazil's enormous Tele Norte Leste Participacoes SA was looking to buy new equipment, Huawei sweetened its bid with a $30 billion credit-line offer from the China Development Bank.[20]

In Western capitals, governments seemed uninterested in a state of affairs that was now becoming obvious: in the crucial sector of mobile infrastructure, the number of companies was thinning out. The formerly so successful Nortel was struggling badly; within a few years, the Canadian firm was to go bankrupt. What would happen if Ericsson or Nokia took a nosedive, too, or left mobile infrastructure altogether?

Watching company after company sign contracts with Huawei, the two Nordic firms concluded that they might have to relinquish their market ambitions in countries content with buying 3G infrastructure. Their edge now was the future 4G technology. But their technical advantage was diminishing. Without its IP advantage, a modern company loses its edge. China had updated its patent legislation as part of joining the WTO, but the legislation unsurprisingly only applied to China, and Western companies had already concluded that the legal system was not going to come through for them there. In Western countries, they had more protection. The US government had just charged two engineers in the San Francisco Bay area with economic espionage for China after discovering they'd been stealing IP from companies, including TSMC, a fast-rising Taiwanese chipmaker, and the FBI had just detained a Chinese-born Motorola software engineer who had been found illegally downloading commercial secrets belonging to the Chicago-based firm.[21] These, though, were rare cases where IP theft was successfully identified. And despite the larger IP risks in China, companies remained eager to be part of the extraordinary Chinese economy. In 2006, it had grown 10.7 per cent, up from 9.9 per cent the year before.[22] A CEO deciding to reduce exposure to China over IP concerns would have seemed myopic. Whatever its provenance, Huawei's mobile infrastructure was by now much better than even a few years earlier.

In Dongguan, Antony Perillo was amazed to see how quickly his Chinese colleagues in the shoe-and-furniture capital had learnt not just the details of running a factory but also the finer details of investments. 'Seemingly all of a sudden, Chinese colleagues in the factories were buying apartments,' he said. 'They'd tell you things like, "I bought another apartment," and you went, "Okay, really? Why have you bought two apartments?" and they'd say, "Oh, it's a good investment." There was rapid education and they were extremely keen to learn.' The investment evangelization was trickling down.

By now, in 2007, there was massive change in the handset world too. The BlackBerry, a device that used a full keyboard rather than the typical 1–9 dial-pad and could send emails and even surf the internet, was taking the world by storm. US Senator Barack Obama, who had discovered the device while serving as a state senator in Illinois, was a devotee. People on more restricted budgets, meanwhile, could opt for less sophisticated relatives of the BlackBerry. The tech-savvy Obama had even begun thinking about how he could use smartphones and the internet to power a run for the presidency.

On the House side of the US Capitol, Mike Turner was almost four years into representing the residents of Dayton. He'd sponsored legislation and resolutions to incentivize brownfield conversion and to commemorate the tenth anniversary of the Dayton Accords, and been appointed to chair the Saving America's Cities alliance, a federal committee concerned with the redevelopment of down-on-their luck cities.[23] He'd represented Congress in Srebrenica when US government investigators returned identified massacre victims to their families. Rather presciently, he'd also sponsored legislation requiring all foreign direct investment in the United States to be matched with equivalent opportunities for US companies in the investor's home country. Americans should be able to invest in China in the same way that Chinese citizens could invest in the United States, Turner argued.[24] The bill failed. In a world that pundits had declared flat, there seemed to be no need for such nationality-based rules.

Now a member of the House Armed Services Committee and the NATO Parliamentary Assembly, Turner also continued to worry about Russia's intentions. 'I based that largely on their views of military structure, their exercises, the modernization of their nuclear weapons,' he told me. 'Most of their programmes have been focused not on defensive structures but being able to intimidate, threaten or invade their neighbours.' Most other politicians, though, were interpreting Russia in much the same way as the Swedish government. Now, in 2006, Gotland was without military defence. And in Washington, lawmakers interested in national security were consumed by the wars in Iraq and Afghanistan, not Russia. Turner was, one might say, a Washington version of Solveig Artsman.

Finland, for its part, was receiving an avalanche of bad news, and it had nothing to do with Russia. It had to do with handsets. Nokia was still enjoying a handset market share of nearly 50 per cent, but even though it had released smartphones it hadn't come up with a compelling offering. A year later, the Finnish giant was quickly falling out of favour with consumers in well-off countries.[25] And in the market for so-called dumb phones featuring voice calls and 0–9 keypads, cheaper competitors were gaining market share. It was a devastating turn of events for the Finnish giant. With people getting hooked on using mobile phones for more than phone calls and texts, there was a whole new generation of phones to be sold. For every 100 Europeans, there were now more than 100 mobile-phone lines. More than one in every four Africans had a mobile phone, and so did one in every three Asians. Globally, almost half the population had a mobile phone.[26]

Less than half an hour by car from John Spellar's constituency, there was finally some good news. In 2005, MG Rover – home to famous brands including Austin and, of course, MG – had gone bankrupt. Despite support of nearly £300 million from the UK taxpayer, the iconic carmaker had not been able to keep up with the competition from other global brands. This had rendered 5,300 workers at its plant in Longbridge – and some 1,000 others employed by suppliers – jobless.[27] Within a year, most of the workers had found work again, but some 2,000 were still unemployed. Then Longbridge's long-suffering residents received manna from heaven, if only a small amount of it: the Chinese carmaker Nanjing acquired MG Rover and would restart production. On 30 May, the Longbridge plant cranked up its machines again in the presence of Nanjing CEO Yu Jianwei. Outside, the Union flag and the flag of China were hoisted. Nanjing had only rehired 130 workers, but it was better than nothing.[28]

In Costa Rica, connecting the country to globalized markets seemed to be progressing so well that Casas-Zamora didn't feel guilty when he bowed out of the government in the autumn of 2007. Still only forty years old, and with a CV that included not just a cabinet post and his doctorate from Oxford but also his status as a World Economic Forum Young Global Leader, Casas-Zamora was definitely a globalization winner. After leaving his ministerial post, he was immediately offered a position with a think tank in Washington, where he could once again write about the health of democracy.

Not far from him, another electoral battle was unfolding, and this time mobile phones had a starring role. 'Presidential candidates John McCain and Barack Obama have very different digital resumes. Their habits were shaped, in part, by what they were doing when the digital age arrived. Obama has been seen walking with his BlackBerry – so absorbed you worry he might bump into something. McCain, on the other hand, says he rarely uses e-mail or the Internet,' NPR public radio reported.[29] Despite having only two years in the Senate under his belt, the Democrats' nominee was polling surprisingly well against his Republican rival. Indeed, thanks in no small part to mobile phones and the internet, the Democrat had managed to make himself a household name and collect plenty of small donations at the same time.

The world had come a long way since Marc Andreessen's launch of the world's first internet browser fifteen years earlier and Yahoo's arrival not long after that. In 2008, almost three-quarters of Americans and Canadians were using the internet, as were nearly half of Europeans, more than a quarter of people in Latin America and the Caribbean, nearly one-fifth of all people in the Middle East and North Africa, more than 4 per cent of South Asians and nearly 4 per cent of sub-Saharan Africans.[30]

People in all these parts of the world were, of course, using mobile phones too, and a rapidly growing number of them were using the internet on their phones.[31] The phone battle was shifting from one between the dumb phone and the smartphone to one between smartphones. Nokia, desperate to shore up its lagging market share, released a smartphone and so did Microsoft and a few other companies. But all these clever devices paled in comparison to a handset created not by a fellow telecoms firm but by Apple. It was June 2007. The iPhone had arrived, and consumers loved it.

6
FRIVOLOUS FINANCIERS CAUSE FINANCIAL TURMOIL

Even as the excitement about smartphones spread among consumers, bankers and policymakers knew that elsewhere something very troubling was afoot. The trouble had begun in early 2007, when scores of subprime mortgage lenders in the United States declared bankruptcy: companies had been selling homes to people who could not afford them, in the expectation that house prices would keep rising. And the malaise didn't stop there. The financial-sector innovation that had started with nifty creations like UBS's 'CDO of CDOs' – collaterized debt obligations squared – had grown even more innovative, and investment bankers had been particularly keen on buying and selling mortgage lenders' mortgages. The bankers had then created ever-craftier ways of slicing the mortgages and selling them – including their inherent risk – to financial institutions around the world. It was a world of securitization and credit default swaps. 'We knew that there were a lot of instruments being created that were hard to understand: derivatives of underlying instruments, securities that were being sliced into different tranches of risk and repackaged,' Michael Cole-Fontayn told me. 'An ever-increasing number of special-purpose vehicles were being created that didn't seem to appear on any balance sheet. The underlying collateral may have been originated by one particular firm, and that loan was then sold along with the underlying rights to the collateral. Sliced, diced many times over, ending up in special-purpose vehicles that were then able to get credit ratings that seemed to be in excess of reality. Those securities were then distributed all around the world.'

Especially during his tenure as chairman of the Italian parliament's House of Deputies' Finance Committee a few years earlier, Giorgio La Malfa – the economics professor and veteran legislator – had been trying to make sense of what was transpiring on the US housing market and what bankers' enthusiastic creation of new derivatives meant for the interconnected global economy. 'I was concerned because it's unimaginable that you can eliminate risk from the economy,' he told me. 'It's obvious that you can't lend money to people who're not able to repay and then sell it to the market, but somehow that basic truth had vanished and they wanted to keep selling these financial instruments. And sooner or later, the illusion that you can eliminate risk by dividing up your assets and selling them to others was going to encounter disaster.'

At one point, La Malfa organized hearings with Italian banking bosses but, as he recalled, 'there was a very negative reaction from the Italian financial-services sector because I was "intruding" on their freedom of choice. What was happening was obviously that they were making enormous amounts of money by for example selling these derivatives to towns and other local entities.' Italian banks had been buying fewer shaky repackaged mortgages than banks in many other countries.[1] For La Malfa, though, it was a matter of fiscal prudence: how could the firms be allowed to keep packaging up risky debts and selling them to less sophisticated outfits?

In August 2007, Paris-based BNP Paribas announced that the assets held by three of its hedge funds lacked liquidity because investors were rejecting its heavily mortgage-focused assets. Other European banks soon made similar announcements. Seven months later the venerable New York investment bank Bear Stearns, facing imminent collapse, had to sell itself for a pittance to JPMorgan Chase. But the crisis kept spreading. In September, the US government saw no choice but to nationalize Fannie Mae and Freddie Mac, the country's two federally backed mortgage insurers. That month Lehman Brothers, one of the world's largest investment banks, declared bankruptcy (though not before having tried to raise liquidity in Hong Kong),[2] while the US government bailed AIG out for $85 billion. The country's largest insurer had made hefty bets in the credit default swap markets. 'You have to be very careful with financial capitalism,' La Malfa told me. 'If you look at the financial crisis, it was obvious even before the first firm went bankrupt that something bad was brewing. Capitalism is unstable, and financial capitalism is even more unstable.'

The global financial system was still extremely shaky when political and business leaders convened in Davos in January 2008, and once again Sergei Guriev – now having been named one of the WEF's Young Global Leaders in a cohort that also included Saif al-Islam Gaddafi and the future Nobel Economics Prize winner Esther Duflo – was back in the Swiss mountain resort.[3] And although the elevation of next-generation leaders like Guriev into the WEF elite was still going like clockwork, something more profound was beginning to shift some leaders' belief in American economic leadership. 'Already then, it was clear that things were not perfect,' Guriev said. 'And in Davos, Russian leaders made the case that Russia could become a safe haven from the global financial turbulence. Russia already had a rainy-day fund – today we know it was a war chest – which was substantial, and in the following two years or so, it did protect the country. And oil prices were high. Financially speaking, Russia was looking good.'

In the United States, McCain and Obama were now neck and neck.[4] But George W. Bush was still in charge, and the financial crisis, which was now also wreaking havoc outside America, made the Enron scandal look like a mild case of flu. The global tribe of bankers employed by interconnected financial institutions had been playing the same apparently irresistible game. The public angrily debated whether bailing out banks that had brought on their own misery was enabling reckless behaviour or taking a painful step to safeguard ordinary people's deposits. In Britain, home to famously unfettered financial markets, Prime Minister Gordon Brown and Chancellor of the Exchequer Alistair Darling faced the same poisoned chalice and decided that they had to save the banks to save the country's economy. As the Norwegian playwright Henrik Ibsen once concluded, 'These heroes of finance are like beads on a string – when one slips off, the rest follows.'[5] That couldn't be allowed to happen. The UK government had to bail banks out.

In virtually every Western country, the taxpayer had to rescue failing financial institutions. 'There was phenomenal coordination by central banks all around the world,' Cole-Fontayn recalled. 'Central banks and finance ministers everywhere were having to persuade the political system, the governments of the day, to borrow extensively, in order to bail out, if you will, financial market participants. And to prevent a crisis like this from happening again, they came up with countless measures to bolster the capital and liquidity of major financial institutions that had never anticipated to be humbled.' Cole-Fontayn's own parents called him, demanding an explanation of what they were reading in the newspaper and why the situation wasn't under control.

At least the summer delivered some respite. Between 8 and 24 August, nearly 11,000 athletes from a record 204 countries and regions competed in the Beijing Olympics. Television audiences around the world loved the Chinese organizers' spectacular pageantry at the opening and closing ceremonies, but most of all they loved the charismatic sprinter Usain Bolt, who won the 100-metre race, and the American swimmer Michael Phelps, who won eight gold medals and set seven world records over a staggering seventeen races. The games, held under the slogan 'One World, One Dream', were a resounding success for China. Despite the pain caused by the bankers, it felt as if the world was on a trajectory of more collaboration and better times for all. *Wandel durch Handel* had defeated fear and pessimism. That feeling had been enhanced a few months earlier, when Russian voters elected Dmitry Medvedev to succeed Putin, who had stepped down after completing the maximum two terms in office. Medvedev, considered a liberal, wanted to modernize his country's economy and even suggested that Russia could create its own Silicon Valley by learning from the original.

But now, with the summer of 2008 nearing its end, Ekaterina Zhuravskaya, Guriev's wife and fellow economist, began suspecting that the new president's ambitious reform plans would come to nought. Indeed, she felt that freedom in Russia was not going to return to what it had been in the nineties, and that the family should leave the country. Guriev himself, though, remained optimistic. 'For a couple of months it looked like freedom would restart,' he told me. He even became an occasional external advisor to Medvedev and was appointed to the boards of state-run companies.[6]

When the Olympics ended, the United States was on the homestretch of its presidential-election campaign, and McCain and Obama were still neck and neck.[7] Even though the financial crisis was rocking the globe, globalization seemed in robust health, with citizen anger united against the global banker tribe rather than a particular country. In fact, the financial crisis had demonstrated the importance of governments working together, and they'd done so not just with their closest friends but most importantly within the G20 – a group formed after the Asian Financial Crisis that comprised leading Western economies as well as countries like China and Russia.

So strong was the new global order that even Russia's brief war against its neighbour Georgia merely seemed like a blip. To be sure, the five days of fighting that saw Russian troops advance into Georgia on the day of the Olympic opening ceremony had rattled the outside world. But an armed conflict confined to select parts of a small country was unlikely to halt the new world order's seemingly unstoppable advance. Indeed, even as the financial crisis kept spooking the world, manufacturing was continuing its march towards greater efficiency and cheaper goods. That autumn, Apple's new MacBook Air retailed for $1,599, whereas the breakout laptop two decades earlier, NeXTcube, had set consumers back $6,500.[8] The British singer-songwriter Ray Davies's song 'Vietnam Cowboys', about empty factories in Birmingham and baby boomers in Hong Kong, was making the rounds. And Mattel, the maker of Barbie, was so certain that the future for its iconic blonde doll lay in China that it was planning to open its very first House of Barbie (featuring a couture collection, a design centre, lots of dolls and even a Barbie bar) in Shanghai.[9]

On 4 November 2008, Obama was elected president of the United States. Michael Chertoff got ready to turn the Department of Homeland Security over to the incoming administration, and he felt confident Obama's team along with prosecutors across the United States would hold to account the bankers who had gambled away ordinary people's money and pushed the global economy to the brink of catastrophe. 'Of course you shouldn't make a performative point of prosecutions,' he told me. 'But if there's a real basis to prosecute, and there's a real violation of law, and you have the evidence to back it up and take it in front of a jury, and if you don't do it, you feed the narrative that the institutions of the government operate for the benefit of the elite.'

There was no doubt that the financial crisis had put the global tribe of bankers in their place, at least reputationally. But even as governments finally managed to stabilize their economies, the population was paying a painful price for bankers' adventures. In the United States, an estimated 5 per cent of homeowners lost their houses, and in October 66 per cent reported that their economy had suffered as a result of the crisis.[10] In every country, the economy shrank; the global economy collectively lost some $30 trillion.[11] 'The financial crisis was the worst economic crisis since the Great Depression but not really comparable in magnitude,' Guriev observed. 'But people had been so optimistic and nobody, myself included, had imagined how big the bubble would be, how many people would lose their jobs, how many banks would go under. At that time, investment banking was the career of choice for virtually everybody in economics and beyond. Financial globalization was at its peak, investment bankers were paid huge bonuses, and they thought of themselves as the masters of the planet, making sure that the world was functioning based on very fast financial transactions around the world. And then, this. The financial crisis was a huge lesson in humility for bankers.' Indeed, it seemed to unite the world – countries, politicians and citizens alike – against bankers.

Western governments still saw no choice but to save banks from bankruptcy to salvage their countries' economies. In Washington, the newly inaugurated Barack Obama, now overseeing an economy that was still seeing hundreds of thousands of Americans lose their jobs each month, convinced Congress to agree to a $838 billion relief package intended to jumpstart the economy.[12]

Such daring rescues by Western capitals succeeded and staved off far worse misery, but in many voters' minds they merely rewarded reckless financiers. Making matters worse, only a handful of bankers went to jail over the crisis. One US banker, a Credit Suisse executive named Kareem Serageldin, who had been working in London, was sentenced to thirty months in prison after pleading guilty to fraudulently inflating the prices of bonds. 'This was far below the presumptive fifty-seven months' imprisonment in the sentencing guidelines. The judge indicated that a departure from the sentencing guidelines was justified in the particular circumstances of this case because Serageldin was operating in a climate in which such wrongdoing was routine,' the *Chicago Law Review Online* explained.[13] Only Iceland and Ireland prosecuted and convicted chief executives for their role in the crisis.[14]

The fact that bankers seemed to have got away with a slap on the wrist provided inflammable fuel for the growing narrative that Western governments operate for the benefit of the elite. Until then, globalization had mostly delivered improvements to people's standard of living, but when Davos Men and Women visited misery on countless innocent people, they suffered no serious consequences. Chertoff was furious, and not because he wanted to see banking bosses suffer. 'It was a mistake not to prosecute,' he told me. 'I understand that these are complicated cases, but the lack of prosecution gave people the perception that they can't know whether they'll have a recourse if they put their money in a bank and lose it. And it created the perception that the law is not being applied equally. People told me, "Why would you have to prosecute this person or that person?" and I'd say, "If you prosecute a kid for committing a theft, why would you not prosecute a rich person for committing a theft that involves a thousand times as much money?"'

His fears came to pass. Five years after the trauma of 2008, a majority of Americans would still feel that the US government hadn't done enough to prosecute the bankers, while only 15 per cent felt the government had done enough.[15] And ten years later, two-thirds of Britons didn't trust banks to work in the best interests of UK society, while 72 per cent believed that banks should have faced more severe penalties for their role in the financial crisis, and 63 per cent worried that banks may cause another financial crisis.[16]

But that lasting damage was yet to manifest itself. While bankers had been humbled and forced by governments to make their globe-spanning trade more resilient to shocks, companies in other sectors didn't view their globalized nature as a source of concern. On the contrary, being globalized was central to their success. That year, Unilever reported 7.4 per cent sales growth and a market divided almost equally between its Western European core market, the Americas and Asia, Africa, and Central and Eastern Europe. Its 174,000 employees worked in 100 countries and 270 manufacturing sites and were led by top managers from twenty countries who that year had spent nearly €1 billion on R&D. The company had just acquired a Russian ice-cream brand, too.[17]

In Helsinki, Maria Ohisalo was now at university, studying social policy, and in Finnish supermarkets she could contribute to Unilever's success by buying products from Lipton, Knorr and Ben & Jerry.[18] The British tea firm, the German maker of soup mixes and the famously alternative ice-cream brand from Vermont that prided itself on social activism were now part of Unilever's universal empire. That too was globalization – the relentless march of consumer-product uniformity Theodore Levitt had predicted in his 1983 *Harvard Business Review* article.

Ohisalo had also found a political party she liked: the Green League. Joining its youth wing, she discovered that there were others like her, people who cared about the less well-off and about the environment. In one of our conversations, she summarized what she'd concluded by then: 'The stratification is tearing our societies apart. Some have all the world's doors open to them – you can study abroad, work abroad, have friends all over the world, and I'm in this fortunate group – while others feel left behind. On the national scale, globalization has created a feeling of social exclusion, and on the global scale it has led to the exploitation of children and other workers in poor countries, who make it possible for people in wealthier countries to live a good life. And it has led to the exploitation of the environment. It's totally unacceptable.'

China, too, had been feeling the pain of the crisis triggered by foreign banks gambling with the American dream of home ownership for all. After pangs of intense economic agony, Beijing had implemented a gargantuan rescue package, and by early 2009 the country was already back on the path towards impressive growth.[19] But, as Western executives in China noticed, something had changed during the financial crisis: Chinese colleagues and especially Chinese officials now seemed less keen on global integration of their economy. Laid-off Western manufacturing workers and Chinese officials might have nothing else in common, but they seemed to be uniting in doubting twenty-first-century globalization. Guriev was harbouring similar thoughts. 'Before the financial crisis, I thought that American banks were more reliable than Russian banks,' he told me. 'I vividly remember American banks going under in those months and people suddenly thinking that maybe Sberbank [the Russian bank majority-owned by the Russian government] was more reliable than Citibank. That was a huge shift.'

Cole-Fontayn noticed the changing mindset too. 'When some of those financial instruments began to unravel, and when Lehman Brothers declared bankruptcy, and the financial crisis was in full glare of publicity, that's when significant question marks arose around the depth and breadth of globalized financial services and cross-border banking,' he told me. 'And it became very clear that banks and investment firms were living globally but dying nationally with consequences for national taxpayers.' Chinese officials didn't want their country dragged into another financial contagion created in America. Yes, their country had pulled off a massive Keynesian intervention by using the rescue package to build an extraordinary collection of roads, airports, railways, housing, village infrastructure and earthquake retrofits, but the financial crisis didn't endear the US-led global economy to those in charge in Beijing and in quite a few other capitals too.[20] And Beijing's recovery measures were prudent, or at least they seemed to be. 'China financed a construction boom, but that left a legacy of very high debt levels and newly built towns and cities inhabited by almost nobody,' Guriev observed. 'Today we know that that created a real-estate bubble and massive debt. But immediately after the financial crisis, the world saw that the US was in recession while China was not. And that was one of the reasons that people around the world began looking at China as an alternative model, and a model that might function better than the American one.'

That winter, the seeping disunity manifested itself in an unlikely place. In the first days of December, delegates from virtually every country in the world descended on Copenhagen for what Gordon Brown, the British prime minister, pronounced 'the most important conference since the Second World War'. By now, the Intergovernmental

Panel on Climate Change's reports were such alarming reading that governments knew they had to agree on steps to reduce CO2 emissions. Such were the hopes for the COP15 conference in the Danish capital – the fifteenth intergovernmental summit on climate change – that supporters dubbed it Hopenhagen. But the summit was a disappointment. China, fronting a bloc of developing nations, rejected the ambitious cuts for all that Western countries and some developing countries proposed.[21] Western observers, for their part, wondered how a country that had just implemented a gargantuan stimulus package could still qualify as a developing country.

Either way, with China displaying enviable growth there was no doubt that Western companies should remain in the country. But among executives, conversations were emerging that went beyond nervousness about which investments, which new product lines, which plant construction to pursue. Their worry wasn't just that Chinese leaders seemed to be getting cold feet regarding a US-led international financial system: the Chinese coolness added to executives' long-standing fears about China's lack of fair play in the globalized economy. Had China ever been all in? It was impossible to know. But now the country most definitely was not all in any more. And with China no longer the scrappy pupil of capitalism it had been in the nineties, IP theft bothered Western companies even more. Executives discussed it amongst themselves but, once again, what could they do? The US International Trade Commission estimated that in 2009, US companies alone had lost more than $48 billion to IP infringement by Chinese companies.[22]

Despite being a member of the inaugural post-Cold War class of Western banking missionaries, Cole-Fontayn began having doubts about the system those bankers and their pupils had created. 'There was not necessarily a level of oversight and understanding by the management of these organizations,' he told me, referring to the financial-services sector. 'And the regulators didn't fully understand the system either. And essentially, financial institutions were living globally. But when they were severely stressed and ultimately died, they died locally, often without leaving much capital or liquidity in the respective countries.' And while financiers were operating globally, prosecutors could only prosecute in their own countries: that, exactly, was the crux. In the global financial crisis, the old world of nation states and the new world of borderless operations clashed.

One avenue of global money, though, was flourishing: Russian money in Britain. Ever since well-connected Russians began acquiring substantial wealth, they had been buying elegant homes in the UK, especially in London's finest neighbourhoods. They'd bought some of Britain's most famous establishments too: Roman Abramovich, for example, had bought the iconic football club Chelsea, while his fellow oligarch Alexander Lebedev (who had worked as a KGB spy in London in the eighties) had bought the London newspaper *Evening Standard*.[23] And thanks to a new version of the so-called golden visas that had first been introduced in the mid-nineties, the arrival of wealthy people from countries like Russia and China kept increasing.[24] The golden visas, which had already been introduced by many other countries and involved the applicant investing a certain sum (in the UK, £2 million), were in fact designed to attract money by offering residency and ultimately citizenship to the winners of globalization. Governments didn't look too closely under the hood. In fact, under the new scheme introduced by the UK government, the government didn't even look at potential risks involving the wealthy foreigners: instead those applicants' lawyers and wealth managers conducted the checks. Between 2008 and 2015, more than 3,000 globalization winners – Chinese, followed by Russians and Kazakhs – were to arrive in the UK on golden visas, and the UK government knew little about the risks they might bring.[25] While on British soil the golden-visa holders would have to play by British rules, and that seemed enough.

Barack Obama, for his part, had his mind set on a major undertaking: improved relations with Russia and a safer world for all. In 2009, the West's Cold War enemy was no longer an arch-rival, but nor had it turned into a fully fledged partner. Indeed, two years earlier Putin had used a speech to leading politicians and security experts to warn that Russia would no longer tolerate the Western-led world the end of the Cold War had produced: 'Russia – we – are constantly being taught about democracy. But for some reason those who teach us do not want to learn themselves. I consider that the unipolar model is not only unacceptable but also impossible in today's world,' he declared.[26]

Russia remained a major power, and Obama knew he had to involve it if he was to succeed in his ambitions to make the world a safer place. That April, he travelled to Prague to present his vision for a world free of nuclear weapons, a goal he thought he could achieve through close collaboration with Medvedev. In fact, the two young leaders had already met to agree on the pillars for a new nuclear-arms-reduction treaty.[27] Three months later, the US president was the graduation speaker at Guriev's New Economic School, Russia's most prestigious university specializing in economics. 'Think about the fundamental questions asked when this school was founded. What kind of future is Russia going to have? What kind of future are Russia and America going to have together? What world order will replace the Cold War? Those questions still don't have clear answers, and so now they must be answered by you – by your generation in Russia, in America, and around the world. You get to decide. And while I cannot answer those questions for you, I can speak plainly about the future that America is seeking. To begin with, let me be clear: America wants a strong, peaceful, and prosperous Russia,' he said.[28] That December, he received the Nobel Peace Prize.[29]

As 2009 gave way to 2010, the world's elite prepared to convene once again for the World Economic Forum's annual meeting in Davos. Obama stayed away; perhaps he sensed it would be unwise to mingle with jetsetters while Americans were struggling to save their homes.[30] The president's cooperation with his Russian counterpart, meanwhile, was beginning to bear fruit. In June 2010, Medvedev travelled to Silicon Valley to gain inspiration for the innovation city he was planning outside Moscow. 'My purpose is not just to see what is going on there. I would like to have my visit be translated into full-fledged relations and into co-operation with those companies,' he explained at a reception in San Francisco hosted by Arnold Schwarzenegger, the governor of California. The companies included Cisco and Google, and Schwarzenegger promised to dispatch California's best tech experts to help Medvedev build his Russian Silicon Valley.[31] During a meeting with Apple's CEO, Steve Jobs, Medvedev received that year's ultimate gift: Apple's not-yet-released iPhone 4.[32]

That December, Michael Treschow announced his resignation. Under his chairmanship, Ericsson had turned the tide; Treschow left it with €4 billion in net cash and 40 per cent of the world's mobile network market.[33] But Treschow was not leaving business. On the contrary, he'd already assumed the chairmanship of an even bigger global operation: Unilever. 'The single most important thing is that we speed up our innovation machine,' he declared.[34] What was true for mobile-technology infrastructure was true for ice cream and laundry detergent, too: innovation was the only way to stay ahead.

7
A PIPELINE BRIDGING DIVIDES (OR SO IT SEEMS)

On the last day of October 2022, I took the bus from the north-eastern German city of Greifswald, a university town with roots dating back to the thirteenth century, to Lubmin, a seaside town of some two thousand residents. It was Reformation Day, a public holiday in the state of Mecklenburg-Vorpommern, and everything, bar one or two cafés, was closed. But buses and trains were running, and a few minutes before my bus's departure I sat down at the bus stop. Two teenage boys were already waiting, and when I enquired about the bus they assured me I was in the right place. I couldn't tell whether the two knew each other, because both were engrossed in their smartphones. On the train from Berlin to Greifswald, an older woman had asked me how to send a WhatsApp message to a new contact; her daughter usually does such things for her, she told me. She handed me her Samsung Galaxy, and after I registered her new contact, she proceeded to text the person.

I remembered what Karl-Henrik Sundström had told me: in the early days of mobile telephony, Ericsson's engineers were determined to create the perfect sound quality. Then they realized that people didn't care that much about the sound: it was the device's personal nature that appealed to them. Now the devices engrossed the whole person, and few if any phone calls were ever made.

About half an hour later I got off in Lubmin, where Achim Langert and Jana Burow live. Burow grew up nearby. In East German times, her father was mayor of Wusterhusen, a somewhat larger town nearby, and his remit also included Lubmin. Langert grew up in Dresden and later worked as a criminal investigator, first with the East German People's Police and after that in reunified Germany. A few years ago he retired and moved north, where he met Burow. From their front door, the beach is a only couple of minutes away. Once there, Burow and Langert can join tourists and locals taking strolls on the sand, or they can opt for a wooden footpath that takes them to the pier, Lubmin's main tourist attraction. If they turn right at the pier, they see a couple of restaurants where locals and visitors like to stop for a hearty meal. But if they keep walking and then climb on top of a low embankment, they can see Nord Stream 1 and Nord Stream 2 emerge from the Baltic Sea.

In the nineties, Burow – emerging from her post-nuclear power plant unemployment – began renting out rooms in her house to tourists. Then, starting in 2009, she got a fantastic string of new guests: geologists and engineers from countries like Britain and Italy who were based in Lubmin for months at a time. She knew they were working on the new Nord Stream 1 pipeline that would stretch from Russia to Germany; indeed, she enjoyed hearing from them about how one lays such a pipe. Since the pipeline would come ashore in Lubmin, the town was a convenient base for the geologists measuring the seabed, the engineers designing and supervising the construction, and of course the workers laying the pipeline.

Around the same time in 2009, Lubmin's newly elected mayor, Axel Vogt, was learning the ropes. A lawyer by training, he'd been victorious in his first run for public office a few months earlier. 'I campaigned to become mayor focusing only on local issues, and then when I became mayor I realized how much global politics we had here in our small town,' he told me. 'All of a sudden, I had constant meetings with the state government in Schwerin, and lots of people made appointments with me.' A long-time Lubminer, he'd known about the plans for Nord Stream 1, which involved not just the undersea pipes stretching 1,224 kilometres from the Russian town of Vyborg to Lubmin but also a land-based facility in Lubmin and pipelines carrying the gas on to other parts of Germany.

But as Vogt took office, Nord Stream 1 was making global headlines, and not always of a positive nature. Globalization supporters viewed the pipeline, jointly owned by a consortium comprising Russia's Gazprom and a minority group comprising the German energy giants Wintershall and E.ON, Engie of France and the Dutch company NV Nederlandse Gasunie, as a stunning success for borderless business. Poland, Ukraine and the Baltic states, by contrast, accused Germany of making itself dangerously dependent on Russia. It was undeniable, though, that Germany's post-war commercial integration with other countries had been a smashing success. Why should Russia be any different? Shouldn't wise foreign policy include optimism regarding other countries' potential, not just worst-case scenarios? That had been the basis of US foreign policy towards West Germany after World War II. Germany, now the world's leading proponent of commerce-based coexistence, was the country that could prove that optimism and commercial links were the right approach. As for Vogt, 'I was open to the idea of Nord Stream,' he told me as we sat down in his office at the Port of Lubmin. In addition to serving as Lubmin's mayor, Vogt is also chairman of the Port of Lubmin and chairman of the regional water authority, and he'd suggested that the port office might be a good place for a conversation.

It was. After Vogt collected me at Lubmin's town hall, we drove to the port office, passing Nord Stream's land-based facility on the way. On this Reformation Day, the port was mostly quiet. 'I've learnt through personal experience that you have to be open to new things,' Vogt told me in the office's conference room, from where I saw several docked vessels, the German federal police's Port of Lubmin office and a hostel ship housing maritime construction workers. 'We had to develop the industrial area so that Lubmin would become an attractive place both for our residents and for those considering moving here. You can't just place all your bets on tourism.'

Vogt's life is the story of geopolitical metamorphosis and its influence on ordinary citizens. As a child he was talent-spotted by East Germany's legendary swimming coaches. He did mandatory military service as a non-commissioned officer in an army battalion responsible for keeping sensitive installations safe from NATO reconnaissance units. He was then slated to study at East Germany's prestigious specialist sports college, which trained national sports coaches and administrators. But when East Germany collapsed, so did Vogt's career plan. He started over and became a lawyer.

When Vogt assumed his mayoral post his predecessor had already agreed to host Nord Stream in Lubmin; indeed, the project's geologists were already inspecting the planned route. The new mayor, reasoning once again that one has to be willing to try new things, embraced the project. 'Lubmin was stagnating,' he told me in the modern port office. 'We had the old nuclear power plant and one other major employer, but that was pretty much it. Our income from business taxes was low, and we didn't really have any prospects for more companies. I needed to do something about getting businesses to come here. Like many other small towns, they'd been hoping for a major employer to arrive, but that never happened.'

Vogt is a decidedly outgoing man; it's easy to see why he enjoyed a good career as a lawyer after having to abandon his plans of becoming an East German sports coach. When I went to see him, nearly a month had passed since the mysterious explosions that disabled both Nord Stream 1 and Nord Stream 2. While official investigators and armchair ones were frenetically gathering clues about what might have occurred, Vogt was busy trying to contain the harm this calamity might cause Lubmin – an unenviable task given his limited powers. He was also increasingly concerned about the fragility of global product supplies. 'We notice the supply chain disruption here at our port too,' he told me. 'Vessels used to arrive on schedule, but now they have delays of seven to ten days. That means that we have to try to process them whenever they arrive so they don't get even longer delays. And those ships bring goods that we need here as well. We notice the difference when ships are late because that means fewer goods on the shelves in the shops in our region.' His own town council had been waiting months for new equipment for the local playground.

The supply chain disruptions caused by Covid-19 and Russia's war against Ukraine had, in fact, given Vogt a new appreciation of the skills he gained in East Germany's notoriously unreliable economy. 'I must say, we former East Germans are having an easier time with supply chain disruption than many others,' he reflected. 'We're just so used to shortages and trading whatever you have, and what you need, with friends and acquaintances. But my kids have no such references.' Indeed, he went on, 'maybe it's not bad to have the skills we learnt in the GDR.[1] If I have a puncture on my bike, I mend the tube. My children's reaction is to go to the store and buy a new tube. But I say, "The tube works perfectly fine if you mend it." And what if there are no new tubes because they're made in distant countries and there are supply chain disruptions?' Vogt was right. If supplies of various goods were to stop, many East Germans and other former Warsaw Pact citizens would know how to make do, and so would the generation that lived through World War II and the rough post-war years, not to mention citizens of emerging economies. Those who've only known efficient global supply chains would struggle.

But Mayor Vogt's main focus, now as in 2009, was Nord Stream. He told me how in 2009, he was convinced that even though his town had failed to attract the one big employer, it had several crucial things going for it. 'We were already a prospective energy hub because we had production, transport and storage,' he explained. 'And we had an additional advantage: our port. We have a railway that goes right to the harbour. Our land is moderately priced. All the services a company might need – water, sewage, power and so forth – are there because the area has been built up around the nuclear power plant. Energy and port-related companies were our opportunity to attract companies here.' So, he recounted, 'we went about promoting ourselves. And after a while the companies began arriving.'

Nord Stream's impending arrival was, of course, the result not just of mayoral charm offensives under Vogt's predecessor but also of great-power politics. The pan-European consortium was officially a Swiss company, but with Russia's government-owned gas conglomerate Gazprom as its majority shareholder and Western European energy giants as minority shareholders, Nord Stream had always been considered a geopolitical undertaking as well as a commercial one. Indeed, ever since the nineties, the Russian government and the EU had tried to find ways of delivering more Russian gas to Europe. Even during the Cold War, when Soviet gas flowed to Europe through land-based pipelines travelling through then-Soviet Ukraine and communist Poland, it was clear that European economies would eventually need more energy than the pipeline could deliver, and by the 1970s nuclear power was decidedly controversial in Western Europe. After the Soviet

Union's collapse, European governments and Boris Yeltsin's Russia concluded there was potential for more Russian gas exports to Europe, and in 1997 the Finnish-Russian company North Transgas Oy was founded to explore a pipeline route through Finland and Sweden. In the same year, governments meeting at the Kyoto Climate Summit agreed to reduce carbon-dioxide emissions by 2020, which made Russian gas an even more attractive option in Europe. Coal emits considerably more carbon dioxide than natural gas does.[2]

Yeltsin's retirement and the arrival of Vladimir Putin didn't change the optimistic pipeline plans. Indeed, the endeavour's odds of success seemed to improve when Putin took charge and set about bringing order to the Russian economy. By the early 2000s, Gerhard Schröder, the German chancellor, was regularly voicing concerns about how his country was going to be able to meet the energy demands of its flourishing economy. In 2003 Gazprom acquired North Transgas, and the following year Wintershall and E.ON joined Gazprom in the undertaking to build two pipelines of more than 1,200 kilometres each from Russia to Germany. Later Engie and NV Nederlandse Gasunie also joined Nord Stream AG, as the company was soon named. The four Western European firms agreed to split a 49 per cent share of the company, with Gazprom maintaining its 51 per cent stake.[3]

Nord Stream 1, whose construction was projected to cost an estimated €4–5 billion, showed the gains cross-border collaboration could achieve, and together with its planned sibling, Nord Stream 2, it was a crucial future addition to Europe's power supply. 'The European Commission has supported the deal as part of the Trans-European Networks (TENs) and as part of the EU's efforts to diversify energy supplies. Russia has promoted the deal as ensuring long-term gas supplies to Europe. The NSGP [Nord Stream gas pipeline] is supposed to deliver 25% of the additional gas import needs of EU25 in 2015,' a European Parliament report explained.[4]

Commercially speaking, Nord Stream was just one of the countless other corporate transactions taking place, but it maintained its decidedly political touch. When executives from Gazprom, Wintershall and E.ON signed the agreement forming Nord Stream AG on 8 September 2005, they were joined by Putin and Schröder. Ten days later, Germany held elections, which Schröder and his SPD lost. A few days after the SPD joined a coalition government led by the Christian Democrat Angela Merkel, Schröder joined Nord Stream AG as chairman of the supervisory board.[5]

For Lubmin, Nord Stream promised to be a boon. The struggling town would benefit not just from the income from long-time lodgers, but also from the permanent jobs maintaining Nord Stream's land-based facility, and most especially from the local taxes the company would pay once Nord Stream 1 and then Nord Stream 2 became operational. Lubmin's location on Germany's north-eastern coast had, in fact, turned out to be an unbeatable asset. To many residents, the Nord Stream news felt like an enormous blessing after years of anguish over the town's future. It's not easy to replace a state-owned nuclear power plant that brings supporting businesses with it. What large company would want to make a bet on a town that is past its prime and whose residents are leaving?

Sitting in her and Langert's living room, Burow told me she was excited when Nord Stream 1's first instalment of expert workers arrived. Langert similarly considered The One – as locals call Nord Stream 1 – an opportunity. 'It would have been different if they'd built it right on the beach,' he told me. 'But the area where it comes ashore is ugly to begin with.'

On Gotland, Solveig Artsman recalled the mysterious summons she received, in 2007, to a municipal council meeting where a new project – it turned out to be Nord Stream 1 – was to be immediately discussed. Specifically, the council members were to discuss leasing Slite harbour on the island's eastern shore to Nord Stream for use during Nord Stream 1's construction. 'It was a very rushed meeting, and the purpose was that we should decide to take a positive view on Nord Stream getting access to Slite harbour for the construction of Nord Stream 1,' she told me. 'A member of my party group had already told Nord Stream that we'd support it. But I said I knew far too little about this project to be able to confirm any support.'

She and a few others managed to get the council to agree to a slight postponement of the vote, and in the days that followed Artsman dug into any material she could find on the proposed pipeline. She presented it to the council. In her notebook, she still has the points her party colleagues made to her that evening: 'You should trust specialists. You're a Russophobe. Europe, especially Germany, needs energy. I trust those who have more expertise than I do. This can be a peace project.'

Artsman fought against the pipeline until the very end, and so did a party colleague of hers. 'But we were instructed by the leaders of our party in the municipal council not to bring up Nord Stream in the council meetings, and we were told what to say if Nord Stream was on the agenda,' she told me. 'The point was that we mustn't jeopardize the deal because doing so would harm Gotland.' So convinced were other council members of the wisdom of Nord Stream's construction that a few of them tried to intimidate Artsman and some of the other dissenters. 'We were told that if we voted against the deal we'd bring down the government,' Artsman recalled. The government in Stockholm had only lodged minor environmental reservations, which Nord Stream had promised to address. Finland, too, approved the deal. Denmark declared that it didn't want the pipeline close to Bornholm, a popular tourist destination, so Nord Stream slightly altered the route. A few parliamentarians brought up their concerns about national security, but they were not in charge.

The only way to have even a chance of stopping the pipeline, Artsman concluded, was to invite a senior member of parliament from her party to see the harbour and the planned storage site for himself. The parliamentarian travelled, accompanied by an aide, from Stockholm to Gotland's Visby Airport, from where Artsman and another Nord Stream dissenter collected them. 'We showed them the storage site and the harbour and gave them information,' Artsman told me. 'When we were sitting at the airport waiting for their departure, I said to the member of parliament: "What will you do regarding this issue?" And he said, "I can't do very much. I have to think about my career within my party, which you surely understand." And I said, "No, I don't." And that was it. Then he left.'

When the council voted, another member joined Artsman in logging an objection: 'The harbour project in Slite is part of the aggressive energy policy by Russia with the aim of increasing Russia's influence in the region. By accepting and approving the project in Slite, Gotland becomes a willing participant in this Russian foreign policy,' he wrote.[6] To most, it felt like an argument hopelessly stuck in the past. Only a quarter of the council members voted against the project. Shortly afterwards, the contract was signed by a local official and Matthias Warnig, Nord Stream's CEO and a former East German intelligence officer.

Today, when Artsman looks back at those anguished months, she's not angry with Nord Stream: she's disappointed in her fellow elected representatives. 'Of course the Nord Stream team was within its rights to ask for the use of Slite harbour,' she told me. 'My concern was that the proposed deal would harm Gotland rather than benefit it. There was a lot of talk about the money we'd get from the deal, but in the contract the amount wasn't specified and I felt you couldn't just assume we'd get the money. I don't even buy a used car without all the details being specified. I had the feeling that Nord Stream was very good at writing contracts, so I suggested that the municipality hire a contract lawyer who could go through the details. But others on the municipal council told me that would be completely unnecessary since we had a municipal lawyer. I said, "There's a difference between municipal law and contract law, just like you don't go to the dentist if your knee hurts." But they just thought I was being difficult.'

At the end of Nord Stream's planned route in Lubmin, the geologists had been followed by engineers, who similarly brought money to the town's small hospitality industry. Then construction of The One began. An Italian firm had designed the pipeline, the pipe material was being provided by a German firm and a Russian one, and the coatings and logistics were to be carried out by a French firm. By day, the experts went out on vessels to measure the seabed and then to lay the pipeline. By night they returned to Lubmin, often going out for drinks or meals in the town's restaurants and takeaways before returning to their rented accommodation in people's homes or on hostel ships. Burow began believing in her hometown once again. It's easy to understand Mayor Vogt's enthusiasm as the world beat a path to his town. Every mayor of every town and city has to attract more businesses to pay for public services, and when mayors do manage to attract new businesses, it's usually smaller companies. Indeed, as Vogt decided early on, holding out hope for one big anchor business of the kind that have sustained small towns in previous generations would be foolish, because any company can pack up and leave. And now a global company was building a base in his town. It would bring significant lodging and hospitality revenue throughout the construction phase, followed by taxes once The One began operating.

Artsman watched the construction begin in Slite, a village of some 1,500 residents. 'As soon as the contract had been signed, ships arrived with various pieces of equipment, and crews began rebuilding the harbour,' she told me. 'It was a lot of people and a lot of heavy traffic. People like me were obviously concerned, but others viewed the construction as jobs for the community, which we did need.' And the arrangement was going smoothly, the workers bringing the parts out to the construction sites in the Baltic Sea by day and returning without incidents. The municipal council's pro-Nord Stream members felt they were shrewdly participating in globalization. But although she had left politics by this time, Artsman couldn't help getting worried about Gotland's sudden dependence on this one foreign company. 'For as long as Nord Stream had access to the harbour – and this was part of the contract – it also got to decide which vessels could dock there,' she explained. 'I don't think that a private company should get to decide which vessels are allowed to dock in a publicly owned Swedish harbour. And what would have happened if there had been a problem at the Port of Visby [Gotland's main port]? We would have risked being cut off.'

There was another thing that worried Artsman as she saw the construction project take shape: 'They built a storage site to house the pipes that were going to be laid, which was part of the contract as well. It was a massive place, and the storage area itself was sturdily built. It had electricity and water and was sealed off by a barbed-wire fence, and there were spotlights too.' Plenty of storage sites, of course, feature fences and spotlights. But Artsman worried that with this piece of land now under Nord Stream's control, the Russian government could force the company to allow non-commercial uses. 'You don't need to be a defence expert to realize that such a site could be used to store weapons too,' she told me. I saw the storage site during a visit to Slite shortly after the construction phase, and it's certainly possible that it could have been used for weapons storage. But in the heady construction days, whenever Artsman made such observations many thought she was positively paranoid. Besides, the pipe-laying crews were working professionally and efficiently. It was globalization in action.

Globalization was marching ahead in other ways too. Martin Luther, the godfather of the Lutheran Church and global Protestantism, was born and lived only a few hours from Lubmin, but on the 507th anniversary of his famous nailing of 95 theses to the door of the Palace Church in Wittenberg I saw few signs of commemoration in Lubmin or anywhere else in the region. Instead I saw pumpkins, Halloween decorations and people in Halloween fancy dress. Three decades ago, this American feast had not yet permeated Europe; in fact, it was virtually unknown. Since then, the global retail industry has ensured its introduction and indisputable success even in Lubmin, where Washington's campaign against Nord Stream had otherwise made many people think ill of America. In Greifswald, a tattoo parlour (closed for Reformation Day) offered, in English, '€400 tattoo flat rate'. At the railway station I found a rare food establishment open on this day: 'Alex's to go', in English. Such percolating habits, too, are a product of the past three decades of unfettered American-led globalization. But as I saw from the bus as we entered Lubmin, an advertising poster from an electrical-goods firm provided a stark reminder of the world's current state of affairs: 'More independence through a heat pump,' it announced.

It's easy to understand why Lubminers were thrilled about the pipeline and why German policymakers were similarly enthusiastic. The pipeline was, after all, not just a symbol for *Wandel durch Handel*; it would also bring energy to Germany and beyond, and help the globalizing economy expand even more. In the early 2010s, opposition still mostly came from Poland, Ukraine and the Baltic states. The European Parliament report summarized the positions on Nord Stream: 'The supporters of the NSGP argue that it is a major Russian–EU infrastructure project which will bring increased energy security for Germany in particular and for the EU as a whole by adding capacity and an additional transit route . . . For transporting the same amount of energy through the Baltic Sea by ship one would have to employ 500–600 LNG tankers or 160–170 oil tankers annually. For others, however, it signals a decline in energy security as it adds to the EU's energy dependence on

Russia. Some fear that Russia could use the pipeline to blackmail other transit countries such as Poland and Ukraine in the future.'[7] Either way, the project was going ahead, because even its detractors could find no fault in the contract, only unease about geopolitics. Besides, the prospect of a major war in Europe seemed mostly a product of paranoia.

Along the pipeline's 1,224-kilometre route, the crews had to tackle hurdles left by the geopolitics of previous eras – mines that had to be found and disabled. They found 170 of them.[8] But then an incident occurred that seemed to some more ominous than unexploded bombs from two world wars. The tariffs for the export of Russian gas to Europe through the existing pipeline via Ukraine were to expire on 31 December, and Russia and Ukraine had failed to agree on new terms. In early January 2009, with governments still battling the global financial crisis, Russia cut off gas exports through the pipeline. Ordinary citizens around Europe quickly felt the pain. 'The crisis has far-reaching consequences. Russia's reputation as a supplier to Europe and Ukraine's reputation as a transit country, are seriously damaged,' researchers at the Oxford Institute for Energy Studies reported.[9]

The gas flow was restarted after only nineteen days, but the interruption had caused permanent damage: Russia had signalled that it was willing to use gas supplies as a weapon. The question was which lesson to draw from the scare. Did it mean Europe should not rely on Russia for gas? Or did it mean that it should import gas from Russia, just not through the Ukraine pipeline? Merkel remained certain of Nord Stream's promise. 'Nothing at all has changed,' she told a news conference. 'We want it to be built quickly. We have an approvals process to complete. Politically, there is a commitment by the German government to this project.'[10]

Like so many other members of the business community he'd joined, Gerhard Schröder was now making regular visits to Moscow. But by late 2009, Ekaterina Zhuravskaya had concluded it was advisable to head in the opposite direction. 'It had become clear that Putin was running the show,' Sergei Guriev explained. 'My wife said once again that we needed to leave. I was running the university at that point, and I thought it was important to train new economists. So I said, "Okay, I will commute." She got a job in Paris, and I began commuting. That's real globalization.'

Some time later, in March 2011, with construction of Nord Stream 1 nearing its completion, Mother Nature struck. A devastating 9.0-magnitude quake hit Japan, causing a tsunami that ravaged the region of Fukushima, where it killed more than 18,000 people and swept away entire towns. The tsunami also reached the Fukushima nuclear power plant, where its massive waves flooded the reactors and caused a nuclear incident that forced more than 150,000 people to evacuate.[11]

Around the world, the accident caused immediate disruption among car manufacturers. The Onahama factory near the nuclear power plant was the world's only supplier of Xirallic, the paint pigment that gives cars a glittering shine. With Onahama – which in true globalization style was German-owned – having to suspend operations, the supply of Xirallic was disrupted and the world's leading car manufacturers forced to suspend completion of some of their cars.[12] Some decided that they'd placed too much faith in global supply chains and began using two suppliers for the pigment.

Angela Merkel drew her own lessons. On 14 March, three days after the disaster, she told a press conference in the German capital that 'the accident at the Fukushima nuclear power plant will have nuclear consequences for the whole world, so we can't go back to business as usual'.[13] Germany would phase out nuclear power. Mayor Vogt realized this would give Nord Stream and his town an even more decisive role.

On 8 November 2011, The One was inaugurated. In the end, the ambitious project had gone significantly over budget, but The One was now ready for use. It would be able to deliver 55 billion cubic metres of natural gas each year, enough to supply 26 million households in Germany and beyond.[14] As an engineering undertaking, the pipeline was a marvel. 'It was the first time that such a long pipeline, nearly 1,200 kilometres on the seabed and some additional kilometres on land, had been built without any intermediate base stations,' Vogt reflected. 'It was amazing to see such a major international project located in our little town in this economically weak part of Germany.'

At the inauguration ceremony, Chancellor Merkel sat in the front row in a party tent raised just a few metres from Mayor Vogt's harbour office. She was joined by President Medvedev, Prime Minister François

Fillon of France, Dutch Prime Minister Mark Rutte, Schröder and, next to him, Matthias Warnig, whose signature Artsman had seen on Nord Stream's contract with Gotland. Seated around them were political leaders from other Baltic Sea states, Britain and Italy. A chamber orchestra played,[15] and Merkel rose to speak. 'Nord Stream is indeed setting new standards in the European energy partnership,' she declared. 'In this respect, we will be closely connected to one another for decades to come. So one can say: the buyer countries and Russia benefit equally from the pipeline. It is an expression of a long-term cooperation that offers great economic opportunities.'[16] Then Medvedev took the floor: 'Today we're watching an event of great symbolic significance, something we've been waiting for for a long time. The operational commencement of the first stage of the Nord Stream pipeline, opening a new chapter in the partnership of Russia with the European Union.'[17] Then Warnig spoke, calling the inauguration a 'truly moving occasion'.[18] The leaders turned on the symbolic tap, and Nord Stream 1 was in operation. It was scheduled to run for fifty years.

Further back among the potentates sat Axel Vogt. On this day, he was simply a local mayor in the company of some of the world's most powerful people, but after their departure that evening it would be his responsibility to ensure that the mighty pipeline enjoyed a peaceful existence in his town. While Smethwick residents had to content themselves with jobs in supermarkets and cafés, Lubmin residents now had a chance of employment looking after crucial infrastructure. Nord Stream, in turn, expected municipal services from sewage to port facilities to run smoothly.

Pauline Neville-Jones, who had seen the weakened Russia up close during the Bosnian War and observed it again during the conflict in Kosovo, saw the news from Lubmin. After leaving the diplomatic service, she had been appointed to the House of Lords and served as security minister. The pipeline seemed like an impressive commercial undertaking, she thought, but the collaboration with Russia felt vacuous. 'We somehow weren't able to find the agenda on which we could actually engage them in a joint enterprise,' she told me. 'Our link with Russia mostly consisted of commerce.' Neville-Jones wondered if commerce was a strong enough link with the on-and-off hegemon.

With the tap now turned on, the Russian gas emerging from the Baltic Sea effortlessly travelled to millions of households in northern Germany and other parts of Europe, just as the planners had intended. Even though he was not in charge of energy distribution, Vogt knew that mayors from struggling towns all over Europe would come to him hoping to learn from this remarkable turnaround. 'I was proud to participate in the inauguration festivities,' he told me. 'And everyone was proud: the engineers, the politicians, everyone. It was a feat that this construction had been completed without a single significant mishap.' And, he added, 'it felt particularly meaningful considering that Fukushima had happened just a few months earlier and the chancellor had decided that Germany should get out of nuclear power.'

We stepped out of his office and walked alongside the quay. 'The chancellor's decision meant that Germany was not going to use nuclear power, and Germany had already decided to stop using coal,' he reflected. 'That meant we, Germany, had to use gas, and that gas was going to come through Lubmin. Both technically and politically, we Lubminers were proud to be part of this effort.' He was looking forward to decades of prosperity for his town.

8
GLOBALIZATION *FLEURS DU MAL*: DECAY AND A FEW LAST HURRAHS

Antony Perillo's Dongguan shoe factory was thriving. It was reliably producing shoes that China's now similarly reliable transportation network of lorries and trains delivered to the Port of Hong Kong, from where cargo ships efficiently delivered them to European ports, from where the shoes travelled to warehouses and eventually shops and customers' homes. The considerable logistics effort was still cheaper than making the shoes in Britain, as the company used to do. But in 2012, things were beginning to change. The production was still reliable and the transportation worked well too. But, Perillo recalled, 'You could sense something. First thing we always noticed was that we could never get any of our IT to work. Our IT just would not work any more, not even the simplest things of trying to Google something or use WhatsApp.' Perillo and his fellow managers knew that it wasn't a technical problem. Digital communications, which had until then worked smoothly, had simply turned clunky. 'The locals would talk about it,' Perillo recounted. 'They would tell you, "If you write something, someone will read it." I would say, "Yeah, maybe. I'm not sure." But after a while I became convinced that was the case. And they didn't try to do it quietly.' Perillo wasn't sure whether the apparent monitoring was being applied to all companies, what kind of information the monitoring concerned, what its purpose was or who was conducting it. But, he explained, 'It was a turning point. People started to realize that things weren't going to continue to be liberal. Things were going to snap back. But no one knew how much.'

Among executives in more technology-focused companies, too, concern was growing. The balance of pros and cons of doing business in China, which for so many years had heavily tilted towards the pro side, was continuing to shift ever so slightly. There was, of course, the continuing headache of competitors getting access to Western companies' secrets, in both legal and illegal ways, and that mattered more now that the Chinese firms were closing in on the Western ones. But there was also the fact that the Chinese Communist Party had elected a new chairman, Xi Jinping, who didn't seem to share Hu Jintao's rather liberal vision of China's future. What would that mean for Western companies there? Nobody knew.

But Western companies had concluded that their IP loss in China was of a more systematic kind: it was pervasive and involved the Chinese government. 'The Chinese had a strategy for building their telecoms industry, and it included basically copying our products,' Karl-Henrik Sundström told me. 'And not just our products but also those of Nokia, those of Motorola, those of Cisco, those of Juniper and so on.[1] And when a huge market like China does it, it becomes a very different thing than what we'd seen in the past. I think we understood what would happen. But we underestimated how fast it would go.'

Sundström and his colleagues also suspected that Huawei had the support of Chinese authorities, both in financial assistance and in getting the IP. 'Huawei and the government were linked together, but it was very hard for us to prove,' he said. 'We also knew that these close links raised security questions, and to be honest we didn't make that point very well.' Western governments, for their part, thought they could handle the dilemma of Huawei's links to the Chinese government by making sure the Chinese kit wasn't used for sensitive communications. 'They liked cheap telecommunications,' Sundström said. 'And they saw it as another company arriving and offering a cheaper solution, which drove the penetration of mobile telephony and allowed more people to use it. So they thought it was good.'

But policymakers' concerns about their companies' endemic IP loss were real, and they seemed to be realizing that China's systematic absorption of Western companies' IP wasn't just commercial rivalry on steroids: it was a new form of geopolitical competition. In advanced economies, countries don't need to compete for land the way they did in the days of agrarian economies. Knowledge has taken the place of land as the pillar of a country's economic performance. Through legal and illegal acquisition of Western commercial secrets, China – its government and its companies – was turbocharging its economy with the goal of rivalling Western countries, especially the United States. The path to becoming a superpower in the twenty-first century was to establish the most sophisticated and the most innovative economy and operate on a large scale. Russia, insinuating to other countries that it might like to take chunks of their territory, was mostly stuck in twentieth-century geopolitics.

China was, in fact, racing fast towards the twenty-first-century version of superpowerdom. It was beyond doubt that China was rapidly upgrading its military, which had been receiving double-digit budget increases for the past one and a half decades. The Chinese navy (the confusingly named People's Liberation Army Navy) in particular had seen its capabilities rapidly expanded thanks to the addition of, among other things, newly acquired destroyers, submarines and anti-ship missiles.[2] But becoming a superpower through economic means was certainly preferable. So concerned were a number of leading American national security experts that they were now writing a report on the growth of IP theft and the harm it was causing America's companies. 'The scale of international theft of American intellectual property (IP) is unprecedented – hundreds of billions of dollars per year, on the order of the size of U.S. exports to Asia,' concluded the authors, who included Jon Huntsman – a recent US ambassador to China – and Admiral Dennis Blair, a former director of national intelligence.[3] The Blair–Huntsman commission blamed Russia, India and other countries for participating in the theft, but concluded that 50–80 per cent was being perpetrated by China.[4]

Nearly every executive, in fact, had a story of when commercial secrets had been taken from them. Keith Krach, who had enjoyed a stellar career at General Motors before switching to the tech industry and had gone on to co-found and lead the business-to-business e-commerce giant Ariba, had such a story too. It involved a Chinese company Ariba at one point considered a potential joint-venture partner. 'But I treated it like an isolated thing,' Krach told me. And like most other Western companies, Ariba had continued to thrive despite the loss. Now the German technology giant SAP had acquired Ariba for more than $4 billion.[5] Krach had become an even wealthier man. But the IP loss bothered him.

By now, parliamentarians and government agencies had documented globalization's Achilles heel of IP theft more than once, but what more could they do? Legislating against it at home would do little to help companies losing IP in China. Now, though, some policymakers were concluding that some of China's most successful companies in technologically advanced sectors might also pose a national security threat. The US House Permanent Select Committee on Intelligence had just finished hearings on Huawei and ZTE, and the committee members were alarmed. The companies posed a threat to US national security, the committee reported, and recommended that 'U.S. government systems, particularly sensitive systems, should not include Huawei or ZTE equipment, including component parts', and the same rule should apply to government contractors working on sensitive systems. 'Private-sector entities in the United States are strongly encouraged to consider the long-term security risks associated with doing business with either ZTE or Huawei for equipment or services,' the committee concluded.[6]

In Russia, Vladimir Putin had just succeeded his protégé Dmitry Medvedev as president, while Medvedev had succeeded him as prime minister. Yes, Putin had gamed the two-term presidential term limit by having Medvedev stand for president and serve one term, but doing so wasn't illegal. And yes, a vocal minority of Russians had expressed their opposition to Putin through protests in Moscow, St Petersburg and a few other cities, which Putin interpreted as signs of Western interference. And yes, there had been allegations of vote-rigging. But the official tally showed the president turned prime minister winning the presidential election with 64 per cent of the votes cast.[7] Now Putin would have at least another six years at the helm of his country. A few months later, in August 2012, Russia fulfilled its long-standing ambition of joining the World Trade Organization.[8]

In January 2013, Sergei Guriev was once again back at the World Economic Forum's gathering in Davos; he even spoke at one of the main stage's key sessions, which focused on Russia. 'Prime Minister Medvedev was there, former Finance Minister [Alexey] Kudrin was there, and we discussed the future of Russia; how Russia would become part of the West,' Guriev recalled. 'There was so much hope.' Medvedev delivered the opening remarks, which were followed by a discussion between Kudrin, Guriev, Aleh Tsyvinski – a Belarusian economics professor at Yale and co-chair of the World Economic Forum's Global Agenda Council on Russia – and Herman Gref, the widely respected CEO of Russia's state-owned Sberbank.[9] Speaking to the audience of global leaders, Guriev noted that with oil prices likely to stay high, it was unlikely that the Russian government would launch structural reforms. But, he added, 'this process is not sustainable in the long term, simply because [the] Russian middle class will continue to grow and demand reform.'[10]

Russia's most prosperous citizens, who might be able to make such demands in the short term, were often not in Russia; instead, they were commuting between Moscow and Western capitals. By now, dozens of wealthy Russians had bought luxury properties in Britain while continuing to build their fortune in Russia. 'Russia is a good example of what happened in crony capitalist countries,' Guriev told me. 'Some people lose because their jobs are destroyed by imports: that always happens. In a country like Sweden, the government retrains these people and gives them free healthcare because the beneficiaries of globalization pay taxes. In a country like Russia, the people who are left behind are left behind. And the beneficiaries of globalization, the people who sell metal or oil to the global economy, don't pay taxes. They take money out to a place like Switzerland or the US or the UK. That's the story of globalization in a crony capitalist country.' Such capital flight makes things even worse for ordinary people at home. Guriev described the situation in Russia: 'Money is going out, the state is under-financed and it's not benevolent. People who are left behind detest globalization. And oligarchs know they are hated by the voters. This is the vicious circle of crony capitalism in a globalized economy.'

Mike Calvey, who had earned his money the proper way through investments in promising firms rather than through shady deals with the state, likewise owned a home in Britain and regularly worked from his office in an upscale part of central London. But even though the Russian economy needed serious reform, Calvey remained convinced of the country's potential. He was said to personally already have attracted billions of dollars in investments to the country.

At Davos, some audience members thought Guriev was being overanxious about Russia's future in the globalized economy. Guriev, though, was far more concerned about Russia's future than he was letting on, and his worry had more to do with Russia's governance than the level of the oil price. 'I was commuting every week, and since there are long university holidays in France, my family could come to Moscow during those breaks,' he told me. 'But when Putin came back, that's when the dark times really started to ascend.' Even though Guriev was rector of the New Economic School, had served as an advisor to President Medvedev and was even a member of Sberbank's board, he no longer felt safe in his home country. Friends and acquaintances suspected that in somewhat openly supporting the opposition activist Alexey Navalny, Guriev had sealed his fate. 'My wife and I are academics on subjects that are of international interest, we speak English, we're published in academic journals: if something happens, we can move,' Guriev told me. 'I thought that would protect me because people would know that I wasn't afraid of them. But it didn't.'

A few weeks after the Davos panel, officers turned up with a search warrant for years' worth of Guriev's emails, apparently looking for evidence of links to the oligarch Mikhail Khodorkovsky, who was still serving his long prison sentence for alleged fraud. 'And then,' Guriev said, 'high-ranking friends of Putin told me, "Look, you shouldn't be here. Any second, you can be arrested. It's better for you not to be here." I was advised to leave as soon as possible. And that day I bought a one-way ticket for the next day, and I left.' On 30 April 2013, Guriev flew to Paris, and soon thereafter he was appointed a professor of economics at the prestigious Sciences Po university.[11] 'My story illustrates globalization,' he told me. 'My skills are portable.'

In London, parliament's Intelligence and Security Committee was now conducting its own inquiry into Huawei. Even though the company's technology already had to undergo security screening at a government-supervised test site near Oxford, the committee was not swayed. 'Building on the perception that the UK is a "friendly face" in its battle to win major overseas contracts, Huawei last year announced a £1.2bn research investment in the UK,' it noted. Indeed, the committee said, Huawei had seized on Britain's welcoming attitude to pressure other countries into affording it similarly helpful treatment.[12] In other countries, the Chinese firm was already becoming a sore point as governments thought ahead to their countries' digital future.

Yet the British government forged ahead. In October 2013, Chancellor of the Exchequer George Osborne, a member of the Conservative-led coalition government elected three years earlier, travelled to Huawei's campus in Shenzhen, met with CEO Ren Zhengfei and returned home bearing gifts: the promise of a new Huawei R&D plant in the UK.[13] The global-trading chancellor viewed the Chinese firm as exactly the sort of company the UK should do business with. 'Some nations wouldn't want Chinese investment in critical infrastructure like water and airports. We welcome it,' he told students at Peking University.[14]

Chinese companies didn't seem very interested in, say, infrastructure investments in regions like the English Midlands. But there had been some good news in this former global manufacturing powerhouse: parcel companies were now setting up depots in the region. From there the delivery behemoths dispatched goods that had travelled to the UK from around the world, on ships crewed by seafarers from countries like India and the Philippines, and whose far-flung production chain had been managed using digital technology. All over the Midlands, Gerard Coyne had seen the excitement over redundancy payments turn into despondence, and now there was hope on the horizon. 'We got quite a few new jobs in warehouses and logistics, things like massive parcel depots,' he told me. 'But this job growth was offset by immigration from Eastern Europe.'

Coffee chains were opening new outlets in the area too. 'We have cafés but no big factories, and that's the problem,' the former screw-factory worker in Smethwick summarized.

Some time after Osborne's visit to Huawei, Ciaran Martin, a senior official with Britain's signals-intelligence agency, GCHQ, travelled there too. Before his departure, he'd received firm instructions from the government: 'This is a really important relationship. Don't fuck it up.' Martin did as he was told. GCHQ had long regarded Huawei as an unofficial extension of the Chinese state and treated the company accordingly in its interaction with the government. The British cyber-sleuths were confident they could continue to operate on that basis, especially since they didn't view the 5G mobile technology now being developed as significantly different from 4G or the previous generations. For them, assessing Huawei's risk in future 5G technology was entirely a technical matter.

But Britain was also, Martin felt, at an odd inflection point. It would not be possible to reconcile America's growing unease over China with the friendly approach pursued by Osborne and Prime Minister David Cameron much longer.

Before Martin or anyone else managed to find a mutually acceptable approach to Huawei, Russia delivered shocking news. In early March 2014, following a pro-European uprising in Ukraine that saw the Moscow-friendly President Viktor Yanukovich resign and leave for Russia, mysterious forces bearing no insignia seized key landmarks on Ukraine's strategic peninsula of Crimea. The peninsula's regional parliament then voted to secede from Ukraine and join Russia, a step approved by 96 per cent of Crimean voters in a referendum condemned by the international community. On 21 March, Russia annexed Crimea, including its crucial Black Sea Port of Sevastopol. By then, the 'little green men', joined by pro-Russian separatists, were fighting against Ukrainian forces in Ukraine's eastern Donbas region.

Days after the annexation, the G8 countries suspended Russia's membership of their illustrious group.[15] Governments across NATO's territory were so alarmed that they increased their defence spending after imposing sanctions on Russia. But the EU's sanctions didn't cover oil and gas. And while the United States did sanction Russia's state-owned oil and gas giant Rosneft and the gas giant Novatek, the sanctions merely blocked the two energy companies from debt financing in the United States.[16] Most businesses continued operating mostly undisrupted in Russia, just as they had during other strife since the early nineties. Even though operating in Russia was frequently infuriating and sometimes even dangerous, it was lucrative. 'Even after Crimea,

Russia remained part of the globalized economy,' Guriev said. Calvey remained optimistic, telling fellow businesspeople from the West that 'there's everything here, growth, creativity, anything you want'.[17] And he put his money where his mouth was, continuing to invest hundreds of millions of dollars.[18] Indeed, such were the opportunities that BP remained in Russia even though the head of its Russian joint venture had been harassed by the security services and had had to leave the country in 2008 after a row over his visa.[19] That executive, Bob Dudley, had gone on to become BP's CEO and a member of the board of the Russian energy giant Rosneft.[20] Despite the annexation of Crimea, he remained on Rosneft's board.[21]

But the discussions about how else to respond to Russia's flagrant violation of international law were intensifying. Ukraine's leaders were pleading with Western governments for help, and as luck would have it, NATO had a summit scheduled that September.

The summit, held in Wales, marked a watershed moment for the alliance. NATO had certainly not been idle since the Soviet Union's collapse: there had been the interventions in the Balkans and the war in Afghanistan, where the alliance led the UN-mandated International Security Assistance Force and then the Resolute Support Mission that saw NATO troops train Afghan ones. In 2014, NATO was eleven years into its mission in Afghanistan, the very country where NATO's original adversary the Soviet Union had been humiliated by local warriors.[22] These missions, though, took place outside the alliance's territory. Now NATO was once again becoming a pillar of its member states' survival, and the member states agreed to move their defence expenditures towards 2 per cent of GDP within the next decade.[23]

Despite other executives' sanguinity, Sundström concluded that Russia had become too risky for business. The Ericsson boss had recently been appointed CEO of the global paper-and-pulp company Stora Enso, which had significant operations in Russia, and now he decided that the company should reduce its operations in the country. 'You can do a lot of business in Russia with good people, and they will honour the deals you've done,' he told me. 'But the authorities treat everybody else like a minor player because they view Russia as a superpower. You never know what they will do. It's extremely unpredictable.'

With trees taking up to a hundred years to grow, political unpredictability is lethal for a paper-and-pulp company. 'Because legislation in Russia was changing from day to day already in 2014, I decided that there was not going to be stability for businesses,' Sundström explained. But other companies kept going. They could always reduce operations if things got worse.

In China, too, business was marching on despite business leaders' growing irritation over lost IP and fears over where Xi might take his country. While the British government took a strong stance over Russia's annexation of Crimea, it was enthusiastically pursuing its relationship with China, both because it saw opportunity and because it was eager to keep up with Angela Merkel and her government. Australia, meanwhile, had been courting its massive regional neighbour so successfully that it had now been its largest trading partner for several years running.

British leaders courted Chinese investments into the UK too, but they were not completely naïve. They noticed how Chinese firms were buying up some of the country's specialist aerospace and technology companies, and how lots of UK technology was becoming Chinese technology. At the same time, Chinese firms had lots of money, and Cameron and Osborne wanted to show off their version of Britain to the world: a forward-looking country attractive to all kinds of investors.

In Ghana, there was success too, especially for mining companies and for Huawei. As in many other developing countries, the Chinese firm was now firmly ensconced in mobile-telephony infrastructure. 'More than ten years ago when I was communications minister, I visited Huawei's headquarters and selected Huawei as Ghana Telecom's equipment vendor,' President John Dramani Mahama declared after meeting the company's deputy chairman and rotating CEO, Guo Ping, in Accra, and went on: 'I'd like to thank Huawei for its efforts in helping Ghana reduce purchase costs. I also appreciate Huawei's contributions to developing the local ICT industry and cultivating a skilled ICT workforce in Ghana.'[24] The Chinese firm, which was already providing 3G equipment across Ghana, had just won a 4G contract.

The larger and more powerful Chinese rivals grew, the more the uneven playing field bothered Western executives. The GM executive, who had first worked in China in the early nineties, recalled how the state of affairs had changed since then, when executives were happy to hand over IP and tolerated other IP being stolen. 'We suddenly realized that we'd created a monster,' he said. 'That's when people began talking about restricting Chinese car imports to the United States.' The same monster was also frightening other Western market leaders. Lenovo, a Chinese PC-maker that in the nineties had made products of such low quality that it had had to focus on sales in the Chinese countryside, was now the global market leader and had acquired the formerly unassailable IBM's PC business.[25] The white-goods firm Haier, the low-quality brand that Treschow hadn't even considered acquiring, was now the world's leading white-goods maker.[26]

In December 2014, the British government signed a deal with CGN that saw the state-owned Chinese energy company take a one-third ownership of the planned new nuclear reactor known as Hinkley Point C. The Chinese firm was also to help build two other new nuclear reactors.[27] Around the same time, Finland approved an agreement that saw Russia's state-owned nuclear-energy corporation, Rosatom, become a 34 per cent owner of a new Finnish nuclear power plant.[28]

In a different part of the world, mysterious objects were beginning to protrude above the water surface. For months, China had been pouring sand and cement onto rocks and reefs in a part of the South China Sea near the coast of the Philippines and Vietnam but far from China. Thanks to the artificial additions, the rocks and reefs were slowly becoming much larger and much higher. In fact, they were beginning to look like islands – and they were located in the middle of a crucial waterway that contains vast natural resources and unique marine wildlife.[29] China, though, claimed the waters were in fact Chinese, since they were on the Chinese side of the 'nine dash line' maritime boundary Beijing had unilaterally imposed in the South China Sea.[30] The Chinese undertaking was causing consternation in the Philippines, Vietnam and other countries, not just because the artificial islands seemed to solidify China's controversial claim on key parts of the South China Sea, but also because the new island base would allow the Chinese military to disrupt global trade and even harm China's neighbours.

Australia's expanding trading links with China, meanwhile, were bearing fruit. 'Since 2009 the benefit to the Australian household of trade with China has increased almost fivefold from $3,400 to $16,985 in 2013,' the Australia China Business Council reported, pointing out that trade per household had increased by 13 per cent in the previous year.[31] That November, Xi arrived for a state visit in the country. Speaking to the Australian parliament, Xi highlighted how China 'will provide a bigger market, more capital and products, and valuable cooperation opportunities for our partners in the region and the world'.[32] But he also called China 'a big guy' and stressed its strategic interests in the region. Alert Australian officials heard the faint sound of alarm bells.

The globalist agenda was, in fact, becoming a bit unfashionable. As the world's elite prepared to gather in Davos for their January 2015 meeting, the Pew Research Center reported that 78 per cent of Americans considered the gap between rich and poor as a big problem for their country. In Africa, where countries have long suffered from an endemic gap between a wealthy elite and a struggling populace, the figure was 93 per cent. In the Middle East, it was 74 per cent; in Asia and Latin America, it was 82 per cent. In Europe, the figure was a staggering 91 per cent.[33] Since most European countries have well-funded social safety nets, the massive concern about a gap between rich and poor instead seemed to be a protest against a society of perceived winners and losers.

Kevin Casas-Zamora wasn't surprised. 'In regions like Latin America, Africa and the Middle East, inequality is obviously a huge issue, but around the world people's unhappiness with globalization is more about privilege,' he pointed out. 'That sense of elite privilege is an irritant that makes people resent much of what the elites are doing, whether or not it's connected to globalization. And this all becomes a toxic cloud that separates those in charge from so-called ordinary people.' This was the globalized economy's domestic flaw in the countries that had so eagerly exported their capitalist systems: globalization had brought cheaper consumer goods for everyone, but even people enjoying those benefits were irked because there seemed to be many more benefits for those who were plugged in. 'Everything we have around us is cheap, clothes are much cheaper, everything is cheap,' Mo Ibrahim observed. 'Nobody actually said thank you for that. All of these goods we have are really so available and cheap because of globalization.' Sometimes the perception of unfair privilege was real: it bothered Guriev to see affluent people take advantage of a financially open world to move their wealth to tax havens.

Casas-Zamora had been continuing his global rise. A few years after his departure from government, the Organization of American States had appointed him its political secretary, which put him in charge of election observation and conflict prevention. And on his way up the political ladder in Costa Rica, Casas-Zamora had been appointed a World Economic Forum Young Global Leader in a cohort that also included PayPal founder Peter Thiel, future Mexican president Enrique Peña Nieto and Sheryl Sandberg, later to become Facebook's chief operating officer.[34] Now, though, he was beginning to have doubts about whether Costa Rica's swift opening up to world markets had been uniformly positive. 'Globalization brought so many good things for my country,' he said. 'It became much more dynamic economically. We created entire new sectors of the economy. But it also had another effect. In the process of creating all these new, very dynamic economic sectors linked to the global economy, we created a two-tier economy.'

Three strikes against globalization were, in fact, emerging at the same time: ordinary citizens were voicing their displeasure with faraway elites, China's failure to play by globalization's rules was becoming impossible to ignore, and so was the fact that some of its companies might pose a national security threat to Western countries. What's more, Chinese and Russian leaders no longer seemed very keen to fully integrate their countries into an economic system originated by the West. The concerns were emerging from different directions and among completely different groups of people, but they were converging into a general wariness of globalization. And countries were discovering what Giorgio La Malfa's intellectual godfather John Manyard Keynes had discerned during the globalizing period between the world wars: that instead of creating peace, interdependence could cause friction, even conflict.[35] Russia's expansionist urge was racking nerves, too. And what about China's naval expansion and menacing behaviour towards its neighbours?

Ordinary citizens had, of course, never been asked whether they supported globalization; for most political parties, it was just a given. Citizens had simply been given access to ever-cheaper, ever-more sophisticated goods. By now, smartphones were so attractive and so affordable that Nokia had been forced to sell its former dumb-phone empire to Microsoft and exit the handset business altogether.[36]

Now many voters had taken to treating elites as proxies for globalization. In the summer of 2014, Republican primary voters in the suburbs of Richmond, Virginia, had ousted their congressman, Eric Cantor, in favour of an obscure college lecturer named Dave Brat. It didn't matter that Cantor was house majority leader and considered a Washington star, that he'd been endorsed by important people or that he'd heavily outspent Brat. Voters then gave the folksy academic a decisive victory in the Congressional election. 'The issue is the Republican Party has been paying way too much attention to Wall Street and not enough attention to Main Street,' Brat explained after winning.[37] By now, nearly two-thirds of Americans owned a smartphone, and whether it was an iPhone or another brand, it was largely made in China.[38] But that such benefits had been delivered by the global business elite was rarely mentioned. It wasn't that people were suffering, economically speaking. Just like Jana Burow and her fellow KKW Greifswald workers, laid-off factory workers in the English Midlands, Ohio, Finland and other places had mostly been able to rebuild their lives after their employers' demise. But the resentment Burow and her fellow citizens in different countries felt wasn't really about money: it was about a feeling of powerlessness.

Treschow was watching unexpected politicians in Brat's mould emerge across the West. In his own home country, an upstart party called the Sweden Democrats was beginning to pick up disillusioned working-class voters who'd previously voted for the Social Democrats on the opposite end of the ideological spectrum. The Sweden Democrats had now made it into parliament. 'In hindsight, governments should have increased support for regions harmed by globalization,' Treschow reflected. 'Companies always try to find new customers; they don't consider social aspects. It's not their job.' And for the most part, they'd delivered spectacularly on their job to increase prosperity in their home countries and beyond. But if ordinary citizens received the increased convenience and were still unhappy because they didn't feel like globalization winners, globalization would be discredited.

Despite the growing unease all around, companies kept up their operations in China and Russia, and governments kept courting investments.

Even with dark clouds appearing on the horizon, David Cameron's British government kept courting China, and in the autumn of 2015 their energetic efforts reached their crowning achievement: Xi Jinping arrived in the UK on a state visit. 'The State Visit will see more than £30 billion worth of trade and investment deals completed, creating over 3,900 jobs across the UK,' the government promised.[39] It pulled out all the stops. The Chinese leader met Queen Elizabeth and rode with the monarch in a golden carriage. He addressed parliament's assembled members. His visit would lift UK–China relations to a 'new height', the Chinese leader declared, and spoke of 'deep mutual affection'.[40] To demonstrate the closeness of the two leaders' relationship, Cameron invited Xi for a beer at a picturesque English country pub photographers in tow.[41] (The following year, a Chinese-owned holding company bought the pub.[42])

Now, though, Cameron had to decide how to handle the increasingly loud voices calling for Britain to leave the European Union. The EU had so successfully smoothed all movement within Europe that Europeans took for granted that goods would easily get to them and they would be able to travel within the twenty-eight-country bloc practically as easily as they roamed at home. But to some, 'Brussels' had come to represent a remote elite that made decisions above people's heads.

So-called ordinary people had made their views known before. When, in the 1890s, the American agitator Mary Elizabeth Lease delivered speeches calling on American farmers to 'raise more hell and less corn', her audiences applauded and agreed with her, but most couldn't raise very much hell except by participating in even more rallies. Now they could use social media. In the United States, 62 per cent of people were on Facebook and 20 per cent were on Twitter. More than 70 per cent of Britons used social media, over two-thirds of them on a daily basis.[43] Seven in ten Facebook users visited the site every day.[44]

In the United States, many people feeling disrespected were turning to Donald Trump, the author of that 1987 open letter accusing Japan of taking economic advantage of America. Nearly two decades later, the first-time political candidate was running for president, shocking the political establishment by picking up large swathes of voters and attacking China for unfairly taking advantage of globalization. Indeed,

Trump was attacking globalization itself. The real-estate developer and reality-television host was joined in his criticism of global capitalism by the far left in America and beyond. When John McDonnell, the British Labour Party's shadow chancellor and a veteran socialist, was asked in an interview whether he thought Trump's criticism of globalization was correct, he responded, 'Of course it is, but he says it as an election slogan and will not deliver on it.'[45]

An astonishing news scoop delivered further fuel for those suspicious of global elites. In April 2016, Germany's *Süddeutsche Zeitung* and a group of newspapers in other countries began publishing information from a gigantic trove of 11.5 million documents belonging to the Panama-based law firm Mossack Fonseca. The leaked documents, soon dubbed the 'Panama Papers', had been handed to journalists by an anonymous source who said he was concerned about income in equality, and it documented extraordinary use of tax havens by the rich and famous all over the world.[46] Vladimir Putin was found to have money in offshore accounts, courtesy of a friend. Prime Minister Nawaz Sharif of Pakistan had an offshore account, and so did Ukrainian President Petro Poroshenko, Prime Minister Malcolm Turnbull of Australia, King Salman of Saudi Arabia, Xi Jinping's brother-in-law, the wife and children of Azeri President Ilham Aliyev, Iceland's Prime Minister Sigmundur Davíð Gunnlaugsson, and scores of ministers and parliamentarians in democracies and autocracies, not to mention business leaders and others with significant assets.[47] Far from every politician and business leader had money secreted away in this manner, and such accounts can be legal, but the fact that the elite were hiding wealth abroad drove home the notion that globalization mostly served the rich. When residents of countries on all continents were polled the month after the revelations, four in five said the discoveries showed there are two sets of rules in the world: one for rich people and one for everyone else.[48]

A few weeks later, the man initially deemed too provocative and policy-ignorant to even have a chance at winning the Republican nomination for president did exactly that. 'Our politicians have aggressively pursued a policy of globalization – moving our jobs, our wealth and our factories to Mexico and overseas,' Donald Trump told supporters in the former steel capital of Pittsburgh.[49]

In Britain, voters decided the country should leave the European Union.[50] David Cameron, the prime minister, had firmly supported remaining in the EU and seemed to think that with all the economic arguments in favour of doing so, his side was certain to win the referendum. And in economic terms, staying in the Union made perfect sense. As the Remain campaign constantly reminded British voters, the UK's contribution to the EU amounted to £340 per British resident per year, while the trade generated by being part of the EU came to £3,000 per British resident per year.[51] But Cameron hadn't fully grasped that in many people's minds neither globalization nor the European Union was just about economics. And the Brexit campaign's famous bus that travelled around the country declaring, 'We send the EU £350 million a week – let's fund our NHS instead' spoke to people weary of faraway decision-makers.[52]

In the Smethwick area, nearly 67 per cent voted to leave.[53] John Spellar was not surprised. 'All through the referendum, and all the way back to when we joined the EU, there had been an elitist tinge to the pro-Brussels side,' he observed. 'And over the years the resentment had only increased. People were rightly or wrongly ascribing many of their problems to the EU, and nobody was responding.'

At the beginning of 2016, Unilever had delivered an impressive annual report that included a turnover growth of more than 10 per cent. It was Michael Treschow's last annual report; he'd completed the maximum nine years as chairman. 'Consistent profitable growth in volatile markets' is how the company summarized its performance, adding, 'We are preparing ourselves for tougher market conditions and high volatility in 2016.' The company highlighted successes during the past year: people were buying more Knorr stock cubes and Hellman's mayonnaise, and Unilever had strengthened its position in the 'premium gelato' business by buying a trendy American company.[54]

At home and during his travels around the world, Treschow had been following news about Brexit and about Trump's unorthodox election campaign. He'd been observing the growing concern amongst politicians and security officials over Chinese technology in sensitive infrastructure. He was, of course, also intimately familiar with China's interpretation of capitalism. Since his first visit to Beijing in the eighties, he'd been to China more than fifty times. 'I've seen the development,' he told me. 'Things were certainly not perfect in the early years; there were concerns about things like human rights in China. But from a market-economy perspective, things were going pretty well. The Chinese made their investments, and they needed our technology. Of course we squabbled with them about intellectual property, but there were no major conflicts. But since then, the squabbling has increased because on top of Western companies being concerned about IP theft, Western governments have realized that, whoops, we have lots of Chinese components across our critical national infrastructure, not just in telecoms systems but in servers and lots of other things too.' And, thanks perhaps to the fact that he still had a home in his childhood village, he'd seen ordinary citizens grow disillusioned not just with global bankers but with global elites altogether, even as they enjoyed the inexpensive consumer goods that the remotely operating elite had made possible.

Now the quintessential Davos Man concluded that the public ought to have been consulted about the changes that would bring such massive changes to their daily lives: 'We as societies should have articulated that in globalization everyone may benefit, but not everyone feels like they're a winner.' Or, as Spellar put it, 'The benefits of globalization are general and thinly spread, while the costs are specific and acutely felt.'

In Lithuania, Gintarė Skaistė remained upbeat. While many of her compatriots were working in service jobs in Britain, Skaistė was finishing her PhD, investigating the potential for a venture-capital sector in her country. The young graduate student had also done another thing that would have been unthinkable when she was growing up: she'd surveyed her country's political parties and joined the one she liked the most, the centre-right Homeland Union. That autumn, she was elected to Lithuania's parliament.

Ivita Burmistre, too, was optimistic. For three years she'd led Latvia's team negotiating the country's accession to the OECD, the prestigious rich-country club. Now Latvia was joining it. 'Some call it a club of rich countries, but I call it a club of countries that have lessons and practices to share. The OECD is not an organization you apply to, it's an organization you're invited to join,' Burmistre observed. 'I visited practically all the OECD's member states to convince them that Latvian accession would be beneficial not just to us but to the OECD since we'd bring our own experience and lessons learnt.' It was an impressive collection of experiences and lessons learnt the hard way, including a period when a fifth of the adult population were out of work.[55] Now, from her perch in Paris, where the OECD is based, the ambassador who grew up dreaming of being able to buy a pink dress had not only worked hard getting her country through the organization's famous doors but had also developed a taste for French fashion and cuisine.

Keith Krach, who'd begun his career helping out in his father's Ohio workshop, was now in his fifth year as CEO of the electronic-document giant DocuSign. 'I never thought I'd go back and do the CEO gig again,' he told me. 'Ariba was such a success that it afforded all of us a pretty bountiful lifestyle.' Krach lived in a nineteenth-century building in San Francisco that used to be home to Russia's consulate in the city. He regularly travelled by private jet.[56] But the IP loss to Chinese competitors kept bothering him. 'I once asked a Chinese executive, "When are you guys going to stop stealing our technology?"' he recounted. 'The response came back, "It's your fault for not protecting your IP." That's when I knew for a fact: they had a different value system.'

In the British manufacturing town of Longbridge, the storied MG Rover plant had just closed for good. SAIC, which had merged with its smaller rival Ninjang years earlier, had turned the plant into an assembly station for car parts delivered, IKEA style, from China. Now the assembly, too, was about to end: MG cars would be fully made in China.[57]

Around the same time, the US regulator approved the sale of GE's appliance division to Haier for $5.6 billion.[58] GE needed to shed divisions to focus on its core business, and what difference would it make to consumers if they bought their washing machine from Haier rather than GE as long as they liked the quality and the price point? But Treschow, who remembered how Electrolux had tried to acquire GE's appliance division only two years earlier and seen the US regulator nix the deal on competition grounds, asked himself whether the American regulators had fully grasped in which direction the world was heading.[59]

9
TRUMP TAKES ON GLOBALIZATION

At the end of October 2016, Joachim Lang signed off as head of E.ON's Berlin office. After a month's leave, he was going to assume the post as secretary general of the BDI, the powerful Federation of German Industries. Leading the association representing German business was a phenomenal professional opportunity and one that Lang felt prepared for after nine years of juggling the complex issues that face every private company providing a crucial public good. With E.ON a part-owner of Nord Stream, Lang had also been a key participant in this high-profile undertaking. He'd seen Nord Stream 1 planned and executed; he'd attended its opening ceremony in Lubmin. And before E.ON, he'd been a senior official in the federal government, where he'd also served as an advisor to Chancellor Merkel. But days after he left his post at E.ON, America's vote counters delivered startling news: Donald Trump had won the US presidential election. Lang knew that the American businessman seemed to dislike Germany, in particular Germany's business success. It was an ominous start to Lang's new job.

On 17 January 2017, having sworn the oath of office on the podium in front of the Capitol, Trump delivered his inaugural address to the nation. 'Today we are not merely transferring power from one administration to another, or from one party to another, but we are transferring power from Washington, DC, and giving it back to you, the people,' the new president declared.

Trump spoke about how the 'establishment protected itself' and hadn't shared its triumphs with the people. He bewailed how 'for many decades, we've enriched foreign industry at the expense of American industry', how 'we've made other countries rich while the wealth, strength and confidence of our country has dissipated over the horizon'.[1]

Watching the inauguration from his constituency office in Smethwick, John Spellar was not surprised that the first-time political candidate had captured the presidency. 'Governments can't just stand back and say, "There's nothing we can do about the effects of global trade", because then the public will say, "Well, then we'll try somebody else who can."' And that's what had happened in the United States.

On the day of Trump's inauguration, participants were concluding the 2017 iteration of the World Economic Forum in Davos. Once again, leaders from politics and business, including showbusiness, were in attendance. Outgoing US Vice President Joe Biden spoke, Jack Ma – by now China's most successful entrepreneur – spoke, Sheryl Sandberg spoke, former US secretary of state and all-around foreign-policy guru Henry Kissinger spoke, Google co-founder Sergey Brin and the singer Shakira spoke. There were panel discussions about 'China's Pivot to World Markets', 'China's Role for Global Prosperity', 'Ending Executive Pay' and 'Investing in Peace'. The closest to a representative of the common man among the speakers was British celebrity chef Jamie Oliver, famous for teaching ordinary Britons how to cook.[2] Perhaps it was a reflection of the world's fears regarding America's new president that Xi Jinping delivered a keynote and received a decidedly warm welcome. The Chinese leader had arrived with one message: globalization was working.[3] The unpredictable Trump could pursue his protectionist ambitions; Xi would take over the mantle of economic leadership being relinquished by the Americans.

The day after Trump's inauguration, the United States announced it would not join the Trans-Pacific Partnership, an ambitious trade agreement involving countries ranging from Canada and Mexico to Vietnam and Malaysia that had been painstakingly negotiated by Barack Obama. In Berlin, Lang was flabbergasted. 'The TPP had been negotiated over such a long period of time, involved so much money and would really have benefited American companies,' he told me. 'Instead the United

States walked away from it.' America's departure was a massive blow to German businesses, because so many had operations in TPP countries, but what mostly baffled Lang was that 'Trump delivered the Indo-Pacific to China on a silver platter.' Trump, though, seemed convinced that protectionism would aid the people left behind by globalization. Indeed, such was the shift in America that Trump's Democratic opponent in the presidential election, Hillary Clinton, who had served as Obama's secretary of state and supported the TPP, now rejected it.[4]

A few days before Trump's inauguration, Jake Bright, a commentator writing for the World Economic Forum, had tried to make sense of what had transpired in Britain and the United States in the preceding months. 'Both the US election and Brexit represent the greatest political backlash to the forces of globalization since the 1999 Seattle World Trade Organization protests. In the world's first- and fifth-largest economies nearly 80 million people (62 million in the US and 17 million in the UK) chose a candidate and referendum rejecting free trade, liberal borders and regional economic integration,' he posited.[5] Had the leaders attending the World Economic Forum's gatherings been more honest with one another, they might have discovered long before the Brexit vote and Trump's election that globalization suffered from fundamental vulnerabilities far beyond the grievances now being advanced by Trump and Brexit voters. They might have had honest conversations about China's subversive business practices, about the fact that trade doesn't inoculate countries against expansionist designs, about the fact that commerce alone doesn't create democracy. But as long as things were mostly going well, why ponder such unpleasant matters?

In truth, Washington had begun to highlight globalization's large blemishes already under President Obama, who had spoken of how 'the middle class has been taking it on the chin even before the financial crisis – too many Americans working harder than ever just to get by, let alone get ahead'.[6] Obama had wanted to fix globalization's unfair practices, especially those practised by China, but where to start? His administration had filed more WTO complaints against China than against any other country. It had even won some of them. It hadn't made much difference.

Trump was taking on the battle in his very own way. 'We can't continue to allow China to rape our country,' he had proclaimed during the election campaign.[7] There were going to be no more toothless IP-theft investigations, polite WTO complaints or pleas for Beijing to play by the rules. Instead, the new president wanted to bring China in line through a massive effort on several fronts. America was going to declare China a currency manipulator. It was going to tackle Chinese IP theft and forced technology transfer. It was going to force China to end export subsidies and adhere to labour and environmental standards.[8] To top it off, the co-author of *The Art of the Deal* planned to negotiate a massive trade deal with China. That all this didn't square with leaving the TPP and making China more attractive to America's allies didn't seem to bother him.

In London, a young communications consultant named Alicia Kearns was becoming aware of another troubling reality of globalized business. After graduating from Cambridge University, she had joined the government as a press officer; at one point, she covered counter-terrorism issues in Iraq and Syria. Now she was in the private sector. Like many other people her age, she also felt strongly about human rights, and for months she had been hearing about massive persecution of the Uyghur people in China's Xinjiang region, where so many Western clothing manufacturers were buying their cotton. 'When I started reading more about it, it helped consolidate my view on China,' she told me. 'China was putting out all this stuff about ISIS recruiting in Xinjiang, which I knew wasn't true. By 2016, I was a China hawk.' China's ISIS allegations, she concluded, was just a strategy to make Westerners fear Uyghurs. Kearns had also joined the Conservative Party and was planning to stand for parliament. Like most of her fellow Conservatives, she was a free-trader. But like a growing number of them, she didn't want trade with China at any price.

On 27 June 2017, a conflict that had been lurking in the shadows burst to the surface. Russian hackers – who were subsequently traced to the Russian state – attacked Ukraine using malware so potent that it brought down the radiation-monitoring system at Ukraine's Chernobyl Nuclear Power Plant along with four hospitals, six power companies, two airports and more than twenty banks.[9] The attack, soon known as NotPetya, was so powerful that it hit Western multinationals too. A. P. Møller Maersk, the Danish shipping giant, was crippled, as were the pharmaceutical behemoth Merck, FedEx's European subsidiary TNT Express, the French construction giant Saint-Gobain, Reckitt Benckiser, a British household-goods leader best known as the maker of Durex condoms, and Mondelēz, the American snack giant that makes Doritos and Oreos. Merck alone lost $870 million and was temporarily unable to manufacture crucial hepatitis vaccines.[10] All told, NotPetya caused damages to the tune of $10 billion. When Western governments attributed the attack to the Russian government, several insurers argued that it should count as an act of war. Globalized business, which has become used to commercially targeted attacks, was now indisputably on the front line in a growing cyber war involving powerful countries.

In Washington, Trump continued issuing new executive orders. He ordered the establishment of a Trade and Manufacturing Office, signed a 'Buy American, Hire American' executive order and an 'Addressing Trade Agreement Violations and Abuses' one. He ordered a national security supply chain review and created a Presidential Advisory Council on Infrastructure to 'advance infrastructure projects that create high-quality jobs for American workers, enhance productivity, improve quality of life, protect the environment, and strengthen economic growth'. Within his first months in office, the new president also blocked a Chinese venture-capital firm from buying a key American semiconductor business.[11] He appeared to have recognized that Chinese firms were no longer primarily interested in acquiring household Western brands: they wanted cutting-edge technology, and as early as possible, because China was marching ahead with its plan to become the globe's high-tech manufacturing superpower. Gone were the days when Beijing was courting low-tech firms like Perillo's shoe company.

Despite accelerating concerns about Chinese practices, despite concluding that Trump was on a collision course with China, and despite steadily harsh rhetoric from Vladimir Putin, executives remained optimistic. '2017 became a boom year for German business,' Lang said. 'The only thing that dampened the atmosphere a little bit was the question of how to achieve Germany's ambitious climate targets, or rather how to combine that with our economic growth. That was the big question we were tackling: will the climate targets put a brake on the German economy, how expensive will it be to meet those targets and how will this affect the competitiveness of German industry? What does it mean for German industry if we're the only major economy with such climate targets? The US didn't have them, nor did China.' Shortly after being sworn in, Trump appointed Scott Pruitt – a man known to question the link between human activities and climate change – to lead the EPA, the US agency in charge of environmental protection.[12]

By the end of 2017, German trade with China would reach €187 billion, an astounding 30 per cent of all EU–China trade. The year before, German companies had invested €76 billion in China; the 5,200 German companies present there employed more than a million people.[13] With volumes like these, it didn't matter all that much that assistance from Beijing had helped China's solar-panel industry cripple German solar-panel makers, who once dominated the market, or that more and more Germans were buying budget-priced Chinese cars.[14] Indeed, so alluring was the arrival of cheaper Chinese goods that the German government had long ago phased out its subsidies for solar-panel users, which resulted in more than 100,000 German solar-industry workers losing their jobs.[15]

Not even the perennial headache of IP loss had caused German companies to fall out of love with China. If there were any nagging headaches, they were around the perennial climate and energy. 'Because everything was going so well for Germany – we had large economic growth, large corporate tax revenue and large corporate profits – the politicians thought along the lines of, "the sky is the limit; we can ask the private sector to contribute a bit more to the climate targets since they're doing so well",' Lang said. 'But we worried that there wasn't enough renewable energy in Germany for everyone to be able to switch to it.'

Ciaran Martin, too, was closely following news from Trump's new administration, but for a different reason. He needed to discern how the president would approach Chinese telecommunications technology. Though still only in his early forties, Martin had already served as director of security and intelligence at the Cabinet Office, the hub of the UK government. Now he was the inaugural CEO of the country's National Cyber Security Centre. If the centre, the first of its kind, was to keep Britain safe from all manner of cyber harm, Martin had to understand how Trump intended to approach Chinese-made communications gear. While the United States used little Chinese technology in its telecoms infrastructure, the UK used a considerable amount, especially equipment made by Huawei, though it had tried to reduce the risks involved. Now, though, Martin and other security officials were increasingly concerned about the risks Huawei and other Chinese technology companies could pose in other rapidly expanding tech areas such as smart cities, where urban furniture collects data from every single person.

Maybe the US had been wise to limit its exposure to Huawei, but for the UK and most other countries the dearth of alternatives – in reality, only Ericsson and Nokia – made Huawei an inevitable option. Martin and the NCSC remained confident that Britain could continue what they considered a prudent approach.

Either way, the United States and Britain needed to agree on how to treat Chinese technology. Was sensitive infrastructure technology from Huawei simply a different commercial offering comparable to that from Ericsson or Nokia, or did it pose a national security threat because of Huawei's ties to the Chinese government? 'We'd talked to the NSA [the US signals-intelligence agency] for two decades about managing Huawei,' Martin told me. 'They didn't much like it, and they didn't do anything themselves, but they knew there was no actual risk to American secrets because we don't transmit NSA and GCHQ exchanges over public networks. It was a political disagreement that didn't jeopardize the day-to-day security cooperation.'

But especially considering Trump's strong and frequently expressed views on Chinese fair play, Martin and his colleagues thought there might be an opening for discussions about Chinese tech in Western infrastructure. A joint Anglo-American approach to China's involvement in Western smart cities, in fact, seemed an eminently sensible idea to propose to the new administration. Martin got in touch with his American counterparts, political officials appointed by the new president. It didn't go well. 'We're practically screaming to them, "We can handle China and 5G, and there are far bigger threats from Chinese tech you want to worry about and we should work together on",' the otherwise soft-spoken Martin recalled.

Trump himself seemed to have far more immediate concerns than Huawei. While in Brussels for his first-ever NATO summit in May that year, he complained that 'the Germans are bad, very bad', prompting a top official to explain that Trump was merely referring to Germany's trade with America. The new president then followed up by tweeting, 'We have a MASSIVE trade deficit with Germany, plus they pay FAR LESS than they should on NATO & military. Very bad for U.S. This will change.'[16]

First, though, Trump wanted to overturn another arrangement that he heartily despised. 'As I have said many times, the Iran deal was one of the worst and most one-sided transactions the United States has ever entered into,' he declared in a speech that autumn.[17] He was announcing that the United States intended to leave the Joint Comprehensive Plan of Action (JCPOA), an extremely comprehensive agreement negotiated over several years by Iran and China, France, Germany, Russia, Britain and the United States and signed in 2015.

Under the agreement, commonly referred to as the Iran Nuclear Deal, Iran had agreed to dismantle large parts of its nuclear programme and allow international investigators to monitor its compliance, while the United Nations, the EU and the United States agreed to lift sanctions in return. The deal, which had come into force in January 2016, was a breakthrough for international diplomacy. The moment the deal took effect, more than $30 billion in Iranian frozen overseas became available and would be used for imports, the country's IRNA news agency reported.[18] Transport Minister Mahdi Hashemi announced that Iran was planning to order more than a hundred Airbus jets to modernize the country's ageing passenger fleet, and he invited airlines and investors: 'Come with your proposals. We would like to have new contracts and serve them immediately and make up for the losses that we suffered from in the past.'[19]

Western companies were thrilled at the prospect of entering the country, which offered a market of nearly 90 million, a comparatively well-educated workforce and massive pent-up demand to boot. 'The flurry of investor excitement and the sheer size of Iran's economy had some analysts comparing it to the reopening of Eastern bloc markets after the fall of communism,' the *Washington Post* reported.[20] Britain's new foreign secretary, Philip Hammond, declared, 'I hope British businesses seize the opportunities available to them through the phased lifting of sanctions on Iran.'[21] Executives began making their way to Iran. Ministerial delegations arrived. Consultants and bankers turned up. Hotel chains, as ever the advance team when a country opens because visiting businesspeople need somewhere to stay, arrived. AstraZeneca, the Anglo-Swedish pharmaceutical giant, signed a memorandum with an Iranian firm that would see AstraZeneca set up manufacturing in the country.[22]

Siemens signed a contract to electrify a crucial 500-kilometre railway line, build a new highway and build 500 trains for the state railway system.[23] The German engineering behemoth also signed an agreement with an Iranian firm for the construction and delivery of twenty turbines and additional generators for Iran's electricity net. 'With these important agreements we're making the long-term partnership come alive again,' announced Siemens CEO Joe Kaeser, a Bavarian so committed to global business that he'd changed his name from the original Josef Käser.[24] So massive was the investor interest that Business Sweden in Iran, an association helping Swedish companies do business in the country, had to find a larger office. 'The lifting of the sanctions and a more business-oriented environment are projected to increase real GDP growth to 4.2 % and 4.6 % in 2016 and 2017, respectively. On the production side, growth will be mainly driven by higher hydrocarbon production. On the expenditure side, consumption, investment and exports are expected to be the main drivers,' the World Bank had explained in its 2016 economic outlook.[25]

Sergei Guriev was now serving as chief economist at the EBRD, the London-based institution that once sent experts like Mike Calvey to help Guriev's own country transform itself into a market economy. 'Since the job of the chief economist is to work in other countries as well, occasionally I would commute not between Paris and London but between Paris and Tirana or Tashkent,' Guriev told me. The young graduate in Moscow who had watched the international economist circuit from the outside and wondered how one joins it was now an international authority to whom transforming economies turned for advice.

In Dongguan, Antony Perillo was getting ready to renew the lease on his company's facilities, as he'd done many times before. 'The way you'd renew a lease was that you went to the local community administration,' he explained. 'The officials there would always follow instructions from the central authorities to the letter.' But this time, there was an unexpected complication: 'We didn't get an instant response, which was odd, especially since we'd always received instant responses in the past.' Perillo and his team waited, and then they waited some more. 'It took a very long time, which was unusual,' he said. 'We started to get a bit suspicious, so we asked someone with good connections to discreetly enquire for us whether there was an issue. Could we clarify anything?

His team received evasive answers. Expats with experience working in China had learnt that when local officials offered non-answers it meant that a central policy had changed and that they were waiting for instructions to communicate that change. 'So,' Perillo said, 'we waited. Then we received a reply with a very, very high increase on the rent. We tried to negotiate, but we didn't get anywhere. Then an acquaintance in the professional services in Hong Kong told me that they were seeing this happen regularly and that their offices in the mainland were being asked to help. And this woman said to me, "You probably won't be renewing that lease." So I immediately started looking for somewhere new, but nobody was keen to lease to us.'

Perillo concluded that their company was no longer desired in Guangdong Province. 'As a businessperson, what you take away from that is that there's a central political directive having to do with a certain aspect of the market, even if it's just the real-estate market,' he told me. 'And you think, "If they can suddenly do that, what else are they capable of doing?" It just wasn't desirable to have companies like us there any more. We had served our purpose. Not renewing leases was an interesting way of going about it, but it worked.' The company had to look for sites in other countries. Apparel-makers had already begun moving factories to nearby countries – a result of China's rising wages, Perillo had thought, but now he realized many had probably been eased out in a similar manner to what he'd just experienced. 'We said, "What are our options in moving our production to Bangladesh, Cambodia and especially Vietnam?" Our manufacturing partners in Guangdong had already set up manufacturing in Bangladesh and Cambodia and Vietnam. So when we slashed our presence in Guangdong, we were really just joining a migration that had already begun,' he recalled.

Making shoes in Guangdong was, at any rate, not as profitable as it had been in the nineties, when Chinese wages were extremely low. China had moved up a few slots on globalization's totem pole, on which apparel resides near the bottom. But Bangladesh, long an also-ran for Western apparel companies, had been cleaning up its reputation for poor worker safety, and now it was attracting firms seeking to leave China. Bringing in firms China no longer wanted in fact seemed a key part of Bangladesh's strategy to tap into the globalized economy.[26] Vietnam and Cambodia, too, were delighted to receive apparel manufacturers.

In truth, for some time Perillo had had an inkling that shoes and clothes were not going to be part of China's plan for ever. He and the other managers had heard of a plan that said certain parts of Guangdong Province would be converted to production of higher-value consumer goods. 'We all assumed it to be things like mobile phones or laptops or something like that,' he told me. 'And now infrastructure was in place, and the workers had been trained in Western management skills. The engine was working very, very well.' The plan Perillo had caught wind of wasn't secret: it was Beijing's Made in China 2025 strategy for manufacturing superpowerdom, presented by the government in 2015. Beijing wanted to focus on biomedicine, high-tech robots, electric cars, high-tech ships and trains, polymers and other advanced manufacturing.[27] Clothes and shoes were out.

John Spellar was happy to have socks and even shoes manufactured in lower-wage countries, but he was far from surprised that China was going more upscale. 'Our doctrine was, "We don't mind shipping out the low-value stuff to be made elsewhere, because we'll keep the high-value stuff,"' he said. 'That assumes that the countries that are doing the low-value stuff and building up the skilled workforce won't get the idea that they might be able to do the high-value stuff as well. Of course they'll get that idea.' Japan, which in the 1950s made mostly clothes and toys, had trodden the path towards higher technology decades ago. Being able to rise up the totem pole of manufacturing was also part of the promise of globalization.

Although only three years and a bit had passed since Xi's cheerful visit to Australia, the regional neighbour was observing the hardening Chinese attitude that Perillo had witnessed, though in a different way. 'There has been foreign interference in Australian politics,' Prime Minister Malcolm Turnbull declared in December 2017. A senator had warned a Chinese businessman and political donor that the latter might be under surveillance, which had prompted the government to commission a report on Chinese influence efforts in the country. When the report uncovered worrying activities by Beijing, the government began preparing legislation that would ban foreign influence-peddling. A year later, parliament passed the legislation, which banned foreign countries from carrying out activities to influence Australian politics. For good measure, the new legislation banned IP theft as well.[28] A few weeks later, Australia banned Huawei and ZTE from its 5G network.

In the happy nineties, and even the noughties, trade and national security had been separate. The reason they'd been separate then was, of course, that most countries didn't have major problems to fight out and even when there were geopolitical disagreements governments were careful not to harm their painstakingly built trade. Now the Australian government began fearing that China would punish Australian companies as proxies for their home government. It would be so easy to do, since neither companies nor the governments could really hit back. Beijing had done so already in 2010, when the Norwegian Nobel Committee – an independent body appointed by the Norwegian parliament – awarded the Nobel Peace Prize to the Chinese dissident Liu Xiaobo. Beijing responded by blocking imports of Norwegian salmon.[29]

Annoying its largest trading partner on national security grounds put Australia in an extremely vulnerable position. But parliament passed the legislation – and, to everyone's relief, China didn't react. Perhaps it was because Australia is a crucial supplier of iron ore for the Chinese industry. Perhaps China was planning to retaliate later. But Australians had to prepare for revenge.

In Iran, there was jubilation as Western investments kept announcing their impending arrival. Maersk signed a contract to ship Iranian oil. GE decided to do business in the country, as did Honeywell, the American technology behemoth. Volkswagen, Citroën, Peugeot and

Renault began investing, as did the Swedish lorry giant Scania.[30] 'The path for the participation of our companies in the global production chain, which is the best way of providing jobs for young workforces, has been smoothened,' Foreign Minister Javad Zarif proudly declared at the 10th International Exhibition of Exchange, Bank and Insurance in 2017, pointing out that foreign direct investment in Iran had skyrocketed by 1,300 per cent during the four years since the election of Hassan Rouhani, the country's reformist president.[31]

But Trump just didn't like the Iran Nuclear Deal. In May 2018, America left the agreement, which the president called 'decaying and rotten' and an embarrassment.[32] US sanctions on Iran would return. Within days, the EU took the extraordinary step of introducing blocking statutes, which prevented EU-based companies from complying with the United States' reinstated sanctions on Iran.[33] But it was a futile attempt. When the world's largest economy – in whose currency most businesses trade – imposes economic sanctions, companies don't dare take any risks. Companies including the previously so enthusiastic Siemens said they would wind down their operations in the country. Even Russia's Lukoil and the Indian oil-refining giant Reliance got cold feet.[34] 'The US leaving the Iran Nuclear Deal had major foreign-policy implications, but for businesses it was like a spring that never managed to blossom,' Lang concluded. 'The deal evaporated before it had properly taken hold. There wasn't enough business activity for it to become a major problem for the companies that had begun investing in Iran. And in combination with the US walking away from the TPP, it was a signal that the US was turning inwards.'

America's decision to walk away from an international treaty was met with disbelief by investors and foreign capitals. If Washington could abandon a treaty it had signed and helped negotiate, what did this mean for other treaties? Any country could simply renege on its commitments and other countries would not be able to cajole it into rethinking.

The new US president had his eye set on his country's allies. 'Germany is a captive of Russia,' he complained to NATO Secretary General Jens Stoltenberg in May 2018, when German authorities were about to certify the new Nord Stream 2 pipeline.[35] A few days later,

Trump imposed tariffs on steel and aluminium from the EU, Canada and Mexico after denouncing these allies' steel and aluminium as a national security threat.[36] 'The United States has been taken advantage of for many decades on trade. Those days are over,' he declared in a statement, while White House Trade Advisor Peter Navarro declared that 'economic security is national security'.[37]

For the third time within less than eighteen months of trade turbulence, Lang was dumbfounded, especially since he knew the new tariffs would cause more damage than America's departure from the Iran Nuclear Deal or even its dismissal of the TPP. While he and the rest of corporate Germany had been concerned about what Trump might do to global trade, they'd thought he'd go after China. Weren't business leaders constantly talking about IP lost to China, and voters about jobs lost to it? That job migration was still having an effect on Americans back home. Between 1982 and 2014, the share of American multinationals' jobs abroad had soared from 30 to 60 per cent, and between 1980 and 2017, the number of Americans employed in manufacturing had fallen from almost 20 million to a little over 12 million.[38]

But instead of tackling China's Janus-headed role in the globalized economy, Trump imposed tariffs on America's friends. 'It was absurd to allege that America's closest allies were suddenly posing a national security threat to the United States,' Lang told me. 'And the tariffs made no sense because at the end of the day they had to be paid by American companies. You have to remember that this was not some primitive steel but extremely high-value steel used in automotive manufacturing. The American companies that needed this steel had to keep buying it and paying the tariffs. It was absolutely infuriating and irrational.' Now German business knew that Trump's scorn of Germany wasn't just election sloganeering: 'You realized that he's serious about this,' Lang said.

The European, Canadian and Mexican steel and aluminium producers' American customers kept buying the goods, now at a higher price, and their bottom lines suffered correspondingly. But Trump, citing the need for America to be able to build tanks and fighter jets using its own steel and aluminium, was not to be swayed. Steelworkers were delighted. 'Jubilant is probably the word. These people are ecstatic,' a steelworker union representative in Granite City, Illinois, whose plants had announced they'd add hundreds of jobs, told a radio interviewer.[39]

What Trump seemed to have forgotten was that by imposing tariffs on rule-abiding countries, the United States was violating the WTO's rules. He also seemed to have forgotten that America needed its European friends in the looming struggle against China. And he'd clearly not taken into account that his tariffs would make crucial manufacturing in America more expensive.

Democrats and even Trump's fellow Republicans were aghast. 'Europe, Canada & Mexico aren't China. You don't treat allies the same way you treat opponents. Blanket protectionism is a big part of why we had a Great Depression. "Make America Great Again" shouldn't mean "Make America 1929 Again",' tweeted Senator Ben Sasse, a moderate Republican.[40] But the tariffs stayed. The EU member states filed a WTO complaint against the United States.[41] When the WTO finally issued a ruling, in December 2022, it was in the EU's favour.[42] But by then, Trump was no longer president.

In 2018, Trump's attacks on America's allies continued. Visiting Brussels for a NATO summit that July, Trump again railed against Nord Stream: 'We're supposed to be guarding against Russia and Germany goes out and pays billions and billions of dollars a year to Russia. We're protecting Germany, we're protecting France, we're protecting all of these countries. And then numerous of the countries go out and make a pipeline deal with Russia where they're paying billions of dollars into the coffers of Russia.'[43]

Solveig Artsman, who had waged her battle against Nord Stream long before Trump ever mentioned the pipeline, felt she should be pleased that the world's most powerful man was now on her side. But instead she wondered why he was so passionate about the pipelines. 'I asked myself what his objective was in trying to stop Nord Stream,' she told me. 'When he came up with the idea that the Americans should buy Greenland soon after that, I began thinking that perhaps it was all about expanding America's power in the High North.' Over several years, China had been buying up companies and real estate on Greenland in anticipation of the Arctic ice melting.

Axel Vogt, the mayor of Lubmin, felt acutely uneasy hearing the president of the United States attacking the pipelines, but he decided that he was probably overreacting. A contract is a contract. A few streets away, Achim Langert too watched the regular news of Trump's tirades against Nord Stream, while sitting a few hundred metres from The One. He was stunned to see the American president take such a confrontational interest in his small part of the world. But what would Trump do?

At first, nothing. In the spring, the US Department of Commerce had found ZTE 'incapable of being, or unwilling to be, a reliable and trustworthy recipient of US-origin goods, software, and technology' after having established that the company had sold goods to Iran and North Korea in violation of international sanctions. The Department banned American companies from selling components to the firm.[44] Six US intelligence agencies including the CIA had, in turn, advised Americans not to use Huawei or ZTE phones.[45] And members of Congress from both parties, many of whom had held hearings and issued reports about Chinese business practices for years, energetically supported the Trump administration's forceful rhetoric on China. Chinese telecommunications companies 'represent a fundamental risk to American national security. We need a comprehensive plan to hold the Chinese and their state-sponsored entities accountable for gross violations of the law and threats to our security,' Senator Chris Van Hollen – a Democrat – told news media. In May, stores on US military bases were ordered to stop selling Huawei and ZTE phones.[46]

But in July, the Trump administration suddenly changed course: the ban on trading with ZTE was reversed.[47] 'That pardon was instructive for us,' Ciaran Martin told me. 'When the ZTE sanction was lifted, we just knew, he's not serious about this. Tech was just a bargaining chip.' Trump himself proved Martin right when he announced, shortly after the ban was lifted, that the step was 'also reflective of the larger trade deal we are negotiating with China and my personal relationship with President Xi'.[48] Trump had jeopardized national security to seal his ambitious trade deal with China – or the risks posed by ZTE had not been very serious to begin with.

In London, Martin and other officials debated what this might mean for Huawei. With Britain and the United States locked in a decades-long embrace, Martin knew that Trump's decisions mattered even more to Britain than they did to other allies. Not that there was any doubt about where Trump stood on Huawei. For months, officials from his administration had been travelling to allied capitals, telling the governments to ditch the Chinese firm from their telecoms infrastructure. But was Trump truly worried about national security, or would Huawei turn out to be another ZTE? In London, officials struggled to interpret the president's thinking. Sir Kim Darroch, the country's ambassador to Washington, could shed no further light on the matter, and in subsequently leaked cables he described an insecure president and a chaotic administration.[49]

That August, the US Congress banned the use of Huawei and ZTE by US government agencies and contractors.[50] Even though Trump and Democratic leaders like Speaker of the House Nancy Pelosi agreed on little else, they were of one mind regarding Huawei. Martin was unsurprised, given the US government's limited use of the Chinese tech. And Trump hadn't said very much about Huawei in recent weeks, which Martin interpreted as a sign that the president had lost interest.

Around the Western world, policymakers and citizens looked back on a discombobulating twelve months. Trump's steel and aluminium tariffs on friendly countries had caused outrage, and he'd seemed to relish threatening German business in particular. European governments cowered in fear lest their country become the next target of the president's anger. In Britain, only 50 per cent of people held a positive view of America under Trump. So did a meagre 44 per cent of Swedes, 42 per cent of Spaniards and 38 per cent of French citizens, 39 per cent of Canadians and 54 per cent of Australians.[51] But in Poland, the US president enjoyed the affection of 70 per cent of the population. With such division amongst themselves, how were Western allies going to find a common strategy to tackle China?

Then matters took an unexpected turn. On 1 December, while changing planes at Vancouver International Airport, a Huawei executive named Meng Wanzhou was arrested by Canadian authorities acting on a US arrest warrant.[52] The warrant had nothing to do with Trump: it had been issued that August by a New York court after prosecutors found evidence that Meng and Huawei had violated US sanctions against Iran and that they had caused Huawei's US bank, HSBC, to also unwittingly violate the sanctions. But Meng wasn't just any executive: she was Huawei's chief financial officer, a member of its board and founder-CEO Ren Zhengfei's daughter. Beijing issued furious denunciations of the arrest. Trump, meanwhile, appeared to have lost his enthusiasm for the trade negotiations with China, which at any rate seemed to have fallen short of his expectations.

A few weeks before Canada's unplanned showdown with Beijing, DocuSign CEO Keith Krach had again made a business trip to China, and now he was having the same realization locally based executives had been having for years. 'I've been going on business trips to China since 1981, but this time I could clearly see the evolution of China's competitive industry having turned into a form of techno-economic aggression,' he told me. Perhaps Western companies had in fact created a monster. And, Krach told me, 'As I was flying home, I wondered if the leaders in Washington were doing anything about it.' But he was a businessman, not a Washington insider.

In January 2019, Sergei Guriev arrived at Davos again, his global star shining brightly even though that of his home country had dimmed. 'I saw my old friends from Sberbank,' he told me. 'At that point, Sberbank had for several years been hosting a breakfast on Russia. They would bring former prime ministers like Tony Blair, current prime ministers like the prime minister of Luxembourg and CEOs from companies like McKinsey to talk about the world, challenges in the current world and globalization, but also about Russia.' Like dozens of other leading corporations around the world, the Russian bank had paid the World Economic Forum a neat sum for the opportunity to partner with the organization and arrange events in Davos. The bank had invited Guriev to speak at its panel.

'At that point, people were very much aware that globalization was creating political problems,' Guriev recalled. 'We discussed the challenges to the Western democratic order, inequalities, injustices created by globalization. That was already a shift in mindset from just a couple of years earlier. The mood was sombre. But nobody was thinking that a session on Russia sponsored by a state-owned Russian bank might soon not be possible any more.' Indeed, many Davos participants seemed more concerned about Donald Trump than about Vladimir Putin or Xi, a keynote speaker once again. A few weeks later, Joe Kaeser announced that Siemens wanted to increase its investments in Russia.[53]

At home in San Francisco, Krach was still trying to decide how he should share the knowledge regarding Chinese business practices that he and other executives had been collecting. He did know one important person: Mike Pence. Krach decided to contact him, and the vice president agreed to see him. 'We're all free-traders,' Krach told me as he recounted the meeting. 'We believe in globalization. But it only works if everyone plays by the rules. And the Chinese don't! If you do all the things the Chinese do, the market is no longer free. It's a fool's market!'

Krach had asked for the meeting as a businessman irate about the conditions under which Western companies had to compete. As the meeting went on, Krach felt that Pence had understood his concerns. The vice president had indeed. 'Have you thought about serving your country?' he asked. Krach hadn't. But since the vice president of the United States asked, of course he would be willing to serve his country.

10
5G BECOMES A GLOBALIZATION LIGHTNING ROD

In July 2019, Keith Krach was getting used to his new digs in the US State Department and his new position as under secretary of state for economic growth, energy and the environment. In his Senate confirmation hearing, Krach had been asked how he could tackle globalization's flaws. 'I said, "I'd use America's three biggest areas of competitive advantage: unify and rally our partners and allies; leverage the innovation and resources of the private sector; and emphasize the moral high ground and democratic values," ' he recalled. 'That's the only strategy you need. But you've got to execute!'

Now it was up to him to execute. To be sure, Krach would not be the only person executing Trump's attempted globalization fix: there was Trump himself, Secretary of State Mike Pompeo, Commerce Secretary Wilbur Ross, US Trade Representative Robert Lightizer and National Security Advisor John Bolton, but they had many other responsibilities. Even though the under secretary of state for economic growth also had a diverse portfolio, Krach knew that economic growth was going to be the focus. That suited him perfectly. On the surface, global business was still in robust health. To be sure, UNCTAD, the UN agency in charge of trade and development, reported that 'economic conditions started deteriorating in the second half of 2018 and further in 2019. The reasons were trade tensions between the United States of America and China, fears of a disorderly Brexit in Europe and a negative global output outlook more generally.'[1] UNCTAD's preliminary data indicated that trade would decline by 3 per cent before the year was over. But investors seemed confident that businesses would make up for such tension and disorder, perhaps in other markets.

Despite Donald Trump's vitriol against business in his grandparents' home country, German companies were doing well too. That year, Frankfurt's DAX stock market soared by more than 25 per cent, compared to 12 per cent growth among London's FTSE 100.[2] 'We saw good times once again,' Joachim Lang said. 'Our goal was mostly to figure out how German companies could become even more successful, how we could improve the investment climate in Germany even further, and how we could improve German companies' opportunities abroad. Every year was getting better.' The government of Italy, for its part, was getting serious about finally replicating German business success in China. That spring, with Xi in Rome on a state visit, Italy endorsed the Belt and Road Initiative.[3] 'This is a very important day for us, a day when Made-in-Italy has won, Italy has won and Italian companies have won,' Deputy Prime Minister Luigi Di Maio declared, and he could point to immediate contracts worth €2.5 billion for Italian companies.[4] But even while Xi was shaking hands with Prime Minister Giuseppe Conte, the move seemed ill-advised to many of his fellow Italians, including members of his own government coalition. Why publicly embrace Xi's marquee initiative just as everyone else seemed to have become more circumspect regarding China?

Huawei embodied the concerns now converging. Since its humble beginnings in the late eighties, the mobile-communications firm had delivered an extraordinary performance. In its most recent annual report, the company had reported revenue growth of 19.5 per cent, which helped the company surpass revenues of $100 billion for the first time. Profits were up by a massive 25.1 per cent,[5] and Huawei was performing well in both the handset market and the telephony infrastructure market. Things had gone the opposite way for Motorola. The pioneering American firm that had helped develop mobile telephony was no more. Or rather, it had been acquired by China's Lenovo, which turned it into a subsidiary.[6] Haier had, of course, bought GM Appliances. Companies across the board presented a similar picture. China Inc's transformation from embryonic manufacturer to industrial behemoth was complete.

To paraphrase the US president in Art Buchwald's famous column about Japanese cars, Donald Trump wanted China to stop making so many damn Chinese smartphones, laptops, washing machines, televisions and other technology-infused products that could outcompete American ones. And in trying to tackle trade imbalances with major rivals, the US president was hardly alone. On the issue of China, the otherwise controversial president still enjoyed bipartisan support in Congress. News media organizations, in turn, were beginning to pay far more attention to Chinese companies' business practices. Investigations by investigative reporters would later establish that Huawei had received as much as $75 billion in grants, credit facilities, tax breaks and other financial assistance from the Chinese government, thanks to which it had been able to underbid Western competitors.[7] 'When the volume of goods going between trading partners becomes too imbalanced, countries usually try to create a balance by creating different rules,' Michael Treschow observed.

On the corporate side, more and more companies were discovering that new Chinese products bore an uncanny resemblance to their own. Over several years, an army of Chinese intelligence officers and state-linked hackers and spies had, for example, targeted Western companies building parts for Boeing's 737 aircraft and the Airbus 320.[8] Although the US had indicted several Chinese intelligence officers over the IP theft, their efforts appeared to have helped China's government-owned aircraft manufacturer Comac speed up its development of a rival to the two warhorses of global aviation.[9]

Then another troubling trend intensified: countries were again willing to harm other nations. Ukraine had, of course, seen part of its territory taken by Russia. And in the South China Sea, some of the islands China had been building were now fully constructed. They hadn't been built for human habitation. Instead military bases featuring airports, missiles, fighter jets and other equipment now graced the waters off Vietnam and the Philippines. The United Nations Convention on the Law of the Sea's tribunal had already ruled in favour of the Philippines. 'A low-tide elevation cannot become a "rock" or an "island" merely because it has been subject to some degree of human manipulation. Equally, a "rock" cannot be upgraded to an "island" by human intervention,' the tribunal declared.[10] The Philippine government was jubilant, but the Chinese government dismissed the 'so-called award' as 'illegal and invalid'.[11] Indeed, China had ignored the ruling and kept building, and now the islands were a fait accompli. That meant the country had territory from which it could attack regional neighbours and which it could use as a staging post for more distant undertakings.[12]

The previously so optimistic Joachim Lang, too, was seeing clouds on the horizon. At the beginning of the year, the BDI had published an extraordinary report by Lang and another BDI executive that outlined how China's business practices undermined competition and called on Germany and the EU to strengthen their defence against such distortion. 'We saw three potential outcomes: China as a partner, China as a competitor, China as a systemic rival,' Lang said. 'It was the first time that someone in a leading position in German industry had given an assessment that was in any way critical of China.' Contrary to expectations in the nineties, China had not developed into a liberal market economy, the report concluded. Inevitably, the country would remain an important export market for German goods, but the practice of Chinese companies exporting their wares to Germany at artificially low prices thanks to government assistance was untenable, the authors pointed out.

In no time, Lang and his co-author began receiving invitations from Washington. The National Security Council got in touch, as did the US Trade Representative's office and the State Department, and soon they were briefing American officials. 'We told them, "We believe that it's the beginning of a trend, since many smaller businesses have already become much more sceptical regarding China. Only the large ones are still euphoric,"' he recalled.

Indeed, while most German multinationals and politicians remained enthusiastic about China, Merkel's government had become a bit more circumspect than it had been in the past. It had already blocked a state-owned Chinese firm from buying a major share in a German power company and instructed a state-owned bank to buy it.[13] And, perhaps motivated by the shock of a Chinese company buying a leading industrial-robot maker and redirecting its focus to China in 2016, it had strengthened its weak screening of foreign investments.[14]

Wealthy countries getting ready to build nationwide 5G networks, for their part, were getting nervous about Huawei. It was fine to do business with the firm, and its advantages vis-à-vis Western firms might even be tolerable. But installing its technology in crucial nation-spanning infrastructure meant to last for years was a different matter. Australia had, of course, already banned Huawei from its 5G network, and elsewhere too civil servants began assessing how to treat the company. Even in London, the passion for China had subsided after Theresa May succeeded David Cameron as prime minister. 'We entered a new phase,' Martin said. 'I asked one of Theresa May's senior political advisors – I said, "I'm a civil servant. What are we going to do about this Huawei stuff? We seem to be operating with Trump's rhetoric but Osborne's policies." And the advisor said to me, "Oh yes, that's absolutely right. We have the same China policy as during the golden era. We just don't like it as much as we used to." '

Time was of the essence. If the UK was going to have the best possible mobile network – and in the globalized economy, countries compete on the quality of their infrastructure – it would have to make a decision soon. Going down the Australian route and banning Huawei from 5G seemed too radical. But if the US took action against Huawei and the UK didn't, the special relationship would be in tatters. That spring, US officials travelled to allied countries to make the case against Huawei. 'They went around all these capitals, and one of my European colleagues called me up and said, "We just had the American show-and-tell",' Martin told me. 'I said, "What was it like?" And he said, "It was a bunch of newspaper articles put on PowerPoint slides and classified as top secret." It was no way to treat allies.'

British officials hoped the increasing focus on national security risks linked to Huawei would instead get Washington interested in the kind of technical precautions the UK had been advocating. Instead matters took a different turn. 'May and Trump had agreed that there would be technical exchanges between the teams,' Martin recalled. 'These meetings were very difficult. There's supposed to be technical analysis of risk and so on, but the US sent over a delegation of politicals. And we say, "Where are the people who understand telecoms security?" We then managed to get the NSA involved. They're technical experts so they know that, for example, if you pipe a piece of metal from China it's not exactly an existential threat. If you build your entire 5G network with everything dependent on Beijing, yes, but there's a lot of grey in between. But the technical experts were in a really difficult position.' The Brits were irked, too, when the Americans made their case to friendly voices among British parliamentarians. One British official recalls meeting with a member of parliament who read out points regarding Huawei from a sheet with US State Department letterhead. When Martin went to see a group of the US-leaning China hawks to discuss Huawei, 'they were perfectly decent but they said, "We trust you on the technical risk-mitigation stuff but we need to send a strong signal to China." '

In Britain, the hawks were in fact gaining the upper hand. Or rather, the UK had entered a schizophrenic stage in its relationship with China. In April 2019, May declared that Huawei would be excluded from 'core' parts of the UK's 5G network. A few days later, Philip Hammond, now serving as chancellor of the exchequer, travelled to China for an investment summit.[15] The following month, the United States put Huawei on the so-called Entity List, which prevents foreign companies listed from doing business with US firms.[16]

In the summer of 2019, other Western countries' intelligence services were independently voicing concerns regarding Huawei. A group of Swedish members of parliament travelled to Washington for meetings with US officials. They knew that Sweden's civilian intelligence agency, SÄPO, and its military intelligence agency, MUST, were apprehensive about potential Huawei participation in the country's 5G network. 'We had a number of briefings with the US government, and the officials made the US position regarding Huawei very clear,' recalled Pål Jonson, a member of the Swedish parliament's Defence Committee and one of the trip's participants. 'They raised the security aspect and the integrity aspect. We also discussed whether there might be some sort of compromise along the lines of what the Brits had suggested, for example having 30 per cent Huawei, but the Americans dismissed those ideas and said that it's not really possible to set a network up that way.' That autumn, the Swedish parliament resolved instead to add a paragraph to the country's telecoms legislation requiring national security issues to be considered in telecoms infrastructure. In Brussels, the European Commission was developing its 5G toolbox, a set of recommendations for safe 5G networks in EU member states.[17]

Around the same time, Ciaran Martin and Britain's national security advisor, Sir Mark Sedwill, travelled to Washington accompanied by a delegation – Martin with his technical counterparts and Sedwill with US National Security Advisor John Bolton. Unlike the Swedes, though, they achieved nothing: following the leak of cables written by Ambassador Darroch – including one in which the ambassador warned that Trump's administration might 'crash and burn'[18] – the White House informed the Britons that their ambassador wasn't welcome. The officials flew back without having conducted so much as a heated discussion. Within days, Sir Kim resigned from his post.

The Britons swiftly made another attempt, now with a skeleton group comprising only Sedwill, Martin and a note-taker, and this time they held a meeting with Bolton. Martin told me how the encounter proceeded: 'We made the case that there had been massive failure in market consolidation. And we told them, "We're with you when it comes to Chinese tech but you need a proper strategy. You guys look like you're flicking through a bunch of Wikipedia pages of major Chinese tech companies and picking them off randomly." This was around the time that Trump decided he wanted to ban TikTok.'

Despite having only been launched in 2017, the Chinese social-media app had quickly gone viral around the world. Its short user-generated videos, glued together by a powerful algorithm, were an addictive combination. But like all apps, it also collected vast amounts of consumer data, which under Chinese legislation it had to hand over if Chinese authorities requested it. That October, Donald Trump banned TikTok from federal government devices. Its 'data collection threatens to allow the Chinese Communist Party access to Americans' personal and proprietary information – potentially allowing China to track the locations of Federal employees and contractors, build dossiers of personal information for blackmail, and conduct corporate espionage,' the Executive Order noted.[19]

During the Britons' meeting with Bolton, Sedwill proceeded with a lengthy explanation of how Britain wanted to support the US in contesting Chinese technology dominance. 'And then,' Martin recounted, 'Sir Mark turned to me for the technical points. I said, "Ambassador Bolton, you've decided that in the epoch-defining clash between Chinese and Western tech some 5G phone masts of not terribly great strategic significance in the English countryside are the epicentre of this battle. It doesn't make any sense." And Bolton just said: "Gotta pick something." '

I asked Bolton about the conversation. He didn't recall the 'gotta pick something' comment but told me: 'The Brits were unhappy about the point we were making. Our point was that you can't just protect your hubs, you have to protect the system. It's impossible to defend the entire system. You have to exclude the threats like Huawei and ZTE.'

These days Martin teaches the practice of government at Oxford. But despite his many years of dealing with officials in different countries, he hadn't realized that in deciding to go all-in for pushback on Chinese technological ambition the Americans had made Huawei a centrepiece, or he hadn't realized it soon enough. The US had never liked Britain's nearly twenty years of Huawei but had never particularly complained about it. Now the UK was caught between its closest ally and a long-standing commercial arrangement.

Misgivings regarding Chinese unfair economic play and fears regarding 5G security risks were, of course, not the same thing, but Western governments were beginning to feel that they needed to put their foot down to stem the many ways in which China was undermining the global economic order they had conceived in the nineties. Australia had gone first by strengthening its espionage laws, but that was hardly going to fix globalization. The issue on which Western countries took a stand needed to be an issue of real national security concern, but it also needed to highlight China's unfair globalization practices. But what would that be?

The United States seemed to have picked Huawei. The UK hadn't yet picked anything. It was perhaps no surprise that the special relationship was enduring a significant amount of shouting, non-meetings and general acrimony when Keith Krach first hung his figurative hat on the seventh floor of the unglamorous Foggy Bottom building that houses the world's still-most-powerful foreign ministry.

The gregarious former top executive began mapping a strategy of how to implement the goals he'd told the Senate he wanted to achieve. He'd already come to one conclusion: there will be no more telling America's friends what to do. 'There had been a whole host of American officials going around to allies saying, "Hey, these guys [the Chinese] are bad guys" and "Don't buy Huawei",' he told me. 'That's exactly people's stereotype of the big ugly American. Nobody likes to be told what to do.' Shortly after taking up his position, Krach was invited to meet an Italian minister visiting Washington. 'I said, "What should we talk about?" and the officials organizing the meeting said 5G. And I said, "What should I say?" They said, "Don't buy Huawei." I said, "That's the stupidest frigging thing I've ever heard in my life." If I was the CEO of a telco and someone said, "Don't buy Huawei," here's what I'd do. I'd go to my chief of staff and say, "Check out Huawei. It must be some really good stuff." '

As Krach worked on his alternative strategy and hired Silicon Valley veterans to join his cadre of diplomats, the UK government formally announced that it would limit high-risk vendors – understood to mean Huawei – to 35 per cent, and non-sensitive parts, of its planned 5G infrastructure.[20] Weeks later, Nancy Pelosi appealed to world leaders assembled at the Munich Security Conference to stay away from Huawei. 'This is the most insidious form of aggression, to have that line of communication, 5G, dominated by an autocratic government that does not share our values,' she explained.[21]

Despite their unease about Huawei's technology, America's friends and allies didn't seem to heed Pelosi's warning. The following week Huawei announced ninety-one new contracts around the world, forty-seven of them in Europe.[22] Indeed, apart from Britain and Australia, America's allies were reluctant to exclude Huawei, in part perhaps because the Trump administration had asked them to. For three decades, globalization had blossomed because it was insulated from geopolitics. National security concerns notwithstanding, why risk upsetting such a successful formula now? And governments knew that excluding Huawei meant risking retaliation by Beijing.

In Helsinki, Maria Ohisalo was now interior minister. That April, she'd been elected to parliament. After weeks of negotiations, Ohisalo's

1. Bilal Ahmed, a young technology advisor in Frankfurt am Main. 'I grew up thinking that the world was moving towards more unity … And now all of that is over … the interconnectedness of the world is leading to more tension, and autocratic states are impeding on our way of life and have leverage over us,' he said.

2. Finland's Green League leader and environment and climate change minister Maria Ohisalo (front) with her fellow party leaders in Sanna Marin's coalition government. Western countries should pursue energy independence from Russia and technology independence from China, she argued.

3. Gintarė Skaistė, Lithuania's minister of finance, visiting the European Commission in June 2023. She had just led her country's economy through a tough period when China blocked imports of Lithuanian goods after Lithuania invited Taiwan to open a representative office in Vilnius.

4. Kevin Casas-Zamora as a doctoral student at Oxford University. He was already one of globalization's winners and was about to embark on a career that would make him vice president of Costa Rica, a respected academic and a top international official.

5. Energy Summit for Central America, with the heads of state of Central America, Mexico and Colombia. Kevin Casas-Zamora (second vice president of Costa Rica) is in the back row, second from right. 'We were very naïve with regard to free trade … We never really thought through the political implications of free trade and the security implications of free trade,' he told the author.

6. Mo Ibrahim (right) participating in the Indian mobile-telephony company AirTel's launch in New Delhi in 1995. Ibrahim realized that sub-Saharan Africa, with its poor infrastructure, was perfectly suited for mobile telephony, and became a billionaire on it in the early 2000s.

7. Michael Treschow (standing) leading an Atlas Copco meeting in 1991. Referring to the early 1990s, he told the author that 'there were unlimited countries to expand to. If a country was too isolationist, you didn't need to bother with it because there were so many other ones.'

8. Katrin Krüger, Lubmin's Lutheran pastor, in her church. Reflecting on Nord Stream's arrival in Lubmin and its subsequent demise, she told the author that 'Billions were spent, the seabed was harmed, countless trees were felled. And the whole thing was for nothing!'

9. Jana Burow and Achim Langert outside their home in Lubmin. In East German times, Burow worked in the town's large nuclear power plant and became unemployed when it closed. She was thrilled when Nord Stream came to Lubmin. 'I was so excited when they did the test run … You could see it far and wide because there was a massive flare,' she told the author.

10. The pier in Lubmin. Nord Stream 1 and Nord Stream 2 come ashore to the right of this view. For Lubmin, which had been home to a large East German nuclear plant dismantled after German reunification, Nord Stream offered the kind of turnaround that countless towns and cities that have lost their largest employer dream of.

11. Lubmin's mayor Axel Vogt in the Port of Lubmin. Behind the worker-hostel ship to the left is the open space where Nord Stream 1's inauguration took place. When Nord Stream 1 and Nord Stream 2 were sabotaged in September 2022, Vogt realized that Russian gas would no longer be flowing to his town.

12. Slite harbour on the Swedish island of Gotland, which Nord Stream used as a depot during the construction of Nord Stream 1. Local politician Solveig Artsman opposed Gotland's commercial agreement with Nord Stream, which gave a company she considered too close to the Russian government exclusive access to one of Gotland's two commercial harbours.

13. An abandoned building in Smethwick, a town in the English Midlands that used to be a manufacturing hub. 'Your factory is part of your social life and may also be a workplace where your children will follow you,' the local member of Parliament, John Spellar, told the author.

14. Pauline Neville-Jones (second from left) at the signing of the Dayton Accords. To her left: Slobodan Milošević, Alija Izetbegović and Franjo Tuđman. Although the Accords ended the Bosnian War, Neville-Jones felt Serbia's ally Russia wasn't fully signed up to the agreement or the post-Cold War world. 'We somehow weren't able to find the agenda on which we could actually engage them in a joint enterprise,' she told the author.

15. Mike Turner (centre, in front of the middle flag) chairing a meeting of the House Permanent Select Committee on Intelligence. Turner, mayor of Dayton when the Dayton Accords were signed, twinned his city with Sarajevo, where he saw the results of the Bosnian War's atrocities. He became concerned that war could return to Europe once again.

16. Sergei Guriev (third from right) speaking at the World Economic Forum in Davos in January 2013. Guriev commented on oil prices and the likelihood of structural reforms in Russia in a scholarly manner, but inwardly he was increasingly concerned about Russia's future and his own future in the country.

17. UK Chancellor of the Exchequer George Osborne (left) enthusiastically pursued business links with China. In October 2012 he visited Huawei Technologies and CEO Ren Zhengfei (right) in Shenzhen and told students at Peking University that 'Some nations wouldn't want Chinese investment in critical infrastructure like water and airports. We welcome it.'

Green League and four other parties formed a coalition government and Ohisalo received the crucial Interior Ministry. A few days later, the Green League elected her its leader. 'For Finland, the 2019 parliamentary elections were the climate elections,' she told me. 'As a country, we realized long ago that the world of cheap flights, people and goods constantly being able to travel around the world, would hit the limits of what the planet could handle, but the IPCC reports from the past few years have really driven home the urgency.'

The state-of-the-climate reports by the Intergovernmental Panel on Climate Change had very much driven home the urgency. With each annual report, the IPCC's team of respected climate experts were documenting even more troubling planetary health data. In its most recent report, released in October 2018, the IPCC had declared that human-induced warming had 'reached approximately 1°C (likely between 0.8°C and 1.2°C) above pre-industrial levels in 2017, increasing at 0.2°C (likely between 0.1°C and 0.3°C) per decade'. There wasn't much time left if the world was to avert a catastrophic two-degree Celsius temperature increase.[23]

Ohisalo's and her fellow Greens' influence could be felt in the coalition government's declaration: the five parties vowed to make Finland carbon neutral by 2035 and thereafter carbon negative, to make the country the world's first fossil-free welfare society, and to make Finland a global leader in the circular economy.[24] As interior minister, Ohisalo was now also the top official in charge of domestic security. But on Huawei, she kept her counsel.

Krach and his team of diplomats and Silicon Valley imports were desperate to convince people like Ohisalo. Their concern was, of course, about Huawei's links to the Chinese government, but it was really about whether globalization could continue in its current form. 'We've seen IP theft, dumping of cheap goods, bullying of countries to get them to buy your goods,' a technology expert who was serving in the Trump administration during this period told me. 'That's no longer free enterprise. That's not what civilized countries do. We don't say, "If you don't buy from Apple we'll cut diplomatic ties."' Krach, in turn, frequently pointed out that globalization had become fundamentally unfair. Paradoxically, he was making much the same argument as Joachim

Lang in Germany; indeed, both were expressing the concerns executives had quietly been voicing for years.

Krach had vast experience in determining what a corporate customer might consider a value proposition, but he'd never before conducted diplomacy with foreign governments and really had no idea what, say, the government of Poland or the government of Bulgaria might consider an attractive value proposition. He decided to go on an international listening tour. 'We met with all these finance ministers and economics ministers, and I'd say, "How is your relationship with China?",' he told me. 'And they'd say, "Well, they're a really important trading partner," and then they'd look both ways as if someone was in the room, and add, "But we don't trust them." That rang bells in my head because, for years, I would tell my DocuSign employees, "We're not in the software business, we're in the trust business. We deal with people's most important documents." Well, 5G is the ultimate trust business.'

On 23 January 2020, Chinese authorities locked down the city of Wuhan after nearly 300 people had fallen ill with a new virus that resulted in a pneumonia-like illness. Japan and South Korea had each detected one case of the virus, too, and the US Centers for Disease Control and Prevention had begun screening airline passengers arriving from Wuhan. But Trump was confident the mysterious virus was just a minor nuisance and tweeted to thank Xi for his – Xi's – handling of the outbreak.[25]

A few days earlier, Trump had signed a trade agreement with China. Though it fell far short of the massive deal he'd been envisaging, it did include a promise by China to buy many billions' worth of additional agricultural products, while the US agreed to halve tariffs on certain Chinese products. So excited was the president by the deal that he held out the prospect of a visit to Beijing. It would later emerge that China had purchased none of the American farm products it had committed to buying.[26]

And China had not been transparent about the virus. More than three weeks before Wuhan went into lockdown, Li Wenliang, a doctor in the city, had sent a message to a group of fellow doctors warning them of the new virus circulating at his hospital and urging them to keep safe. Even though the virus was at that point known to the authorities, they didn't inform the public or the World Health Organization. Indeed, when one of the doctors shared Li's message, the authorities forced the ophthalmologist to sign a statement saying he'd been making false statements.[27] The following day, when Taiwanese authorities contacted their Chinese counterparts and the WHO to say they had heard of a mysterious string of pneumonia cases in Wuhan and wanted to take precautions, they received no response.[28] When the Chinese authorities finally acknowledged the virus, known as Covid-19, and imposed the Wuhan lockdown, it was too late.

It was under the cloud of an approaching global pandemic that Britain celebrated its departure from the European Union that 31 January 2020. There were countdown parties and Boris Johnson – who had succeeded Theresa May as prime minister – gave a televised speech, but in the end the event so desired by many Britons was a mostly muted affair.[29] The divorce negotiations with the EU had been drawn out and fiendishly complex, an easily predictable reality that the pro-Brexit side had failed to mention during the campaign. And though the complicated future was not a hot topic on Brexit Day, Britain was facing the world alone just as the established order was beginning to stumble.

By the beginning of February, a string of countries had declared public-health emergencies and were evacuating their citizens from Wuhan, but the virus was already spreading within their countries. Trump remained optimistic. 'One day – it's like a miracle – it will disappear,' he declared on 27 February.[30] By that time, the Italian town of Codogno had already imposed Europe's first lockdown. Xi, in turn, had introduced a zero-Covid policy that meant lockdowns would be imposed wherever a Covid case was detected.

Companies that had spent the past three decades building global supply chains to maximize efficiency and value faced a furious scramble to secure supplies and fulfil contracts. 'Already in February it was clear that there was a production problem in China,' Lang said. 'When someone got Covid, factories had to completely close. The BDI's companies with operations in China told us that there would be implications for manufacturing in Germany because parts from China would be missing, and they told us, "You'll be getting this problem too." ' They quickly did; on 4 March, Germany had 262 Covid-19 cases.[31] Two weeks later, the country went into lockdown.[32] The WHO had declared the virus a global pandemic only a few days earlier, and governments around the world began suspecting that Beijing had been exerting pressure on this supposedly neutral body.[33] By mid-March, countries around the world were under lockdown. Schools and most workplaces were closed; theatres, cinemas and sports facilities too. Normal life was suspended. The countries that couldn't afford lockdowns made do with improvised facemasks and other small measures. But regardless of wealth, countries and individuals of all income levels suffered.

For businesses, the different lockdowns created the double hazard of operations at home being disrupted and supplies not arriving from China. 'We knew the situation in China would have consequences for German companies because they'd be missing components,' Lang said. 'They quickly tried to shift their supply chains by finding an alternative supplier somewhere else in Asia, in Latin America or somewhere else, and sometimes it was just a matter of hours before a competitor got there first. And then there were the logistics problems, especially in ports.' Everything companies needed from China suddenly took much longer, if it arrived at all. In one US survey, three-quarters of companies reported supply chain disruptions, four-fifths expected disruptions in the near future, 62 per cent reported delays in receiving goods and 53 per cent reported difficulties in getting information from China.[34] Manufacturers and retailers frantically searched for alternative suppliers – if there was any point looking.

But most urgently, Covid-19 was a public-health emergency.[35] With medical products desperately needed at home, Germany banned exports of such products, as did other countries and even the EU.[36] Although factories quickly switched production from, say, gin to hand sanitizer and from speciality clothing to personal protective equipment, there were desperate shortages, especially in Italy, Covid's first European victim. But when Italy asked fellow EU countries for help, for a few painful days nothing happened.[37] And despite having caused the tragedy by denying the virus's existence, Beijing was willing to exploit other countries' export bans for power-projection purposes. In early March, a Chinese flight landed in Italy to great fanfare, carrying 31 tonnes of medical supplies. Beijing also dispatched facemasks to Spain, France, the Czech Republic, Serbia and the EU and eagerly publicized this fact, neglecting to mention that the EU had sent it facemasks in the pandemic's early stage.[38] Huawei, which was trying to increase support for its 5G equipment, sent facemasks to Italy, Spain, the Netherlands, Poland and Greece.[39] The number of facemasks sent by both Beijing and Huawei was decidedly modest, but what counted was the symbolism: China was ready to help when European countries were not.[40]

In March 2020, Krach and his team were given the authority to design a last-ditch effort to prevent China's potential domination of 5G communications.

The energetic businessman turned politician rushed to visit allied capitals before they imposed lockdowns. Trust, he had decided, would be his winning argument. 'Trust is the most important word in any language,' he told me. 'You partner with people you trust, buy from people you trust. The US is definitely not perfect, but people trust us more than they trust the Chinese.'

Knowing he was in a fight against time, Krach tried to conduct as many foreign meetings as possible. 'We went around to governments and companies and said, "Who do you trust with your citizens' data and your government's most sensitive information?"' he explained. He visited NATO. He visited the European Commission. As chance would have it, the EU's commissioner for the internal market, the official responsible for 5G, was an acquaintance of Krach's from the business circuit. To him, too, Krach made his case for more trust-based decisions.

Asking countries not to use Huawei was a highly symbolic step. But if American leaders were serious about reducing America's vulnerability to whatever Xi's government might think up, they also needed to make sure that high-tech products could be manufactured at home. Most fundamentally, that meant incentivizing companies to manufacture computer chips in America. That spring, Democratic and Republican members of Congress were in the throes of composing the CHIPS Act, proposed legislation that would see the US government provide tens of billions of dollars to companies committed to building microchip manufacturing in the United States.[41] Krach, meanwhile, proposed an idea of his own to Congress: legislation for massive government funding of research and development in the United States. Two leading senators – one Democrat and one Republican – took on his idea and co-sponsored a bill, the Endless Frontier bill.

The legislators were in a hurry because America needed to regain some of its R&D advantage over China, and because manufacturing of microchips is a hugely complex process that is astronomically expensive to set up. In a truly globalized manner, the world had increasingly come to rely on a small number of chip-manufacturing plants, several of which were located in Taiwan. Indeed, Taiwan's TSMC, with its massive operations in Taiwan and even some in China, had become an indispensable hub of global chip production. In the mid-2010s, such country specialization had seemed acceptable and even desirable. Now, in 2020, it had become a source of enormous concern, and not just because it was obvious that a pandemic could disrupt supply chains. In many capitals, fears of a Chinese invasion of Taiwan were growing. Hadn't China just built and militarized a string of islands in the South China Sea? A military conflict between China and Taiwan would decimate global chip production and cripple modern economies, indeed the modern way of life. It surprised no one when Democrats and Republicans united around both the CHIPS and Endless Frontier Acts.

At the end of March, the US closed its border to foreign nationals. Other countries, too, banned entry to foreigners, with various degrees of rigidity. China closed its borders, and so did Russia.[42] Global aviation, which had survived ash clouds, terrorism and the global financial crisis, ground to a standstill.

After his string of meetings with foreign officials, Krach felt that they agreed with him that without trust, globalization wasn't going to work. But just as America's concern about Huawei wasn't just about the security of 5G, Krach's mission wasn't just about philosophy. If countries agreed with him that trust is necessary but then didn't follow up and ban Huawei from their 5G networks, Krach would have failed. 'You can't just say, "We're going to break Chinese subversion of globalization!" ' he told me. Instead of taking the whole world on, Krach said, the first step had to be to 'defeat and neutralize' the Chinese telecommunications industry. And as Krach saw it, Huawei had to be tackled not just because its infrastructure posed a national security threat but also because it was reducing the global telecoms infrastructure price level and thus distorting the market. 'Huawei's artificially low prices had left only Ericsson and Nokia as serious competitors on the global market,' Krach observed. 'And if Huawei can underbid competitors, who's going to enter that business? It's not profitable! We needed to neutralize Huawei in order to lift the price umbrella.'

Washington's fight against Huawei was about national security threats and market distortion relating to one company, but in reality it concerned the conduct of globalized business itself. Karl-Henrik Sundström, whose long telecoms career had been accompanied by the steroid-fuelled rise of Huawei, was watching the battle. 'It was clear already in 2006 and 2007 that Huawei's participation in the globalized economy wasn't going to be smooth,' he told me. 'We saw them entering a lot of markets, and we tried to block them. Everybody in the industry knew that they were stealing IPRs [intellectual property rights]. But treating them as a national security issue just wasn't on the agenda. And the big operators liked Huawei, because they got a good product, basically a copy of Nokia and Ericsson at a much lower price.'

While Ciaran Martin and his fellow British officials were insisting on treating Huawei as a 5G security issue, and countries including Sweden and Australia took a similarly narrow national security approach, across Washington the firm was now a symbol of globalization's dysfunction. And for Krach, all those reasons made Huawei the lowest-hanging fruit as he pursued his mission to level the playing field. 'We wanted to use 5G as a beachhead,' he told me. 'A beachhead is something that's small enough that you can own it and big enough that you can live off of it for a while. Ideally it's defensible, and ideally it's strategic high ground from which you can attack adjacent markets. The objective was to use 5G to build an alliance of democracies. 5G was the kernel, and it was perfect!'

Britain's approach of allowing a little bit of Huawei in its 5G network was becoming untenable. 'The government said that the risk-mitigation model no longer worked because of the force majeure created by the Americans,' Martin explained. In July 2020, as Britain had just emerged from its first Covid lockdown, UK Secretary of Digital, Culture, Media and Sport Oliver Dowden delivered a statement to the House of Commons. 'These sanctions are not the first attempt by the

US to restrict Huawei's ability to supply equipment to 5G networks. They are, however, the first to have potentially severe impacts on Huawei's ability to supply new equipment in the UK,' he told the legislators.[43] And, he added, 'From the end of this year, [UK] telecoms operators must not buy any 5G equipment from Huawei.'[44] Martin had lost the battle.

The 5G showdown had turned into the most bruising fight the US–UK relationship had had in a long time. Martin still maintains that Huawei and other Chinese firms posed real security risks, but that those risks had little to do with 5G gear. 'The Americans achieved their objectives,' he told me. 'But were they the right objectives? Forcing countries like the UK and others to forgo Huawei doesn't necessarily make the UK or these other countries any safer. They were cooking up proposals about creating alternatives, but there was no substance in any of the proposals at that time on telecoms. And they weren't turning their attention to more strategically important things like smart cities or synthetic biology.' The UK National Cyber Security Centre – the agency led by Martin – had already intervened when the town of Bournemouth wanted to use the Chinese technology giant for new smart-city installations. 'We had to ask them nicely not to do it because we had no legal powers over them and there was no viable Western alternative they could go with,' Martin noted. It was in such installations, he maintained, that Huawei's risk still lay, not in most 5G infrastructure. The former technology advisor to the US State Department has no time for such arguments. 'The UK position on Huawei was a bit like, "I don't want a tumour in my heart but it's OK to have a tumour on my arm." Sure, it's better to have it on your arm, but with technologies like this one, the tumour is going to spread. And secondly, even if it doesn't spread, why would you accept it on your arm? Their position was a self-contradiction,' he told me. Either way, the Anglo-American 5G battle was over.

'5G was a means to an end,' Krach said. 'And as we were going around the world making the case, nobody could say that we were just promoting American alternatives. We don't have one!' Other countries fought the battle less aggressively than the United States, but they too had concluded that they couldn't stake their telecommunications fortune on a company that wasn't a straightforward commercial provider of the kind they'd thought globalization would provide. In the many seemingly golden years of collaboration with China, though, countries had neglected to insure themselves for the eventuality that their enormous trading partner turned out to be a problem in other areas – national security, say. Industrial policy, which sees government intervene in the market to ensure the country produces certain goods and services, had been treated as a thing of the past.

Fortunately, Nokia and Ericsson had survived the bruising battles of the free market and were still there to provide first-rate technology. But their existence was not the result of clever advance thinking by governments: it was the result of constant innovation, adaptation and competition even under unfair conditions. 'The advantage of our system is free and open enterprise,' Martin reflected during a conversation in early 2022. 'But that's also a weakness, because it makes it much harder to strategically manage your capabilities, particularly beyond nation-state level. Even the Americans struggle. In fact, when it comes to 5G they don't have anything. We've abandoned industrial strategy, never mind doing it in conjunction with each other. The Americans were kneecapping Chinese tech, but they didn't have a strategy for how to build up American tech.' Now they were energetically trying to fix that.

Something even more fundamental than 5G equipment was shifting too: the public mood about China. While some activists and politicians like Alicia Kearns – who had won a seat in the UK parliament in the 2019 elections – had for years been highlighting China's subversion of globalization, its domestic human-rights violations or both, the wider public had mostly been indifferent to the country's practices. Indeed, ordinary citizens had little chance of knowing about IP theft or other unfair business practices. But now the public around the world had learnt about Chinese authorities' obfuscation about the proliferating virus in Wuhan. Such behaviour in the face of a deadly virus didn't just offend people; it had killed their friends and family members too. By the beginning of August 2020, the virus had killed nearly three-quarters of a million people.[45]

When polled by the Pew Research Center that summer, 77 per cent of Americans said they had little or no confidence in Xi, an increase of

27 percentage points over the year before. Meanwhile, 79 per cent of Australians distrusted the Chinese leader, up from 54 per cent. Italy: 75 per cent, up from 54. Germany: 78 per cent, up from 61. Netherlands: 70 per cent, up from 53. Britain: 76 per cent, up from 60. Sweden: 82 per cent, up from 67. Around the Western world, a median of 78 per cent professed to have no confidence in Xi.[46]

In the United States, the presidential election campaign was in full swing, and Trump and his Democratic challenger, Joe Biden, were trying to outdo each other in their scepticism of globalization and China. The Trump campaign ran attack adverts calling Biden 'Beijing Biden' and accusing him of being 'China's puppet' and of supporting China while 'China cripples America'. The Biden campaign counter-attacked by highlighting Trump's praise of Xi. In reality, dislike of globalization's erstwhile star pupil China united the two sides.

As the turbulent year drew to a close and people in most countries had been allowed to emerge from lockdown at least once, Krach was seeing his strategy bear fruit. 'The imperative was to take away Huawei's momentum,' he explained. 'We had a scoreboard where we measured our success. And remember that there's power in unity and solidarity.' Perhaps countries had also independently reached decisions similar to his. Either way, that November Sweden announced that it would not include Huawei or ZTE in its 5G network.[47] The list of countries announcing plans to ban Huawei also included many unexpected entrants: Bulgaria, Canada, the Czech Republic, Denmark, Estonia, France, Greece, Latvia, Poland, Romania. Elsewhere, telecommunications companies announced that they'd voluntarily forgo Huawei kit.

Mo Ibrahim, the mobile communications engineer turned billionaire, was following the standoff with anguish. 'As we say in Africa, "When the elephants fight, the grass suffers,"' he reflected. 'And we Africans are the grass. Mobile telephony is just one area of the fight.'

11
GLOBALIZATION BECOMES A WEAPON AS XI HITS BACK

Scott Morrison is a man used to plain speaking. In fact, he's got such a knack for the common touch that in 2019, in his first election as leader of Australia's Liberal Party, he led the party to a surprise victory. In April the following year, with Covid-19 ravaging his country and every country, Morrison decided to call for an international investigation. 'This is a virus that has taken more than 200,000 lives across the world. It has shut down the global economy. The implications and impacts of this are extraordinary. Now, it would seem entirely reasonable and sensible that the world would want to have an independent assessment of how this all occurred, so we can learn the lessons and prevent it from happening again,' he declared.[1] Those numbers became obsolete the moment he spoke them, so rapid was Covid-19's destructive march.

When Malaysia Airlines flight MH17, flying over eastern Ukraine, was shot down in 2014, not only did the passengers' and crew's home governments call for an investigation; they launched one. Now, with more than a million people worldwide infected with Covid-19 and nearly a quarter of a million having lost their lives to it,[2] the Australian prime minister's call for an investigation into the virus's emergence might have seemed prudent. Over the next few months, Morrison made the proposal a few more times. In September 2020, speaking at the United Nations' ghostlike General Assembly – which Covid forced global potentates to attend via video link – he pointed out that 'this virus has inflicted a calamity on our world and its peoples. We must do all we can to understand what happened for no other purpose than to prevent it from happening again.'[3]

But Morrison knew that criticism of Chinese authorities would expose Australia to retaliation by Beijing. In the spring, after calls for Covid investigations by other Australian politicians, the Chinese Communist Party's English-language newspaper, *Global Times*, had suggested such reprisal was coming. 'Australia is always there, making trouble. It is a bit like chewing gum stuck on the sole of China's shoes. Sometimes you have to find a stone to rub it off,' the paper, which functions as a mouthpiece for the country's authorities, wrote. China's ambassador to Australia, meanwhile, told an Australian newspaper that 'maybe the ordinary people will say "Why should we drink Australian wine? Eat Australian beef?" '[4]

Far away from the world of chewing gum and Australian wine, Lithuania was holding elections. Gintarė Skaistė was re-elected, and when centre-right parties formed a coalition government a few weeks later, she was given the crucial Ministry of Finance. The new government had gutsy foreign-policy ambitions. Presenting its coalition agreement, it mentioned Taiwan, and it went further still: 'We will actively oppose any violation of human rights and democratic freedoms, and will defend those fighting for freedom around the world, from Belarus to Taiwan,' it declared.[5] It was a momentous moment for Taipei, which had spent years seeing its small band of nation-state supporters decline as one after the other switched their diplomatic recognition to China. Vilnius wasn't switching its diplomatic recognition from Beijing to Taipei, but even mentioning support for Taiwan was bold.

Skaistė is a soft-spoken woman not given to sabre-rattling. If she were not a politician, she'd make an excellent professor of economics. But Skaistė was now in charge of her country's financial well-being. She knew that the move would trigger anger in Beijing, and she also knew of the *Global Times'* threats to Australia. Lithuanian companies exporting to China were a likely target, she concluded. But, she told me, 'the exports to China were below one per cent of total exports from Lithuania, so we didn't expect that reaction might harm our economy very much'.

In Canberra, Morrison and his government were taking Beijing's threats with similar calm. With China dependent on crucial Australian goods like iron ore, it seemed unlikely that Beijing would weaponize trade. Then China's embassy in Canberra handed Australian news media an extraordinary document. In the note, Beijing accused Canberra of trying to 'torpedo' China's infrastructure projects in Australia and took it to task for the Australian media's 'unfriendly or antagonistic' reports on China. The list, which soon became known as the 14 Grievances, also included complaints about Australian government funding for 'anti-China' research at an Australian think tank and alleged raids on Chinese journalists and academic visa cancellations. And the list went on: Beijing disliked Canberra 'spearheading a crusade' in multilateral forums on Taiwan, Hong Kong and Xinjiang, its calling for an independent Covid investigation, its ban on Huawei and its blocking of a range of Chinese investments and acquisitions in Australian infrastructure and agriculture.[6]

Before globalization's Big Bang, circumspection concerning foreign direct investment was considered common sense. During its glory days, such scrutiny instead came to be seen as an unnecessary hurdle. When Western countries began exporting their market economy coupled with a dose of democracy, it seemed inconceivable that their trading partners could pose risks that would require scrutiny of foreign direct investments. Many countries did away with FDI screening altogether. Now, with antagonism rising again, Beijing seemed unable to accept criticism of its approach to coexisting with other countries. 'China is angry. If you make China the enemy, China will be the enemy,' a Chinese government official told an Australian reporter.[7]

In other Western capitals, governments were still nurturing hope that 'change through trade' would at least have convinced Chinese officials that it would be futile to try to dictate the actions of other countries' governments and civil society. Canberra's silence, though, seemed to further enrage Beijing. A few weeks later, it banned imports of Australian wine. More precisely, it imposed tariffs so punitive – up to 218 per cent – that Australian winemakers swiftly lost their largest export market.[8] Chinese imports of coal, copper, nickel, woodchips, lobster, cotton, barley and beef were suspended or the bans on them expanded, while Australian goods China would struggle to replace – especially iron ore – were left untouched.[9] Chinese authorities issued various nebulous statements citing issues including beetle infestations and ecological health, but to Australian politicians and business executives it was clear what was happening: Australian companies were being punished for statements by the country's politicians and even its journalists and academics.

Sweden was facing similar wrath. It was civil servants at the Post and Telecom Authority (PTS), an independent government agency, who had decided, on national security grounds, to exclude Huawei from the country's planned 5G network. But the agency's technical experts hadn't reckoned with the mighty in Beijing. 'With no evidence, Sweden takes national security as a pretext to slander Chinese companies, openly oppress Chinese telecom companies and politicize normal economic cooperation,' government spokesman Zhao Lijian complained. Sweden should correct its 'mistake' and 'avoid negative impact on China–Sweden economic cooperation,' Zhao ominously advised.[10]

Beijing had badly wounded Australia's vintners and farmers. But it seemed to be losing the war of global public opinion. The country, which had been admired for its efficiency ever since Deng Xiaoping began opening it up to global business, was instead beginning to look overly rigid. Its draconian zero-Covid policy meant that workplaces and neighbourhoods were repeatedly being put under strict lockdown even as other countries were opening up. And in the race for a Covid vaccine, Chinese researchers were lagging far behind their Western colleagues. In early December, the world's first Covid-19 vaccine was approved: one developed by German scientists and the American pharmaceutical giant Pfizer.[11] Days later, a Covid vaccine developed by the Anglo-Swedish pharma concern AstraZeneca received its approval. When December 2020 turned to January 2021, nearly 100 million people had been infected by the virus and some 2 million had lost their lives to it.[12] But the end of the Covid misery was in sight – for those able to access the Western vaccines.

In the United States, Joe Biden had won the US presidential election. Shell-shocked as they were from the turbulent Trump years, people around the world had followed the election campaign and then the vote counting, and now they were following the election's chaotic aftermath as an enraged Trump tried to portray Biden's victory as invalid. America's allies were not so secretly delighted with Biden's victory: now they wouldn't have to worry about becoming Washington's targets. Indeed, they might even be able to face China together rather than apart. But Biden's election caused a conspiracy epidemic so severe that a few days into the new year, a large mob managed to force its way into the Capitol with the goal of thwarting the election's certification. A global public was relieved when the election deniers failed and democracy held firm.

In Stockholm, Ericsson CEO Börje Ekholm was in no doubt as to the meaning of Zhao Lijian's call for Sweden to reverse its Huawei decision and 'avoid negative impact on China–Sweden economic cooperation'. Ever since those first years in China, Ericsson had held a large share of the Chinese telecoms infrastructure market. In recent years, though, that share had steadily been declining as Huawei's sales continued to rise. Still, China was a crucial market for the Swedish telecoms giant – at 8 per cent of Ericsson's revenues, far more significant than its home market. And all this time, Ericsson had publicly voiced no complaints about the way Chinese authorities ran the country or the way Chinese businesses conducted themselves. Indeed, Ekholm was also a director of Jack Ma's Alibaba, which now accounted for a staggering one-quarter of the world's online retail.[13]

But Ekholm could see the writing on the wall. He texted Sweden's minister of trade, Anna Hallberg: 'At the moment Sweden is a really bad country for Ericsson,' he wrote.[14] Such was Ekholm's desperation that he pleaded with Hallberg to 'talk to' the PTS. Ekholm's messages made it to the news media. 'Our soul is in Sweden, it's Ericsson's base. But if Sweden doesn't support free trade it is a complication for us,' he explained in a subsequent interview, pointing out that 'we make 99 percent of our turnover outside Sweden'.[15] Minister Hallberg declined to intervene. Ericsson had to brace itself for a backlash from China over Sweden's 5G.

Ekholm is a skilled executive and a quintessential Davos Man. Now, though, he was facing the globalized executive's rapidly approaching dilemma: growing international hostility was leaving globalized companies in the line of fire, and the occasionally frustrating but always lucrative strategy of relying on China for sales, manufacturing or both was suddenly an obvious vulnerability. Should he try to keep his company in China despite the risks, or should he begin a withdrawal that would cause immediate harm to the bottom line?

A couple of weeks later, the World Economic Forum convened again, forced into cyberspace by the Covid pandemic. Once again Xi Jinping was a featured keynote speaker, as were other world leaders including Angela Merkel, President Emmanuel Macron of France and India's Prime Minister Narendra Modi.[16] 'Economic globalization has never and will not veer off course. Countries around the world should uphold true multilateralism,' he declared.[17] Perhaps the Chinese leader thought it was the message the global elite wanted to hear. But the world was already proving him wrong. Three days later, Biden was inaugurated as president – under strict Covid protocols, of course – and he had very clear ideas about what needed to be done about globalization.

When February arrived, so did news that Chinese authorities had approved the country's own Covid vaccine. Its efficacy, though, was so low that administering it was virtually guaranteed to cause continued lockdowns.[18] At the same time, China was refusing offers of Western vaccines to help inoculate its own population. Predictably, the disruptions continued. For German businesses, Beijing's refusal of the Western vaccine offers was not merely an inconvenience: it was an eye-opener. 'We learnt that the ideologically infused Covid strategy – the idea that "we don't use any Western vaccines" – was more important than economic success because not accepting Western vaccines meant constantly keeping workplaces closed even when other countries reopened,' Joachim Lang observed. 'But China was prepared to pay this steep price so as not to have to acknowledge that the West had better Covid vaccines. That's how we realized that in today's China ideology trumps business.' Indeed, the government didn't seem bothered by the fact that its Covid strategy was resulting in the departure of many Western managers. 'The Chinese leadership gave the impression that they didn't mind their country becoming isolated in this way, because when expat managers didn't return they were replaced by Chinese managers,' Lang said. 'And having more Chinese managers gave the government more power even in Western companies.'

Indeed, the constant lockdowns made expat life in China less attractive than it used to be. And something else was changing too. Over the past decade, a government-run internet surveillance system had blocked first a few, then an increasing number of websites Beijing considered a threat. Now the list of apps and websites inaccessible to internet users in China spanned the most popular ones: Google, Facebook, YouTube, Instagram, WhatsApp, Spotify, Twitter, Pinterest, Snapchat. Western news media including the BBC, Reuters, the *New York Times*, the *Wall Street Journal*, the Australian Broadcasting Corporation and the *Washington Post* were blocked too. To be sure, those really determined to access Western news and social media could do so using VPN connections, but the firewall could detect VPNs too.[19] Living behind an increasingly thick firewall, and now having to contend with constant lockdowns, meant that assignments in China were no longer the boon it once was for Western managers. 'It used to be a career advantage in business if you had spent some time in China,' Lang said. 'At the very latest with Covid, that began to change.'

While the Great Firewall was a nuisance to the expats remaining in the country, it had been shaping the minds of Chinese teenagers and twenty-somethings now coming of age. They were possibly even more sealed off from outside information than Gintarė Skaistė, Ivita Burmistre, Sergei Guriev, Jana Burow and Achim Langert had been behind the Iron Curtain, where ordinary citizens could often receive Voice of America, the BBC World Service and Radio Free Europe. Much like authoritarian regimes through the ages, Beijing was also infusing daily life with belligerent rhetoric. 'The Communist Party has been ramping up its nationalistic propaganda, promoting the idea that a diminishing West, especially the United States, is determined to thwart China's rise. The Chinese government still invokes the idea that China suffered "a century of humiliation" in the hands of these "imperialist powers",' a Human Rights Watch researcher wrote.[20] With young professionals in China growing up instructed to think of the West as China's enemy, perhaps it was no surprise that Beijing's punitive tariffs on Australian wine, the most popular kind sold in China, seemed to encounter minimal rebellion.[21]

In Taiwan, pineapple farmers were getting ready to harvest their famously juicy fruit. But just before they could do so, China – the largest export market for Taiwanese pineapples – imposed a blockade on the fruit, claiming that its inspectors had found 'harmful organisms'. The Chinese authorities provided no evidence of a spike in harmful creatures.

Taipei concluded that the blockade was instead a signal to the government of President Tsai Ing-wen, which had successfully battled Covid and dared to highlight its achievements as a vibrant democracy with a successful economy. That economic success, of course, depended on exports to China. If Taiwan's famous pineapples had to rot on the island, it would send an unmistakable message to not just Taiwan but other countries too.

But Taiwan was defiant. 'Taiwanese pineapples are stronger than fighter jets. Geopolitical pressures cannot squeeze their deliciousness,' tweeted Vice President Lai Ching-te,[22] while Tsai tweeted that 'After Australian wine, unfair Chinese trade practices are now targeting #Taiwanese 🍍 pineapples 🍍. But that won't stop us. Whether in a smoothie, a cake, or freshly cut on a plate, our pineapples always hit the spot. Support our farmers & enjoy delicious Taiwanese fruit!'[23] Taiwan's Western friends heeded her call. Ordinary citizens began tweeting support under the new #FreedomPineapple hashtag, just as they had tweeted in support of #FreedomWine when Australia's vintners were targeted. On Facebook, the American Institute in Taiwan shared a photo of its director with three pineapples on his desk, while the Canadian Trade Office in Taipei posted a photo of staff with a pineapple pizza.[24] Within four days, the pineapples that would ordinarily have been exported to China had been snapped up by companies and ordinary citizens.[25]

Commercial blockades are nothing new. During World War I, Britain tried to starve Germany and Austria into submission by blocking supplies, and one might argue that certain Western economic sanctions against countries like Iran have constituted commercial blockades. Since joining the globalized economy and gaining heft in it, China has occasionally tried out commercial coercion. Five years after punishing Norway's fishermen, it banned South Korea's popular K-pop bands from performing in China and disincentivized Chinese tourism to South Korea. The boy bands could never have predicted the ban, because it had nothing to do with them: it was retaliation against Seoul's decision to host on South Korean soil a US THAAD missile defence system for protection against North Korea.[26]

But now, in 2021, China seemed to be exploiting globalization in proliferating ways. There was the long-standing headache of its IP appropriation and unfair support of its own companies, and now any business could become a target as Beijing sought to punish words or deeds by Western governments. And the harmful business practices didn't exist in isolation. Over the preceding few years, China had not just built its artificial islands and turned them into military fortresses; its formidable, 16,966-vessel long-distance fishing fleet had also been fishing other countries' waters dry, and the People's Liberation Army Navy had kept expanding.[27] The PLAN now had some 350 ships and submarines, including more than 130 major warships, and the ability to launch long-range missile strikes against land targets. That made it the world's largest navy.[28]

Speaking to Congress that April, just a few months into his presidency, Joe Biden articulated what was happening to the post-Cold War world order: 'We're in competition with China and other countries to win the 21st Century. We're at a great inflection point in history.'[29] It wasn't just a feeling. In 1990, world trade made up 37 per cent of world GDP. Just before the global financial crisis, the figure was 59 per cent. In 2020, it was 52 per cent. In 1990, bank loans to borrowers in other countries accounted for 27 per cent of global GDP. In 2007, it was 56 per cent. Now, in 2021, the rate had fallen to 36 per cent.[30]

Whilst Taiwan's pineapple farmers were frantically rerouting their ripening fruit, Ericsson seemed to have accepted that it would be unable to maintain its market share in China, let alone grow it, and that the quality of Ericsson's technology was of no importance in the matter. When the company presented its quarterly report that July, the figures showed that between March and June, the company's sales had grown by a healthy 8 per cent worldwide. In China, they had decreased.[31] A few days later, China Mobile, the world's largest telecoms provider, announced its latest round of infrastructure contracts. As in the previous round, Huawei and ZTE won by far the largest shares. But Ericsson, which in the previous round had won 11 per cent of the contract, won a mere 2 per cent.[32]

Nokia, which had won nothing in the previous round, won 4 per cent. Around the same time as the PST excluded Huawei, the Finnish parliament had passed a law to protect communications infrastructure against espionage. The Finnish legislators' concern was clear, but they didn't name any companies. That, explained the *Global Times*, would stand Nokia in good stead. 'Finland's approach is more flexible, leaving more room for repositioning,' a Chinese analyst interviewed by the paper noted, favourably comparing Finland with Sweden. He added that the Finnish government 'is alive' to the opportunities this provided for Finnish companies on the Chinese market.[33] Then: the surprise win for Nokia. Ohisalo and her government colleagues had been wise to keep their counsel.

Another attack against Swedish business was under way too. Just as Ericsson's Chinese sales slump was becoming apparent, H&M's Chinese sales began slumping badly too. The fast-fashion retailer had been removed from large ecommerce platforms and its store locations removed from online maps. Chinese app stores mysteriously no longer included H&M's app, and almost two dozen of its shops had to close after sudden problems with the landlords.[34] When the retailer presented its quarterly report that July, sales in China had nosedived by nearly a quarter: a nightmare scenario in a country that makes up 5 per cent of H&M's total sales.[35]

H&M had been opening stores in China ever since setting up its first one in 2007. And like so many other companies, it had been relying on China both for manufacturing and for sales to Chinese consumers. It was a major buyer of Xinjiang cotton, grown and processed in the province by suppliers that catered to international apparel companies. But around the time that Alicia Kearns learnt about human-rights abuses against Xinjiang's Uyghurs in 2015 and 2016, so did many others. In 2018, a United Nations panel estimated that some 2 million Uyghurs had been forced into 'political camps for indoctrination', where they were to be disabused of wishes to freely practise their Muslim faith or their local customs. Beijing was concerned that without such intervention, the Uyghurs might act on their long-standing desire for Xinjiang to gain independence. The UN panel had also established that many of them were being used as forced labour by companies supplying cotton and other goods.[36] Then news media discovered that H&M and other apparel companies had indirectly been using Uyghur forced labour through their supply chains. Together with other firms in the sector, the Swedish firm quickly tried to distance itself from such practices; together they formed an industry group called the Better Cotton Initiative.[37]

In the summer of 2020, the group issued a statement calling for better labour practices in Xinjiang.[38] Ten, even five years earlier, such a statement would have been so innocuous as to be boring. And when the statement went out, nothing happened. Then, in early 2021, the Chinese consumer boycott of H&M appeared, and it featured not just the purge of the fashion chain's retail channels but a social-media campaign by the Central Communist Youth League (the Chinese Communist Party's youth wing) as well. The boycotters directed their rage against other targets, too, especially the quintessentially British brand Burberry and the quintessentially American brand Nike, two other Better Cotton participants.[39] Curiously, the boycott erupted just as Beijing sought to punish Sweden for excluding Huawei, and just as the EU, Britain and the United States had imposed sanctions on Chinese officials involved in the mass internment of Uyghurs.[40]

The geopolitical neutrality that H&M and other global businesses had been nourishing for so long had done nothing to protect them. And because it's not illegal to boycott a company or not award it contracts, the companies' home governments could do nothing to help them. Across the Western world, executives were taking note. In a global risk survey that spring of 2021, an extraordinary 48 per cent of executives said they were concerned about deteriorating relations between China and the West. Twenty-one per cent were concerned about growing economic nationalism, the promotion of reshoring and national champions. Only 12 per cent were concerned about civil unrest linked to lockdowns.[41] Two years earlier, the biggest concern for executives had been trade sanctions at 31 per cent, followed by political violence at 22 per cent.[42]

In Ohio, Mike Turner was seeing these fears spread among the Dayton area's manufacturers. To be sure, the businesses were mostly not the sort of household names that might be targeted directly, but they could suffer harm through their supply chain. 'We've had product manufacturing move to China, but that has made manufacturing companies that remained here become dependent on parts coming from China,' he told me. 'That puts Chinese companies in an extremely strong position, and it gave China the opportunity to take advantage of it. That has led to a lot of anxiety among manufacturers, because it makes the whole manufacturing chain vulnerable. And manufacturers know that China doesn't hesitate to use its economic influence for state goals. China and Chinese companies are blurred together.'

In Vilnius, Skaistė bore in mind the Australian vintners, the Taiwanese pineapple farmers, Ericsson and the global fashion retailers as her government deliberated over how to best manifest its support for Taiwan. A few days after H&M and Ericsson presented their disappointing quarterly results in China and impressive results elsewhere, the Lithuanian government announced that it would invite the island to open a representative office in Vilnius.[43] It was a daring move. The last time a European country had allowed Taiwan to open a representative office was Slovakia in 2003, and China was much weaker then. What's more, Lithuania would allow the de facto embassy to use the name Taiwan rather than the more low-profile, and much more common, Taipei.[44] But Skaistė was confident that even if China decided to try to punish Lithuanian businesses, with only 1 per cent of exports going to China Lithuania would suffer little harm.

Across the border in Russia, another high-stakes test of globalized business was in progress. Mike Calvey, the American private-equity boss who had been living and investing in Russia since its first post-Soviet years, was on trial. The convoluted case involved a business dispute with a protégé of a Putin advisor, and ever since the American's arrest in 2019, investigators had been trying to prove his guilt. Prominent business leaders suggested the case was a misunderstanding. 'This is transformative. This kills FDI [foreign direct investment] stone dead forever . . . This sends the message, can you use the security services against your business rivals over a few million dollars? Yes, you can,' a source told a reporter, while a Western hedge-fund investor in Russia declared that the case proved Russia was no longer interested in Western investments.[45] Calvey was facing ten years in prison.

In early August 2021, Calvey's trial for alleged embezzlement was about to conclude. Prosecutors had been struggling to pinpoint his guilt, and even Putin's commissioner for the rights of entrepreneurs had criticized the prosecution.[46] In his final statement to the court, Calvey delivered a desperate plea. Speaking in Russian, he told the court that an acquittal would 'be a big positive signal proving that courts are independent and investors' rights are protected [that could] attract billions of dollars in new investments to Russia and create thousands of new jobs'.

But Russia no longer seemed concerned about making itself attractive to new Western investments. Indeed, it had made no efforts to bring back its perhaps most celebrated economist and trainer of future economists, Sergei Guriev. Instead, Guriev was training future economists in Paris; after his tenure at the EBRD, he'd been appointed scientific director of Sciences Po's master's and PhD programmes in the subject. On 5 August, Calvey was found guilty and given a five-and-a-half-year suspended sentence.[47] A few days later, China withdrew its ambassador in Vilnius and demanded a reciprocal move from Lithuania.[48] An unsettling reality had also taken hold in the South China Sea. The UN's tribunal ruling on China's artificial islands five years earlier, which faulted China for building the islands, had sided with the Philippines. Now, though, the Philippines president, Rodrigo Duterte, seemed to want to forget about his country's tribunal victory and the ruling itself.[49] 'They filed a case, we won. That paper in real life between nations, that paper, it is nothing,' he'd recently declared.[50] Policymakers far beyond the islands' immediate surroundings were taken aback. China seemed to be able to break international laws and get away with it.

Western businesses, for their part, were beginning to make contingency plans for China. Some thought about moving a factory or two to another country (but which one?), while others looked for alternative suppliers. LinkedIn and Yahoo announced they were leaving altogether, though given the existence of the ever-thicker Great Firewall, their departure was hardly surprising.[51]

In Vilnius, Skaistė and her fellow ministers were monitoring Lithuania-related outbursts from Beijing. 'We saw statements in their official media, and if you know Chinese media, you understand that when an official newspaper of China's government says something, that means it's official, even if it's not a government document,' the unflappable Skaistė explained. 'And the comments in their media outlets were along the lines of, "You will see what will happen."' That November, the Taiwanese representative office opened.[52] As embassies and de facto embassies go, it was a modest bureau. Its meaning, though, was enormous.

Skaistė had underestimated the harm China could inflict on her country. 'Very quickly, Lithuanian companies began telling us that their goods were stuck in Chinese customs and couldn't move,' she told me. Their cargo was simply being held in Chinese ports. There were no official statements; just a Kafkaesque situation involving containers with Lithuanian goods arriving in Chinese ports and prevented from travelling on, and nobody being able to provide answers to concerned companies or the Lithuanian government. Lithuania had just disappeared from China's customs registry.[53] And it wasn't just Lithuanian products being blocked; Skaistė began hearing that all products containing Lithuanian components would be affected. 'Their reaction was overwhelming,' Skaistė told me. 'Our exports to China dropped to zero and their exports to us dropped too. But China also tried to break our supply chains.'

Foreign companies that had built factories in the Baltic state as part of their supply chains now saw their goods languish in Chinese ports. Hundreds of German companies, for example, had direct investments in Lithuania, among them two major automotive suppliers that had just expanded their production in the Baltic state as part of their global supply chain – which also included China.[54] Now they couldn't get their parts from Lithuania to their factories in China. Companies that had spent three decades building precisely such global supply chains, and which had no influence over prospective statements by the government in any of the supply chain's countries, were alarmed. And with the EU's economies being intimately integrated, Lithuania's problem was now the EU's problem.

Most other EU member states would not have wanted to provoke China by inviting Taiwan to open a de facto embassy, but now the EU had to step in. 'Imports from Lithuania are no longer processed by Chinese customs. This affects many ports and different goods. We are also concerned that we are increasingly receiving reports of blocked imports from other member states as well,' EU Trade Commissioner Valdis Dombrovskis declared just before Christmas.[55] Even Lang's

Federation of German Industries felt compelled to speak up. 'The latest measures China has adopted against Lithuania amount to a trade boycott that will impact the whole of the EU . . . In the long term, the escalation by China is a devastating own goal. It shows that China is prepared to decouple economically from "politically undesirable" partners,' the association noted.[56] Australian winemakers, meanwhile, were taking stock of the damage Beijing's tariffs had done. Their exports to their most important export market had plunged by 97 per cent.[57]

In Washington, Joe Biden signed into effect a new law targeting human-rights abuses in China. During the Cold War, Western countries had tried to cajole Warsaw Pact countries into better treatment of dissidents, but they could do little more than plead. Now, with only one member opposing, Congress had passed the Uyghur Forced Labor Prevention Act, which banned goods made in Xinjiang from entering the United States unless the importers could prove that the goods had involved no forced labour.[58] America was showing support for the persecuted Uyghurs – and incentivizing American manufacturers to reduce their dependence on China.

The following month, after efforts by the EU to resolve the issue with China had gone nowhere, Dombrovskis's office filed a complaint against the country with the WTO. And while he was at it, the feisty former prime minister of Latvia also filed another complaint against China.[59] It concerned an equally aggrieving matter: China's habit of blocking European firms from enforcing their high-tech patent rights vis-à-vis Chinese companies, even in European courts. In an effort to at least partially prevent Chinese companies from illegally taking their commercial secrets, some European companies had been suing them in European courts – only to find the lawsuits blocked by so-called anti-suit injunctions filed by the Chinese government.[60] Now Dombrovskis wanted the WTO to tackle the matter. The EU didn't have much chance of success: China could oppose the EU's request for WTO mediation, and even if it agreed, the process was likely to drag on.[61] But given the state of relations with China, the EU had nothing to lose.

Biden, too, seemed to feel the globalized world could no longer be kept together. His administration had just added a group of Chinese quantum-computing firms to the Entity List of companies with which

American firms are banned from doing business.[62] Not very long ago, quantum had been the new mobile telephony or the new internet: the nirvana on which scientists collaborated across borders. The twenty-first century would see quantum computing, for sure, but it would be different versions, developed by competing teams. In another illustration of a connected world splitting apart, the US government had announced a diplomatic boycott of the upcoming Beijing Winter Olympics in protest against the country's human-rights abuses, prompting government spokesman Zhao to ominously announce 'resolute countermeasures'.[63] Earlier in the year, US Secretary of State Antony Blinken had outlined the administration's China policy: invest at home, align with allies, compete against China.[64] Krach was thrilled. 'The Biden administration has picked up on almost all our China initiatives,' he told me. Indeed, Biden was about to go further still.

In the meantime, Huawei had turned to the Swedish courts. While Sweden's planned 5G network was small compared to that of more populous countries, the Chinese firm took exception to its exclusion. In fact, Huawei seemed determined to make a statutory case of Sweden. When a lower court ruled against the Chinese firm, noting that the PTS had the right to exclude companies on the basis of national security concerns, Huawei appealed.[65] For good measure, it also took the case to the European Court of Justice.[66] Some months later, in January 2022, the Chinese firm further upped the ante, taking Sweden to the International Centre for Settlement of Investment Disputes, an institution operating under the World Bank.[67] But the telecoms giant's court cases in Sweden, the EU and with the World Bank were not just about Sweden: they were a shot across the bows of any other countries that might dare to exclude it.

Michael Treschow was seeing the world he and his comrades had built unravel. 'I've been to China so extremely often, starting in the early eighties, and have met most of their top officials, including Xi Jinping,' he observed in one of our conversations. 'I've met with Chinese politicians more often than I met with Swedish ones. The first times I met them, there were absolutely no signs that China may want to change the way it conducted its trade with the world. It was always about, "How do we make this better?" There was never any funny business along the lines of not wanting to continue along this path. Yes, it was always capitalism their way, but things got freer and freer. Arrangements moved from licensing agreements to joint ventures and eventually you might get the opportunity to set up a fully owned subsidiary in China. Everything worked, and everything grew.'

And now, executives lived in fear of punishment by the country that had seemed capitalism's most adept pupil, albeit one with very specific ideas. Lang was coming to a frightening realization. Not only was trade unable to prevent hostility between countries; protagonists were also willing to forgo trade with one another. 'The discussion around geoeconomics was morphing from an academic one into a very real threat for companies,' he observed. 'But we, the private sector, were not prepared for it because we always assumed that everyone was equally interested in maintaining free trade.' The private sector had been wrong.

12
RUSSIA INVADES UKRAINE

Axel Vogt, the mayor of Lubmin, still remembers the day Nord Stream 1 was inaugurated. As we sat in his office at the harbour, he pointed to the quay opposite. That's where the tent stood in which Angela Merkel, Dmitry Medvedev, François Fillon, Mark Rutte, Gerhard Schröder and all the other dignitaries ceremonially inaugurated the new pipeline on 8 November 2011. Soon thereafter, they were gone; Lubmin is not the sort of town where potentates or other visitors linger during the colder months. In the summer, people spend time on the beach. But as Vogt concluded the moment he moved to Lubmin, tourism is at best a partial source of income.

That's why The One and its sibling-to-be, The Two, were such a breakthrough for Lubmin. Its gas would flow year round, bringing the town tax revenues of more than €5 million each year. Its facility by the port, handling the transfer of gas from the Baltic Sea pipeline to the terrestrial one transporting it to its eventual destinations, would provide highly skilled jobs for local residents. Reassured by the arrival of such a major outfit, several other companies had already expressed an interest in setting themselves up in Lubmin. Vogt, an exceptionally friendly man with a warm handshake, could even live with the fact that the pipeline was generating some controversy. The nuclear storage site next to the old power plant had also generated controversy over the years, he reminded himself. Imagine if the old East German nuclear power plant were still in operation: environmental campaigners would stage constant protests in his town.

Vogt was proven right. A Canadian company trading in canola soon made Lubmin its German arrival port. A mid-sized oil company set up shop in Lubmin, which became its arrival port too. And when nearby Baltic Sea offshore wind construction took off in earnest, the town became a base for crews and equipment. Like the Nord Stream 1 teams, the workers often stayed in the hostel ship docked right at the harbour or rented accommodation from Lubmin residents. After years of decline, the people of Lubmin felt that destiny was finally on their side. East Germany joining West Germany and then the global economy hadn't been too bad in the end.

And things were about to get better still. 'Shell and four European companies – ENGIE, OMV, Uniper and Wintershall – signed financing agreements with Nord Stream 2 AG, the company responsible for the planning, construction and future operation of the Nord Stream 2 pipeline. The 1,220-kilometer pipeline will be able to transport a total capacity of 55 billion cubic meters of natural gas per year. It will run from the coast of Russia via the Baltic Sea to Greifswald in Germany, acting as a direct link between Russian reserves and European consumers,' the oil and gas giant Shell had announced when plans for the pipeline were finalized in August 2017.[1] The five energy companies had each committed to provide financing and guarantees for up to 10 per cent of the total cost, around €9.5 billion, and would also provide additional funding and guarantees of some €1 billion.[2]

Local pastor Katrin Krüger remembers the period before construction began. 'For months the pipes were lying here on a field that the company used as a storage site, waiting to be brought to the seabed,' she told me in the church's small kitchen. 'And it was clear to me that the government's various approvals and certifications of Nord Stream 2 were just a formality. You don't buy the pipes and bring them here unless you're completely certain that the pipeline will be approved. We're tearing up the Baltic Sea's seabed and countless trees are having to be felled where the new pipeline comes ashore. But there were no protest marches, nothing. I thought, how is this possible?' In early 2018, Merkel's government gave permission for the construction to commence on the German side. And once again, engineers and construction workers descended on Lubmin. Or rather, they arrived in Lubmin to a warm welcome.

Krüger didn't mind the engineers and construction workers and certainly valued the income they brought, but she was hurting for the trees and wondering why everything had to happen so quickly. 'It truly felt like a cloak-and-dagger operation,' she told me. 'And I thought, what sort of money must be involved when they can do this kind of thing?' Cloak-and-dagger or not, Lubmin had hit the jackpot again.

In 2018, Donald Trump was still in charge in Washington, and he most certainly didn't like Nord Stream. And on this issue, he was of one mind with most Democrats; the US Senate had already passed, with a 98–2 vote, a sanctions bill that fined Nord Stream 2's European minority investors.[3] He and other powerful people in the American capital of course didn't know Pastor Krüger or that she too, for very different reasons, was sceptical about Nord Stream. In fact, they'd never visited Lubmin, nor had they had a conversation with Mayor Vogt. He would have been delighted to tell them why he considered Nord Stream such an asset to his town, and he might also gently have pointed out that no German politician would dream of trying to block an infrastructure project in the United States.

The Senate's sanctions, though, had forced the pipeline's European participants to suspend their active participation.[4]

But Nord Stream 2's troubles didn't end there. In December 2019, Trump's firebrand new ambassador to Germany, Ric Grenell, began writing letters to German companies warning of further US sanctions if they participated in the project.[5] Then two Republican senators, Ted Cruz and Ron Johnson, wrote to a Swiss company involved in the construction, threatening it with 'crushing and potentially fatal legal and economic sanctions', as they put it.[6] That month, the Senate overwhelmingly passed a new sanctions passage, this time targeting the companies involved in the construction.[7] The Swiss firm immediately withdrew.

But the targeted firms, and many others, were baffled: how were companies supposed to operate if a legal contract could be overturned by a government or parliament that decides to punish a project for geopolitical reasons? The American legislators pushing punishment of the

European energy firms had apparently also failed to consider the implications of such unilateral sanctions against law-abiding companies: in 2019 the United States was still the world's strongest nation, and the dollar was still the world's most important currency and thus the most-used one in commercial transactions. America had the power to intervene in globalization on geopolitical grounds, and imposing sanctions on companies was one way in which it could do so. But in a not-too-distant future, China could become the world's most powerful country, with companies regularly trading in its currency. That would give Beijing the chance to unilaterally impose sanctions on commercial projects that had incurred its wrath, including commercial projects involving American companies.[8] As 2020 made its troubled march through the world, Beijing proved that it could repeatedly punish Western companies for geopolitical reasons, and that Western governments were powerless to stop it.

In May 2021, Joe Biden waived the Nord Stream 2 sanctions on the grounds that the pipeline was at any rate nearly complete.[9] And Germans were adamant that the construction should continue. That month, three-quarters of Germans polled in a survey thought Nord Stream AG should keep building the pipeline despite US opposition.[10] Four months later, the construction crews completed The Two, though the German government announced it would suspend the pipeline's certification on technical grounds.[11] Nevertheless, the pipeline was complete, and Mayor Vogt knew that whenever the certification was issued, there would be demand in Europe for the 55 billion cubic metres of gas the pipeline was capable of transporting each year. And like the Nord Stream 1 gas, the gas from The Two would come ashore in his town, which could double the fees paid by Nord Stream AG.

After decades in the downward spiral known to countless towns that have lost their main employer, Lubmin was looking forward to extremely prosperous times courtesy of an interlinking world. 'I was so excited when they did the test run of Nord Stream 2,' Jana Burow told me. 'You could see it far and wide because there was a massive flare. And I thought, "Hooray, it's almost there." I thought, "It doesn't matter what some people in the press or the government say, because there are contracts and you have to stick to them."'

That December, Mayor Vogt heard alarming news about Russia sending nearly 200,000 troops to the border with Ukraine. Soon American intelligence agencies began sharing warnings of an imminent invasion.[12] On 14 January 2022, US intelligence agencies warned that Russia could invade Ukraine 'within a month'.[13] But 14 February came and went. The following day, the Kremlin announced it had initiated a partial withdrawal from the Ukrainian border.[14] The American spies seemed to have misjudged Russia's plans.

In London, a little-known body called the Joint War Committee convened, and its members were not convinced that Russia had changed its mind about invading Ukraine. Despite its governmental-sounding name, the JWC is a maritime insurance body, composed of industry executives and advised by a security company comprising former military and intelligence officers. Because the global insurance industry is concentrated in London, the JWC convenes there. And because insurers are in the business of risk, on matters of wars and almost-wars they rely on the JWC to assess such prospects for the world's bodies of waters. It does so by means of a country-ratings index: the riskier the situation, the higher a body of water ranks on the index and the more shipping companies wanting their ships to traverse it need to negotiate with their insurers. For years, the waters off Libya, Nigeria and Somalia had been a perennial presence on the JWC's so-called Listed Areas.

'We meet quarterly, and since we had met in December our next meeting was not scheduled until March,' the JWC's secretary, Neil Roberts, told me. But in mid-February the committee decided that the matter of a potentially imminent war in Europe couldn't wait until March. The members convened for an emergency meeting. 'The advisors gave their view that there was an 80 per cent likelihood of Russia invading within the next two weeks,' Roberts recounted. 'That advice was quite different from what other advisors in the market were saying; their opinion leaned towards fifty–fifty. But our advisors took into account the large amount of specific information about Russia's invasion plans that US and British intelligence had made available to the media, and an 80 per cent likelihood is good enough to change the risk rating.' That day, the Joint War Committee put out a notice to the insurance industry saying it had added the Sea of Azov and the Russian and Ukrainian parts of the Black Sea to the Listed Areas.

That meant that any shipping company wanting to enter those waters had to inform its insurers and get agreement. There is a seven-day implementation plus a grace period for changes to the JWC's risk areas, which meant that starting on 24 February any ships wanting to sail through the Sea of Azov and the Russian and Ukrainian parts of the Black Sea would have to notify their insurers, who would review the risk before deciding whether to accept the journey. It would be a lot more hassle for the shipping companies.

Political-risk insurers had already drawn similar conclusions. By the end of January, fifty-seven of the sixty companies that offer political-risk coverage – which includes contingencies like insurrections, coups and government seizure of companies in countries deemed even somewhat hazardous – had stopped issuing coverage in Ukraine.[15] And without access to political-risk insurance, foreign companies would be wary of operating in the country. In January, international companies had already begun leaving Ukraine, the Ukrainian hryvnia had lost value and Ukraine's sovereign dollar bonds had slumped, while the cost of protection against a Ukrainian default had increased.[16] Simply by massing soldiers at the border, Putin was causing immense harm to Ukraine – and doing so was not illegal. To many, the insurers looked paranoid.

Indeed, on the same day that maritime underwriters decided war was likely, Olaf Scholz was visiting Russia for meetings with Putin. Like President Emmanuel Macron of France, the German chancellor had travelled to Moscow to try to avert war, and he seemed to have succeeded. At the press conference that followed, Vladimir Putin immediately addressed the two countries' business links: 'I got the impression that the Chancellor is willing to continue working pragmatically and mutually beneficially with Russia. This relates above all to our business links, which have traditionally been very intensive. After the People's Republic of China, Germany ranks second among Russia's foreign trade partners,' the Russian president observed, noting that trade between the two countries had increased in 2021. 'Altogether there are about 4,000 companies with German capital in Russia,' he pointed out, and reminded the journalists that Russian oil and gas covered more than a quarter of Germany's energy needs.[17] Then he spoke a bit about the need for more Russo-German collaboration on climate change.

Scholz seemed cautiously optimistic. After agreeing with his Russian counterpart about the vital nature of the two countries' business links, he urged Putin to withdraw the troops massed at the Ukrainian border. 'Let's continue discussing these matters through a dialogue. We mustn't end up in a dead-end street. That would be a misfortune for us all,' Scholz pleaded.[18] In London, the UK government issued a warning to the Kremlin and the Russian elite by cancelling its golden-visa scheme.[19] The United States had already sent a consignment of ammunition to Ukraine, to be used in case of a Russian invasion, and the Baltic states had promised to send weapons.[20]

The 2022 Winter Olympic Games now under way in Beijing were at least spreading a bit of cheer around the world. There was jubilation when Finland won its first-ever Olympic gold in ice hockey, beating its perennial rival Russia. But there was controversy when Eileen Gu, a freestyle skier born in San Francisco to a Chinese single mother – and investment banker active in the United States and China – chose to compete for China. Gu won two gold medals. The closing ceremony was as well executed as the one fourteen years earlier, but the games' motto – Together for a Shared Future – seemed to convince no one.

At least the Olympics had temporarily quelled the war fears. Putin would not dare spoil Xi's show, the reasoning went. After the closing ceremony, the world held its breath. What would Putin do? The answer came a few hours later. The Russian leader signed decrees recognizing the independence and sovereignty of the so-called Luhansk People's Republic and Donetsk People's Republic, Ukrainian territories that had broken away from Ukraine in 2014. Then he ordered Russian troops to be sent there.

The United States, the EU and the UK responded immediately – by targeting Russia's role in the globalized economy. First came a cocktail of sanctions on Russian banks, bans on Western investment in the annexed regions and travel bans on leading Russian officials and oligarchs, many of whom maintain homes in the West. The EU imposed an export ban on certain goods and technologies, cut Russia's access to the EU's capital and financial markets and services, and added more travel bans and asset freezes for leading Russian personalities. Australia added its weight, banning Aussie banks from trading with five of Russia's largest banks and imposing travel bans on Russian officials. And Japan joined in, imposing restrictions on its banks' trade with Russian banks.[21] Officially, the sanctions were imposed to punish Russia for its annexation of the two regions in the Donbas, but in reality the Western powers hoped that the swift punishment would deter the Kremlin from launching any further aggression against Ukraine.

The Japanese government imposed its sanctions in the early hours, local time, of 24 February. A few hours earlier, President Volodymyr Zelenskyy of Ukraine had delivered a televised address to the people of Russia. 'We know for sure that we don't need the war. Not a Cold War, not a hot war. Not a hybrid one. But if we'll be attacked by the [enemy] troops, if they try to take our country away from us, our freedom, our lives, the lives of our children, we will defend ourselves. Not attack, but defend ourselves. And when you will be attacking us, you will see our faces, not our backs, but our faces,' he said.[22] He looked drained. For weeks, he'd been downplaying America's invasion warnings, knowing that investors and international markets would get even more nervous about his country if he, too, started speaking of war.

The sanctions and Zelenskyy's plea were in vain. At virtually the same time as the Japanese government issued its announcement, Russian national television aired an address by Putin. 'Today, I again consider it necessary to come back to the tragic events taking place in the Donbas and the key issue of ensuring Russian security,' the Russian president began. 'Let me start with what I said in my address of February 21. I am referring to what causes us particular concern and anxiety – those fundamental threats against our country that year after year, step by step, are offensively and unceremoniously created by irresponsible politicians in the West. I am referring to the expansion of the NATO to the east, moving its military infrastructure closer to Russian borders.'[23] While television stations were airing the speech, Russian troops launched a coordinated attack on Ukraine. Soldiers poured across the Russian–Ukrainian border into the Chernihiv, Kharkiv and Luhansk regions in the east. Naval forces attacked the Black Sea cities of Odesa and Mariupol. Yet other troops attacked from occupied Crimea and from Belarus, where Putin ally Aleksandr Lukashenko was providing friendly territory. Explosions were heard in the Ukrainian capital of Kyiv. In Odesa alone, eighteen people were killed by a missile strike.[24]

When Solveig Artsman woke up and turned on the radio app on her smartphone, she heard the news. It brought instant memories of her Nord Stream battles. 'I vividly recalled how during the debate before the municipal council signed the contract, one of the members wanted us to understand that the Cold War was over and that Nord Stream was a peace project. I tried to make the point that it really wasn't. But many others said, "Of course it is. Now we'll get cheap gas and we'll trade with each other." At one point a senior person in the party pointed at me and said, "What are we going to do about people who suffer from Russophobia?" I don't know if these people have suppressed what they said, or if they recall it. But I remember it.'

In Helsinki, Maria Ohisalo received the news, and though she was horrified and fearful for her own country, she felt vindicated. 'Like many Finns, I was shocked,' Ohisalo told me. 'At the same time, I thought this was a long time coming. My party had been extremely critical of Putin's regime and the oppression of the opposition parties in Russia. But until Russia invaded Ukraine, this criticism was mostly ignored in Finland.' That may have been because Russia was Finland's sixth-largest export market and its main supplier of oil and natural gas.[25]

Waking up in his home outside London, Neil Roberts heard the news too. 'I said to myself, "Our advisors are very gifted." We were set up for what happened on that morning,' he told me. 'The troubling part from a shipping perspective was that there were eighty-five ships that had previously docked in Ukrainian ports and were stuck there.' The merchant vessels and their crews hadn't left quickly enough and were caught in a sudden warzone.

Axel Vogt, too, heard the news in the early hours. 'I couldn't believe it; it was like 9/11, that kind of shock,' he told me. 'And it immediately became clear to me that we'll never see gas flowing through Nord Stream 2. That was a feeling we'd been having for some time. But I still thought that our contracts with Nord Stream would keep going and that the gas that was already flowing through Nord Stream 1 would keep being delivered. My lawyer self said, it's a contract, there's just no way that they can just stop delivering the gas.'

Pauline Neville-Jones, now a member of the UK House of Lords, looked back to the Dayton negotiations and her perception that the Russian and Serbian negotiators felt they were being overpowered by the West. Some of Russia's narrative of Western aggression went back to this experience involving a group of people – Serbs – that Russia perceived as belonging to its sphere of influence, she thought. But Neville-Jones was self-critical too. 'We were convinced by our own propaganda and by our strong desire to think the best of them,' she told me. 'Putin pulled off a coup in Crimea and interfered in Syria and he got the feeling that we, the West, were feeble, that we mostly seemed interested in money and wouldn't say boo to a goose. And he got the idea that he could do anything.' Mike Turner, now the top Republican on the House Intelligence Committee, likewise thought back to the Dayton Accords and what he'd seen while helping Bosnians rebuild their communities. 'I believe that those atrocities that were committed in Bosnia were a precursor of what we're seeing in Ukraine: the attacks on civilians, the massacres,' he told me. 'The disintegration of Yugoslavia and the atrocities in Bosnia are tied to what we're seeing Russian soldiers do in Ukraine today.'

Vogt's lawyer self was right: the gas kept flowing. But in Washington, Brussels, London and other Western capitals, governments knew they needed to respond even though Ukraine was not a member of NATO or any other Western defence alliance. They struck by again targeting the Russian economy. 'Today, we imposed an unprecedented package of financial sanctions and export restrictions in lockstep with our Allies and partners that will isolate Russia from the global financial system, shut down its access to cutting-edge technology, and undercut Putin's strategic ambitions to diversify and modernize his economy,' US Deputy National Security Advisor for International Economics Daleep Singh told a press conference in Washington that afternoon. He listed the specifics: the US would sanction Russia's two largest banks, Sberbank and VTB, by freezing Sberbank's access to the US financial system, freezing VTB's assets in the US and banning Americans from trading with the two banks. It would freeze the assets of three further Russian banks and ban trade with them. It would restrict US investors from financing thirteen crucial state-owned enterprises. And it didn't stop there: the United States also sanctioned executives in the companies as well as other high-profile Russians.[26] In coordination with other Western allies, Washington banned exports to Russia of sensitive technology that could be used by the Russian military. It sanctioned Belarusian banks, defence companies and officials too.[27]

The British government delivered another blow by freezing Russian bank assets in the country and shutting off Russia's banking system from the UK's powerful capital markets. London also banned Russian state-owned companies and key private ones from raising funds on the British financial markets. Cole-Fontayn's colleagues who had spent their careers specializing in Russia on a purely capitalist basis woke up to a new reality where a bank's nationality mattered a great deal. So did the nationality of famous personalities going in and out of Britain. The UK government imposed sanctions – comprising asset freezes and visa bans – on more than a hundred Russian companies and leading personalities and imposed export control on goods used in Russia's high-tech and strategic sectors. It banned Aeroflot, the Russian flag carrier, from UK airspace and cut off British bank access for wealthy Russians, including Kirill Shamalov, Putin's former son-in-law and Russia's youngest billionaire.[28] The European Union banned Russian airlines from its airspace and sanctioned Putin, Foreign Minister Sergei Lavrov, a string of other leading Russian personalities and Russian banks. Like the United States and Britain, it imposed export bans on dual-use goods – which can be used for both civilian and military purposes – and a range of technology exports.[29] Australia added sanctions of its own, as did Japan, Taiwan and Canada. Even Iceland added to the economic punishment of Russia. The EU banned aviation companies based within the European Union from leasing aircraft to Russian airlines, a crippling blow as 515 of the 980 passenger jets registered in Russia were foreign-owned. The EU politicians gave the companies thirty days to get their aircraft out of Russia.[30]

Western governments could impose this massive economic punishment on Russia precisely because the country had spent the past three decades and some integrating its economy with the West. And the economic retribution continued. Three days after the invasion, the

United States, Germany, France, Italy, the European Commission, the UK and Canada collectively announced that some Russian banks would be removed from the SWIFT system, with which international transactions are made, to prevent Russia's Central Bank from deploying reserves to undermine sanctions.[31] Allies also followed Britain's lead and limited the popular golden visas, which had for so long allowed wealthy Russians to gain residence in their countries.[32]

The following day, Russia hit back, banning Western airlines from traversing Russian airspace. Western governments had, of course, already done the same with Russian airlines, but their bans didn't make much difference since Russian airliners rarely cross Western airspace, except when travelling to a Western country. Russia's overflight ban, by contrast, crippled European airlines' massive Europe–Far East market segment just as they were getting ready to resume flights suspended by Covid. As late as October 2021, after the US aviation industry had pleaded with the US State Department, Russia had agreed to issue more overflight rights to American airlines.[33] In 2019, the last normal year before Covid-19 devastated all manner of movement, more than 300,000 flights had travelled through Russian airspace.[34] And now, no Western flights at all.

Aviation executives were prepared – up to a point. Ever since Russian rebels in eastern Ukraine shot down a Malaysian Airlines plane over Ukraine in 2014, they'd been worrying about aviation incidents should Russia launch a full-scale invasion. By the time Russia invaded, most Western airlines had already stopped flying to Ukraine. But now Western airlines would have to circumvent Russia's vast airspace while airlines based in China, the Middle East and other countries that hadn't sanctioned Russia could keep traversing it. The Europe–Far East globalization commute had been crippled.[35]

Something very fundamental was changing. When American and other leaders began voicing doubts about globalization, Germany had kept its belief in the power of markets to moderate nation-state behaviour. Now even Germany was beginning to question globalization's power to convert. 'We are living through a watershed era. And that means that the world afterwards will no longer be the same as the world before. The issue at the heart of this is whether power is allowed to prevail over the law. Whether we permit Putin to turn back the clock to the nineteenth century and the age of the great powers. Or whether we have it in us to keep warmongers like Putin in check,' Olaf Scholz told the Bundestag's assembled members on 27 February.[36] A watershed era – *Zeitenwende* was the word Scholz used – meant not just the change into a new era but also the crumbling of German belief in the markets' ability to mollify countries' most aggressive instincts. And now that this turning point had arrived, the German government launched a massive project to launch offshore terminals that could receive liquefied natural gas (LNG) from countries like Qatar and the United States so Germany wouldn't be dependent on Nord Stream any more.[37]

In France, Finance Minister Bruno Le Maire informed a radio station that 'we're waging an all-out economic and financial war on Russia. We will cause the collapse of the Russian economy.'[38] His words rapidly spread among the world's insurers, who became extremely nervous. War is unsurprisingly excluded from standard business insurance, and until very recently, it had been clear what constituted a war. But now? NotPetya had caused war-like devastation, and less severe cyberattacks had brought disruption or massive money loss too. A ransomware attack on the crucial Colonial Pipeline, which supplies the US East Coast with oil, had wreaked havoc on American drivers in May 2021.[39] Underwriters racked their brains to determine what Le Maire's inadvertent declaration of economic war might have on their clients' coverage. The clients themselves were desperately trying to decide whether to stay in Russia, Ukraine or both – or whether they should leave at any cost.

Le Maire quickly withdrew his comment, but it had already made its way to Moscow.[40] One week later, the country's ruling party, United Russia, announced that a government commission had approved the first step towards nationalizing assets of foreign firms that leave the country in connection with the West's economic sanctions.[41]

Business had been weaponized, and because globalization had intimately linked countries' economies, that would have incalculable consequences. The fact that the economies were so interlinked was, of course, the reason that Western governments could even attempt to punish Russia without using military means. When the Soviet Union invaded Afghanistan in 1979, there was little even the most sympathetic governments could do in support of the Afghans apart from send them weapons, as the United States ended up doing, and when the Soviets invaded Czechoslovakia in 1968, Western governments could do little more than voice outrage and receive Czechoslovak refugees. But now, Western governments could punish Russia not just by sanctioning leading personalities and crucial enterprises, but also by forcing their own companies to stop doing business with the country. Globalization might not be able to turn autocracies into liberal democracies, but it proved useful as a tool with which to punish regimes that violate international law.

And Western allies kept responding to Ukraine's desperate pleas for help. By mid-March, the United States had approved $2 billion worth of military aid, and one month later it had pulled ammunition, radars, drones, armed personnel carriers, armoured vehicles, helicopters, body armour and other equipment out of the US military's own inventory to send to the Ukrainian armed forces.[42] Estonia had dispatched anti-tank missiles.[43] Governments were frantically looking to see what they could quickly send to the battlefield. Even Australia had prepared a delivery of infantry vehicles.[44] But Germany was struggling to fully adjust to the world's brutal turn. Defence Minister Christine Lambrecht could only bring herself to promise the Ukrainians helmets and some marginally useful equipment the Bundeswehr had inherited from East Germany.[45] Even the equipment other countries had sent was far, however, from sufficient. Although Ukraine swiftly recaptured the Kyiv region, its armed forces needed to fight off the Russians in the north, east and south. In truth, Western governments were nervous: what would happen if they sent Ukraine powerful weaponry including tanks and fighter jets and Russia retaliated against them?[46]

On 14 March, the Russian Duma passed a law allowing the government to confiscate Western-owned planes leased by Russian firms: a swift response to the EU's order obliging Western aviation companies to withdraw their planes leased to Russian airlines.[47] Would the European aviation companies be able to get their aircraft out before Russian authorities took them? Aircraft owners and their insurers were facing combined losses of $10 billion.[48] Russia won: the ink was barely dry on the legislative papers when the Russian government seized hundreds of Western-owned aircraft.[49] They were no longer allowed to leave the country.

A month later, the JWC met anew and raised the entirety of Russia – including its ports – to the highest risk rating. 'It was a big step,' Roberts said. 'We took the precaution of consulting the relevant departments in the UK government, and I explained that if we do this, it may be perceived as the West upping the ante and the markets saying that there was a terrible situation within Russia. But the Committee considers a number of perils, not just kinetic ones, and the one we were concerned about was the risk of confiscation since the Russian government had already confiscated so many Western aircraft.' The JWC had to prevent Western-owned ships from being seized by Russia in a similar manner.

The UK government gave the JWC the green light. 'So we acted,' Roberts told me. 'And we don't act for political reasons; we act for business-exposure reasons. Vessels going to Murmansk, vessels going to the Sakhalin project [ExxonMobil's oil-and-gas production with Rosneft off Russia's eastern coast], they'd have to report to their underwriters. The insurance industry C-suite demanded transparency regarding the risks in Russia. Having lost all these aircraft, they were very sensitive about losing ships.'

Bosses at multinational companies swiftly convened emergency meetings. Many were in sectors so severely affected by sanctions that remaining in Russia made little sense, while others decided it was commercially or ethically unwise to remain. BP announced that it would divest its 19.75 per cent stake in Rosneft. Equinor, Norway's state-owned energy company, said it was withdrawing from its Russian joint ventures. Exxon said it would pull out of Sakhalin-1, one of the Sakhalin exploration sites. The American energy giant had a 30 per cent stake in the project, which it jointly owned with Rosneft, a Japanese and an Indian company.[50] Shell announced it was leaving a joint venture with Gazprom and pulling out of Nord Stream 2.[51] Pulling out meant billion-dollar losses for almost all the firms, though the war was also allowing energy companies make enormous windfalls.[52] But withdrawing seemed the only viable option, also because Western insurers were getting concerned about unwittingly violating sanctions by insuring energy operations in Russia.

The departures spread to consumer products. Starbucks announced its exit, as did Coca-Cola, Ferrari and Ford. Unilever said it would suspend all imports and exports in and out of Russia, though it didn't announce any closure of its factories there.[53] Caterpillar, the heavy-equipment giant, said it was leaving, and Mercedes-Benz and Harley-Davidson said they'd stop exporting their wares to Russia. The German DIY chain OBI Baumarkt announced that it would donate its Russian operations to a suitable taker. (Four months later it did so, giving 60 per cent of its assets to a Russian entrepreneur for around €10.)[54] Every day, more companies joined the list of businesses announcing they'd depart from Russia or curtail their operations there.[55]

Even McDonald's took its leave.[56] After thirty-one years in Russia, years that had included a coup, a near civil war, two wars in Chechnya, an invasion of Georgia and the annexation of Crimea, the golden arches were leaving for good. One month later, the Illinois-based empire sold its Russian operations to a local entrepreneur, who renamed the firm Vkusno & tochka ('Tasty and that's it'). He informed news media he'd paid a 'symbolic sum' for the acquisition.[57]

Far from all Western companies operating in Russia were affected by the sanctions, which by March were mostly focused on Russian banks and dual-use technology that could benefit the Russian military. Insurers, always concerned about sanctions exposure among their clients, made an even more expansive interpretation than the governments of which companies were covered by the sanctions, and the prospect of operating without insurance prompted many companies to start packing their bags. But even then, plenty of consumer-product companies, retail chains and enterprises in the food sector would have been free to remain. Like McDonald's, some had quickly decided to leave anyway, concluding that the war was going to be a far bigger affair than the annexation of Crimea or any other upheaval over the past three or so decades. To some, leaving or slashing operations felt like the morally right thing to do, even though doing so meant sending Russian employees into unemployment. Others planned to remain until they'd found a humane plan for such local personnel. Some merely suspended operations, leaving factories, inventories and staff in place. Others only suspended exports to Russia or contracts with Russian clients, or contracts with the Russian government. Suspending contracts with the Kremlin is, of course, far less costly than withdrawing altogether. The companies bravely announcing a complete departure also faced the risk of incurring the Kremlin's wrath.

In Lubmin, Mayor Vogt still couldn't decide what the upheaval might mean for Nord Stream 1. In Stockholm, Karl-Henrik Sundström was aghast, but in a guilty sort of way he was also relieved that Stora Enso now only had a relatively light presence in Russia. Two months after the invasion, it divested.[58] Companies that, by contrast, had kept going in Russia, hoping for another quarter of tolerable conditions and tidy profits, now faced considerable disruption whether they stayed or tried to leave. Those opting to leave discovered that Russian authorities were already putting up hurdles.

All told, one month after the invasion, 450 Western companies had announced some sort of retreat from the Russian market: a unique corporate response to a geopolitical event.[59] The US government took its next step, sanctioning a slew of Russian defence manufacturers, most of the Russian Duma's members and Sergei Guriev's former board colleague Herman Gref.[60] The Sberbank CEO, though, had years earlier moved his wealth to offshore accounts.[61]

But while some companies tried to hurriedly leave Russia, others saw the invasion as just another hiccup of the kind globally operating companies regularly witness. They'd seen the coup against Gorbachev, Moscow's bid to militarily crush Baltic independence the same year, Saudi Arabia's proxy war against Iran in Yemen, Myanmar's 2021 military coup, the civil war in the Democratic Republic of the Congo. Every time, businesses had made adjustments to keep their operations safe. While governments condemned and sometimes punished egregious acts by other governments, businesses made commercial risk assessments. In the globalized world, globally operating companies could assume they'd never become a wholesale target when governments squabbled. The arrangement ultimately benefited everyone. When Russia annexed Crimea in 2014, Joe Kaeser even stepped up Siemens's investment in Russia.[62] Geopolitics was a matter for politicians.

Making that assessment once again, Nestlé, the Swiss consumer-products giant that makes everything from chocolate bars to cat litter, decided it should stay in Russia. So did Uniqlo, the Japanese apparel chain. 'Clothing is a necessity of life. The people of Russia have the same right to live as we do,' Tadashi Yanai, the CEO of Uniqlo's parent company Fast Retailing, explained in early March, adding that war was despicable and announcing that his company was making a donation to UNHCR, the United Nations' refugee agency.[63]

But something had changed. Moments after the two firms announced their respective intentions, social-media users began venting their anger. 'Did we mention today that @Nestle likes Russian blood money?! Well . . . #BoycottNestle,' an account named @AnonOpsSE tweeted.[64] 'The primary ingredient of @Nestle's chocolate is blood,' tweeted user @DrGJackBrown.[65] '#Uniqlo has decided to keep Russia's shops open. I have decided that I will stop buying #Uniqlo until they reconsider their position,' Twitter user @partymola opined.[66] The companies' social-media punishment accelerated at unimagined speed. Even Volodymyr Zelenskyy weighed in. 'Business in Russia works even though our children die and our cities are destroyed,' he told an anti-Nestlé protest in Bern.[67]

Clearly taken aback by consumers' suddenly strong opinions on geopolitics, both companies rapidly reversed course. Within a couple of days, Uniqlo declared that it was closing its Russian stores. Nestlé announced that it had suspended production of most of its brands in Russia and said it would only sell essential products like infant food and promised to donate its profits to charitable causes.[68]

Maria Ohisalo, who had left the Interior Ministry to become minister of the environment and climate change, was following the news from Ukraine. She was shaken by the brutality Russian troops were now visiting on the Ukrainians, and she knew that her own country, which has a more than 1,300-kilometre-long border with Russia and bravely fought back against Soviet invaders during World War II, was in a perilous position. Fortunately for Ohisalo and her fellow ministers, Vladimir Putin didn't seem obsessed with Finland the same way he was with Ukraine, and Finland boasted impressive defence involving not just the military but the private sector and ordinary citizens too. Still, war waged by a neighbour against another neighbour was a calamitous turn of events. Finnish companies, which had been trading heavily with Russia, scrambled to find alternative markets, and many of them began closing their operations in Russia.

But something even more unexpected was transpiring across the country: ordinary Finns, who had lived through Soviet-imposed neutrality during the Cold War and resolutely remained outside NATO since the Soviet Union's demise, decided they wanted to join the alliance. Sixty per cent were now in favour of Finland joining NATO, a leap from 26 per cent the previous autumn.[69] Next door in Sweden, too, public support for NATO membership was growing: 49 per cent were now in favour, up from around 40 per cent in previous months.[70] Would the two countries, which had for decades built their security policy on jointly remaining outside NATO, dare to apply for membership? Russian officials had long threatened that there would be consequences if they took such a step.

In Lubmin, Achim Langert went to speak with Mayor Vogt about the war's meaning for their town. 'I told the mayor, "Sanctions against Russia, that's like cutting our own flesh. They can live without our money, but we'll struggle without their gas," ' he recounted. ' "And now we constantly hear how businesses have to close because they can't afford the energy bills. The Russians are managing to sell their gas anyway and we're struggling to get energy. The only winner is the United States because their energy prices have remained low and European companies are moving production there. It makes absolutely no sense for a country like Germany to halt its energy imports from Russia." ' But Vogt was merely a small-town mayor, albeit the mayor of a town situated right in the collision zone between globalization and geopolitics. And he knew he had to make contingency plans in case gas stopped flowing through Nord Stream 1. 'In early March, when I submitted our annual risk assessment for the harbour, I noted that attacks on the infrastructure were a possibility, and I must tell you that our state interior minister and other officials thought I was a bit ridiculous,' he told me in his harbour office. 'They responded along the lines of, "Well, there aren't any indications; don't worry about it." '

The sanctions continued, and so did the construction of an LNG terminal off the coast of Lubmin that would allow ships delivering liquefied gas to dock and transfer their crucial cargo. Burow and Langert could make no sense of what was happening. Why, with gas still flowing through The One, would the country start building infrastructure for gas from other countries? Like Artsman on the other side of the Nord Stream debate one and a half decades earlier, the couple felt bulldozed by people and instructions far more powerful than them.

By May, ordinary Finns and Swedes had made their views on NATO so clear that politicians decided to follow their lead. Three months into the war in Ukraine, 188 of Finland's 200 members of parliament, including Ohisalo and her Green League, voted in favour of Finland applying to join NATO. Only eight voted against.[71] And in Sweden, the Social Democrat minority government, supported by the country's centre-right parties, announced that Sweden too would apply for membership.[72]

A few weeks later, the EU announced sanctions on Russian seaborne crude oil. The United States and Britain imposed more sanctions, too. So did Canada, Japan, New Zealand, even Switzerland. Soon thereafter, Nord Stream turned The One off for maintenance, and once again journalists from all over the world descended on Lubmin, seemingly oblivious to the fact that such maintenance had been taking place every summer.[73]

At the town council and the financial committee, Vogt and his fellow members had discussed many times what they'd do if the gas stopped flowing, but the prospect seemed so remote that they didn't settle on an answer. Now, during the maintenance break, Vogt read everything he could get his hands on, from EU statements to media reports and, he said, 'I realized that it was possible that Russia would use the gas as a weapon, or that Europe would stop receiving it. I told the financial committee, "Now we have to decide what to do if Europe stops receiving the gas or if Russia stops delivering it."' The finance committee and city council revised their finances to account for the massive €2.75 million gap the town might face. Not that long ago, the town had drawn up a budget that also included the fees Nord Stream 2 was expected to deliver. Now the town faced the prospect of life without both pipelines, a certain €5 million loss in 2023. It was a good thing that the council had been prudent and put money aside over the years.

'And,' Vogt told me, 'at this point it dawned on me that it could be over for Nord Stream 1.'

In late August, Nord Stream again closed The One for maintenance – and on 5 September, the company announced that the pipeline would remain closed indefinitely. Vogt had been watching the news from Ukraine. He'd seen the footage of the atrocities Russian troops were committing in the Kyiv suburb of Bucha, the images of Kyiv residents gathering in subway stations for protection. He'd watched the destruction of Mariupol. He remembered the terrifying prospect of war from his days as an East German conscript. Even so, Nord Stream 1's unexpected pause and Nord Stream 2's delayed launch filled him with sadness over what could have been.

Precisely three weeks later, Vogt awoke to find the catastrophe had arrived. Someone had caused the two gas-filled pipelines to explode, and suddenly the Ukraine war was no longer just a tragedy in a remote country: a part of it had spread to his small part of the world. The explosions had rendered unusable the extraordinary pieces of infrastructure conceived of more than two decades earlier to link former antagonists and provide energy for a growing globalized economy. 'I don't want to say that I was expecting it,' Vogt explained. 'Sure, when I went to bed in those weeks I didn't assume it would happen, but I did consider it possible. In the morning of that day, lots of officials arrived, the Bundespolizei [federal police] was on call. And we had a meeting involving all the entities around the port to decide what needed to be done. I immediately thought of the security of all the facilities. I cancelled all my meetings and we held security discussions all day.' That's how the day transpired. After a day full of emergency meetings, Axel Vogt went home. Lubmin's unexpected starring role in the globalized economy, and its surprising reprieve from poor financial prospects, was over. 'And that was it,' Vogt told me. 'Russian gas would not be coming any more. It's a good thing we were prepared.'

Katrin Krüger saw the news on her smartphone, though she could have heard it from a neighbour just as quickly. 'Billions were spent, the seabed was harmed, countless trees were felled,' she reflected. 'And the whole thing was for nothing!'

In reality, it was an allegory of globalization. 'A couple of explosions sufficed to completely disable these pipelines, and now Germany has to scramble to get energy from somewhere else,' Krüger reflected. 'When Covid hit, we struggled to get facemasks because they were all made in China and at that point suddenly everyone wanted them. It just feels extremely perilous to build a society on the expectation that other countries will always provide us with the goods we need.'

A few weeks before my visit, Burow, Langert and some 3,000 other people had participated in a demonstration in Lubmin, demanding that Nord Stream 2 be certified.[74] Now it was too late. In fact, just a few days earlier construction crews had arrived in Lubmin to start building the new offshore LNG terminal.

Axel Vogt knew that the LNG terminal would bring the town revenues, albeit more modest than those Nord Stream had delivered. A few days before Nord Stream's demise, the German government had announced that Lubmin and Rostock, a city located some one and a half hours west of Lubmin, were going to become the country's energy ports. Lubmin had suddenly been given a role almost as prominent as hosting Nord Stream, and one less geopolitically infected, since the German government had resolved only to import this new energy from friends.[75] As we stepped out of his office to walk along the quay, Vogt was upbeat about Lubmin's future in the curtailed global economy. 'We'll get new taxpayers, both through the new hydrogen facilities and the LNG terminals that will be located just off the harbour,' he said. 'And we'll have the transformer for the wind power from the new offshore wind farms. We have our oil refinery. And the good thing is that thanks to Nord Stream we have the infrastructure to transport this energy on to other parts of the country and Europe. Despite the war, we're using energy infrastructure that was created in conjunction with Russia.' Just before Christmas, tugboats towed the massive *Neptune* ship – the key part of the LNG terminal – into the Port of Lubmin, from where engineers connected it to the pipes that once transported Nord Stream's gas around Germany and Europe.[76]

Achim Langert agreed with his wife that switching from Russian gas to LNG that had to be delivered by ship from faraway countries like the United States didn't make sense, but what could he do? 'Global power games are being played here in our town,' he decided.

A few days later, the United States held mid-term elections that saw the Republicans win a slight majority in the House, while the Democrats won a one-seat Senate majority. For the eleventh time, voters in Dayton chose Mike Turner to represent them in Congress, and when Congress reconstituted itself in the new year, he assumed the chairmanship of the House Permanent Select Committee on Intelligence. As the world entered a rapidly deteriorating period of undetermined length, Turner would be one of Congress's most powerful voices on national security. And throughout his two decades in Congress, the former mayor of a town hit by offshoring had kept making the case for domestic manufacturing. Now the two areas, which just a few years earlier had seemed to be entirely disconnected, were suddenly two sides of the same coin.

13
GEN Z OPENS A SECOND FRONT

Twenty-four-year-old Louis Weise, who comes from the eastern German city of Leipzig and studies international relations in Berlin, constantly monitors foreign news. When Russia invaded Ukraine, he hung a Ukrainian flag out of his window. When I spoke with him seventeen months later, it was still there.

Like other members of Generation Z (people born after 1996), Weise is an undiluted participant in the globalized economy. While his parents and grandparents lived through East Germany's error-prone command economy, Weise grew up the post-Cold War way. He wore Western clothes made in China, then, perhaps, Bangladesh. He rode in German cars made partly in Eastern Europe and partly in China, and used American electronics made from parts manufactured around the world. His family's fridge and washing machine collected parts in a string of countries before being assembled and then transported to the Weise home. When his parents and grandparents tell him about the hand-cranked washing machines many East Germans were still using in the eighties, or that buying one of East Germany's ridiculed Trabants once involved a years-long wait, he can't conceptualize what such a life was like. But like many other Gen Z-ers, Weise has concluded that the globalized economy poses a threat to the planet. 'The vast majority of my friends and I don't eat meat any more, we try to travel in an eco-friendly way, we buy second-hand clothes, etcetera,' he told me. 'We weigh the pros and cons of our globalized consumption. I also feel we have a bigger awareness of the problems of globalization and a willingness to act on that than some of the older generations.'

Even though Weise hadn't needed Greta Thunberg in order to arrive at his conclusions about the climate, he was part of Generation Greta. Perhaps the Swedish teenager simply spoke for many of her contemporaries when, in 2018, she launched her solitary 'School strike for the climate' in front of the Swedish parliament. Two years later, Thunberg's Friday for Future marches had soared to a global movement that on one occasion saw some 4 million protest, the world's largest climate march to date.[1] By then, Greta (as everyone called her) had spoken at COP24 in the Polish city of Katowice, where she'd told the delegates that 'what I hope we achieve at this conference is that we realize that we are facing an existential threat'.[2] But the assembled leaders had only reached a modest agreement; indeed, Donald Trump was so opposed to the conference that he'd stayed home.[3] And the youngsters' protests continued. Greta became a global activist celebrity, was nominated for the Nobel Peace Prize and named *TIME*'s Person of the Year.[4] She spoke at COP25 in Madrid; she told Davos participants that 'I want you to panic . . . and act.'[5] And Generation Z members weren't just walking in protest marches: like Weise (and Greta), many of them had become vegetarians or vegans to try to save the climate.[6]

By 2022, nearly four in five Gen Z-ers were planning to go meatless once a week, thus returning to a lifestyle that was commonplace before globalized agriculture made cheap meat available to all.[7] But the COP summits' modest achievements were reflected by the deteriorating climate. When 2022 arrived, figures showed that 2021 had been the world's sixth-warmest year and that the years between 2013 and 2021 were all among the world's ten hottest years on record.[8] Globalization had contributed to this state of affairs. Livestock cultivation, a particularly egregious greenhouse-gas emitter, had increased explosively as countries like China grew more prosperous and began eating more meat. But Weise, Greta and their fellow Gen Z-ers couldn't expect climate activism from their contemporaries in China. China's would-be Greta had already been harassed by the authorities.[9]

Now Russia's invasion of Ukraine, and the often hard-to-verify statements by companies about their future operations in Russia, added another strike against the world of borderless commerce, Weise thought: 'We shouldn't have greenwashing or sportswashing, but we also shouldn't have warwashing.'

'Warwashing' may not be in the dictionary, but after Russia's invasion of Ukraine Weise and many others felt that companies were saying the right thing about the war but refusing to act accordingly. Weise wanted to register his protest against such corporate behaviour, and he knew that he might achieve at least a tiny impact by boycotting companies still active in Russia, but, he told me, 'it's just that they're so big that I couldn't think of a way to boycott them'. Harming a conglomerate that operates multiple consumer brands through a consumer boycott is, in fact, a tall order. But in the weeks and months after the invasion, Weise's fellow German consumers identified a suitable target: Ritter Sport. The family-owned German confectioner, which had kept selling its famous chocolate bars in Russia, quickly found its Facebook page inundated with invectives. 'Still in Russia among the war criminals, that's unacceptable,' one user wrote. 'I always had the impression that Ritter Sport was a sustainable and socially conscious company. Until now, I've been a good customer. That will change now. Ritter Sport keeps delivering to Russia and that's hypocritical,' wrote another.[10]

CEO Andreas Ronken tried to explain: 'Ending our business in Russia wouldn't really help end the invasion, but it would have a direct and major impact on our employees in Russia and at the end of the day also on us as an independent family-run enterprise, all the way to the cocoa farmers in the supply chain,' he told a German newspaper.[11] Ronken's predicament perfectly summarized globalization's unexpected quandary. Ronken and his fellow executives, accustomed as they were to making decisions based purely on commercial considerations, had reckoned neither with geopolitical trembles nor with consumers.

But Russia's invasion of Ukraine had triggered a desire among many consumers – especially younger Western ones – to use their consumer power against the companies they felt were enabling the war. They could try to boycott businesses still operating in Russia and advertise their anger on social media. A few weeks into the war, 76 per cent of Germans said they were basing their consumption choices on whether a company was still doing business in Russia.[12] A nationwide US poll, in turn, found that Americans overwhelmingly wanted companies to take a stand. Seventy-five per cent wanted American firms to stop conducting business with Russia, to stop doing business with Russian partners and to stop selling their goods and services in the country, while 74 per cent wanted companies to close their factories and offices in the country.[13] In Sweden, a centre-right student group called on fellow students to boycott companies doing business in Russia.[14] And Russia was not the only country on consumers' minds. Ever since China had begun intensifying its surveillance of the Uyghurs in the late 2010s, the plight of the Uyghurs had captured the attention of citizens and politicians across the Western world. By 2021, 70 per cent of Americans said it was important to work to promote human rights in China, even if doing so harmed economic relations, while 58 per cent of Germans advocated a tougher stance even if it harmed economic relations.[15] China, for its part, perceived Western support of Uyghur human rights as a concealed effort to help the Uyghurs split off from China. And while Western sentiments straddled the generations, Generation Z was taking the lead – because it has become used to making demands on brands. In 2021, a study found that more than half of American Gen Z consumers researched brands to ensure the brands aligned with their 'position on corporate social responsibility'.[16]

Other surveys found that Gen Z was the generation most willing to boycott companies.[17] 'We're a generation that's a lot more aware of global issues,' reflected Hana Azari, an eighteen-year-old of Albanian origin who lives in a suburb of Washington, DC. 'If a company makes a decision that negatively influences a lot of people, young people will take that into account. They reason that if they buy products from such a company, they contribute to that suffering.'

In a small town outside Latvia's capital, Riga, sixteen-year-old Mārcis Vanags too saw Russia's invasion on the news. Even though his small country is situated across the border from Russia and had been under Russian occupation when Mārcis's parents grew up, Mārcis had not focused much on matters of war and peace. Instead he had lived much like teenagers across the Western world and indeed like youths in Russia, China, the Gulf and the many other countries involved in globalization: enjoying increasing prosperity and with access to quality goods at reasonable prices. When he saw Russia's invasion of Ukraine, Mārcis decided that he had to do his bit. 'If a brand stays in Russia, I won't buy it,' he told me.

In Frankfurt am Main, twenty-six-year-old technology advisor Bilal Ahmed kept buying Ritter Sport, but he stopped using software by the Russian firm Kaspersky, reasoning that it might no longer be safe. And when he had to buy a computer security key and discovered that Google's key was partly manufactured in China, for security reasons he instead opted for one that was fully manufactured in Europe. Next on Ahmed's list: boycotts in support of the Uyghurs. 'I come from a Muslim background, and in that circle of friends people are aware of the persecution of the Uyghurs and want to boycott companies that use Uyghur forced labour,' he told me, adding that he'd already started trying not to buy products made with Uyghur forced labour.

But even though Ahmed simply wanted to support the Uyghurs' right to live free from persecution, punishing and rewarding companies over the issue was extraordinarily complicated. 'It's extremely hard to find out who uses forced labour in Xinjiang,' he explained. 'I can go on the internet and the companies all say they don't use forced labour, but what about second- or third-tier suppliers?'

Global crises make the news haphazardly. The Ukraine war dominated the northern hemisphere's news cycles for weeks, but like all news it then began fading. In late 2021, forced labour in Xinjiang, Chinese hostage diplomacy, Chinese boycotts of Australian wine, Taiwanese pineapples and the entirety of Lithuania's industry had cropped up on occasion, and so had conflicts like Saudi Arabia's proxy war in Yemen. Ben Hitimana, a twenty-three-year-old tech worker whose parents arrived in Britain as wartime refugees from Rwanda, told me he and others his age want to weigh in on geopolitics: 'Russia and China are the big things, but there are so many other ones. Palestine is one. There's a really big swing towards support for Palestine; people like me are taking a look at whether companies actively support Israel.'

But, as Ahmed and Weise had discovered, punishing a company isn't straightforward in a globalized economy. Ritter Sport's boycotters may inadvertently have harmed the livelihood of cocoa farmers in West Africa. At the same time, they spared companies that had merely announced they were leaving Russia without completing the departure – and the details of multinational operations are so difficult to ascertain that even talented sleuths may not know whether an enterprise has followed through on its promise. Such complexities of globalization, though, get lost when consumers feel the urge to use their power to punish companies.

A few months after the invasion, Tom Mulholland, a nineteen-year-old British student, attempted to categorize how he thought companies should behave: 'Global brands have a responsibility, for example with regard to Ukraine and human rights in China,' he told me. 'I try to stay away from firms that do business in Russia. But with regard to China, everything is made in China. China is the factory of the world. And here in the UK, we're in the middle of a cost-of-living crisis. If you're a student during a cost-of-living crisis, the reality is that price trumps location.'

Indeed, the geopolitically motivated consumer boycotts powered by Generation Z that had their breakthrough during the Ukraine war's first weeks differed from past generations' boycotts, where success was mostly measured in the effect on a company's bottom line. The new generation of consumer boycotts could simply be a group of people, formally organized or not, attacking a company on social media while still buying its products. 'Social media makes it easier to take a position,' Mulholland said. 'You can say on social media that you're boycotting but then you might buy the product anyway.' Brand boycotts had become what one might call 'Gen Z Sanctions': optics over substance, but effective all the same.

In her classroom at New York University's Stern School of Business, Alison Taylor had reached a similar conclusion. Taylor, a lecturer in corporate ESG (environment, social, governance) issues, had joined academia from the business world, and already before the Ukraine war she had noticed a politicization of commerce among Generation Z. 'In my classes, I get the impression that students may consider voting every four years but mostly they try to get political things done through their employers and the brands they use,' she told me. 'We're redirecting energy in a really dangerous way. Brands are embracing the perception that they're a legitimate conduit for political issues.' Russia's invasion of

Ukraine didn't seem to stir most of her students into action, but the mindset was the same: they could use their consumer power to push for changes that past generations would have tried to achieve through protest marches or the ballot box.

That's also the paradox of the Gen Z-led boycotts that came to the fore in the days and weeks following the invasion: by obeying the loudly expressed opinions of vocal activists – who may have acted with the purest intentions – companies were making themselves lightning rods for other political and geopolitical issues of the day. And, said Taylor, 'when companies try to do the right thing, there's a kind of gotcha element. They say they're doing the right thing in one area and then people will say, "But what about this other issue?"' The ethics of gotcha aside, Sara Cutrona, a young office worker in the Italian city of Bologna, was certain the campaigns would continue because businesses feared them. 'Companies pay attention to young people's social-media campaigns from a reputational perspective,' she observed. 'They know that people pay attention to what they do and don't do, and that they'll suffer consequences if they do something people perceive as wrong. Companies are very sensitive.'

But while a core group of passionate consumers might loudly articulate their views on geopolitical issues du jour, large chunks of the Western army of consumers – those most likely to have the ability and inclination to boycott brands – didn't expect companies to follow up their departure from Russia with a departure from other geopolitically iffy countries. Some, in fact, remained geopolitically oblivious. 'There are people in my high school who don't pay attention to international politics, but I feel they're in a bubble,' Azari said, as the Ukraine war was entering its second year. 'I could go around the school and ask, "Is the war in Ukraine over?" and many people will say, "Yes, I think it is."' On the other hand, she added, 'I've seen people in fan bases who immediately when someone posts an offensive remark they'll stop buying.'

In 2022, companies selling all manner of product had already accepted having to take a position on social issues of the day; for some, such positioning had even become a useful marketing strategy. When Russia invaded Ukraine, the notion that companies could remain geopolitically neutral came to a screeching if not complete halt.

Executives, though, were now facing the randomness observed by Azari. When Russia annexed Crimea in 2014, consumers were not outraged enough to launch campaigns against the companies remaining in Russia. Eight years later, by contrast, they were outraged by the invasion of Ukraine. They were not irate about Saudi Arabia's proxy war in Yemen, but they were, on and off, incensed by China's use of Uyghur forced labour in Xinjiang factories, Myanmar's military coup and Israel's treatment of Palestinians. In the world of cybersecurity, where Israeli companies are world leading, many young people like Hitimana were now talking about refraining from buying certain products – and from working for companies that did business with Israel. 'The issue of Israel is massive,' Hitimana told me. 'Do you really want to work for a company that does a lot of business with Israel? The places we work, the products we buy, there's a concerted effort to address inequalities and injustice.' While countless members of Gen Z still took jobs based on the salary and perks rather than a company's political positions, they were keeping politics on the corporate agenda.

As companies realized that they were becoming a twenty-first-century equivalent of political parties, which citizens could support or oppose, they not only found that consumer anger was unpredictable, they also concluded that while the majority might never express a view on geopolitics, a small group of activists could explode in anger over a particular issue and cause real harm to the companies targeted. That made it extremely difficult for executives to chart a course. And they knew the dilemma would only increase as the global standoff intensified. Cutrona began worrying that hostile governments might even create disinformation that would cause Generation Z to boycott an innocent brand.

It was easier to predict what China's young consumers would find unacceptable – and they had opened a second front in the emerging battle of consumers. Unlike Western consumers, the Chinese consumer brigade almost always struck in response to corporate wrongdoing in the same areas: alleged opposition to Chinese rule over Hong Kong, Taiwan and Tibet; alleged opposition to China's treatment of the Uyghurs; alleged support of Hong Kong's democracy protests; and political disputes between China and the company's home country.

The Italian fashion house Versace was oblivious to conflicts, geopolitics and consumer boycott brigades when, in 2019, it released world tour T-shirts featuring cities and the countries in which they were located. Hong Kong was paired with Hong Kong – unsurprising given its special status. Nobody at Versace had considered that the T-shirt might attract interest beyond its aesthetic qualities. But Chinese consumers launched a boycott, and the Italian fashion house was swiftly forced to declare that it 'respects the sovereignty of China's territorial state', while creative director Donatella Versace explained that 'never have I wanted to disrespect China's National Sovereignty and this is why I wanted to personally apologize for such inaccuracy and for any distress that it might have caused'.[18]

Just one day after Versace's unplanned row with Chinese consumers, the American fashion brand Coach also released a world tour T-shirt, and this garment too contained cities paired with countries, while Taipei was paired with Taiwan and Hong Kong was listed alone.[19] The celebrated French fashion house Givenchy's world tour T-shirts, released the same day, featured similar pairings. Even though both brands almost instantaneously issued humble apologies reiterating their support of Chinese sovereignty, their Chinese brand ambassadors quit and Chinese consumers struck with force.[20] The campaign against Coach quickly reached a billion views on the social-media network Weibo, a Chinese alternative to the blocked Facebook and Twitter.[21]

When the designer brands posted their annual results for 2019, revenues in China were healthy. But the campaigns had caused the companies harm that was much more difficult to remedy: reputational damage.[22] Almost four years later, Google searches of Givenchy and China, and Versace and China, returned articles about the row among their top results. Motivated Chinese consumers had powerfully demonstrated their might against geopolitically offending global businesses.

Had the temples of fashion been paying attention to geopolitics, they would have known that when President Nicolas Sarkozy of France announced he would not be attending the 2008 Beijing Olympics in protest against China's persecution of Tibetans, Chinese consumers swiftly launched a boycott against the French supermarket chain Carrefour.[23] They would also have remembered China's boycott of

Korean boy bands over the installation of American THAAD radar systems in South Korea a couple of years earlier. To be sure, such campaigns had been rare. But in 2015 and 2016 their number suddenly grew. The following year there were seven boycott campaigns, in 2018 there were ten, and in 2019 the campaigns skyrocketed to thirty-four.[24] The campaigns almost exclusively targeted brands from Europe, North America, Japan and South Korea operating in the apparel, automotive and food and beverages sectors. By 2021, brands had been so frightened by the experiences of Versace, Coach, Givenchy and others that there were few Hong Kong- and Taiwan-related offences to campaign against. Now Chinese consumers were instead training their digital guns on brands deemed critical of China's treatment of the Uyghurs, an issue fast gaining attention in the West.[25] While trying to please Western consumers, H&M and its fellow Better Cotton Initiative participants had exposed themselves to counterfire from Chinese consumers. The corporations were also convenient proxies for their home governments as China sought to avenge the Xinjiang-linked sanctions imposed on Chinese officials.

Consumers weren't just acting on government prompts. Though analysts at a Swedish think tank identified direct government links to the boycott in one-third of the campaigns they observed, Chinese consumers were perfectly capable of being incensed over geopolitics without government instruction. 'The growing number of consumer boycotts, especially those targeting US and European companies, seems to be connected to a general rise in online nationalism,' the analysts concluded, and continued: 'Overall, online criticism of behaviour seen as insulting to China has grown in popularity in the Chinese information environment since at least 2016. As the presence of younger people online is comparatively high, this trend could be related to increasingly hawkish views among the younger generation, which have been documented by some surveys.'[26] The Great Firewall of China had helped turn consumers into a powerful force that could strike against giants of globalization deemed critical of the country.[27]

With Chinese consumers ready to retaliate if global brands voiced support for the Uyghurs, and Western consumers possibly ready to boycott brands that didn't sufficiently speak up for the Uyghurs, executives realized they faced a two-front war. On top of that, executives faced retaliation by Chinese authorities. It was hardly surprising that by 2022 China had become the country in which the largest number of companies reduced or avoided investments. In 2020, the top slot had been held by Iran, followed by Libya, Argentina, Russia and Zimbabwe. In 2021, it had been Egypt, South Africa, Argentina, Russia and (due to Brexit) Britain. Now Venezuela, Iran, Nigeria and Russia followed China.[28]

In a small university town in Texas, the increasing geopolitical tremor and the reach of commerce had left twenty-one-year-old Erin Hodgson grappling with what was her moral obligation and what was simply commerce. Should she boycott Amazon even though she had no way of establishing whether its tentacles reached, say, Russia or camps in Xinjiang? Or was it naïve to think that she could somehow make a dent against such an all-encompassing behemoth? Then she thought about Shein, the Chinese fast-fashion retailer that was selling its wares at lower prices than even H&M could muster. Thanks to its explosive growth, Shein was now one of the world's top fast-fashion purveyors, together with Zara's Spanish owner Inditex, H&M and Japan's Fast Retailing (the owner of Uniqlo). 'It's really popular among women my age, but I know if something is made with forced labour of course I'm not going to buy it,' she told me. In theory, Shein's clothes involved no forced labour, since the Uyghur Forced Labor Prevention Act had now come into effect. That meant that Shein had been able to prove it didn't use forced labour, and the company insisted it didn't. Still, members of Generation Z and legislators in Washington had their doubts.[29] Azari, too, had heard the discussions but concluded that teenagers would keep buying the clothes anyway. 'Shein: if you want a cute going-out top, six bucks,' she observed. 'Leather pants, fifteen bucks. It's so cheap. Shein keeps up with every single microtrend, and trends change so quickly. Every couple of weeks there's something new on TikTok.'

Azari wasn't exaggerating. Together, Shein's unbeatable prices and TikTok's virality had also created a true globalization-age phenomenon: teenagers showing off their Shein hauls on TikTok. Azari did try to stay away from Shein, and was definitely wary of TikTok, but she'd concluded it made little sense even to try to influence the companies' behaviour.

And there were Western behemoths she and her fellow Gen Z members felt equally incapable of influencing, whether the issue concerned ethics or geopolitics. 'You're just not going to stop buying from Apple because they do business in China and cooperate with the Chinese government!' she decided. 'Same thing with Amazon. Where else are you going to get free shipping within two days? How are you going to show your concern when companies almost have monopolies?'

And despite Meta – formerly known as Facebook – launching a video app that closely resembled TikTok, the Chinese firm still ruled the digital video waves. By now, even the least geopolitically interested citizen knew that TikTok stored massive amounts of user data that it could pass on to the Chinese authorities. Still, it was hard to imagine life without the addictive app. In Norway, twenty-nine-year-old Justice and Public Security Minister Emilie Enger Mehl was taken to task by parliamentarians for using the app on her government phone – and announced that she'd arranged to receive a new phone on which she could use TikTok and other social media.[30]

By late 2022, Shein was America's largest fast-fashion retailer, and its fully digital selling strategy was doing well in European countries too, though it had been the subject of a hashtag boycott campaign over accusations of plagiarism.[31] When the year ended, TikTok had been downloaded a record 676 million times around the world – not including China, where TikTok's milder sister company Douyin operates.[32]

A plethora of other legislators, including Italy's Silvio Berlusconi, were on the app too.[33] Indeed, TikTok seemed the best way of reaching Generation Z, not just in order to sell them goods but also to get them to vote. Had globalization proceeded as envisioned by its founding fathers and mothers, politicians and government officials using a Chinese viral-video app would not have caused concerns about national security; instead, it would have been lauded as a sign that China was truly becoming like the West. But globalization had unfolded very differently. In late 2022, the US Congress banned the app from government-owned devices.[34] India had already done so.[35]

Young people in the West were also beginning to react to globalization's flaws by articulating a further-reaching desire than the punishment of companies: they wanted their countries to partially retreat from the turbulent interconnected world. In late 2022, when the Pew Research Center conducted focus-group conversations with young people from the United States, Germany, Britain and France, it found that the next generation, both on the left and on the right, wanted their countries to limit their international engagement and, for example, become more energy-independent. The desire for energy independence, in fact, strongly united the left and the right.[36]

Gen Z's views notwithstanding, some companies did seem to be getting away with doing business in war-mongering or dictatorial countries because they were too big. And as Weise, Ahmed, Hodgson, Azari and plenty of others had discovered, many businesses also had supply chains too complex to scrutinize. Then there was the issue of standards. Opposing one war or one unjust regime through boycotts should logically mean boycotting all companies operating in any country involved in wars or persecution. When Germany decided to boycott Russian gas it was a good thing, Weise thought: 'But straight away ministers flew to Qatar to increase our ties with the Qataris. Is this the sort of partner we should be trading with? Then again, we need partners.' Azari decided that she should keep an eye on Ukrainian businesses and other companies run by 'an oppressed group of people or those who may benefit from an increase in consumers', and try to buy from them in the same way that people around the world had bought 'Freedom Pineapples' to support Taiwanese pineapple farmers. Through such actions, she thought, Gen Z could yield its consumer power in a positive way.

Cutrona, for her part, was convinced that Italians would counter-attack if Chinese consumers launched a campaign against one of Italy's marquee brands again. 'I'm convinced young Italians would push back online,' she said. 'But that would only happen if the brand had taken a stand, not if it was a mistake. The brand would have to communicate to the public that it was taking a stand.' In this two-front war over geopolitical support, brands simply couldn't please both sides.

Although the European Commission had been trying to be a moderating force, one that could salvage key parts of globalization, it also represented a continent that prided itself on its support for human rights. Now it presented plans for an import ban on goods made with slave labour.[37] The proposals didn't mention any countries, but it was clear to everyone that one manufacturing superpower appeared to be home to particularly widespread use of forced labour. The Commission was planning to ban TikTok from its devices too.[38] One move concerned persecution of minorities, the other Western countries' national security; they just happened to coincide, timing-wise. Western companies, adapting to the new ways of the world, decided that backlash from Xi's forces was only a matter of time.

14
FRIENDSHORING SETS SAIL

The sun had already set when, on 2 August 2022, Nancy Pelosi landed in Taipei. Even more than China hated the idea of Taiwan being listed as a country on haute couture T-shirts, it hated the idea of a leading American politician visiting the island and meeting with its president. Indeed, so predictable was Beijing's anger over official visits to an island it considers a renegade region that no senior US policy-maker had dared to visit Taiwan in a quarter of a century. During that time, Western relations with China had flourished, then decayed. And now Pelosi had arrived, accompanied by fellow members of Congress and global fascination.

It didn't seem to matter, to Pelosi or her host, President Tsai Ing-wen, that Beijing had retaliated in advance by suspending a vast range of food imports from Taiwan.[1] It also didn't matter that China's top diplomat, Wang Yi, had warned that American politicians were 'playing with fire'.[2] And it didn't matter that China was now voicing its extreme displeasure by preparing naval exercises around Taiwan. Pelosi had arrived on the island. Even though the veteran congresswoman from San Francisco didn't represent the US government, the signal was unmistakable: American leaders were willing to visit Taiwan despite Chinese fury, military exercises, commercial retaliation and whatever other means of revenge Beijing might think up. 'Our delegation came here to send an unequivocal message: America stands with Taiwan,' Pelosi said during a ceremony at the presidential palace.[3]

Such a visit would have been unthinkable just a few years earlier. The globalized economy had made China such an indispensable part of Western societies' well-being that political leaders were even afraid to offend the country by, say, issuing invitations to the Dalai Lama. Not even Nobel Peace Prize winner Oscar Arias could deny the great-power writing on the wall: he'd switched Costa Rica's official recognition from Taiwan to China.[4]

Now the leadership in Beijing was rattled by the latest unambiguous manifestation of America's rapidly changing attitude towards China. The mighty People's Liberation Army Navy launched live-fire drills and Chinese authorities banned exports of natural sand to Taiwan.[5] For good measure, they also banned imports of Taiwanese fish and citrus fruits, including the island's famous pomelo, which was just about to be harvested. Once again, Beijing had chosen its commercial victims well: 95 per cent of Taiwan's pomelo exports ordinarily go to China.[6] Now it was too late to find alternative export destinations.

But Taiwanese food companies had watched this show once or twice before. After banning imports of Taiwanese pineapples the previous year, Beijing had also banned Taiwanese grouper, then Taiwanese Chardonnay. Many Taiwanese food producers began cultivating alternative export markets in Europe and North America, in Japan and elsewhere in Asia. Such efforts couldn't bear immediate fruit, but they were a long-term strategy to keep Taiwanese agriculture viable.

International companies were watching too, and they were similarly unsurprised by China's commercial retaliation to Pelosi's visit. It was simply an escalation of the weaponization of globalization they'd been witnessing for a long time. And they, too, had been preparing to make themselves less dependent on the powerful, lucrative and increasingly vindictive country. Some had quietly been shifting IP-sensitive operations to other countries for some time. Lower-tech outfits like Perillo's shoe firm had, of course, felt they were being pushed out of the country years earlier. Shortly after Pelosi's visit, Apple announced that it would start manufacturing some of its new iPhone 14s in India.[7] Friendshoring, a concept that had been gestating in manufacturing circles, presented itself to the global public.

To be sure, Apple would keep most of its manufacturing at Foxconn's massive iPhone City in China. But its announcement was so pivotal because the American tech firm had, ever since the first-generation iPhone's manufacturing launch in China, been one of the corporate world's most enthusiastic believers in the country.[8] China-based production, in fact, had helped make Apple the world's most valuable brand. CEO Tim Cook had himself signed a massive deal that saw the tech giant invest $275 billion in China in exchange for 'relaxed pressure on its business', and Apple had consented to having its Chinese users' data stored on a server in China and managed by a Chinese company.[9]

Now this fervent supporter of China said it was moving some of the production of its top-of-the-line iPhone to India. Soon the tech giant from Cupertino also announced plans to make some of its MacBooks in Vietnam.[10] Apple's fiercest rival, South Korea's Samsung, announced it was moving some production of its top-end device, the Galaxy S23 smartphone, to India.[11] Google announced plans to move part of its Pixel-phone production to Vietnam.[12] Intel said it would transfer its Chinese chip manufacturing to South Korea and commit more than $100 billion to new fab – chip-factory – sites in Ohio, Europe and elsewhere in Asia.[13] LG Electronics, Hyundai Motor and Kia Motors had already begun moving production from China.[14] Perhaps inevitably, Chinese companies were drawing similar conclusions. Some solar manufacturers, for example, were moving production to Southeast Asian countries.[15]

At the Paris Motor Show a few weeks later, the global automotive executive Carlos Tavares even thought aloud about the possibility of having no factories at all in China.[16] Tavares, who had previously voiced concerns about Chinese political interference in business, merely articulated a concern many other executives had flagged in political-risk surveys. But the fact that he dared to do it illustrated the state of Western executives' trust in China. A short time later, Tavares – the CEO of Chrysler owner Stellantis – concluded that China also no longer offered the cost-and-efficiency combination that had once made the country so attractive to business leaders. China is 'not the only one and not even the best' manufacturing location, he said, pointing to 'plenty of options' including India, Mexico and parts of North Africa and Asia.[17]

When the American Chamber of Commerce in Shanghai surveyed its members that autumn, only 47 per cent projected year-on-year revenue growth that year, a 29-percentage point plunge compared to 2021 and the lowest figure in ten years. Forty-seven per cent of the companies surveyed expected revenue growth in China to outpace their companies' worldwide growth within the next three to five years, 22 per cent lower than in 2021. Fifty-two per cent said their headquarters' confidence in China's economic management had worsened over the past year, and only 18 per cent ranked China at the top of their company's global investment plans, down from 27 per cent the year before. Only 55 per cent were optimistic about China's five-year business outlook, the lowest-ever figure in the Chamber of Commerce's surveys. Nineteen per cent were already reducing investment in China.[18] Some companies were significantly expanding their Chinese operations – but they were mostly retailers and other consumer-product behemoths like McDonald's, Starbucks (with plans for some 3,000 new coffee shops in China) and Ralph Lauren, outfits keen to sell to China's consumers but not making sophisticated goods in the country.[19]

Even among Germany's previously enthusiastic businesses, China was losing its lustre. Yes, giants like Volkswagen and Siemens remained committed, and VW seemed especially eager to hang on to the Chinese market, where it had recently slipped to second place after the Chinese brand BYD.[20] But a divide was opening up in German business: while many multinationals fervently stuck with their China focus, small and mid-sized companies were getting uneasy about the country. When surveyed by the German Chamber of Commerce that winter of 2022, only 51 per cent of German companies were planning to grow their investments in China, compared to 71 per cent a year earlier. Forty-nine per cent said that China had become less attractive compared to other markets, and 10 per cent were planning to leave the country altogether.[21] A survey conducted by the European Union Chamber of Commerce in China, meanwhile, showed that 23 per cent of Western firms were considering moving operations away from the country.[22] In Britain, Tony Danker, the director general of the Confederation of British Industry, explained that 'every company that I speak to at the moment is engaged in rethinking their supply chains because they anticipate that our politicians will inevitably accelerate towards a decoupled world from China'.[23]

The top reasons businesses gave for their loss of interest in China concerned the frequent disruptions caused by the government's zero-Covid policy, but they were also deterred by the increasing legal uncertainty for foreign businesses in the country. Many were put off by the Chinese authorities' support of Chinese companies at the expense of foreign firms. Twenty-nine per cent of German firms reported having been discriminated against in favour of Chinese companies.[24]

In an extraordinary confluence of events, China's harsh zero-Covid policy had arrived just as politicians were getting seriously concerned about the country's behaviour at home and in the world. China's role in spreading the virus on the world had made citizens distinctly wary of Xi Jinping's regime. And for Western businesses, zero-Covid had added to their long-standing frustration at the unlevel playing field for operations in China. They were further spooked by Xi's increasing hold over the country. In 2018, he'd arranged for the Chinese Communist Party's two-term leader limit to be lifted, which would allow him to keep standing for election. In October 2022, that came to pass. At the CCP's 20th National Congress, Xi was re-elected to a third term as the party's – and thus the country's – leader.[25] He spelled out his goal without ambiguity: to make 'China into a great modern socialist country that leads the world in terms of composite national strength and international influence by the middle of the century'.[26]

Just as the juncture that could force companies to choose their path was becoming clear, the Biden administration struck with an order prohibiting companies around the world from selling advanced chips to China if they were made with American technology, software or machinery.[27] It was a harder blow than any Trump had attempted to land.[28] China's masterfully executed rise from the world's shoe factory to the world's high-tech factory would be delayed. No sooner had the US ban arrived than India's Tata Group conglomerate announced that it would begin making smartphone microchips in India – where Apple was, of course, proceeding with plans to build top-line iPhone manufacturing.[29]

The same week, Apple announced that its long-standing chip supplier, Taiwan's TSMC, would build a chip factory in Arizona. 'And now, thanks to the hard work of so many people, these chips can be proudly stamped Made in America,' Cook – who'd made his career expanding Apple in China – declared.[30] The United States, Japan, South Korea and Taiwan launched an initiative to reduce the semiconductor industry's dependence on China.[31] Intel was already building two advanced fabs in Ohio. 'Crews have already moved roughly 62,000 dump truck loads of earth,' one journalist reported.[32] The technology giant was even going to spend $100 million to train young locals for work in the futuristic factories.[33] Mike Turner, who like so many other Ohioans had spent decades hearing that manufacturing had little future in his state, was delighted. 'All those who believed at one time that China would become like us are learning that it's not possible,' he told me. 'Capital will begin fleeing China. With Intel's commitment to build the largest chip-making factory in the world in Ohio you're seeing an understanding of the risk of being China-dependent.'

In Italy, a new government had taken office. It included Italy's first-ever minister of enterprises and Made in Italy, and two other ministerial portfolios reflecting the shifting circumstances in the world: a minister of agriculture, food sovereignty and forestry and a minister of the environment and energy security.[34] The European Commission, for its part, was continuing its battle for fair play. That December, its WTO complaints against China's blockade of Lithuanian goods having made no difference, it took the next step and requested WTO adjudication. It also requested adjudication over China's use of anti-suit injunctions, the strategy of blocking Western companies from suing Chinese companies over patent violations.[35] Virtually nobody, though, expected the efforts to achieve much. The WTO seemed like a remnant from happier times.

In corporate headquarters, executives were beginning to map how they might be able to reduce exposure to China – the very exposure they'd spent decades building. Michael Treschow thought back to the dozens of times, beginning in the eighties, that he'd visited the country for business. 'Initially it was always "the new China", "the better China",' he observed. 'It continued like that until Xi Jinping took over and introduced significant changes that nobody had conceived might happen. We were all a bit naïve and thought that China could handle being a socialist country with a market economy, and there came Xi Jinping with his new policies, which really were a radical change of course.' But even then, few people realized that Xi's arrival marked a fork in the road. Now, though, Treschow told me, 'I realized the CCP had discovered that the market economy was taking over the leadership of the country. It concluded that it needed to take back control over the country and the market economy.'

Indeed, the political interference that bothered Carlos Tavares and other multinational CEOs wasn't just affecting Western companies operating in China: it targeted Chinese companies too. Jack Ma, the fast-rising entrepreneur Guriev had first met at Davos in 2001, had taken his Alibaba from fledgling e-commerce platform to an all-around digital service now holding a quarter of the global e-commerce market.[36] Then he had built his Alipay payment platform in an equally successful fashion. But in 2020, Alipay had seen Chinese regulators cancel its stock-market launch.[37] Now Chinese authorities imposed rules on Alibaba and other home-grown tech giants, supposedly to curb monopolistic behaviour.[38] A hefty fine for Alibaba followed, and other companies were called in for a meeting and instructed to 'pay full heed to the warning of Alibaba's case'.[39] Under Xi as under Deng Xiaoping, the cat catching mice could be of any variety, but it had to demonstrate loyalty to the regime. So perilous was the situation even for China's tech titans that Ma vanished from public view and resurfaced as a resident of Tokyo.[40] If such misfortune could strike even China's most illustrious companies, it was hardly surprising that Western companies were now looking for friendlier shores. 'The Chinese government got worried about citizens' connection with the world that globalization was providing,' Treschow concluded. 'Part of the reason globalization is in trouble is that it goes hand in hand with digitalization and modernization. The Chinese leaders discovered that such connectivity between their citizens and the world was a threat to the political system. For as long as Xi remains in charge, he'll want to maintain this control over society. Global trade leads to more democracy and fewer violations of human rights. If you don't want that, it's clear that you'll want to limit your country's participation in global trade.'

Joachim Lang decided that the Chinese government's attitude had changed, not just towards its own companies but towards the globalized economy too. 'China is essentially saying, "Now we're economically as strong as the United States, and as a result we want to be treated as an equal." I know from my conversations with Chinese officials that they're always happy to talk to us Europeans but that they're primarily interested in what the Americans think of them. They're fixated on what America thinks of them. What they can't accept is any form of US dominance over them.' If the US wasn't willing to accept China as a fellow economic superpower but was instead getting nervous about Chinese unfair play and national security risks, Beijing didn't seem to mind easing a few Western companies out the door to demonstrate how little Western loss of trust bothered it.

China in the 2020s was, Lang thought, like the United States in the 1910s. 'At the beginning of the twentieth century, the United States was politically not very important but became so thanks to its economic power,' he explained. 'Economic power automatically translates into political power. It's about respect. If China got respect from the United States, it would react in a measured way if the US did something that other countries might criticize.'

That November, Olaf Scholz tried to steer cross-border commerce back to happier days by leading a business delegation on a visit to Beijing. But it was a truncated visit. Due to China's zero-Covid rules, the German chancellor spent a mere eleven hours on Chinese soil, though he did find time to remind Xi Jinping that Germany opposed Beijing's belligerence towards Taiwan and its persecution of minorities – and to ask him to help get Russia to end its war against Ukraine. The plea was in vain.[41]

Indeed, unlike the United States, which as a rising power in the 1910s eventually convinced itself it should support the Allied powers and help defeat the aggressors, Beijing insisted on neutrality in Russia's war against Ukraine. And the war, which Russia had conceived as a 'special military operation' that would be over within days, was dragging on. As 2022 drew to a close, the United Nations reported that since February, 17,831 Ukrainians had been killed or maimed by Russian weapons. It cautioned, though, that the real figure was likely to be far higher.[42] The war was thought to also have claimed the lives of some 80,000–100,000 Ukrainian soldiers and even more Russian ones.[43] More than 4 million Ukrainians had found refuge in EU countries and additional ones elsewhere in Europe, which – Europeans' astounding hospitality notwithstanding – had put a strain on both the refugees and their hosts.[44] Ukraine's economy was struggling to stay afloat, and the rising energy prices resulting from the war had triggered inflation across Europe, North America and other parts of the world.[45] European countries, the United States, Canada, Japan, Australia and other Western countries in turn kept trying to end the war by punishing Russia with one sanctions package after another and assisting Ukraine with weapons packages. At the end of January, even Germany decided it was time to send tanks to Ukraine.[46] Beijing still declined to intervene, declaring instead that it wanted a peace deal.[47]

Or rather, China intervened in a different way, by buying oil now discounted by Russian suppliers desperate to replace its declining sales to the West.[48] Chinese companies also picked up significant business as Western companies withdrew from Russia. By early 2023, Chery was, for example, enjoying exponential Russian growth thanks to the war, and Chinese smartphones had increased their market share to 80 per cent, from 45 per cent before the invasion.[49] Customs data also revealed that China was supplying Russia – once its decidedly superior patron – with technology featuring both civilian and military applications.[50] Western sanctions, once a potent weapon, were losing their sting because China and some other countries that were economic bit players during the Cold War were now powerful enough to thwart them. Turkey's trade with Russia was booming.[51] Fourteen months into the invasion, India's imports of Russian petroleum products had grown by 157 per cent, its imports of coal-related products by 206 per cent and fertilizers by 307 per cent. Indian imports of Russian crude oil had soared by an astounding 1,144 per cent.[52] And Russia's GDP figures showed that, despite the unprecedented sanctions, its GDP had only declined by 2.1 per cent during 2022.[53] Many Western companies had also published their figures and forecasts for Russia, and it was a painful tale: for the brewers Carlsberg and AB Inbev, losses of more than $1 billion each; VW, $550 million; Nissan, $687 million; Renault, $867 million; Crédit Agricole, $500 million; Société Générale, €3.2 billion; the German household-goods giant Henkel, €1 billion; McDonald's, $1.4 billion. But the biggest losses were in the energy sector: Equinor, more than $1 billion; ExxonMobil, $3.4 billion; Shell, $5 billion; Total

Energies, $10.7 billion; and BP, an astonishing $24 billion.[54] Businesses from Russia, the Middle East and other countries had acquired the departing companies' assets at bargain prices.

Had globalization blunted economic sanctions as a tool the West could deploy to punish misbehaving countries? Turner didn't think so. 'Even though not every country abides by the sanctions and the consumer economy in Russia hasn't collapsed, you're still seeing an impact on the part of the economy that the Russian state depends on,' he told me. 'The aerospace industry, the military-industrial complex, their ability to make sophisticated weapons systems: in these areas they're losing abilities that countries not abiding by the sanctions can't balance out.' China, though, had achieved such rapid technological advance that it looked likely to be able to soften the blow of even such sophisticated sanctions in the future.

Keith Krach, too, was following the news from Russia, from Ukraine, from China. After leaving government, he'd not returned to CEO life but instead launched an organization to help protect Western science and technology innovation. Now he concluded that Jack Ma's professional demise was a warning to Western companies. 'Speaking as a businessman: it doesn't take an invasion of Taiwan for China to become very unsafe for Western businesses,' he told me. With businesses of all sizes taking a pessimistic view on future opportunities in China, it was hardly surprising they were looking for friendlier shores. They were, in fact, doing so even though setting up shop somewhere else would involve significant expense and, in Western countries, higher wages. The executives were simply betting that relying on China for significant chunks of manufacturing, sales or both would become too risky as the West and China continued to square off. When the insurance broker WTW released the 2023 edition of its political-risk report, which documents how much money multinationals have lost to political risk – disturbances including expropriation, political interference, coups and war – China was once again in the top three, beaten only by Russia.[55] And labour in China was no longer nearly as cheap as it used to be. Between 1999 and 2022, average annual wages in the country had risen from less than CNY 7,500 to some CNY 107,000.[56]

The West also saw a steady drip of new rules and laws governing business with China – some relating to forced labour, others to sensitive technology. In Germany, for example, a clean supply chain law obliging German firms to ensure human rights were upheld in their supply chains had just come into effect.[57] In early 2023, the computer giant Dell announced it was going to stop using chips made in China, and Panasonic decided to move some aircon manufacturing home to Japan.[58] When Germany's famous *Mittelstand* of small and mid-sized companies were surveyed on their supply chains, two-thirds said they were growing their supplier base and one-third said they'd increase production in Western Europe.[59] Friendshoring delivered another novelty: public endorsement of industry bosses. In the United States, nearly seven in ten Americans said companies should strive for supply chains run through friendly countries, even if it led to higher prices.[60] In fact, citizens of liberal democracies seemed to be tiring of the whole concept of globalization. When polled in 2016, citizens in Western countries had mostly seen globalization as a force for good, though many in France did not.[61] But when polled five years later, South Korea was the only liberal democracy where a majority thought globalization had been a good thing for their country.[62] Citizens' coolness towards the movement that had brought them unprecedented levels of material comfort was perhaps also prompted by the fact that *Wandel durch Handel* was shifting direction: Western companies, and even their home countries, were the ones being forced to adjust. It wasn't just boycotts like the import ban on Norwegian salmon. Hollywood had years ago begun making its movies to suit Chinese censors, and by the mid-2010s few politicians dared to invite the Dalai Lama any more.[63] Western citizens didn't like hearing that a Taiwanese flag on Tom Cruise's bomber jacket in *Top Gun* had been removed to suit Beijing.[64] Moods were turning more pessimistic outside the West too. By 2021, only 34 per cent of Russians thought globalization was a good thing for their country. Perhaps it should have come as no surprise that Putin went to war despite knowing it would trigger unprecedented economic punishment.

Thanks to the shifting opinions among citizens, politicians and business leaders, somewhat Western-aligned manufacturing-savvy countries now found themselves extraordinarily attractive. Vietnam was emerging as a frontrunner, accompanied by India, even Indonesia and the Philippines. Mexico, too, was becoming more attractive. Barbie-maker Mattel even said it would turn its Mexico factory into its largest plant anywhere in the world.[65] Companies paid visits to Bangladesh, Cambodia, Turkey and Latin American countries. Eastern Europe again became more desirable. Germany's vice chancellor and economy minister, Robert Habeck, called on companies to diversify their Asian supply chains.[66] Taipei advised start-ups to expand to Japan rather than China.[67] Kyocera, a Japanese electronics firm and stalwart of China-based manufacturing, concluded that manufacturing in China was no longer a promising prospect. 'It works as long as [products are] made in China and sold in China, but the business model of producing in China and exporting abroad is no longer viable,' the company's president, Hideo Tanimoto, told the *Financial Times*.[68] And during a meeting with Indian tech leaders in Bengaluru, US Secretary Janet Yellen declared that the United States wanted to friendshore with India.[69] Even though Prime Minister Narendra Modi was making headlines with nationalist policies that resulted in skirmishes, he was also energetically trying to recruit Western companies of all kinds, and they were keen finally to succeed in India. A generation after manufacturing executives like Michael Treschow had seen their Indian plans thwarted by red tape and constant logistical challenges, business leaders hoped India's moment had finally arrived. China's *Global Times* let it be known what Beijing thought of the friendshoring: 'The transfer of manufacturing of a few companies is not going to be significant enough to really alter China's core place in the global supply chain,' the government's official English-language newspaper declared.[70]

That was certainly true in the near future, but 3D and other technological advances now made it easier to set up factories on a smaller scale. Africa's best-governed countries might even have a chance at positioning themselves as manufacturing hubs, perhaps for goods headed for consumers in nearby countries. But Mo Ibrahim, who'd built a company operating infrastructure in sub-Saharan Africa, wasn't optimistic. 'Power is missing; half the population in Africa don't have access to power,' he told me. 'Without power, how can you have industry? How can you have anything, education, health, or anything else? We also need to improve our infrastructure, and most importantly we need to develop the internal African market.'

Friendshoring, though, might also involve African tech firms taking their innovative solutions to friendly countries abroad. Slightly over a decade after founding his software company, Robert Okine was doing precisely that. 'Years ago I realized that my company shouldn't just market itself to Ghanaian universities but universities across sub-Saharan Africa, so I moved to Accra and began to market our services in other countries,' he told me. 'Then we got our first project with the United Nations and I thought, "There's always an opportunity to team up with like-minded people in other countries. That's one of the advantages of globalization."' In early 2023, his company had contracts in twenty countries and the UN, and he'd just opened an office in Washington. 'A couple of centuries ago, you could aspire to be the best in the village,' he reflected. 'But today you compete with the whole world. Whatever you do, there may be someone who does it better and you have to compete to become better than them.'

While Okine hadn't received US government subsidies to set up his new Washington office, the United States was in fact trying to bring more companies to America, especially those with cutting-edge production. Through the CHIPS and Science Act, the US government was beginning to spend some of the nearly $80 billion Congress had allocated to the establishment of semiconductor manufacturing and the $200 billion it had set aside to support scientific R&D and help turn it into products.[71] Congress had also passed the mystifyingly named Inflation Reduction Act, a key legislative achievement for President Biden that had little to do with inflation and a great deal to do with creating green jobs in America. 'The Inflation Reduction Act makes a historic commitment to build a new clean energy economy, powered by American innovators, American workers, and American manufacturers, that will create good-paying [*sic*] union jobs and cut the pollution that is fueling the climate crisis and driving environmental injustice,' the White House declared in its summary of the legislation, thanks to which the government would be able to provide generous grants, loans and other incentives to companies setting up manufacturing of greenhouse-gas-reducing goods.[72] Thanks to the IRA, America stood to slash its carbon emissions by a massive 40 per cent.[73]

In fact, going green, creating jobs and reducing dependence on China seemed to form a rare win-win-win scenario. US and foreign companies announced plans to build electric-car factories in Michigan and the southern US states.[74] Ford was planning a new American battery factory.[75] Highlighting companies' typical business-first approach, Volkswagen announced that it would build an electric-car factory in South Carolina and was planning to build a battery factory in the United States too – which meant forgoing plans to build it in the EU. 'We've been contacted by many US states and they all highlight the IRA. When we put the figures together, the conditions they offer are much more interesting than the conditions they offer in Europe,' a VW executive told news media.[76] European countries, realizing that Uncle Sam's grants and subsidies were likely to entice European companies to set up manufacturing in America rather than at home, didn't much like this green protectionism.[77] But they couldn't do much about the IRA: supporting friendshoring includes accepting one's friends as they are. The EU quickly devised a mini-IRA, the Green Industrial Plan.[78]

Fortunately for Xi Jinping, his apparent conclusion that globalized commerce was undermining the Chinese Communist Party's rule came at a time when China had brought its companies up to Western standards or thereabouts. As apparel-makers had realized years earlier, once China no longer needed Western businesses' expertise, they could diplomatically be shown the door. Beijing might not be all that sad to see some of the friendshorers reduce their presence.

In the world of finance, a bit of separation had commenced years earlier. So unsettled were governments by the 2008 financial crisis that many of them began insisting that banks' national operations be shielded from their global ones. 'Until the financial crisis, financial institutions lived globally but died nationally, and it was that "dying nationally" that was brought home in a very painful way for many countries during the financial crisis,' Michael Cole-Fontayn – who had now left his executive banker career in favour of corporate board appointments – observed. 'The post-crisis reforms have since sought to strengthen and segment capital, liquidity and governance so that each subsidiary of a global corporation has to express itself as a legal entity with its own source of capital, liquidity and governance.' If one market gets infected, the thinking went, it shouldn't cause banks' collective global operations to get the virus too.

Such new national rules, of course, didn't change the fact that banks were still operating around the world; the rules were merely there to prevent one geographical part of banking from dragging other parts into the abyss. But they were a recognition that even among friends, borderless enterprise brought risks. China had long been particularly adamant that it didn't want its citizens to pay the price for reckless behaviour involving bankers and consumers in the United States.[79]

But a much more profound financial separation by China from the Western world had also been taking place: although some Western banks were expanding their activities in the country,[80] China's financial sector no longer had much need for Western bankers. 'These days, to work in finance in China you need a deep understanding of the language and the political, regulatory and supervisory environment,' Cole-Fontayn pointed out. 'It's really Chinese citizens who have been educated in a global context who are coming back to China who are optimally suited to take these jobs. In this way too markets are becoming localized as knowledge is reimported from those students who've had glittering careers overseas.' When Cole-Fontayn and his fellow bankers first arrived in China, they mostly spoke no Chinese and were not experts in China's financial system. That system was, of course, just being constructed according to capitalist rules and Cole-Fontayn and his ilk possessed the expertise required for its construction. But now expat bankers were leaving, worn down by the country's zero-Covid rules and spooked by the authorities' increasing heavy-handedness. Like the expat manufacturing managers, they weren't being replaced.[81] Xi's sudden lifting of some zero-Covid rules in December 2022 hadn't stopped the exodus of the expats.[82] Indeed, giants including Goldman Sachs and Morgan Stanley were scaling back their Chinese expansion plans.[83] 'Now that China has the economy it wants, with Chinese characteristics, it can operate pretty autonomously and independently,' Cole-Fontayn observed. Countries whose economies have advanced clearly no longer need expats to teach them, but successful economics attract professionals of many nationalities. China no longer seemed interested in attracting such people. Even the country's hundreds of international schools were haemorrhaging expats as teachers (40 per cent of the total in 2022) and pupils left and were not replaced by new arrivals.[84] The human link between China and the West was weakening along with the commercial one.

In early 2023, luminaries from business and politics once again gathered in Davos. But this time, the celebrities were not quite as illustrious as they had been in years past. Xi wasn't there. Biden wasn't there. Indeed, the only G7 government chief present was Olaf Scholz. The star attraction on site was instead Ukraine's first lady, Olena Zelenska. Volodymyr Zelenskyy spoke by video-conference from his besieged country, a searing symbol of how the leaders convening in the Swiss mountains had failed in their mission to improve the state of the world.[85] The deflated atmosphere on the mountain was hardly surprising. Sergei Guriev, who wasn't there, reflected on how this time it would have been unthinkable to have a state-owned Russian bank host a conversation about Russia. The sanctioned Sberbank was at any rate unable to wire the World Economic Forum its sponsorship fee.

A couple of days earlier, Scholz had travelled to Lubmin to inaugurate the new LNG terminal that had been built at record speed and would be crucial to keeping German households and companies going now that Nord Stream was no more. 'This is all part of a plan with which we want to ensure that Germany can keep importing all the gas that it used to import,' he told the audience, which this time included no foreign dignitaries.[86] The audience did, however, include Mayor Vogt, who once again got to converse with the German chancellor and was relieved to see his town's suddenly stalled Nord Stream income partially replaced by funds from another company. It was a sign of the times that most of the forty-two crew members on the LNG terminal were from a friendly country: Norway.[87] Russia and China, meanwhile, continued their own friendshoring: by September 2022, China's imports of Russian LNG had soared above 0.8 million tonnes, up from less than 0.3 tonnes in January.[88]

Achim Langert wasn't sure what to make of the symbol of Globalization-Made-in-2023 that had arrived in his town. 'It's like a patient who's lost his leg because the doctor made a mistake and is given a prosthesis as a consolation,' he told me. 'Sure, life goes on, but it would have been preventable. The LNG terminal became necessary only because our politicians here in Germany insisted on phasing out nuclear power and thought we could keep the country going with the wind and the sun. That was one of the reasons Nord Stream became so crucial. And now we're having to import expensive LNG.' Bilal Ahmed, more than a generation younger than Langert and with no emotional attachment to the old KKW Greifswald, had reached a similar conclusion. 'Why did we shut down our nuclear reactors?' he asked. 'Now we're using coal and importing LNG instead. This is the sad price we're paying for German politics over the last decade. I feel so frustrated because my generation had no say in it.'

Burow, too, was frustrated: once again global politics was having an effect on Lubminers, and once again she felt decisions had been taken above the Lubminers' heads. 'Who will want to come on holidays here when several large ships arrive every day and spread noise and diesel?' she asked. Pastor Katrin Krüger, too, worried about the noise generated by the round-the-clock-operating terminal and the environmental harm the delivery ships' diesel was likely to cause. 'And how come we're even considering importing shale gas from the United States, which Germany until recently rejected for environmental reasons?' she asked. Germany's other new LNG terminal, in Wilhelmshaven near the Dutch coast, had already begun receiving gas from Louisiana, and Russia's war against Ukraine had indisputably increased the need for American shale gas.[89] In 2022, European companies had signed ten contracts with American producers of LNG, which is typically fracked in Texas and Louisiana.[90]

So aggrieved were Lubmin residents by the noise generated around the clock by the terminal's engines that the state government forced the LNG operator to reduce it. I thought of the residents of 1990s Smethwick, who'd just let decisions happen to them. No more. Globalization's retreat, and the humbling of the elites, seemed to be giving so-called ordinary citizens a sense of empowerment. The noise and pollution, though, were secondary to the terminal's crucial mission of bringing energy to Germany. The terminal remained, albeit somewhat quieter. As globalization convulsed and refashioned itself into regionalization, Lubminers once again formed its front line. 'Many people here are angry with America,' Burow said. 'I know that not all Americans are the same. But for some people here, America has become an enemy. It's a huge shame.'

A few weeks after the Lubmin terminal's inauguration, international trade figures arrived and – to the surprise of many – seemed to suggest that the US–China trade relationship was in robust health. In 2022, the two countries had exchanged goods worth a record $690.6 billion.[91] China had delivered $536.8 billion worth of goods to the United States compared to only $153.8 billion worth of goods going in the other direction.[92] It was symbolic of China's transformation from low-tech to high-tech manufacturer that while toys remained a pillar in its exports, mobile phones formed a second mainstay.

In some quarters, the figures caused bewilderment: had globalization suddenly recovered? Announcing friendshoring is, alas, one thing; executing it quite another. The nineties offshoring boom had taken Western companies years to implement. Presenting plans for a new factory in Vietnam, India or Mexico and quietly discontinuing one in China was just one step. Then came the hard work of setting up new facilities and suppliers, only after that, producing things.

Leaving Russia had, in fact, become a valuable warm-up for companies with operations in China. As the Ukraine war wore on, Western firms trying to make good on their vow to leave Russia discovered that they were stuck. It wasn't just the prospect of laws permitting government confiscation of the assets of departing companies that kept Western companies from leaving; it was the increasing bureaucracy involved in dismantling operations, not to mention receiving government permission to sell the assets. Four months after the invasion, Nokian Tyres, Nokia's erstwhile tyre-making branch, which had been manufacturing 80 per cent of its tyres in Russia, announced it was leaving. Four months after that, it had only just found a buyer, and the sale hadn't been completed.[93] The CEO of Philip Morris International, Jacek Olczak, admitted that he'd discussed a takeover of PMI's Russian business with at least three potential buyers but 'the talks have stalled because nobody knows how I can make it work'.[94] Sure, PMI would be able to just walk away from its Russian business, effectively donating it to the Russian government – but because globalization had made Russia one of the tobacco giant's largest markets, shareholders were unlikely to accept such a move. At any rate, any company wishing to leave Russia didn't just need the authorities' approval but also had to make a 'voluntary' donation to the Russian treasury – or defer taking the proceeds.[95] And despite their promises of slashed operations in Russia, some companies seemed eager to get at least another quarter or two out of their operations there.

Vladimir Putin was, if anything, turning more belligerent. 'The promises of Western leaders, their assurances that they were striving for peace in Donbass turned out to be a sham and outright lies. They [the West] were simply marking time, engaged in political chicanery, turning a blind eye to the Kiev regime's political assassinations and reprisals against undesirable people, their mistreatment of believers. They increasingly incited the Ukrainian neo-Nazis to stage terrorist attacks in Donbass,' he told the Duma that February.[96] Dmitry Medvedev, the once liberal reformer, offered support from the sidelines. Having already declared that he hated the West, he delivered regular threats, noting, among other things, that 'every day when they provide Ukraine with foreign weapons brings the nuclear apocalypse closer'.[97]

Some companies faced additional difficulties leaving because sanctions prevented them from negotiating a departure with Russian officials. BP saw dividends locked in Russian bank accounts.[98] VW, which had been operating a plant that employed a workforce of 4,000, found its departure plans thwarted when a court blocked its assets.[99] And at the end of March 2023, a Russian government commission announced that the voluntary donation asked of companies would be changed to a mandatory one.[100] It was like Hotel California, where 'you can check out any time you like, but you can never leave'.[101]

Since Russia had already burnt its bridges to the world's Davos-style political and economic corridors of power, it could add any other harm it liked. Companies fretted about scenarios involving laid-off staff members damaging the departing company's facilities. Or, they worried, the government could simply seize their facilities and other assets and reopen the company as a government-owned one. Chinese authorities had, after all, already expanded their tactic of punishing Western companies as proxies for their home governments far beyond Australian vintners and Taiwanese pineapple farmers. The defence contractors Raytheon and Lockheed Martin had been sanctioned, other firms had been fined and Japan's pharma giant Astellas had even seen an executive detained.[102] What would be next, and who? Many executives remembered how, at the height of his power, Venezuela's Hugo Chávez simply nationalized foreign-owned companies.[103] Even consultancies found themselves devising an exit strategy in haste: several had suddenly been raided by police.[104]

Withdrawing from a massive market is painful enough; separating one's supply chain from one of its nodes is a Gordian knot. Antony Perillo, whose footwear firm had gently been pushed out of the country years earlier, was counting his blessings. 'Even when they saw what happened to us, a lot of companies stayed in China because they figured it was a roll of the dice and they'd stick with it until they were pushed out,' he recalled.

When Perillo's company realized that it would have to leave the country, it began by tackling the most basic of tasks. 'We did a lot of travelling,' Perillo explained. 'We did a lot of talking with different people in different industries. We would try and actively seek out people like political journalists. People in the hotel industry were excellent, because not only do they invest large sums of money, they're also very politically savvy. We tended to ignore Western media, because we found that they were very slow to pick up what was sort of going on in many of these places.'

Moving shoe production, though, is straightforward compared with relocating the complex manufacturing – factories, supplies and logistics – required for higher-technology products. China had brilliantly been executing its plan to transform itself from the world shoe factory to the world's factory of high-end smartphones, not to mention solar panels, electric-car batteries and medical technology, which made finding new homes for such operations even more complex and Hotel California-esque. In key components featuring in modern technology, too, China had worked hard to make itself indispensable. By early 2023, the country led the world in thirty-seven of forty-four technologies crucial for current and future advanced economies: nanoscales materials and manufacturing, advanced radio-frequency communications including 5G's successor-to-be, 6G, supercapacitors, electric batteries – and much more.[105] 'It's a long tail bringing manufacturing and supply chains out, especially in sectors like automotive that are technology-heavy and also have a large market in China,' Krach reflected.

Or, as Volkswagen's CEO Herbert Diess admitted, 'China probably doesn't need VW but VW needs China a lot.'[106] The German carmaker was even setting up a training academy for its electric-car production in China – and planned to include Huawei software in the cars.[107] A top executive declared that he'd seen no sign of forced labour at the company's plant in Xinjiang. But because it was 2023, not 2013, such comments immediately provoked fury among Western activists, legislators and even a major VW investor.[108] In March 2023, the China Development Forum, China's version of Davos, was held in person for the first time since the pandemic – and this time, many Western business leaders stayed away.

Now companies also had to worry that China would go down a Russia-like path and thwart those wishing to leave. The legendary emerging-markets investor Mark Mobius said that was already happening to his own money, held at an HSBC account in Shanghai.[109]

Executives also had to worry that Beijing would punish their firms if they publicized any departure plans. To be sure, Xi and his government had been happy to see apparel companies leave, but high-tech companies were a different matter. China was, after all, not yet technologically self-sufficient. Then there was the executives' fear that, while they were trying to friendshore operations, their home governments might say or do something that would provoke Chinese retaliation of the kind that had befallen Ericsson or Australia's winemakers.

Gintarė Skaistė had managed to shore up her country's economy after China's temporary blockade. Or rather, she and Lithuania's industry had mostly salvaged the economy. And Skaistė had drawn firm conclusions from the experience. 'Today, when you look at countries' relations, you understand that geopolitics matters a great deal,' she observed. 'The national economy is changing, and we're moving towards safer supply chains and strengthening links with countries that we have good relations with.' Even for this ardent supporter of open markets, globalization was no longer just about economics. And because it wasn't just about economics, it was destined to struggle. 'It's about geopolitics but also about trust,' she reflected. 'When a crisis like Covid happens, if you're not on the same page as your trading partners, things will become very difficult, and that will affect supply chains too.' Geopolitics was having a direct effect on Lithuania in other ways too. By early 2023, the country had gained 81,000 new residents, 85 per cent of them Ukrainian refugees.[110] In Berlin, Olaf Scholz had just acknowledged the reality of war in Europe and agreed to send some of Germany's first-rate Leopard 2 tanks to Ukraine.[111] The United States, Britain, the Netherlands, Norway and Spain had also decided to give Ukraine some of their mighty Leopards.[112] A step that had seemed too audacious just a few months earlier had now become inevitable. In Sweden, Pål Jonson was now defence minister in the country's new centre-right coalition government, and he was overseeing Sweden's gift to Ukraine of the country's famous CV90 infantry fighting vehicles and Archer Artillery Systems along with assault rifles, anti-tank weapons and much else besides.[113] On Gotland, Solveig Artsman had heard nothing from her fellow councillors who, a decade or so earlier, had accused her of being a Russophobe.

And in Helsinki, Maria Ohisalo was gearing up for Finland's parliamentary elections. More than a year into the war, she felt she'd been proven right not just regarding the nature of Vladimir Putin's regime but also about the need for her country to reduce its dependence on oil and gas – and regarding the need for a new kind of green economy. 'And if we're aiming for energy independence from countries like Russia, we should also aim for technology independence,' she told me. 'Today we're simply too dependent on Chinese electronics. Reducing our technology dependence would also reduce our complicity in human-rights violations in countries like China.' Friendshoring did indeed offer the prospect of bringing existing manufacturing jobs home or to friendly countries while at the same time allowing countries to act more ethically because they wouldn't be so beholden to China.

Then there was climate change. Individual governments, especially in Western Europe, were trying hard to limit CO2 emissions. But 2022 had delivered shocking statistics. It was the world's sixth-hottest year on record; Europe registered its worst drought in 500 years; twenty-eight countries recorded their hottest-ever year.[114] At COP27 that December, the world's countries had agreed to a set of rather modest pledges including the phasing out of coal.[115] But that year, China had approved a massive new group of coal-fired plants.[116] At the beginning of 2023, the world recorded its seventh-highest average temperature since records began in 1850. North America had its fifth-warmest January on record; Africa had its sixth-warmest January on record; and the Arctic saw its third-smallest ice mass on record.[117] Citizens around the industrialized world almost unanimously considered climate change a severe threat: 86 per cent in Greece; 82 per cent in Italy, Japan and South Korea; 81 per cent in France; 78 per cent in Spain; 75 per cent in Britain; 71 per cent in Australia. The United States was the straggler at 54 per cent, a reflection of the country's ideology-fuelled attitude to climate change.[118]

With countries now trying to conduct a green transformation that included the switch from petrol-fuelled vehicles to battery-operated ones, companies and countries would be reliant on China, at least initially. Years before the split between China and the West was becoming obvious, Chinese companies had established a near-monopoly in the processing of rare-earth minerals. By 2021, the United States had managed to increase its processing and thus reduced China's dominance, but China was still far ahead of every other country, with more than 60 per cent of the world's rare-earth processing. The United States in second place was far behind, followed by Myanmar and Australia.[119] China also has the world's largest rare-earth mineral reserves, followed by Vietnam, Russia, Brazil and Madagascar.[120] Expanding rare-earth processing outside China was a race against time as the climate kept deteriorating and the risks involved with dependence on China increased. Companies building and buying electric batteries might have no problem getting the required rare earths from China – but they might also see supplies suddenly cut off in an act of geopolitical vengeance. It was a sign of the times when, in March 2023, the United States and the EU agreed to begin talks to mutually secure supplies of rare-earth minerals.[121]

China had seemed the unbeatable amalgam of what globalized companies needed: a capitalist economy, complete with a well-trained labour force and efficient logistics, combined with centralized rule that provided the unfailing stability that democracies lack. But even the best-managed autocracy will at some point slide towards dictatorial rule. Before leaving for a visit to China together with President Emmanuel Macron of France, the European Commission's president, Ursula von der Leyen, summarized how China had changed and thus the EU's ability to cooperate with it. 'We have seen a very deliberate hardening of China's overall strategic posture for some time,' she said, highlighting Xi's 'no-limits friendship' with Putin and going on to warn that China 'has now turned the page on the era of "reform and opening" and is moving into a new era of security and control'.[122] The ambitious EU–China Comprehensive Investment Agreement, negotiated in 2020, wasn't even discussed in the two Europeans' meeting with the Chinese leader.[123] China's ambassador to the EU, Fu Cong, was incensed at the separation now under way. 'Who in their right mind would abandon such a thriving market as big as China?' he asked. Countries were doing so 'at their peril', he warned.[124]

But with China's increasingly authoritarian turn had come the realization – first among Western business leaders and now among political leaders and the public – that trade simply was not going to make the country more democratic. Treschow had seen it all before. 'If the public at home or foreign governments expect companies to advance democracy, that simply won't work', he told me. During Treschow's tenure as chairman of Unilever, good governance in Bulgaria was so insufficient that the company told the government it would have to leave the country. It left – and returned when matters had improved. 'That's, I think, how you have to behave as a business,' Treschow said. 'You do business according to standards of morals and ethics and hope that others will do the same. Then you can collectively help achieve change in authoritarian or otherwise difficult countries. But as a business leader, you shouldn't be thinking of yourself as some sort of saviour of unfree countries.'

While a dictatorship is stable, leadership-wise, it's also hostage to the caprice of its rulers. Now that many previously enthusiastic corporate supporters of China and Russia were concluding that free markets without freedom brings risk in the long term, the conclusion was just the accumulation of doubts they'd been collecting for years. And during their years of collecting doubts, their operations in both countries had helped them deliver stunning results. It had been a good run.

15
GOODBYE GLOBALIZATION

The winter of 2022 and early 2023 had been mild in Bilal Ahmed's part of Germany, indeed in most of Europe. From a consumer perspective, that was a good thing, since friends and foes alike had predicted that the skyrocketing energy prices caused by Russia's war against Ukraine would cause misery during the winter months.

But Ahmed was struggling to make sense of what was happening around him and around Germany. 'I grew up in a globalized world; this is the only world I know,' he said. 'We didn't even have national service in Germany when I turned eighteen. I've never had to do military service or even think about the Bundeswehr. I grew up thinking that the world was moving towards more unity. I studied abroad and had the opportunity to interact with people from all over the world. In my company, we worked with Russian and Belarusian IT engineers. And now all of that is over. We all thought that globalization would expand the footprint of liberal democracies. Instead the interconnectedness of the world is leading to more tension, and autocratic states are impeding on our way of life and have leverage over us! The more globalized we've become, the more leverage authoritarian countries have gained over us. That really troubles me.'

This was the world that optimists in positions of power in the 1990s, 2000s and 2010s had bequeathed to the new generation, just as their 'economics-is-everything' mindset had delivered a world now approaching unprecedented climate-change peril. People like Ahmed were supposed to grow up in a peaceful and prosperous world, and instead they were being presented with war in Europe, climate emergencies and the prospect of snowballing conflict in Europe, perhaps even a war involving China.

But the decision-makers that had bet so heavily on trade and porous borders weren't all optimists: globalization simply seemed destined to happen. 'I'm exercising self-critical reflection,' said Kevin Casas-Zamora, now secretary general of IDEA, an intergovernmental organization promoting democracy. 'We were very naïve with regard to free trade; very naïve. We never really thought through the political implications of free trade and the security implications of free trade. And those implications are dawning on us now.'

At the beginning of 2023, NATO Secretary General Jens Stoltenberg returned to speak at the annual conference organized by the Confederation of Norwegian Enterprise, NHO. He'd first spoken there in the early nineties, when he was Norway's minister of business and energy. 'In particular,' he told the assembled business leaders at his return visit, 'I remember the restructuring package in Sør-Varanger municipality, after we shut down the mine and the pellet plant. An important part of this was to invest heavily in trade and investment across the newly opened border with Russia. It was a new and optimistic time.' He went on: 'We had unfaltering faith in globalization, free trade and growth. Now I'm standing here again, at NHO's annual conference. In a completely different world. No more tearing down rusted up walls. But building new, upgraded fences. Detente has turned into high tension – and new war. Authoritarian regimes are rising. Democracy is retreating. Globalization is declining.'[1] In Beijing, Xi told members of his country's rubber-stamp legislature that 'Western countries, led by the US, are implementing all-round containment, encirclement and suppression against us.'[2] His new foreign minister, Qin Gang, declared, 'If the United States does not hit the brake, but continues to speed down the wrong path, no amount of guardrails can prevent derailing and there surely will be conflict and confrontation.'[3]

It was a sign of the times that when Americans were polled in early 2023, 50 per cent of them believed that China was America's greatest enemy, compared to 35 per cent who thought it was Russia, 7 per cent who thought it was North Korea, 2 per cent who thought it was Iran and 1 per cent each who thought it was Afghanistan or the United States itself. In 2018, only 11 per cent thought China was the United States' greatest enemy; back then, North Korea led at 51 per cent.[4] In early 2023, only 15 per cent of Americans had a favourable view of China: a record low.[5]

A few months earlier, Morris Chang, the CEO of TSMC and the father of Taiwan's world-dominating semiconductor industry, had made an unexpected intervention. Riding on the crest of globalization and digitalization, TSMC had built itself into a global behemoth supplying the whole world with chips crucial to all kinds of products. But in December 2022, Chang declared that 'globalization is almost dead'.[6] One and a half years earlier, Perillo had told me, 'I give globalization another twenty-four months.' I felt he was exaggerating. Now it turned out he'd been right on the money. In a move illustrating the emerging new world order, the German government announced it was banning key parts of Huawei's 5G technology – not because of national security concerns relating to the components but because of fears that using Huawei could make Germany dependent on China.[7]

In globalization's heady days, people like Casas-Zamora and Stoltenberg – and most men and women in charge of governments, businesses, universities, media organizations and other pillars of society – had had no reason to doubt the maxim that when goods cross borders, soldiers won't. What they failed to consider, though, was that trade might not be able to change countries' domestic arrangements, just like they failed to realize that ordinary citizens may have desires beyond cheaper consumer products.

Instead the two globalizing countries that were also strong enough to form geopolitical counterweights to the West chose a different track. Their decision not to couple market economies with liberal democracy upended globalization's premise of goods versus soldiers – and interdependence became a source of vulnerability for the countries in Western Europe and North America that had so enthusiastically exported their market economies and assumed that everyone, laid-off workers perhaps excepted, would endorse the globalized way of life. 'There was a moment when global politics and technology created a unique opportunity for companies to build around the world,' Robert Okine reflected. 'The technology is still available, but the political conditions have changed.'

If the coexistence of countries were simply a matter of economics, Casas-Zamora pondered, Europe should 'buy gas from Russia for ever and ever, because that's what comparative price advantage dictates. Well, it turned out that things were more complicated than that. And now security concerns are trumping whatever diktats emerge from the economic logic of free trade.' The same, he added, went not just for high-tech goods made in China but also for crucial components going into products like Taiwanese computer chips: 'Free trade would dictate that we should keep buying chips from providers in Taiwan, because those guys are very efficient at producing computer chips. Well, it turns out that there's a risk that one fine day Taiwan could be taken over by China and the whole global economy could grind to a halt. That means it might be advisable to try to produce computer chips somewhere else.'

The somewhere else, Joe Biden and a majority of the US Congress had decided, could be the United States.[8] Not only would the Inflation Reduction Act make America safer: it would, of course, create modern factory jobs. 'Too many have been left behind amid the economic upheaval of the past four decades. They remember the jobs that went away and wonder whether a path even exists anymore for them to succeed. But I know we can forge a path of building an economy where no one is left behind,' the US president tweeted in early 2023.[9] Because Biden and Congressional leaders had forgotten the effect the IRA would have on America's closest friends, they were trying at least to retrofit a few small parts of the gigantic funding package. Rearranging the globalized world order maddeningly complicated.

So certain were many political leaders of a future with less dependence on trade with China that more of them dared to extend a hand to Taiwan. 'Today, I spoke with the president of Taiwan Tsai Ing-wen. I thanked her for her congratulations and I assured her that Taiwan and the Czech Republic share the values of freedom, democracy, and human rights. We agreed on strengthening our partnership,' Petr Pavel – a former general and chairman of NATO's Military Committee, and a first-time politician – tweeted two days after being elected president of the Czech Republic.[10]

Despite the risk of politically motivated retaliation and the other growing risks in China, Czech companies would continue trading with the country. Indeed, all kinds of Western companies were still doing so. Hundreds of companies were operating in Russia, many while also trying to leave. Countless others were selling their wares to Saudi Arabia and similarly lucrative nations not governed by liberal democracy. The original exporters of market economy could, in fact, keep trading with friends and almost-friends in Central and Eastern Europe, in Latin America, in North Africa, the Middle East, Asia and sub-Saharan Africa. The countries in Central and Eastern Europe were, of course, incontrovertible proof that countries could turn themselves into market economies and liberal democracies and integrate themselves into a globalized world based on trade and shared values. Yet the belief that exporting market economies would automatically deliver democracy had vanished. That the leaders of globalization's two crown jewels had turned out to be keen on a Western lifestyle but not a Western way of life was regrettable, but it was their right.

Paradoxically, laid-off factory workers and other ordinary citizens who had been questioning globalization – and been greeted by patronizing snickering by well-educated members of society – had been proven right. 'China has been helpful on one level because everything has become cheaper,' Gurinder Singh Josan, a businessman and community representative in the Midlands, observed. 'But as a result, our industry barely exists any more. People have been benefiting from cheaper products, but that doesn't help them in the long run.' Laid-off workers could, of course, not have predicted Xi Jinping's authoritarian turn or Vladimir Putin's murderous one, nor could they have known that globalization would be undermined by pervasive unfair play. They had sensed, though, that moving large chunks of industry to faraway countries would cause harm at home. 'But,' Solveig Artsman reflected, 'the world outside the big cities didn't seem to matter to decision-makers.'

Unusually among top politicians, Casas-Zamora was willing to admit errors of political judgement. 'We were very blind and very naïve about the implications of free trade, not just about how it would create a two-tier society in our countries but about the potential return of geopolitics,' he said. 'And geopolitics can curtail and in many cases trump the economic logic of globalization. That will renationalize or at the very least regionalize economic activities.' Rather paradoxically, Beijing seemed eager to drive home the point that separation was needed. After Elon Musk tweeted a new US government report suggesting Covid-19 may have been a lab leak, the *Global Times* responded, asking if he was biting the hand feeding him.[11] At that point, more than half of the manufacturing of Musk's Tesla cars was located in China, and more than a quarter of the cars were sold there.[12]

Maybe some countries, especially the United States, were marching too fast in wanting to reduce their dependence on China. And to leave China and Russia, companies would indisputably need much more time than they did after leaving Iran in 2018. It was remarkable, though, how citizens' concerns, businesses' worries about unfair play and governments' concerns about national security were converging with increasing Chinese authoritarianism and belligerence, Russia's plunge into the geopolitical abyss and the emergence of an informal bloc led by Beijing. The United Nations' Human Rights Council's decision, in late 2022, to reject a motion to debate China's treatment of the Uyghurs seemed like another indicator of the world's now unmistakable split into two camps. While Western countries voted in favour of the motion, sub-Saharan African countries, Pakistan, Qatar and the United Arab Emirates voted with China.[13]

With manufacturers now scouting for alternatives to their Chinese facilities and suppliers, it was clear that the answer would not be one country, not even India. They'd have to replicate whatever operations they planned to withdraw from China (or replicate outside it) in a cluster of countries. 'After the Cold War, we built a global structure, global supply chains, global business models, a global management that could be moved around to different countries, and now a sudden brake is being applied on this whole global machinery,' said Treschow, who was seeing his decades of commercial achievement collide with forces stronger than commerce. 'We're having to revise everything we built up. Companies will be forced back to island-style operations. And the risks of disruption to global supply chains means they'll go from global to regional.' A few weeks later, the US and Japanese governments put forward a plan for precisely such an island of friendly nations cooperating on chip production.[14] Perillo wondered what would happen to geographically isolated nations like his home country of New Zealand, whose biggest trading partner by far was China.[15]

The world of free-market commerce could indeed retreat to the string of figurative islands on which Cold War executives operated. This time, though, the central island would be much larger, comprising not just Western Europe, North America, Japan, South Korea, Australia and New Zealand but also the Central and Eastern European countries that had joined the European Union. This group, in turn, was connected to a string of countries ranging from Costa Rica to Vietnam that during the Cold War were, at best, thorny islands. 'The West will have more friends than enemies, so there will be more integration between these countries,' Guriev, now provost at France's prestigious Sciences Po, pointed out. What's more, technology was allowing companies to create more efficient regional hubs than was possible in the seventies and eighties. 'This whole transformation will create jobs in different places,' Treschow said. 'It won't be a literal return to the seventies and eighties but a more modern version with the internet and a digital lifestyle. Things will be different, but they won't be global.' It was not for nothing that Apple was moving manufacturing to India, Vietnam and the United States. It was even planning to open its first Apple stores in India.[16] And Bolivia, home to vast reserves of lithium, the metal crucial to batteries used in digital devices and electric vehicles, had cast its die. Following a billion-dollar deal with three Chinese firms to explore the reserves,[17] it had now signed a $1.4 billion agreement for lithium exploration with another Chinese company and a division of Russia's state-owned Rosatom.[18] The agreements followed another deal, worth $2.3 billion, signed between Bolivia and a Chinese firm in 2019.[19] And because it was 2023, not 2003, that meant China and Russia were on their way towards a monopoly on lithium in the country with the world's largest reserves by far.[20] Any hopes of a summer lull in the global standoff came to nought in early July, when China imposed export curbs on gallium and germanium, two other metals critical to semiconductor production.[21]

I thought of John Spellar, the parliamentarian whose sympathy for laid-off factory workers had for years made him seem almost anachronistic. Now factory jobs were on the verge of returning. Britain wasn't splurging on subsidies for new manufacturing in the same manner as Washington – indeed it was struggling mightily to make its departure from the thoroughly integrated European market work – but many companies were likely to friendshore under their own steam. Some of them, British or otherwise, might set up production in the very area that brought the world the Industrial Revolution. Could the world's geopolitical strife bring an unexpected second wind to the Midlands? Spellar was hopeful: 'We need to start training people in anticipation of the kinds of jobs that may arrive.'

Such jobs, making products so sophisticated they might involve lab coats, could also deliver a reputational upgrade of the often-disparaged blue-collar worker. 'Future supply chains will be a lot more localized with a high degree of automation,' Sundström pointed out. 'Companies will automate their processes, and you will see global products. But it will be a lot more local supply chains with a very high degree of automation. And that means that we'll also need to change the workforce.' The advanced manufacturing now in ascendance might even be an opportunity to eradicate the unfortunate divide between blue-collar and white-collar workers.

Martyn Richardson, who with his brothers had managed to massively grow his real-estate development company from their headquarters in the Midlands town of Oldbury, was optimistic too. At one point, the town had a Toys 'R' Us in addition to supermarkets, but then the chain went bust. It would be redemptive if some of the jobs lost to China returned and were joined by new ones in, say, green manufacturing. The Richardsons had recently bought the site of a factory that used to make automotive components. 'The manufacturing knowledge base is still here!' Martyn said. Manufacturing had changed a great deal since the nineties, and making, say, solar-panel components bears little relation to making screws. But locals, both those who'd once worked in factories and those too young to have done so, were eager to see jobs return. And for many locals, good jobs in manufacturing were far more desirable than jobs in hospitality or logistics.

But Gerard Coyne, the veteran local trade-union boss, had his doubts. 'Technological innovation will begin to fill many of the jobs that were lost to globalization,' he said. 'We'll see more automation and more driverless freight. Many of the jobs we lost won't return, and since German engineering giants will be making many of those robots our workers won't benefit there either. It's absolutely terrible for workers. If they feel isolated and excluded now, imagine how they'll feel when they're replaced by more technology. And imagine when middle-class jobs begin to be affected by robots.' In 2023, the advance of artificial intelligence was causing precisely such job losses, with Goldman Sachs reporting that 300 million jobs were at risk.[22] But the arrival of the robots was an unexpected recompense for the West's manual workers. Goldman found that office professions – including management – were likely to be killed by AI, while blue-collar jobs – including machine operators, miners and lorry drivers – were extraordinarily safe. Only 7 per cent of assemblers and machine and plant operators in the EU were, for example, likely to lose their jobs to AI, compared to 29 per cent of managers.[23] Friendshoring mining and manufacturing companies were already desperate for workers.[24]

Antony Perillo was already part of the new friendshored world. After completing his company's exit from China, he'd led operations in Bangladesh and Vietnam. Now he was based in Britain, an executive with a high-end apparel company with an international customer base but with production exclusively in the UK. Yes, making leather bags in Britain was more expensive than in a low-wage country, but consumers were willing to pay a bit extra for 'Made in Britain'. Lower-end makers of clothes, bags and shoes were, at any rate, making this work rather well in Bangladesh and the other countries that had been welcoming them in recent years. Now mobile phones, solar panels and electric cars were making the same journey as Perillo – but their speed depended on factories finding workers.

Even though it would certainly be complicated for companies to move manufacturing from China, and no country could hope to replace China as a one-stop shop, Perillo thought companies likely to succeed where his own company had succeeded years before. 'Our technological advancement is huge in comparison to the eighties,' he pointed out. 'The digital ability for us to execute friendshoring and to get consistency but also allow for a degree of segmentation is going to be different compared to how it was in the eighties.' The manufacturing about to return was so fundamentally different from the kind that left in the eighties that it hardly even resembled factory work any more. What's more, artificial intelligence could help companies get a complete overview of their extremely complex supply chains, which involve not just direct suppliers but second-tier, third-tier and fourth-tier ones, sometimes even more. Technological advances also made it possible to set up production in friendly and moderately friendly countries without dispatching the armies of expat managers that had been required when Perillo, Cole-Fontayn and their ilk had first arrived in China. And it would be possible to manufacture products that didn't all look the same. It would, for example, 'be wonderful to see a German-designed and German-made mobile phone,' Perillo suggested. If the globalized world of products foretold by Theodore Levitt in 1983 seemed destined to give way to new variation.

China, meanwhile, was enticing countries to join the informal bloc emerging under its leadership.[25] Bangladesh and Myanmar appeared to be leaning in that direction, and the UN vote rejecting a debate on the Uyghurs was a strong indicator of which countries were leaning towards the Beijing-led bloc.[26] Another indicator of China's ambitions to create an informal alliance had arrived in March 2023, when the country brokered an agreement that would see arch-enemies Iran and Saudi Arabia resume diplomatic relations.[27]

A few days later, the heavily sanctioned Iran announced that Russia, now even more heavily sanctioned, had in the past year become its largest foreign investor. 'We define our relations with Russia as strategic and we are working together in many aspects, especially economic relations. China and Russia are our two main economic partners [and] Iran is going to expand its relations with them through implementing strategic agreements,' Iran's finance minister, Ehsan Khandouzi, told a reporter.[28]

Russia and China, in turn, performed a public embrace soon after the International Criminal Court had issued an arrest warrant for Vladimir Putin over war crimes in Ukraine.[29] Even though Putin was now the first leader of a permanent UN Security Council member state to have an arrest warrant to his name, Xi Jinping very publicly travelled to Moscow on his first state visit since being elected to a third term. 'No matter how the international landscape may change, China will stay committed to advancing China–Russia comprehensive strategic partnership of coordination for the new era,' a Chinese foreign ministry statement explained.[30] Putin returned the expression of loyalty by telling Xi that Russia would be able to export even more energy to support China's growing economy.[31] During the Cold War, the Soviet Union and China had maintained a utilitarian relationship with the Soviets as the senior partners. Now Putin and Xi's budding relationship involved both commerce and diplomacy, even the military. And this time, China was the senior partner.

Countries on the geopolitical fence, in turn, found a much-desired opportunity to tell the West to stop lecturing them on domestic issues. At the very least since the end of the Cold War, unsolicited Western advice about governance and human rights had irked governments of less-than-democratic countries. Now, as vital participants in the globalized economy, they could subtly make the point that such lecturing had to stop or they'd join China's emerging camp. Western countries must 'separate politics from trade and the economy', the United Arab Emirates' trade minister, Thani bin Ahmed Al Zeyoudi, explained.[32] That, too, was a return to the Cold War, when Western–Soviet competition for aligned countries was so intense that human rights took a back seat, or no seat at all.

When considering prospective new countries for their production and entire supply chains, manufacturers now had to consider political developments involving not just Russia and China but also the countries that might join the Chinese-led camp. Conversely, they had to plan for harm they might inadvertently cause their own supply chains. Nobody wanted to be like Lithuania's manufacturers, who unwittingly caused a scare to their supply chains when China punished them to avenge Vilnius's friendly overture to Taipei.

There was also the matter of how long companies might be able to sell to geopolitical rivals' consumers. In the crucial Chinese market, it wasn't just Huawei that had been catching up with Western market leaders; Chinese fast-fashion brands, carmakers and technology companies had done so too. It was precisely because China had attractive domestic alternatives that Chinese consumers could stage boycotts against brands like H&M. 'We need new strategic alliances in the world,' Tony Danker, the secretary general of the Confederation of British Industry, told a reporter.[33] In the meantime, the global geopolitical standoff would intensify even as countless Western companies operated significant manufacturing, supply chains and sales in China and the bloc emerging around it. It was no wonder executives were extremely nervous about the harm that might come to their operations – and the additional harm that the two-front war involving opinionated consumers in the West and China respectively could cause.

The world of finance wasn't facing the same segmentation as manufacturing, and of the $1.08 trillion in US treasury securities – that is, US government debt – held by foreign governments, $870 billion was held by China, second only to the amount held by Japan.[34] But so fearful were investors of what might come that by early 2023 top Chinese tech companies had seen their market value drop by $300 million since the beginning of the pandemic, while the value of US tech companies had soared by $5 trillion.[35] How much minds had shifted became even clearer when Rishi Sunak flew to California to join Joe Biden and Australia's Prime Minister Anthony Albanese in officially presenting the three countries' new AUKUS submarine programme. China is 'an epoch-defining challenge to us and to the global order', declared the recently installed British prime minister, a former banker and globalization winner who had long believed in good relations with China.[36]

Technology would also keep operating globally, but not as globally as its many godfathers and godmothers had intended. Telecommunications and the internet were, in fact, emerging as the reconstituted global system's new fault line. It wasn't just the battle over Huawei and the concerns over Chinese government access to TikTok users' data; it was also the fear that adversaries could cut the undersea cables attaching countries to the lifeline of modern societies: the internet. A few weeks into 2023, Chinese commercial vessels did exactly that, severing the undersea cables connecting Taiwan's Matsu Islands to Taiwan proper and thus the world.[37] 6G, the next-generation mobile-communications system being conceived once again, featured collaboration involving a great number of brilliant engineers. Now, though, the borderless teamwork that had characterized previous generations of mobile telecommunications had vanished. Countries looked likely to have to choose between a Chinese 6G architecture and a Western one.

With Russia's invasion of Ukraine well into its second year, Russia's military was so closely matched by Ukraine's tenacious armed forces and their now steady supply of Western weapons that Russia seemed unlikely to want to attempt any further invasions. Then again, recent years had taught policymakers, business executives and ordinary citizens not to take peace for granted, and the risk of a world war triggered by a potential Chinese attack on Taiwan was keeping policymakers and business leaders up at night. Sergei Guriev, meanwhile, had just been declared a 'foreign agent' by the Kremlin for the misdeed of 'speaking negatively about the servicemen of the Russian Armed Forces' and spreading 'false information about decisions Russia's state bodies make and policies they implement'.[38]

No country had believed more fervently in the combination of global peace and global commerce than Germany, which for reasons known to all had decided that war was an unmitigated disaster. Perhaps it was no surprise that more than any other country Germany was now struggling to find its feet in a world moving away from the commerce-fuelled peace that had proven such a blessing for it. But the country that had been so committed to Nord Stream and that had seen its chancellor make the trip to Davos even after his Western peers had opted to stay home was also the country where Scholz's deputy, Robert Habeck, had now advised companies to diversify supply chains away from China and introduced stricter export controls on companies wanting to invest in China.[39] 'What's the identity of Germany in this new world?' Bilal Ahmed asked. 'It feels like my country is having an identity crisis.'

Mostly, though, globalization's original supporters and detractors alike seemed relieved. To be sure, some German and other Western companies were planning to invest more in China, but as Lang observed, 'every euro that they invest in China is duplicated by another euro that they invest in another Asian country'. Post-Cold War globalization had been an honourable undertaking, and it had benefited countless people, but it had run its course. It hadn't taken the climate into account. It had overestimated democracy's power to convert. It had underestimated countries' proclivity to compete for power. It had neglected the voice of grassroots citizens. 'Ideas, knowledge, art, hospitality, travel – these are the things that should of their nature be international. But let goods be homespun whenever it is reasonably and conveniently possible; and, above all, let finance be primarily national,' John Maynard Keynes wrote in 1933.[40] His words seemed to be coming true.

In suburban Washington, DC, Hana Azari was watching the shift away from the only world she'd ever known, and she decided it was logical. 'Globalization was supposed to improve relations between countries, but having our manufacturing in China hasn't helped our foreign policy,' she reasoned. Maria Ohisalo was optimistic too – not because she enjoyed seeing global strife but because globalization's decline offered an opportunity to fix fundamental problems. In 2021, Finland had imported 34 per cent of its energy from Russia, mostly natural gas.[41] Now the tragedy in Ukraine was forcing Finland to wean itself off its convenient but environmentally harmful dependence on Russian energy, and ending that dependence could only strengthen Finland's national security. In the first instance, Finland had to do a 'Lubmin': a hastily arranged LNG terminal had been brought in to bring American gas to the country.[42] But that was only intended as a temporary fix, and Ohisalo saw the disappearing dirty energy as an opportunity to create new green jobs in her country. 'The war has taught us that we can't rely on fossil fuel from other countries,' she told me. 'We need more renewable energy made at home. Fossil fuel has never been just about business; it has always been about power politics too. As a Green politician, I obviously like to think of the whole world as one, but the green shift creates a lot of opportunities for green jobs at home.'

This, Ohisalo thought, might even be the starting point for a new green Nokia – or several green Nokias. 'When Nokia lost its prime position for handsets, it was a great loss for the country, and for years we've been talking about what the new Nokia might be,' she observed. 'I hope the new Nokia will be a company in the area of green tech.' Ohisalo realized Finland wasn't going to single-handedly pioneer the green shift, but in green tech as in mobile technology it could be the advance team. 'People will say, "What can a small country like Finland do to tackle global climate change?"' she told me. 'Well, we can prioritize companies that are making the green shift. That's something that can hopefully inspire other countries as well.' Having recovered from the shock of America's IRA, the EU had just presented a €369 billion package known as the Net-Zero Industry Act that would subsidize the development of new solar technologies, onshore and offshore wind, battery, heat pumps and geothermal energy, renewable hydrogen, biomethane, nuclear, fission and grid tech.[43] At least 40 per cent of the EU clean tech should be made domestically by 2030, the EU said.[44]

The green jobs now looming on the horizon might in fact go far beyond the EU's plan for clean energy. With cheap consumer goods having led to enormous waste and harm to the environment, now was the chance to create longer-lasting consumer products in all kinds of categories. I thought of Axel Vogt, who as a native of East Germany knew how to mend bicycle tyres, while his own children – natives of capitalist united Germany – responded to flat tyres by buying new ones. For the green innovation to take off, though, allied countries would need to work together even more closely so that new products and inventions could be sold in large quantities. A large market, Guriev pointed out, was indispensable if the emerging Western-led alliance was to have a shot at saving the climate.

Despite its cruelty, the Ukraine war in fact presented an unexpected opportunity to accelerate the world's much-needed green transition. In April 2023, the Intergovernmental Panel on Climate Change delivered another stark state-of-the-climate assessment: human-caused climate change would, among other things, harm water availability, agricultural production, livestock productivity and fishing yields, and increase flooding and droughts.[45] Together with green energy transition triggered by the war, friendshoring might, at least in Western countries, bring the transformation COP summits and Davos meetings had failed to deliver. But the West would need to work with China, Russia and the other countries in the emerging Beijing-led bloc to halt climate change even as the two sides battled over power.

While green planning accelerated, news media delivered a steady stream of theories about who caused Nord Stream's demise. A pro-Ukraine commando was the likely culprit, some news organizations reported, while other outlets said a Russian submarine had been seen near the sites days before the explosions.[46] A captivated global public kept sleuthing and speculating about what might have occurred at the bottom of the Baltic Sea during those September days the year before. Nord Stream 1 and 2's Western European minority owners, investors and insurers, though, faced a potential battle over billions of euros. If Russia or another state was the perpetrator, the sabotage could count as an act of war, which regular business insurance doesn't cover. If the perpetrator was a private group thinking it was doing a good deed for a government, or a private outfit operating on behalf of a government, a legal fight over the billions that had gone into the pipelines loomed. It was easy to sympathize with Mayor Vogt's bafflement over the turn global politics had taken since he saw Angela Merkel turn on the tap that cheerful day in November 2011.

But the rift was producing another result too: for some major companies, it was a reason to grow their presence in China. In case of an even more severe split, they wanted their Chinese operations to be able to function independently of their Western ones.[47] That's what twenty-first-century commercial islands would look like.

With such tremors under way, the low prices consumers had taken for granted were likely to dissipate. 'It doesn't take a genius to think cheap goods and cheaper goods may be a thing of the past,' Danker told an interviewer. China's unique fusion of a massive workforce, low wages and considerable efficiency, not to mention centralized power to make things happen, had been irresistible. It has been mostly benign – but it couldn't last.

Reducing commercial intimacy with China and other countries likely to be part of Beijing's new bloc wasn't just a matter of protecting manufacturing and supply chains; now it seemed prudent to try to reduce the blocs' financial interdependence too. In the case of another regional financial crisis, countries would certainly have to ask their bloc partners for a bailout, and countries in the other bloc might be reluctant to help. But, as Ohisalo saw it, reducing the commercial links with China and Russia was also a matter of ensuring that Western countries could continue exercising their values at home. 'If we want to become more energy-independent, more technology-independent, if we want to implement the absolutely necessary climate policies and respect human rights, then we'll have to reverse away from the way globalization is set up today,' she pointed out. 'And staying in China brings risks. Just think about China's use of data.' Nobody seemed to know quite what to do about TikTok. A bit like post-Cold War globalization itself, what had begun life as enjoyable consumption was beginning to seem distinctly sinister. The app had now been banned from work phones not just by the US Congress and the US government but by EU institutions and a number of member governments too.[48] The Kremlin had weighed in by banning officials involved in the 2024 presidential election preparations from using iPhones – also citing national security concerns.[49] The Western institutions stopped short, though, of banning TikTok from officials' personal phones, let alone ordinary citizens' use of it. '150 million Americans love our app,' CEO Shou Zi Chew reminded US lawmakers.[50]

Post-Cold War globalization's premise of efficiency, lower consumer prices and democratization – an extraordinary win-win-win – may only have existed in theory. There was no doubt that globalization had created efficiencies, but it had failed to democratize key participants; and the cheap goods hadn't endeared it to ordinary citizens. Mo Ibrahim was not the only decision-maker baffled by consumers' apparent lack of gratitude. Perhaps that had to do with the fact that people crave something beyond material comfort. And because people's lives were not just about economics, office workers across the Western world had responded to Covid-19 lockdowns by deciding that they quite liked being at home. Before Covid, only a small percentage of the world's workers had been mostly working from home: from freelancers and small-business owners in high-income economies to artisans and seamstresses in emerging ones.[51] Three years after the pandemic struck, working from home – at least a couple of days a week – was normal.[52]

Solveig Artsman had made the acquaintance of some new WFH-brigade members in her village on Gotland. Since the beginning of Covid, the island had gained some 2,000 residents and now had a total of more than 61,000. 'Before the pandemic, my village was pretty desolate, but that changed during the pandemic when people moved here and began working from home,' she explained. 'They seem to enjoy going for walks rather than being stuck in traffic commuting to work. And then, of course, we have the military.'

Yes, the military was back on this strategic island in the Baltic Sea. In 2016, soldiers had begun arriving to replace the ones that had been withdrawn at the beginning of the century. By 2019, the island had a functioning tank battalion looking after its security. Now the battalion was being expanded and enhanced. 'The armed forces' return has already created new jobs and will create more,' Artsman pointed out. 'And when Sweden joins NATO we're likely to have NATO troops here every now and then.'

The armed forces as a major employer, the magical pipeline up in smoke and Sweden about to join NATO: what a sharp turn local and global matters had taken since Artsman first heard about Nord Stream. Across NATO, military spending had been increasing for years, and since Russia invaded Ukraine many of its members had spent large chunks of their GDP to support the invaded country. Estonia, Latvia, Lithuania and Poland had committed more than 1 per cent of their GDP, or almost that share, to aid for Ukraine. Bulgaria, Slovakia, Denmark, the Netherlands, the Czech Republic, Portugal, Austria, Sweden, Greece, the United States, Slovenia, Germany, Spain, Finland, Norway, Britain and Croatia had all committed at least 0.3 per cent of their GDP to aid for Ukraine. China had committed nothing.[53] Germany and Poland were hosting around a million Ukrainian refugees each; Bulgaria, more than 150,000; Romania, almost 120,000. Estonia, with a population of 1.3 million, was looking after nearly 40,000 Ukrainians.[54]

In July, NATO's thirty member states were about to convene for another summit, where they were planning to announce the establishment of a NATO-Ukraine Council.[55] This time they would also be joined by their thirty-first member, Finland, which had joined the alliance in the spring.[56] Ohisalo, though, wasn't able to celebrate her country's seminal step from a ministerial position: in the elections that April, voters had passed the government reins to a centre-right coalition.[57]

Because Turkey objected to the presence of Kurdish militants in Sweden, Artsman and her fellow Swedes were still waiting for their country to be able to join the alliance.[58] Sweden had reintroduced national service in a new selective format also involving young women, and 61 per cent of Germans now supported bringing national service back in their country.[59] Suddenly Bilal Ahmed was constantly hearing national service discussed. The PLAN, China's Navy, for its part, was continuing its massive expansion.[60] Iran, the globalization era outcast, had just joined the Shanghai

Cooperation Organization, a Eurasian organization led by China and Russia focused on economic, political and military cooperation.[61]

With the world developing in this direction, Treschow concluded that a loose Western-led trading coalition, perhaps like a resurrected and beefed-up TPP with more members, wasn't a bad thing. Yes, corporate revenues were likely to decline in the first years as companies withdrew from hostile countries, but an alliance of friends and almost-friends would allow the countries involved to set up stable collaboration with an open door for any country wishing to join. It would be a bit of a repeat of the late eighties and early nineties, but beginning with a larger group.

After a couple of decades of such a split world, countries might be ready to give globalization another try – less naïvely this time, and addressing issues, such as climate change, that they had failed to consider in the nineties. 'It will be Globalization 2.0,' Treschow predicted. 'And with it, we'll need to correct all the things that have gone wrong in this round. It will require time and money, and not all companies will survive. We'll see lots of consolidations. But we'll also need lots of new infrastructure in places like Ukraine. We have to hope that there are wise leaders in charge in the US, in Russia, in China and in Europe, all at the same time, and that they conclude that we can't keep going like this.' This new wave of globalization, eventually led by Gen Z, was bound to be more successful. But such harmony was years away. In 2023, regionalization seemed an attractive proposition.

As July arrived and greeted the world with the hottest week ever recorded,[62] the *Wall Street Journal* correspondent Evan Gershkovich was beginning his fourth month in a Russian jail. He'd been arrested by the FSB security service that spring, accused of spying for the United States, and now faced twenty years in prison.[63] The *Wall Street Journal* denounced the charges as ludicrous, but what mattered wasn't Gershkovich's guilt: his detainment was a signal to Americans and other Westerners that they were no longer safe in Russia. The White House strongly warned Americans not to travel to the country.[64]

Michael Cole-Fontayn was following Gershkovich's fate, which was such a brazen assault on the freedom of the press that Western news organizations made a point of keeping the reporter in the news. But even more, he was following new legislation in China. An amended espionage law passed in the spring had just come into effect, banning the sharing of 'documents, data, materials, and items related to national security and interests' – without defining national security and interests.[65] Any expat, and indeed Chinese citizens, now risked arrest on espionage charges. 'It makes the business of business much more complicated,' Cole-Fontayn observed. 'Of course China is within its rights to pass whatever laws it wants to, but we thought we had a liberal order where trade reduced the risk of conflict. Now geopolitics is trumping every trade and business decision. Three-year, five-year, seven-year investments will be seen through a geopolitical lens.' So concerned were underwriters about China's direction that companies found it virtually impossible to get political-risk insurance – the sort of insurance that protects against expropriation and political interference. Foxconn, the Taiwanese company making Apple's iPhones and other devices in its vast Chinese factories, was already beginning to move operations from China to Vietnam and Mexico. 'We hope peace and stability will be something the leaders of these two countries will keep in mind. But as a business, as a CEO, I have to think about what if the worst case happens?' the company's chairman and CEO, Young Liu, told media.[66]

Cole-Fontayn looked back at the world in which he'd spent virtually his whole career. 'It was a wonderful lived dream that we were seduced into thinking was the new reality,' he summarized. 'That new reality existed for thirty years, and now it's rapidly unwinding. The unwinding began in the context of IP theft and then it accelerated under Covid and was vastly accelerated again by Russia's invasion of Ukraine. The world won't be the same again.' Three decades and a bit after the Iron Curtain's fall, it was descending again, with a new combination of nations on its respective sides.

On 8 July, Ukraine marked the 500th day of Russia's invasion of its territory. President Zelenskyy – who had surprised both the Russians and large parts of the world with his ability to inspire the nation, not to mention his skill in convincing Western governments to send his country weapons – travelled to Snake Island, the Black Sea outpost where Ukrainian soldiers had heroically pushed back the invaders during the war's first days.[67] The United Nations reported that the invasion had claimed at least 9,000 civilian lives.[68] The following week brought news that President Recep Tayyip Erdoğan of Turkey had given the green light for Sweden to join NATO.[69] Twenty-six years after enfolding Russia into their midst, G7 leaders announced their nations would formalize their 'enduring support' of Ukraine and promised to continue to send Kyiv weaponry 'across land, air, and sea'.[70] NATO leaders convened in Vilnius, where they promised Ukraine they'd ease its path into the alliance.[71] In Britain, a parliamentary committee found that the British government had been 'so keen to take Chinese money that it has not been watching China's sleight of hand whilst it overtly penetrated the UK's Energy and Industry sectors'.[72]

Hollywood was supposed to deliver relief from the world's woes with a movie about Barbie, that foremost symbol of Western commercial expansion. But while young and old alike were looking forward to fluffy summer entertainment, the movie caused diplomatic controversies even before its release. Film studios had globalized, too, and by now Hollywood depended on the Chinese market if their moves were to make profits. And a film's access to the Chinese market depended on it passing muster with Chinese censors. Wanting to eliminate every risk, Hollywood studios often bent over backwards. *Barbie*'s map of the South China Sea featured Beijing's unilaterally imposed nine-dash line. Vietnam banned the movie and the Philippines permitted its release only with the line blurred.[73]

In Berlin, the government released its new China strategy, and it was a far cry from the past few decades' commercial optimism and *Wandel durch Handel*. 'China is endeavouring to influence the international order in line with the interests of its single-party system and thus to relativize the foundations of the rules-based international order, such as the status of human rights,' the government paper stated, pointing out that China 'is deliberately bringing its economic power to bear to achieve its political goals'.[74] Germany needed to change its approach to China, the paper concluded.[75] Beijing did not respond kindly to its closest Western trading partner's cooling attitude. Germany had succumbed to 'ideological bias and competitive anxiety', China's Berlin embassy declared.[76] Even Siemens was rethinking the borderless commerce that had served it so well. A few weeks after announcing a €140 million investment in the southern Chinese city of Chengdu, the German engineering giant announced it would invest seven times as much in Germany.[77] The same week saw the anniversary of the UN's ruling on China's artificial South China Sea islands, which prompted Beijing to declare the ruling the result of the United States 'ganging up' on China.[78]

A climate emergency, a major land war, globe-linking commerce fracturing: even though globalization had indisputably delivered enormous convenience and a great deal of prosperity to countless citizens of many kinds of countries, the world that Generation Z would eventually take over was also under extreme strain. Has *Wandel durch Handel* failed? I asked Ahmed. Yes, he said, 'and it has failed spectacularly. I have to say this even as a German. It was our big idea for the world, it was how we wanted to change the world. But in which direction is the change happening? Are we, liberal democracies, changing the world, or are autocracies changing us? Today it seems to be the latter. The notion that we have big ideas and are exporting them, well, we were mistaken. The opposite is happening. And we have to beware of more such influence because things will get worse. How Hollywood and other companies have been adjusting to China's wishes, it's very dangerous. We have to be careful that we don't give up on our values.'

If anything was good about the fracturing world, it was that it was fracturing so decisively that there would be no doubt a remake was needed. That remake was certain to include vigorous cross-border trade, but the next version would have to include all those things post-Cold War globalization had neglected to address: citizens' views, job losses, the inevitability of geopolitical friction among some trading partners, the need for an even playing field – and, of course, climate change. Globalization 2.0 was certain to be better.

On Gotland, Artsman thought back to her opposition to Nord Stream. She recalled how, on one occasion, fellow Gotlanders circled her, showing her new YouTube clips of Putin. Wearing an elegant tailored suit, he was singing Fats Domino's classic 'Blueberry Hill' in English to an audience that included Sharon Stone and other Hollywood celebrities.[79] 'And they said, "What a sweet man, do you really believe he'd start a war?"' It was a parable of post-Cold War globalization. Returning to a world of islands for a couple of decades might not be a bad idea.

INTERVIEWEES

Note: titles indicate position at the time of the interviews. All interviewees spoke to the author in a personal capacity.

Bilal Ahmed, tech worker (Germany): interviewed March and July 2023
Solveig Artsman, pensioner, Gotland (Sweden); former local politician: interviewed September 2022 and March 2023
Anders Åslund, former economic advisor to the Russian government: interviewed December 2022
Hana Azari, high-school student (US): interviewed January and March 2023
Ivita Burmistre, Latvian diplomat: interviewed October 2022
Jana Burow, resident of Lubmin (Germany): interviewed October 2022
Kevin Casas-Zamora, director general, International IDEA; former second vice president, Costa Rica: interviewed November 2022 and February 2023
Michael Chertoff, former secretary of homeland security (US); former federal prosecutor: interviewed October and November 2022
Michael Cole-Fontayn, professional board member; former chairman and CEO Europe, Middle East and Africa, BNY Mellon: interviewed in September and October 2022 and February 2023
Gerard Coyne, former labour union executive (UK): interviewed January 2023
Sara Cutrona, office worker (Italy): interviewed February 2023
Sergei Guriev, provost, Sciences Po (France); former rector, New Economic School (Russia): interviewed September 2022 and February 2023
Ben Hitimana, tech worker (UK): interviewed January 2023
Erin Hodgson, university student (US): interviewed January 2023
Mohamed (Mo) Ibrahim, founder and former chairman and CEO, Celtel: interviewed October 2022 and January 2023
Pål Jonson, chair, Swedish Parliament Defence Committee: interviewed April 2021
Alicia Kearns, chair, UK Parliament Foreign Affairs Committee: interviewed September 2022
Keith Krach, chairman, Krach Institute for Tech Diplomacy; former US under secretary of state for economic growth, energy and the environment; former chairman

and CEO, DocuSign; former chairman and CEO, Ariba; former vice president, General Motors: interviewed October 2022 and January 2023

Katrin Krüger, pastor, Lubmin (Germany): interviewed October 2022

Joachim Lang, former director general, Federation of German Industries; former senior government official: interviewed October 2022 and January 2023

Achim Langert, resident of Lubmin (Germany): interviewed October 2022

Giorgio La Malfa, former chairman, Italian Parliament Finance Committee; former minister of European affairs; former minister of budget and economic planning: interviewed December 2022

Ciaran Martin, professor of the practice of politics, University of Oxford; founding CEO, UK National Cyber Security Centre: interviewed December 2021 and by email

Tom Mulholland, university student (UK): interviewed January 2023

Pauline Neville-Jones, member of the UK House of Lords; former diplomat and Dayton Accords negotiator; former security minister: interviewed October 2022 and February 2023

Maria Ohisalo, minister of the environment and climate change, Finland; leader of the Green League: interviewed August 2022 and by email

Robert Okine, tech entrepreneur, Accra (Ghana): interviewed November 2022

Antony Perillo, footwear executive: interviewed October and December 2022

Martyn Richardson, businessman, Oldbury (UK): interviewed January 2023

Neil Roberts, secretary, Joint War Committee: interviewed December 2022

Gurinder Singh, businessman, Sandwell (UK): interviewed January 2023

Gintarė Skaistė, minister of finance, Republic of Lithuania: interviewed October 2022 and by email

John Spellar, member of the UK Parliament (Labour); senior opposition member on the Defence Select Committee: interviewed October 2022 and January 2023

Karl-Henrik Sundström, professional board member; former CFO and executive vice president, Ericsson; former CEO, Stora Enso: interviewed September and November 2022

Alison Taylor, clinical professor, New York University Stern School of Business: interviewed February 2023

Michael Treschow, professional board member; former chairman, Unilever; former chairman, Ericsson; former CEO, Electrolux; former CEO, Atlas Copco: interviewed March, September and November 2022 and by email

Michael (Mike) Turner, chair, US House of Representatives' Permanent Select Committee on Intelligence; member of the US House of Representatives Armed Services Committee; former mayor of Dayton, Ohio: interviewed March 2023

Mārcis Vanags, secondary-school student (Latvia): interviewed December 2022

Axel Vogt, mayor of Lubmin (Germany): interviewed October 2022

Louis Weise, university student (Germany): interviewed July 2023

ENDNOTES

EPIGRAPH

1. Anatoly Chernyaev, 'The Diary of Anatoly S. Chernyaev 1991', https://nsarchive2.gwu.edu/NSAEBB/NSAEBB345/The%20Diary%20of%20Anatoly%20Chernyaev,%201991.pdf, p. 28 (p. 29 if using online numbering).

INTRODUCTION

1. Jenny Nilsson, 'Artsman vägrar "sälja" Gotland', *Gotlands Tidningar*, 17 July 2007.
2. 'Kommunfullmäktige Protokoll', 17 March 2008, Gotlands Kommun, https://www.gotland.se/36964.

CHAPTER 1: THE BIG BANG

1. David Lane, 'Russian Banks and the Soviet Legacy', University of Cambridge, 2001, https://www.jbs.cam.ac.uk/wp-content/uploads/2020/08/wp0109-1.pdf, p. 6.
2. David McClintick, 'How Harvard Lost Russia', *Institutional Investor*, 12 January 2006, https://www.institutionalinvestor.com/article/b150npp3q49x7w/how-harvard-lost-russia.
3. Kari Liuhto, 'Foreign Investment in Estonia: A Statistical Approach', *Europe-Asia Studies*, 47, no. 3 (May 1995), p. 508, https://www.jstor.org/stable/pdf/152573.pdf?refreqid=excelsior%3A1b5d84558dbc03d7b1c9bf7ad4f10033&ab_segments=&origin.
4. Engines of the Red Army in WW2, 'GAZ-A Staff Car', https://www.o5m6.de/redarmy/gaz_a.php.
5. 'Fiat's Soviet Venture', *New York Times*, 23 January 1972, https://www.nytimes.com/1972/01/23/archives/fiats-soviet-venture.html.
6. 'Togliatti(grad)', Esodoc, https://esodoc.eu/index.php/projects/507-togliatti-grad.
7. Stuart Dowell, 'Coca-Cola Arrived in Poland 50 Years Ago This Week and Brought With It a Taste of Freedom', *First News*, 21 July 2022, https://www.

thefirstnews.com/article/coca-cola-arrived-in-poland-50-years-ago-this-week-and-brought-with-it-a-taste-of-freedom-31885.

8. 'Die Internationale Spedition der DDR', Zeitreisen Deutsch-Deutscher Alltag, https://www.geschichte-doku.de/deutsch-deutscher-alltag/themen/?a=deutrans.
9. Arthur Sullivan, 'Russian Gas in Germany: A 50-year Relationship', *DW*, 3 September 2022, https://www.dw.com/en/russian-gas-in-germany-a-complicated-50-year-relationship/a-61057166; NATO, '1979: The Soviet Union Deploys its SS20 Missiles and NATO Responds', 4 March 2009, https://www.nato.int/cps/en/natohq/opinions_139274.htm.
10. David E. Hoffman, 'Reagan Approved Plan to Sabotage Soviets', *Washington Post*, 27 February 2004, https://www.washingtonpost.com/archive/politics/2004/02/27/reagan-approved-plan-to-sabotage-soviets/a9184eff-47fd-402e-beb2-63970851e130; George W. Ball, 'The Case Against Sanctions', *New York Times Magazine*, 12 September 1982, https://www.nytimes.com/1982/09/12/magazine/the-case-against-sanctions.html; Bernard Gwertzman, 'Reagan Lifts Sanctions on Sales for Soviet Pipeline; Reports Accord with Allies', *New York Times*, 14 November 1982, https://www.nytimes.com/1982/11/14/world/reagan-lifts-sanctions-on-sales-for-soviet-pipeline-reports-accord-with-allies.html.
11. Licence production is the manufacturing of companies' goods under special government permit in another country. This method was common for the production of Western goods in the Warsaw Pact. See, for example, Aleksandra Komornicka, 'Socialist Poland's Opening Towards the West, 1970–1980', doctoral thesis, EUI, June 2021, cadmus.eui.eu/bitstream/handle/1814/71778/Kormornicka_2021_HEC.pdf?sequence=1&isAllowed=n.
12. Ceri Parker, 'The World Economic Forum at 50: A Timeline of Highlights from Davos and Beyond', World Economic Forum, 20 December 2019, https://www.weforum.org/agenda/2019/12/world-economic-forum-davos-at-50-history-a-timeline-of-highlights.
13. 'When Was the First British Airways Flight to China?', China-Britain Business Focus, 2 May 2022, https://focus.cbbc.org/when-was-the-first-british-airways-flight-to-china/#.Y0HvSXbMI2w; 'Welcome to China', *Spiegel*, 6 July 1980, https://www.spiegel.de/wirtschaft/willkommen-in-china-a-2020b833-0002-0001-0000-000014329920.
14. '1982–1991: Neue Marken, neue Märkte', Volkswagen, https://www.volkswagenag.com/de/group/history/chronicle/1982-1991.html; Matt Gasnier, 'China 1986–1995: VW Santana Launches Chinese Motorisation', *Best Selling Cars Blog*, 7 January 1996, https://bestsellingcarsblog.com/1996/01/china-1986-1995-vw-santana-launches-chinese-motorisation; 'Foreign companies in China in the early days of reform and opening up', Invest in China, updated 24 January 2019, https://investinchina.chinadaily.com.cn/s/201901/24/WS5c78effe498e27e3380395a7/foreign-companies-in-china-in-the-early-days-of-reform-and-opening-up.html.
15. Theodore Levitt, 'The Globalization of Markets', *Harvard Business Review*, May 1983, https://hbr.org/1983/05/the-globalization-of-markets.
16. Ilan Ben-Meir, 'That Time Trump Spent Nearly $100,000 on an Ad Criticizing U.S. Foreign Policy In 1987', *Buzzfeed News,* 10 July 2015, https://www.buzzfeednews.com/article/ilanbenmeir/that-time-trump-spent-nearly-100000-on-an-ad-criticizing-us.

17. Bonnie Campbell (ed.), 'Regulating Mining in Africa: For Whose Benefit?', Nordiska Afrikainstitutet, Uppsala, 2004, https://www.diva-portal.org/smash/get/diva2:240515/FULLTEXT02.pdf.
18. George White, 'U.S. Firms Lift Taboo on Doing Business in China', *Los Angeles Times*, 1 December 1990, https://www.latimes.com/archives/la-xpm-1990-12-01-fi-4865-story.html.
19. 'Mobile Phones – From Luggables to Pocket Phones', Ericsson, https://www.ericsson.com/en/about-us/history/products/mobile-telephony/mobile-phones–from-luggables-to-pocket-phones.
20. Fred Hiatt, 'Russian Bankers, Fearing for Their Lives, Schedule a Protest', *Washington Post*, 7 December 1993, https://www.washingtonpost.com/archive/politics/1993/12/07/russian-bankers-fearing-for-their-lives-schedule-a-protest/aa1a9c45-2e54-4dd6-b7bf-a76a5e489125.
21. 'Atlas Copco: 140 Years of Achievements by One of the World's Most Innovative and Sustainable Companies', Atlas Copco, https://www.atlascopco.com/content/dam/atlas-copco/microsites/history/documents/atlas-copco-140-years-2018-version.pdf, p. 89 (p. 105 in the PDF).
22. Juan Carlos Hidalgo, 'Growth without Poverty Reduction: The Case of Costa Rica', CATO Institute, 23 January 2014, https://www.cato.org/economic-development-bulletin/growth-without-poverty-reduction-case-costa-rica.
23. Ibid.
24. Kevin Rafferty, 'China's Grasp and Hong Kong's Golden Eggs', *Harvard Business Review*, June 1991, https://hbr.org/1991/05/chinas-grasp-and-hong-kongs-golden-eggs.
25. Mārtiņš Bitāns and Vilnis Purviņš, *The Development of Latvia's Economy (1990–2004)*, Latvijas Banka, https://www.bank.lv/images/stories/pielikumi/publikacijas/citaspublikacijas/Bitans_Purvins_EN.pdf, p. 140 (p. 4 in the PDF).
26. Daniel Silva, 'GDP Shrinks 2 Percent as Latvia Battles Russian Crisis', *Baltic Times*, 8 July 1999, https://www.baltictimes.com/news/articles/2400.
27. Leonardo Pataccini, *Western Banks in the Baltic States: A Preliminary Study on Transition, Europeanisation and Financialisation*, 2020, p. 7, https://geofinresearch.eu/wp-content/uploads/Pataccini-2020-GEOFIN-WP-11-final.pdf.
28. Ibid.
29. 'As China Opens Its Doors, Coca-Cola Pours In', *Los Angeles Times*, 8 November 1993, https://www.latimes.com/archives/la-xpm-1993-11-08-fi-54690-story.html.
30. Deng Xiaoping, 'Excerpts from Talks given in Wuchang, Shenzhen, Zhuhai and Shanghai', 18 January–21 February 1992, https://olemiss.edu/courses/pol324/dengxp92.htm.
31. Mark Buckle, 'Black Cat, White Cat', *China Daily*, 8 February 2018, https://www.chinadaily.com.cn/a/201808/02/WS5b728ae4a310add14f385b4a.html.
32. 'Our Mission', World Economic Forum, https://www.weforum.org/about/world-economic-forum.
33. Nicholas Snow, 'If Goods Don't Cross Borders', Foundation for Economic Education, https://fee.org/resources/if-goods-dont-cross-borders.
34. Until the early 2004s, *Wandel durch Handel* was often called *Wandel durch Annäherung*.
35. 'A Strong Partnership: 25 Years of SKODA and Volkswagen', Skoda, press release, 30 March 2016, https://skodamedia.com/en-gb/releases/660.

36. 'Warum die Kernenergie in der DDR als "sicher" galt', NDR, 4 March 2022, https://www.ndr.de/geschichte/schauplaetze/Wo-die-Atomenergie-als-sicher-galt-Das-DDR-KKW-Lubmin,kernkraft102.html.

CHAPTER 2: COMPANIES WITHOUT BORDERS

1. 'The History of Mobile Phone Technology', Red Orbit, 4 May 2018, https://www.redorbit.com/reference/the-history-of-mobile-phone-technology.
2. 'Power Up! The Amazing Evolution of the Cellphone Battery', Microsoft Windows blog, 25 May 2011, https://blogs.windows.com/devices/2011/05/25/power-up-the-amazing-evolution-of-the-cellphone-battery.
3. Nigel Linge, 'Motorola Brought Us the Mobile Phone, But Ended Up Merged Out of Existence', *The Conversation*, 13 January 2016, https://theconversation.com/motorola-brought-us-the-mobile-phone-but-ended-up-merged-out-of-existence-33967.
4. Kent German, 'Nokia: A Long and Innovative History', CNET, 25 February 2018, https://www.cnet.com/pictures/nokia-a-long-and-innovative-history-photos.
5. 'China Plant for Motorola', *New York Times*, 28 March 1992, https://www.nytimes.com/1992/03/28/business/china-plant-for-motorola.html.
6. Tom Gnau, '6 Businesses That Helped Build Dayton', *Dayton.com*, 11 July 2020, https://www.dayton.com/business/economy/businesses-that-helped-build-dayton/TSftUOIDYav5EhXDYudD3M.
7. Samuel Staley, 'Dayton, Ohio: The Rise and Fall of a Former Industrial Juggernaut', Reason Foundation, 11 August 2008, https://reason.org/commentary/dayton-ohio-the-rise-and-fall.
8. 'Wright-Patterson Air Force Base: The First Century', WPAFB, https://www.wpafb.af.mil/Portals/60/documents/Index/History-of-WPAFB.pdf.
9. 'Overview: Preface to the IPCC Overview', Intergovernmental Panel on Climate Change, https://www.ipcc.ch/site/assets/uploads/2018/05/ipcc_90_92_assessments_far_overview.pdf, p. 52.
10. 'The Richardson Business was Founded More Than 70 Years Ago in Oldbury, Part of the Black Country and Still Home to the Midlands Office Today', https://www.richardsons.co.uk/our-family-business.
11. Johan Peter Murmann et al., 'Huawei's Intellectual Property Management Transformation', in X. Wu, J. Murmann, C. Huang and B. Guo, *The Management Transformation of Huawei: From Humble Beginnings to Global Leadership*, Cambridge: Cambridge University Press, 2020, pp. 347–80, https://www.cambridge.org/core/books/abs/management-transformation-of-huawei/huaweis-intellectual-property-management-transformation/0B6C66CABAE9A2835F20663247128A26, p. 349.
12. Ibid., p. 362.
13. Paul Wiseman, 'In Trade Wars of 200 Years Ago, the Pirates Were Americans', Associated Press, 28 March 2019, https://apnews.com/article/b40414d22f2248428ce11ff36b88dc53.
14. Murmann et al., 'Huawei's Intellectual Property Management Transformation', p. 362.
15. 'Investing in China as Its Economy Starts to Take Off in the 1990s', Association for Diplomatic Studies and Training, 17 May 2021, https://adst.org/2021/05/investing-in-china-as-its-economy-starts-to-take-off-in-the-1990s.
16. Again, unless noted otherwise, 'the West' refers throughout to liberal democracies in Europe and North America as well as Japan, South Korea, Australia and New Zealand.

17. Lynn D. Nelson and Irina Y. Kuzes, *An Assessment of the Russian Voucher Privatization Program*, Virginia Commonwealth University and Znanie-sila, 23 March 1994, i, https://www.ucis.pitt.edu/nceeer/1994-808-01-3-Nelson.pdf.
18. Ericsson, Annual Report, 1994, https://www.annualreports.com/HostedData/AnnualReportArchive/l/NASDAQ_ERIC_1994.pdf, p. 7 (p. 8 in the PDF).
19. Al Ehrbar, 'The Great Bond Market Massacre', CNN Money, 17 October 1994, https://money.cnn.com/magazines/fortune/fortune_archive/1994/10/17/79850/index.htm.
20. Laurence J. C. Ma and Chusheng Lin, 'Development of Towns in China: A Case Study of Guangdong Province', *Population Council*, 19, no. 3 (September 1993), p. 590, https://www.jstor.org/stable/pdf/2938467.pdf?refreqid=excelsior%3A11e5dc0ddd89be6e134fab990432c5d9&ab_segments=&origin.
21. 'Xinjiang, China's Restive Northwest', Human Rights Watch, 31 October 2000, https://www.hrw.org/news/2000/10/31/xinjiang-chinas-restive-northwest.
22. Nicolas Becquelin, 'Xinjiang in the Nineties', *China Journal*, no. 44 (July 2000), p. 81, https://www.jstor.org/stable/pdf/2667477.pdf?refreqid=excelsior%3A328b6d549e18c21764bc66d17b78e47e&ab_segments=&origin=&acceptTC=1.
23. Michael Haynes, 'The Evolution of the Economy of the West Midlands 1750–2007', working paper, University of Wolverhampton, January 2008, https://www.researchgate.net/publication/311666902_2008_The_Evolution_of_the_Economy_of_the_West_Midlands_1750-2007.
24. 'A Brief History of NSF and the Internet', National Science Foundation, 13 August 2003, https://www.nsf.gov/news/news_summ.jsp?cntn_id=103050.
25. 'Investing in China as Its Economy Starts to Take Off in the 1990s', Association for Diplomatic Studies and Training, https://adst.org/2021/05/investing-in-china-as-its-economy-starts-to-take-off-in-the-1990s.
26. Naveed Hussain, 'Jolie Highlights the Continuing Suffering of the Displaced in Bosnia', UN Refugee Agency, 6 April 2010, https://www.unhcr.org/en-us/news/latest/2010/4/4bbb422512/jolie-highlights-continuing-suffering-displaced-bosnia.html.
27. *Bosnia, 1995 – Operation Deliberate Force*, Brookings Institution, https://www.brookings.edu/wp-content/uploads/2017/04/9780815732419_ch1.pdf, p. 3.
28. Peter Green, 'For Daewoo Group, Eastern Europe Remains Mostly in the Red', *New York Times*, 7 November 1999, https://www.nytimes.com/1999/11/07/business/business-for-daewoo-group-eastern-europe-remains-mostly-in-the-red.html.
29. 'Sony Closes Hungary Plant, Will Move to Malaysia', Manufacturing Net, 3 June 2010, https://www.manufacturing.net/home/news/13231903/sony-closes-hungary-plant-will-move-to-malaysia.
30. 'Goodyear Tire & Rubber Company Form 10-K', https://doc.morningstar.com/Document/a76ddfa57d6cc4f5.msdoc/original?clientid=globaldocuments&key=52dbc583e1012395. See also Jeffry A. Frieden, *Global Capitalism: Its Fall and Rise in the Twentieth Century, and Its Stumbles in the Twenty-first*, New York: W. W. Norton (reissue edn), 2020, p. 432.
31. Tom Wilson, 'Oligarchs, Power and Profits: The History of BP in Russia', *Financial Times*, 24 March 2022, https://www.ft.com/content/e9238fa2-65a2-4753-a845-ce8129f93a0c.
32. Volkswagen, *Annual Report 1996*, https://www.volkswagen-group.com/en/publications/corporate/annual-report-1996-2314, p. 37 (p. 39 in the PDF).
33. Ericsson, *Annual Report 1996*, https://www.annualreports.com/HostedData/AnnualReportArchive/l/NASDAQ_ERIC_1996.pdf, p. 6 (p. 8 in the PDF).

34. Art Buchwald, 'Up in Arms', *Washington Post*, 7 May 1981, https://www.washingtonpost.com/archive/lifestyle/1981/05/07/up-in-arms/b94dcf78-b556-44bd-9ba9-e8bd80c7b76c.
35. 'The New Ford Everest Starts Production in China; Marks Expansion of 20-year Partnership Between Ford And JMC', Ford Media Center, 19 August 2015, https://media.ford.com/content/fordmedia/fap/cn/en/news/2015/08/19/the-new-ford-everest-starts-production-in-china–marks-expansion.html.
36. George Parker, 'A Fiscal Focus', *Financial Times*, 7 December 2009, https://www.ft.com/content/5f0bf460-e36d-11de-8d36-00144feab49a.
37. 'Speech by President and CEO Michael Treschow', Electrolux Group, 27 April 1999, https://news.cision.com/electrolux/r/speech-by-president-and-ceo-michael-treschow,c8558.
38. 'The Electrolux Group Forms New Joint Venture in India', Electrolux Group, 30 September 1998, https://news.cision.com/electrolux/r/the-electrolux-group-forms-new-joint-venture-in-india,c4070.
39. Kester Eddy, 'Investor Profile: Takeover is Hungarian Rhapsody for Electrolux', *Financial Times*, 29 November 2010, https://www.ft.com/content/4a7a13b4-fb50-11df-b576-00144feab49a.

CHAPTER 3: BANKERS CONQUER NEW TERRITORY

1. Alan Cullison and Thomas Grove, '"Last Man Standing": An American Investor in Russia Takes a Fall', *Wall Street Journal*, 31 July 2019, https://www.wsj.com/articles/last-man-standing-an-american-investor-in-russia-takes-a-fall-11564603365.
2. 'Inside Perspectives: An Interview with Michael Calvey of Baring Vostok', Global Private Capital Association, 27 March 2013, https://www.globalprivatecapital.org/research/inside-perspectives-an-interview-with-michael-calvey-of-baring-vostok-2.
3. Ilaria Maria Sala, 'Story of Cities #39: Shenzhen – From Rural Village to the World's Largest Megalopolis', *Guardian*, 10 May 2016, https://www.theguardian.com/cities/2016/may/10/story-of-cities-39-shenzhen-from-rural-village-to-the-worlds-largest-megalopolis.
4. 'Expanding Its Commitment to China, Goldman Sachs Opens Offices in Beijing and Shanghai', Goldman Sachs, https://www.goldmansachs.com/our-firm/history/moments/1994-beijing-shanghai.html; 'The Shanghai Stock Exchange Reopens in 1990', Goldman Sachs, https://www.goldmansachs.com/our-firm/history/moments/1990-shanghai-stock-exchange-reopens.html.
5. Carl Quinn and Dylan Schulz, 'Banking in the 1990s: Challenge and Change', Federal Reserve Bank of Chicago, October 1992, https://www.chicagofed.org/publications/chicago-fed-letter/1992/october-62.
6. Ivan Turok and Nicola Edge, *The Jobs Gap in Britain's Cities: Employment Loss and Labour Market Consequences*, Joseph Rowntree Foundation, 1999, https://www.jrf.org.uk/sites/default/files/jrf/migrated/files/1861347685.pdf, p. 43.
7. Michael Haynes, 'The Evolution of the Economy of the West Midlands 1750–2007', working paper, University of Wolverhampton, 2008, 17, https://www.researchgate.net/publication/311666902_2008_The_Evolution_of_the_Economy_of_the_West_Midlands_1750-2007.

8. 'Asian Financial Crisis: July 1997–December 1998', Federal Reserve History, https://www.federalreservehistory.org/essays/asian-financial-crisis.
9. 'GDP Growth (Annual %) – Thailand', World Bank, https://data.worldbank.org/indicator/NY.GDP.MKTP.KD.ZG?locations=TH.
10. Harry Bouwman et al., 'How Nokia Failed to Nail the Smartphone Market', Leibniz-Informationszentrum Wirtschaft, 2014, https://www.econstor.eu/bitstream/10419/101414/1/794346243.pdf, p. 4.
11. Gordon Kelly, 'Finland and Nokia: An Affair to Remember', *Wired*, 10 April 2013, https://www.wired.co.uk/article/finland-and-nokia.
12. Joseph Kahn and Timothy L. O'Brien, 'Easy Money: A Special Report', *New York Times*, 18 October 1998, https://www.nytimes.com/1998/10/18/business/easy-money-special-report-for-russia-its-us-bankers-match-wasn-t-made-heaven.html.

CHAPTER 4: 9/11, ENRON AND OTHER DISRUPTIONS

1. Margot Hornblower, 'Mafia "Commission" Trial Begins in New York', *Washington Post*, 19 September 1986, https://www.washingtonpost.com/archive/politics/1986/09/19/mafia-commission-trial-begins-in-new-york/32605294-3cc3-4498-afdb-08bed52d463f.
2. Ed Magnuson, 'Headhunters: A Jury Convicts Eight Mobsters', *Time*, 1 December 1986, https://content.time.com/time/subscriber/article/0,33009,962969,00.html.
3. Dick Carozza, 'An Interview with Michael Chertoff', *Fraud Magazine*, March/April 2009, https://www.fraud-magazine.com/article.aspx?id=236.
4. Harumi Ito and Darin Lee, 'Assessing the Impact of the September 11 Terrorist Attacks on U.S. Airline Demand', *National Library of Medicine*, 28 October 2004, pp. 75–95, https://www.ncbi.nlm.nih.gov/pmc/articles/PMC7112671.
5. 'Richard Reid's Shoes', US Federal Bureau of Investigation, https://www.fbi.gov/history/artifacts/richard-reids-shoes.
6. 'Lithuanian Human Development Report', United Nations Development Programme in Lithuania, 2000, p. 28, https://hdr.undp.org/system/files/documents//lithuania2000enpdf.pdf.
7. Max Seddon, 'Gleb Pavlovsky, Russian Spin Doctor, 1951–2023', *Financial Times*, 10 March 2023, https://www.ft.com/content/9a101862-7f39-4894-9bf6-ac0636f2e08f.
8. Ian Traynor, 'No Softening as Putin Plans Direct Rule for Chechnya', *Guardian*, 6 May 2000, https://www.theguardian.com/world/2000/may/06/chechnya.russia.
9. The WEF Global Leaders for Tomorrow programme was a precursor to the WEF Young Global Leaders.
10. 'Our Companies', Investor, https://www.investorab.com/our-investments/?company=astrazeneca; Henry Sender and Connie Ling, 'Softbank to Invest $20 Million In Hong Kong's Alibaba.com', *Wall Street Journal*, 18 January 2000, https://www.wsj.com/articles/SB948202996877749173.
11. 'WEF/Global Leaders for Tomorrow/2001', WikiSpooks, https://wikispooks.com/wiki/WEF/Global_Leaders_for_Tomorrow/2001.
12. John O'Loughlin et al., 'A "Risky Westward Turn"? Putin's 9-11 Script and Ordinary Russians', *Europe-Asia Studies*, 56, no. 1 (January 2004), https://www.jstor.org/stable/pdf/4147436.pdf?refreqid=excelsior%3Afcc1ecf52224a5671b21a16dbe62b550&ab_segments=&origin=&initiator=&acceptTC=1, p. 2 (p. 3 in the PDF).

13. 'China in the WTO: Past, Present and Future', Permanent Mission of China to the WTO, December 2011, https://www.wto.org/english/thewto_e/acc_e/s7lu_e.pdf.
14. 'Trade in Goods with China', United States Census Bureau, https://www.census.gov/foreign-trade/balance/c5700.html.
15. Andre Barbe and David Riker, 'The Effects of Offshoring on U.S. Workers: A Review of the Literature', *United States International Trade Commission Journal of International Commerce and Economics* (June 2018), p. 3, https://www.usitc.gov/publications/332/journals/offshoring_and_labor_final.pdf.
16. 'Unilever Chairman Michael Treschow', Hunt Search Group, https://www.huntsearch.com/viewnews.asp?id=667.
17. Phil Taylor, '"India Calling to the Far Away Towns": The Call Centre Labour Process And Globalization', *Work Employment and Society*, 19, no. 2 (June 2005), p. 262, https://www.researchgate.net/publication/258200336_'India_calling_to_the_far_away_towns'_The_call_centre_labour_process_and_globalization/link/6096915b92851c490fc53057/download.
18. 'SEC Charges a Former High-Ranking Enron Official with Fraud', Securities and Exchange Commission, press release, 21 August 2002, https://www.sec.gov/news/press/2002-126.htm.
19. Frances Ann Burns, '"Crazy Eddie" Sentenced to 12 Years', UPI, 29 April 1994, https://www.upi.com/Archives/1994/04/29/Crazy-Eddie-sentenced-to-12-years/2707767592000.
20. Seth Mydans and Erin E. Arvedlund, 'Police in Russia Seize Oil Tycoon', *New York Times*, 26 October 2003, https://www.nytimes.com/2003/10/26/world/police-in-russia-seize-oil-tycoon.html.
21. 'Funnies: Report Card from "Fiasco Junior High"', ABC News, 20 November 2005, https://abcnews.go.com/ThisWeek/story?id=1330895.
22. Salman Ahmed, 'U.S. Foreign Policy for the Middle Class: Perspectives from Ohio', Ohio State University and Carnegie Endowment for International Peace, 2018, https://www.policymattersohio.org/files/research/tradereport.pdf, p. 3.
23. Mark Williams, 'Ohio Unemployment Rate Lowest since August 2001', *Columbus Dispatch*, https://www.dispatch.com/story/business/2015/11/20/ohio-unemployment-rate-lowest-since/24149508007.
24. Alysha Webb, 'GM Probes Alleged Case of Car Theft by Chinese Automaker', *Autoweek*, 16 July 2003, https://www.autoweek.com/news/a2100061/gm-probes-alleged-case-car-theft-chinese-automaker.
25. 'GM Settles Case with Chery', Associated Press, 19 November 2005, https://www.dailynews.com/2005/11/19/gm-settles-case-with-chery.
26. 'Arbeitslosengeld II – Hartz IV – Bürgergeld', Landeszentrale für politische Bildung Baden-Württemberg, https://www.lpb-bw.de/hartz-iv.
27. *Nedläggning av P18*, Region Gotland, 3 March 2004, https://www.gotland.se/servlet/GetDoc?meta_id=13379.
28. US Department of Justice, 'United States v. Jeffrey K. Skilling', press release, 21 June 2013, https://www.justice.gov/criminal-vns/case/united-states-v-jeffrey-k-skilling#:~:text=A%20federal%20jury%20found%20Skilling,On%20Jan.
29. Frederic Wehrey et al., 'Economic Expansion: The IRGC's Business Conglomerate and Public Works', in *The Rise of the Pasdaran: Assessing the Domestic Roles of Iran's Islamic Revolutionary Guards Corps*, RAND Corporation, 2009, pp. 55–76,

https://www.jstor.org/stable/pdf/10.7249/mg821osd.12.pdf?refreqid=excelsior%3A4c737c1427c797bd8a5d1f02cb12c8df&ab_segments=&origin=&initiator=&acceptTC=1, p. 58.
30. Philip H. Gordon, 'The Crisis in the Alliance', Brookings Institution, 24 February 2003, https://www.brookings.edu/articles/the-crisis-in-the-alliance.

CHAPTER 5: THE RACE FOR MOBILE-TELEPHONY SUPREMACY

1. Ray Le Maistre, 'Huawei Reports 2008 Revenues of $18.3B', *LightReading*, 22 April 2009, https://www.lightreading.com/huawei-reports-2008-revenues-of-$183b/d/d-id/667148; Murmann et al., 'Huawei's Intellectual Property Management Transformation', p. 364.
2. 'Cisco Sues Huawei Over IP "Theft"', *Register*, 24 January 2003, https://www.theregister.com/2003/01/24/cisco_sues_huawei_over_ip.
3. Mark Chandler, 'Huawei and Cisco's Source Code: Correcting the Record', *Cisco Blogs*, 11 October 2012, https://blogs.cisco.com/news/huawei-and-ciscos-source-code-correcting-the-record.
4. Natalie Obiko Pearson, 'Did a Chinese Hack Kill Canada's Greatest Tech Company?', Bloomberg, 1 July 2020, https://www.bloomberg.com/news/features/2020-07-01/did-china-steal-canada-s-edge-in-5g-from-nortel?leadSource=uverify%20wall.
5. Tom Blackwell, 'Exclusive: Did Huawei Bring Down Nortel? Corporate Espionage, Theft, and the Parallel Rise and Fall of Two Telecom Giants', *National Post*, 20 February 2020, https://nationalpost.com/news/exclusive-did-huawei-bring-down-nortel-corporate-espionage-theft-and-the-parallel-rise-and-fall-of-two-telecom-giants.
6. Siobhan Gorman, 'Chinese Hackers Suspected in Long-Term Nortel Breach', *Wall Street Journal*, 14 February 2012, https://www.wsj.com/articles/SB10001424052970203363504577187502201577054.
7. Alexandra Harney, 'Huawei – the Challenger from China', *Financial Times*, 10 January 2005, https://www.ft.com/content/fb6f52ac-6339-11d9-bec2-00000e2511c8.
8. Jenny C. Aker and Isaac M. Mbiti, 'Mobile Phones and Economic Development in Africa', *Journal of Economic Perspectives*, 24, no. 3 (Summer 2010), p. 207, https://pubs.aeaweb.org/doi/pdfplus/10.1257/jep.24.3.207.
9. Ibid., p. 207.
10. Ibid., p. 211.
11. 'Mo Ibrahim: Sudanese-British Entrepreneur', *Britannica*, https://www.britannica.com/biography/Mo-Ibrahim.
12. 'Trade and Development Report, 2005', UNCTAD, https://unctad.org/system/files/official-document/tdr2005_en.pdf, p. v.
13. 'World Investment Report', UNCTAD, https://unctad.org/system/files/official-document/wir2006ch1_en.pdf#page=2, p. 4 (p. 3 in the PDF).
14. Chinese Loans to Africa Database, Boston University Global Development Policy Center, https://www.bu.edu/gdp/chinese-loans-to-africa-database.
15. Dan Strumpf, 'ZTE's State Owner to Cut Its Stake', *Wall Street Journal*, 31 March 2019, https://www.wsj.com/articles/ztes-state-owner-to-cut-its-stake-11552477396.

16. 'China's Mighty Telecom Footprint in Africa', New Security Learning, http://www.newsecuritylearning.com/index.php/archive/75-chinas-mighty-telecom-footprint-in-africa.
17. 'China in Africa: 11. The Role of China's Financial Institutions', Institute of Developing Economies Japan External Trade Organization, https://www.ide.go.jp/English/Data/Africa_file/Manualreport/cia_11.html; 'China in Africa: 6. China's Telecommunications Footprint in Africa', Institute of Developing Economies Japan External Trade Organization, https://www.ide.go.jp/English/Data/Africa_file/Manualreport/cia_09.html.
18. 'China Citizen Pleads Guilty to Unauthorized Access of a Software Company with Intent to Defraud', US Department of Justice, 7 July 2004, https://www.justice.gov/archive/criminal/cybercrime/press-releases/2004/shanPlea.htm.
19. 'Costa Rica: Increase in Mobile Phone Penetration', Central American Data, 27 February 2018, https://www.centralamericadata.com/en/article/home/Costa_Rica_Mobile_Phone_Penetration_Grows.
20. 'Huawei's $30 Billion China Credit Opens Doors in Brazil, Mexico', Bloomberg, 25 April 2011, https://www.bloomberg.com/news/articles/2011-04-25/huawei-counts-on-30-billion-china-credit-to-open-doors-in-brazil-mexico?leadSource=uverify%20wall.
21. 'Two Engineers Indicted in Economic Espionage', *Los Angeles Times*, 27 September 2007, https://www.latimes.com/archives/la-xpm-2007-sep-27-me-espionage27-story.html; 'Suburban Chicago Woman Sentenced to Four Years in Prison for Stealing Motorola Trade Secrets before Boarding Plane to China', FBI, https://archives.fbi.gov/archives/chicago/press-releases/2012/suburban-chicago-woman-sentenced-to-four-years-in-prison-for-stealing-motorola-trade-secrets-before-boarding-plane-to-china.
22. David Barboza, 'Chinese Economy Grows 10.7 Percent in 2006', *New York Times*, 25 January 2007, https://www.nytimes.com/2007/01/25/business/worldbusiness/25iht-yuan.4345858.html; John Wong, 'China's Economy in 2005: At a New Turning Point and Need to Fix Its Development Problems', Wiley Online Library, 5 April 2006, https://onlinelibrary.wiley.com/doi/abs/10.1111/j.1749-124X.2006.00010.x#:~:text=1%20%E2%80%9CChina's%20economy%20grew%20at,Daily%20(%2026%20January%202006).
23. Katie Logisz, 'Speaker Hastert Calls for Open Lines of Communication with Mayors', United States Conference of Mayors, 9 February 2004, https://web.archive.org/web/20090404115336/http://www.usmayors.org/usmayornewspaper/documents/02_09_04/hastert.asp.
24. 'Reciprocity and Fairness in Foreign Investment Act', *Congress.gov*, https://www.congress.gov/bill/109th-congress/house-bill/4959?s=6&r=16.
25. Dave Lee, 'Nokia: The Rise and Fall of a Mobile Giant', BBC News, 3 September 2013, https://www.bbc.com/news/technology-23947212.
26. 'Global ICT Developments', International Telecommunications Union, https://www.itu.int/ITU-D/ict/statistics/ict/#:~:text=By%20the%20end%20of%202007,Asian%20have%20a%20mobile%20phone.
27. 'The Closure of MG Rover', UK Parliament House of Commons Committee of Public Accounts, 12 July 2006, https://publications.parliament.uk/pa/cm200506/cmselect/cmpubacc/1003/1003.pdf, p. 5.
28. 'MG's New Chinese Owners Restart Production', *Manufacturing Business Technology*, 30 May 2007, https://www.mbtmag.com/global/news/13061829/mgs-new-chinese-owners-restart-production.

29. David Kestenbaum, 'The Digital Divide Between McCain And Obama', NPR, 1 August 2008, https://www.npr.org/2008/08/01/93185393/the-digital-divide-between-mccain-and-obama.
30. Hannah Ritchie et al., 'Internet', Our World in Data, https://ourworldindata.org/internet.
31. Hannah Ritchie et al., 'Internet', Our World in Data, https://ourworldindata.org/internet#internet-access.

CHAPTER 6: FRIVOLOUS FINANCIERS CAUSE FINANCIAL TURMOIL

1. Silvia Merler, 'Bad Banks and Rude Awakenings: Italian Banks at a Crossroads', Bruegel, 26 January 2016, https://www.bruegel.org/blog-post/bad-banks-and-rude-awakenings-italian-banks-crossroads.
2. 'Issues Raised by the Lehmans Minibonds Crisis: Report to the Financial Secretary', Securities and Futures Commission, December 2008, https://www.sfc.hk/sfc/doc/EN/general/general/lehman/Review%20Report/Review%20Report.pdf.
3. 'WEF/Young Global Leaders/2006', WikiSpooks, https://wikispooks.com/wiki/WEF/Young_Global_Leaders/2006.
4. 'Gallup Daily: McCain 48%, Obama 44%: McCain Has Held Significant Lead for Last Four Days', Gallup, 11 September 2008, https://news.gallup.com/poll/110227/gallup-daily-mccain-48-obama-44.aspx.
5. Jeffry A. Frieden, *Global Capitalism: Its Fall and Rise in the Twentieth Century, and Its Stumbles in the Twenty-first*, New York: W. W. Norton (reissue edn), 2020, p. 182.
6. Ellen Barry, 'Economist Flees as Russia Aims Past Protesters', *New York Times*, 29 May 2013, https://www.nytimes.com/2013/05/30/world/europe/economist-sergei-guriev-leaves-russia-abruptly.html.
7. Oliver Alexander, 'The Nord Stream Andromeda Story: What We Know and What We Don't', 9 March 2023, https://oalexanderdk.substack.com/p/the-nord-stream-andromeda-story-what.
8. Evan Comen, 'Check Out How Much a Computer Cost the Year You Were Born', *USA Today*, 22 June 2019, https://www.usatoday.com/story/tech/2018/06/22/cost-of-a-computer-the-year-you-were-born/36156373.
9. Ray Davies, 'Vietnam Cowboys', https://www.youtube.com/watch?v=thLpJxoWKSs; Doug Young, 'With Barbie Revamp, Mattel Eyes China Growth', Reuters, 12 January 2010, https://www.reuters.com/article/us-mattel-interview/with-barbie-revamp-mattel-eyes-china-growth-idUSTRE60B1DM20100112; 'Exhibit: House of Barbie Shanghai Flagship Store', *Communication Arts*, https://www.commarts.com/exhibit/house-of-barbie-shanghai-flagship-store; 'Mattel Shuts Flagship Shanghai Barbie Concept Store', BBC News, 7 March 2011, https://www.bbc.com/news/business-12670950.
10. Camille François and Oliver Waine, 'A Social Portrait of the Subprime Crisis', Metro Politics, 14 May 2021, https://metropolitics.org/A-Social-Portrait-of-the-Subprime-Crisis.html; Jeffrey M. Jones, 'Views on the Financial Crisis', Gallup, 2 October 2008, https://news.gallup.com/poll/110797/views-financial-crisis.aspx.
11. 'You Asked, We Answered: Why Didn't Any Wall Street CEOs Go to Jail After the Financial Crisis?', *Marketplace*, https://features.marketplace.org/why-no-ceo-went-jail-after-financial-crisis.

12. 'American Recovery and Reinvestment Act', *Britannica*, https://www.britannica.com/topic/American-Recovery-and-Reinvestment-Act.
13. Joe McGrath, 'The Making of a Mismarker: The Case of the Only Banker Jailed in the U.S. for His Role in the Financial Crash', *University of Chicago Law Review Online*, 7 January 2020, https://lawreviewblog.uchicago.edu/2020/01/07/the-making-of-a-mismarker-the-case-of-the-only-banker-jailed-in-the-u-s-for-his-role-in-the-financial-crash-by-joe-mcgrath; 'Ireland Jails Three Top Bankers Over 2008 Banking Meltdown', Reuters, 29 July 2016, https://www.reuters.com/article/us-ireland-banking-court/ireland-jails-three-top-bankers-over-2008-banking-meltdown-idUSKCN10912E.
14. Richard Milne, 'Olafur Hauksson, the Man Who Jailed Iceland's Bankers', *Financial Times*, 9 December 2016, https://www.ft.com/content/dcdb43d4-bd52-11e6-8b45-b8b81dd5d080.
15. Michael Erman, 'Five Years after Lehman, Americans Still Angry at Wall Street: Reuters/Ipsos Poll', Reuters, 15 September 2013, https://www.reuters.com/article/us-wallstreet-crisis/five-years-after-lehman-americans-still-angry-at-wall-street-reuters-ipsos-poll-idUSBRE98E06Q20130915.
16. Simon Youel, 'Polling: 10 Years after the Financial Crisis, the British Public Still Don't Trust Banks', Positive Money, https://positivemoney.org/2018/08/british-public-dont-trust-banks.
17. Unilever, Annual Report and Accounts, 2008, https://www.unilever.com/files/origin/a4c5f3a134f722d776bd1f4ed9203ce489005c39.pdf/ir-ar08-annual-report.pdf.
18. Katherine Klein, 'How Ben & Jerry's Got Bought Out Without Selling Out', University of Pennsylvania Wharton School, 15 January 2016, https://knowledge.wharton.upenn.edu/article/ben-jerrys-got-bought-without-selling.
19. Christine Wong, 'The Fiscal Stimulus Programme and Public Governance Issues in China', *OECD Journal on Budgeting*, 11, no. 3 (2011), p. 4, https://www.oecd.org/gov/budgeting/Public%20Governance%20Issues%20in%20China.pdf.
20. Ibid., p. 6.
21. David Carlin, 'Why Copenhagen Fell Apart and the Lessons It Offers for COP 27', *Forbes*, 17 November 2022, https://www.forbes.com/sites/davidcarlin/2022/11/17/why-copenhagen-fell-apart-and-the-lessons-it-offers-for-cop-27/?sh=610b71aa5476.
22. 'China: Effects of Intellectual Property Infringement and Indigenous Innovation Policies on the U.S. Economy', US International Trade Commission, May 2011, https://www.usitc.gov/publications/332/pub4226.pdf, p. xv.
23. James Olley, 'Roman Abramovich Has Sold Chelsea, But What is His Legacy at the Club and in England?', ESPN, 31 May 2022, https://www.espn.com/soccer/chelsea-engchelsea/story/4677672/roman-abramovich-has-sold-chelseabut-what-is-his-legacy-at-the-club-and-in-england; Luke Harding and Mark Sweney, 'Russian Oligarch Alexander Lebedev to Buy London *Evening Standard*', *Guardian*, 14 January 2009, https://www.theguardian.com/media/2009/jan/14/russian-oligarch-alexander-lebedev-buy-london-evening-standard.
24. 'UK Scraps Rich Foreign Investor Visa Scheme', BBC News, 17 February 2022, https://www.bbc.com/news/uk-politics-60410844; John Heathershaw et al., 'The UK's Kleptocracy Problem', Chatham House, December 2021, https://

www.chathamhouse.org/sites/default/files/2022-10/2021-12-08-uk-kleptocracy-problem-heathershaw-mayne-et-al.pdf, p. 15.

25. Heathershaw et al., 'The UK's Kleptocracy Problem', p. 15.
26. 'Speech and the Following Discussion at the Munich Conference on Security Policy', Kremlin, 10 February 2007, http://www.en.kremlin.ru/events/president/transcripts/24034.
27. 'Remarks by President Barack Obama In Prague As Delivered', White House, press release, 5 April 2009, https://obamawhitehouse.archives.gov/the-press-office/remarks-president-barack-obama-prague-delivered.
28. 'Remarks by the President at the New Economic School Graduation', White House, press release, 7 July 2009, https://obamawhitehouse.archives.gov/the-press-office/remarks-president-new-economic-school-graduation.
29. 'Today in History: October 9, Obama Wins Nobel Peace Prize', Associated Press, 9 October 2022, https://apnews.com/article/today-in-history-barack-obama-nobel-prizes-che-guevara-ee23adc9d336085ac4c67c9eb9094d52. (The Nobel Prizes are announced in October; the ceremonies take place in December.)
30. Bradley S. Klapper, 'Obama Administration Presence Thin in Davos', NBC News, 20 January 2010, https://www.nbcnews.com/id/wbna34957429.
31. Andrew Clark, 'Dmitry Medvedev Picks Silicon Valley's Brains', *Guardian*, 23 June 2010, https://www.theguardian.com/business/2010/jun/23/dmitry-medvedev-silicon-valley-visit.
32. Ibid.
33. 'Ericsson Chairman Treschow Resigns', *Fierce Wireless*, 5 December 2010, https://www.fiercewireless.com/europe/ericsson-chairman-treschow-resigns.
34. Lucy Killgren, 'Unilever Turns to Treschow as Chairman', *Financial Times*, 12 January 2007, https://www.ft.com/content/8ddcc6ea-a22d-11db-a187-0000779e2340; 'Unilever Chairman Michael Treschow', Hunt Search Group, https://www.huntgroup.com/viewnews.asp?id=667.

CHAPTER 7: A PIPELINE BRIDGING DIVIDES (OR SO IT SEEMS)

1. German Democratic Republic (East Germany).
2. Catherine Tamme, 'Nord Stream 1 and 2: Das Tauziehen ums Gas aus Russland', NDR, 18 November 2022, https://www.ndr.de/geschichte/schauplaetze/Nord-Stream-1-und-2-Der-Zoff-ums-Gas-aus-Russland,nordstream622.html; 'Electric Power Sector CO2 Emissions Drop as Generation Mix Shifts from Coal to Natural Gas', US Energy Information Administration, 9 June 2021, https://www.eia.gov/todayinenergy/detail.php?id=48296.
3. Tamme, 'Nord Stream 1 and 2; 'Who We Are', Nord Stream, https://www.nord-stream.com/about-us/#:~:text=The%20five%20shareholders%20of%20the,Nederlandse%20Gasunie%20and%20ENGIE.
4. *The Nord Stream Gas Pipeline Project and Its Strategic Implications*, European Parliament, 2007, https://www.europarl.europa.eu/RegData/etudes/note/join/2007/393274/IPOL-PETI_NT(2007)393274_EN.pdf.
5. Tamme, 'Nord Stream 1 and 2'.
6. Rolf K. Nilsson, 'Reservation i ärende om avtal med Nord Stream', Gotlands Kommun, 17 March 2008, https://www.gotland.se/36924.
7. *The Nord Stream Gas Pipeline Project and Its Strategic Implications*, European Parliament.

8. 'Nord Stream Preparing for Munitions Clearance', Nord Stream, press release, 2 October 2009, https://www.nord-stream.com/press-info/press-releases/nord-stream-preparing-for-munitions-clearance-366.
9. Simon Pirani, Jonathan Stern and Katja Yafimava, *The Russo-Ukrainian Gas Dispute of January 2009: A Comprehensive Assessment*, Oxford Institute for Energy Studies, February 2009, https://www.oxfordenergy.org/publications/the-russo-ukrainian-gas-dispute-of-january-2009-a-comprehensive-assessment.
10. 'Merkel Urges Progress on Baltic Pipeline', Reuters, 16 January 2009, https://www.reuters.com/article/russia-ukraine-gas-nordstream/merkel-urges-progress-on-baltic-pipeline-idINBAT00262520090116.
11. 'Fukushima Disaster: What Happened at the Nuclear Plant?', BBC News, 10 March 2021, https://www.bbc.com/news/world-asia-56252695.
12. Deepa Seetharaman, 'Automakers Face Paint Shortage after Japan Quake', Reuters, 26 March 2011, https://www.reuters.com/article/us-japan-pigment/automakers-face-paint-shortage-after-japan-quake-idUSTRE72P04B20110326.
13. 'Nach Fukushima: Angela Merkel läutet Atomausstieg ein', SWR2 Archivradio, 14 March 2011, https://www.swr.de/swr2/wissen/archivradio/nach-fukushima-merkel-laeutet-atomausstieg-ein-2011-100.html.
14. 'Nordstream liefert Gas', *Frankfurter Allgemeine Zeitung*, 8 November 2011, https://www.faz.net/aktuell/wirtschaft/pipeline-eroeffnung-nord-stream-liefert-gas-11521668.html.
15. 'Nord Stream Pipeline Inauguration', Nord Stream AG, YouTube, 8 November 2011, https://www.youtube.com/watch?v=zXILH32nYGs.
16. 'Speech by Chancellor Angela Merkel on the Occasion of the Commissioning of the Nord Stream Pipeline', Die Bundesregierung Press and Information Office of the Federal Government, 8 November 2011, https://www.bundeskanzler.de/bk-de/aktuelles/rede-von-bundeskanzlerin-angela-merkel-anlaesslich-der-inbetriebnahme-der-nord-stream-pipeline-470702.
17. 'Nord Stream Pipeline Inauguration', Nord Stream AG.
18. Ibid.

CHAPTER 8: GLOBALIZATION *FLEURS DU MAL*: DECAY AND A FEW LAST HURRAHS

1. Cisco and Juniper are US communications infrastructure companies.
2. Richard Bitzinger, 'Modernising China's Military, 1997–2012', OpenEdition Journals, 2011, https://journals.openedition.org/chinaperspectives/5701.
3. 'The IP Commission Report: The Report of the Commission on the Theft of American Intellectual Property', The National Bureau of Asian Research, NBR, May 2013, https://www.nbr.org/wp-content/uploads/pdfs/publications/IP_Commission_Report.pdf, p. 1 (p. 9 if using online numbering).
4. Ibid., p. 3 (p. 11 if using online numbering).
5. 'SAP to Expand Cloud Presence with Acquisition of Ariba', SAP, press release, 22 May 2012, https://news.sap.com/2012/05/sap-to-expand-cloud-presence-with-acquisition-of-ariba.
6. 'Investigative Report on the U.S. National Security Issues Posed by Chinese Telecommunications Companies Huawei and ZTE, 112th Cong., 8 October 2012', https://republicans-intelligence.house.gov/sites/intelligence.house.gov/files/documents/huawei-zte%20investigative%20report%20(final).pdf, p. vi.

7. Kathy Lally and Will Englund, 'Putin Wins Election as Russian President; Opponents Claim Widespread Fraud', *Washington Post*, 4 March 2012, https://www.washingtonpost.com/world/russians-voting–and-watching/2012/03/04/gIQA3j6CqR_story.html.
8. 'Russian Federation and the WTO', World Trade Organization, https://www.wto.org/english/thewto_e/countries_e/russia_e.htm#:~:text=The%20Russian%20Federation%20has%20been,WTO%20since%2022%20August%202012.
9. World Economic Forum, Annual Meeting 2013, Programme, 23–27 January 2013, https://www3.weforum.org/docs/AM13/WEF_AM13_Programme_3fqmv173dw.pdf.
10. 'Davos 2013 – Scenarios for the Russian Federation', YouTube, https://www.youtube.com/watch?v=_RpOpnREXlg.
11. Ellen Barry, 'Economist Flees as Russia Aims Past Protesters', *New York Times*, 29 May 2013, https://www.nytimes.com/2013/05/30/world/europe/economist-sergei-guriev-leaves-russia-abruptly.html.
12. *Foreign Involvement in the Critical National Infrastructure: The Implications for National Security*, Intelligence and Security Committee, 2013, https://isc.independent.gov.uk/wp-content/uploads/2021/01/20130606_ISC_CNI_Report.pdf, p. 7.
13. George Osborne, Twitter, 16 October 2013, https://twitter.com/george_osborne/status/390398892279619584.
14. 'Chancellor's Speech to Students at Peking University', HM Treasury, 14 October 2013, https://www.gov.uk/government/speeches/chancellors-speech-to-students-at-peking-university.
15. Jim Acosta, 'U.S., Other Powers Kick Russia Out of G8', CNN, 24 March 2014, https://www.cnn.com/2014/03/24/politics/obama-europe-trip/index.html.
16. 'US Sanctions Russia's Rosneft, Novatek', *Argus*, 16 July 2014, https://www.argusmedia.com/ja/news/915846-us-sanctions-russias-rosneft-novatek#:~:text=The%20US%20sanctions%20against%20Rosneft,of%20transactions%20with%20those%20companies.
17. Alan Cullison and Thomas Grove, '"Last Man Standing": An American Investor in Russia Takes a Fall', *Wall Street Journal*, 31 July 2019, https://www.wsj.com/articles/last-man-standing-an-american-investor-in-russia-takes-a-fall-11564603365.
18. Max Seddon, 'Committed Russia Investor Michael Calvey Tripped Up by Politics', *Financial Times*, 22 February 2019, https://www.ft.com/content/aabd47a2-369b-11e9-bd3a-8b2a211d90d5.
19. Max Seddon, 'Calvey's Arrest Sends Chill Through Russia's Foreign Investors', *Financial Times*, 18 February 2019, https://www.ft.com/content/fc2f021a-32ae-11e9-bd3a-8b2a211d90d5.
20. 'BP Exiting Stake in Russian Oil and Gas Company Rosneft', *Economic Times*, 27 February 2022, https://economictimes.indiatimes.com/news/international/business/bp-exiting-stake-in-russian-oil-and-gas-company-rosneft/articleshow/89877896.cms?from=mdr.
21. Dudley resigned from the Rosneft board after Russia's invasion of Ukraine in February 2022.
22. 'NATO and Afghanistan', NATO, 31 August 2022, https://www.nato.int/cps/en/natohq/topics_8189.htm.

23. 'Wales Summit Declaration', NATO, 5 September 2014, https://www.nato.int/cps/en/natohq/official_texts_112964.htm.
24. 'Ghanian President Eyes Broader and Deeper Cooperation with Huawei', Huawei, press release, 18 May 2016, https://www.huawei.com/en/news/2016/5/jiana-zongtong.
25. Johan Nylander, 'How Lenovo Became the Largest PC Maker in the World', *Forbes*, 20 March 2016, https://www.forbes.com/sites/jnylander/2016/03/20/how-lenovo-became-the-largest-pc-maker-in-the-world/?sh=6ac431383 88b; Tim Bajarin, '10 Years Later, Looking Back at the IBM – Lenovo PC Deal', *PC Magazine*, 4 May 2015, https://www.pcmag.com/opinions/10-years-later-looking-back-at-the-ibm-lenovo-pc-deal.
26. 'Haier – the Number 1 Global Major Appliance Brand for 12 Years Running', *ERT Magazine*, 14 January 2021, https://www.ertonline.co.uk/news/haier-the-number-1-global-major-appliance-brand-for-12-years-running.
27. 'Three-year Extension Agreed to Hinkley Point C Contract', *World Nuclear News*, 2 December 2022, https://www.world-nuclear-news.org/Articles/Three-year-extension-agreed-to-Hinkley-Point-C-con.
28. Murat Temizer, 'New Russian Nuclear Power Plant Sparks Debate in Finland', Anadolu Agency, 10 February 2014, https://www.aa.com.tr/en/world/new-russian-nuclear-power-plant-sparks-debate-in-finland/114479.
29. Luis Martinez, 'Why the US Navy Sails Past Disputed Artificial Islands Claimed by China', ABC News, 6 May 2019, https://abcnews.go.com/Politics/us-navy-sails-past-disputed-artificial-islands-claimed/story?id=60993256; Mike Ives, 'The Rising Environmental Toll of China's Offshore Island Grab', *Yale 360*, 10 October 2016, https://e360.yale.edu/features/rising_environmental_toll_china_artificial_islands_south_china_sea.
30. U.S. – China Economic and Security Review Commission, 'South China Sea Arbitration Ruling: What Happened and What's Next?', 12 July 2016, https://www.uscc.gov/sites/default/files/Research/Issue%20Brief_South%20China%20Sea%20Arbitration%20Ruling%20What%20Happened%20and%20What%27s%20Next071216.pdf.
31. *The 2014 Australia – China Trade Report Synopsis*, Australian China Business Council, 2014, https://business.nab.com.au/wp-content/uploads/2015/03/2014_Australia_China_Trade_Report_Synopsis.pdf.
32. 'Full Text of Chinese President Xi Jinping's Address to Australia's Parliament', *Straits Times*, 19 November 2014, https://www.straitstimes.com/asia/australianz/full-text-of-chinese-president-xi-jinpings-address-to-australias-parliament.
33. Richard Wike, 'Inequality is at Top of the Agenda as Global Elites Gather in Davos', Pew Research Center, 21 January 2015, https://www.pewresearch.org/fact-tank/2015/01/21/inequality-is-at-top-of-the-agenda-as-global-elites-gather-in-davos.
34. 'WEF/Young Global Leaders/2007', WikiSpooks, https://wikispooks.com/wiki/WEF/Young_Global_Leaders/2007.
35. John Plender, 'Why Trade Couldn't Buy Peace', *Financial Times,* 23 September 2022, https://www.ft.com/content/a3c224d1-c604-4393-9c32-922f634ab36a.
36. 'Microsoft to Acquire Nokia's Devices & Services Business, License Nokia's Patents and Mapping Services', Microsoft, press release, 3 September 2013, https://news.microsoft.com/2013/09/03/microsoft-to-acquire-nokias-devices-services-business-license-nokias-patents-and-mapping-services.

37. Reid J. Epstein, 'Who is David Brat? Meet the Economics Professor Who Defeated Eric Cantor', *Wall Street Journal*, 10 June 2014, https://www.wsj.com/articles/BL-WB-46414.
38. Aaron Smith, 'U.S. Smartphone Use in 2015', Pew Research Center, 1 April 2015, https://www.pewresearch.org/internet/2015/04/01/us-smartphone-use-in-2015/#:~:text=Today%20nearly%20two%2Dthirds%20of,for%20online%20access%20other%20than.
39. 'UK Welcomes President Xi Jinping for China State Visit', Gov.UK, press release, 20 October 2015, https://www.gov.uk/government/news/uk-welcomes-president-xi-jinping-for-china-state-visit.
40. 'Xi Jinping Visit: UK – China Ties "Will Be Lifted to a New Height" ', BBC News, 20 October 2015, https://www.bbc.com/news/uk-34571436.
41. 'Chinese Buy President Xi and David Cameron Visit Pub', BBC News, 5 December 2016, https://www.bbc.com/news/uk-england-beds-bucks-herts-38212539.
42. Ibid.
43. Maeve Duggan, 'The Demographics of Social Media Users', Pew Research Center, 19 August 2015, https://www.pewresearch.org/internet/2015/08/19/the-demographics-of-social-media-users; *Taking Part Focus On: Social Media,* UK Department for Culture Media & Sport, April 2016, https://assets.publishing.service.gov.uk/government/uploads/system/uploads/attachment_data/file/519678/Social_media_-_FINAL.pdf.
44. Duggan, 'The Demographics of Social Media Users'.
45. 'McDonnell Shares Trump's Fears Over Impact of Globalisation on Workers', *Belfast Telegraph*, 15 November 2016, https://www.belfasttelegraph.co.uk/news/uk/mcdonnell-shares-trumps-fears-over-impact-of-globalization-on-workers-35216309.html.
46. Ivana Kottassova, 'Panama Papers' "John Doe" Says Inequality Concerns Drove Leak', CNN, 6 May 2016, https://money.cnn.com/2016/05/06/news/economy/panama-papers-john-doe-manifesto/index.html.
47. 'Hidden in 11.5 Million Secret Files: 140 Politicians From More Than 50 Countries; Connected to Offshore Companies In 21 Tax Havens', International Consortium of Investigative Journalists, https://www.icij.org/investigations/panama-papers/the-power-players.
48. 'Panama Papers', Ipsos, 2016, https://www.ipsos.com/sites/default/files/2017-07/Panama-Papers-Report.pdf.
49. 'Full Transcript: Donald Trump's Jobs Plan Speech', Politico, 28 June 2016, https://www.politico.com/story/2016/06/full-transcript-trump-job-plan-speech-224891.
50. 'EU Referendum Results: UK votes to LEAVE the EU', BBC News, https://www.bbc.co.uk/news/politics/eu_referendum/results.
51. Sarah Chappell, 'Brexit or Bremain: The Arguments at a Glance', *Euronews*, 12 May 2016, https://www.euronews.com/2016/05/12/brexit-the-arguments-at-a-glance.
52. Emer O'Toole, 'Boris Johnson Says £350m Brexit Bus Figure was an "Underestimation" ', *National*, 7 July 2021, https://www.thenational.scot/news/19426977.boris-johnson-says-350m-brexit-bus-figure-underestimation.
53. 'EU Referendum Local results', BBC News, https://www.bbc.co.uk/news/politics/eu_referendum/results/local/s. Smethwick is located in the Sandwell district.

54. 2015 Full Year Results, Unilever, https://assets.unilever.com/files/92ui5egz/production/0d13c41e4cf97352308280a30e8b36ace32bd4ff.pdf/q4-2015-full-announcement.pdf; 'Our Process', Talenti, https://www.talentigelato.com/us/en/our-process.html#:~:text=Then%20he%20brought%20this%20craft,that%20will%20capture%20your%20heart.
55. Aaron O'Neill, 'Latvia: Unemployment Rate from 2002 to 2001', Statista, 19 October 2022, https://www.statista.com/statistics/375253/unemployment-rate-in-latvia.
56. Nikolay Shevchenko, 'The Unknown 165-Year History of Russia's San Francisco Consulate', Russia Beyond, 2 September 2017, https://www.rbth.com/arts/history/2017/09/02/the-unknown-165-year-history-of-russias-san-francisco-consulate_832632.
57. 'MG to End UK Car Production at Longbridge with Switch to China', BBC News, 23 September 2016, https://www.bbc.com/news/uk-england-birmingham-37449289.
58. Tomas Kellner, 'Done Deal: GE Sells Its Appliances Business to Haier for $5.6 billion', GE, 6 June 2016, https://www.ge.com/news/reports/done-deal-ge-sells-its-appliances-business-to-haier-for-5-6-billion.
59. 'Acquisition of GE Appliances Not to Be Completed', Electrolux, 7 December 2015, https://www.electroluxgroup.com/en/acquisition-of-ge-appliances-not-to-be-completed-21617.

CHAPTER 9: TRUMP TAKES ON GLOBALIZATION

1. 'Full Text: 2017 Donald Trump Inauguration Speech Transcript', Politico, 20 January 2017, https://www.politico.com/story/2017/01/full-text-donald-trump-inauguration-speech-transcript-233907.
2. 'World Economic Forum Annual Meeting', World Economic Forum, https://www.weforum.org/events/world-economic-forum-annual-meeting-2017/programme.
3. 'Full Text of Xi Jinping Keynote at the World Economic Forum', CGTN, 17 January 2017, https://america.cgtn.com/2017/01/17/full-text-of-xi-jinping-keynote-at-the-world-economic-forum.
4. Doug Palmer, 'Clinton Raved About Trans-Pacific Partnership Before She Rejected It', Politico, 8 October 2016, https://www.politico.com/story/2016/10/hillary-clinton-trade-deal-229381.
5. Jake Bright, 'Globalization and the US election: We Need To Take The Voices Of The Discontented More Seriously', World Economic Forum, 9 January 2017, https://www.weforum.org/agenda/2017/01/globalization-and-the-us-election-we-need-to-take-the-voices-of-the-discontented-more-seriously/.
6. 'Remarks by the President on Opportunity for All and Skills for America's Workers', White House, press release, 30 January 2014, https://obamawhitehouse.archives.gov/the-press-office/2014/01/30/remarks-president-opportunity-all-and-skills-americas-workers.
7. Ryan Hass and Abraham Denmark, 'More Pain Than Gain: How the US – China Trade War Hurt America', Brookings Institution, 7 August, 2020, https://www.brookings.edu/blog/order-from-chaos/2020/08/07/more-pain-than-gain-how-the-us-china-trade-war-hurt-america.
8. Ibid.

9. Andy Greenberg, 'The Untold Story of NotPetya, the Most Devastating Cyberattack in History', *Wired*, 22 August 2018, https://www.wired.com/story/notpetya-cyberattack-ukraine-russia-code-crashed-the-world; 'NotPetya', CFR, July 2017, https://www.cfr.org/cyber-operations/notpetya.
10. Greenberg, 'The Untold Story of NotPetya'; 'NotPetya Ransomware Disrupts Merck Vaccine Production', University of Hawai'i – West O'ahu, 4 August 2017, https://westoahu.hawaii.edu/cyber/regional/gce-us-news/notpetya-ransomware-disrupts-merck-vaccine-production.
11. Avalon Zoppo, Amanda Proença Santos and Jackson Hudgins, 'Here's the Full List of Donald Trump's Executive Orders', NBC News, 14 February 2017, https://www.nbcnews.com/politics/white-house/here-s-full-list-donald-trump-s-executive-orders-n720796.
12. Doina Chiacu and Valerie Volcovici, 'EPA Chief Pruitt Refuses to Link CO2 and Global Warming', *Scientific American*, 10 March 2017, https://www.scientificamerican.com/article/epa-chief-pruitt-refuses-to-link-co2-and-global-warming.
13. 'BDI präsentiert 55 Forderungen zum Wettbewerb mit China', BDI, press release, 10 January 2019, https://bdi.eu/artikel/news/bdi-praesentiert-55-forderungen-zum-wettbewerb-mit-china.
14. 'Auferstehen aus Ruinen', IG Metall, 29 June 2022, https://www.igmetall.de/politik-und-gesellschaft/umwelt-und-energie/solarindustrie-auferstehen-aus-ruinen.
15. 'Bundesregierung kürzt Solarförderung früher als geplant', *Die Zeit*, 23 February 2012, https://www.zeit.de/wirtschaft/2012-02/solarfoerderung-kuerzung; 'Auferstehen aus Ruinen', IG Metall.
16. Louis Nelson, 'Trump: Our Relationship with Germany is "Very Bad for U.S."', Politico, 30 May 2017, https://www.politico.com/story/2017/05/30/trump-germany-relationship-tweet-238930.
17. Stephen Collinson, Kevin Liptak and Dan Merica, 'Trump Says Iran Violating Nuclear Agreement, Threatens to Pull Out of Deal', CNN, 13 October 2017, https://www.cnn.com/2017/10/13/politics/iran-deal-decertify/index.html.
18. Michael Birnbaum, 'Europeans Line Up to Do Business with Iran While Americans Wait', *Washington Post*, 17 January 2016, https://www.washingtonpost.com/world/middle_east/europeans-line-up-to-do-business-with-iran-while-americans-wait/2016/01/17/87a9745e-bc99-11e5-85cd-5ad59bc19432_story.html.
19. 'Iran Plans to Buy 114 Airbus Planes', *Guardian*, 24 January 2016, https://www.theguardian.com/world/2016/jan/24/iran-plans-to-buy-114-airbus-planes.
20. Birnbaum, 'Europeans Line Up'.
21. Ibid.
22. 'Svenska företag sonderar i Iran', *Ystads Allehanda*, 10 February 2017, https://www.ystadsallehanda.se/tt-ekonomi/svenska-foretag-sonderar-i-iran.
23. Sabine Kinkartz, 'Iran lässt deutsche Wirtschaft träumen', *DW*, 3 March 2016, https://www.dw.com/de/iran-l%C3%A4sst-deutsche-wirtschaft-tr%C3%A4umen/a-19090526.
24. Ibid.
25. 'Iran's Economic Outlook – Spring 2016', World Bank, 2016, https://www.worldbank.org/en/country/iran/publication/economic-outlook-spring-2016.
26. Achim Berg, Harsh Chhaparia, Saskia Hedrich and Karl-Hendrik Magnus, 'What's Next for Bangladesh's Garment Industry, After a Decade of Growth?',

McKinsey and Company, 25 March 2021, https://www.mckinsey.com/industries/retail/our-insights/whats-next-for-bangladeshs-garment-industry-after-a-decade-of-growth.

27. '"Made in China 2025" Plan Issued', State Council of the People's Republic of China, press release, 19 May 2015, http://english.www.gov.cn/policies/latest_releases/2015/05/19/content_281475110703534.htm.
28. 'Australia Passes Foreign Interference Laws Amid China Tension', BBC News, 28 June 2018, https://www.bbc.com/news/world-australia-44624270.
29. Ivar Kolstad, 'Too Big to Fault? Effects of the 2010 Nobel Peace Prize on Norwegian Exports to China and Foreign Policy', working paper, Chr. Michelsen Institute, Bergen, Norway, 2016, https://www.cmi.no/publications/5805-too-big-to-fault.
30. 'Doing Business with Iran: EU – Iran Trade and Investment Relations', Every CRS Report, 25 October 2017, https://www.everycrsreport.com/reports/IN10809.html.
31. Behrooz Imeni, 'FINEX 2017 Underscores Iranian Economic, Investment Rebound', *Financial Tribune*, 15 April 2017, https://financialtribune.com/articles/economy-business-and-markets/62470/finex-2017-underscores-iranian-economic-investment.
32. Krishnadev Calamur, 'Trump Rips Up a "Decaying and Rotten Deal" with Iran', *Atlantic*, 8 May 2018, https://www.theatlantic.com/international/archive/2018/05/trump-iran-deal/559082.
33. 'EU to Block US Sanctions on Iran for European Companies', *DW*, 17 May 2018, https://www.dw.com/en/eu-to-reactivate-blocking-statute-against-us-sanctions-on-iran-for-european-firms/a-43826992.
34. Ellen R. Wald, '10 Companies Leaving Iran As Trump's Sanctions Close In', *Forbes*, 6 June 2018, https://www.forbes.com/sites/ellenrwald/2018/06/06/10-companies-leaving-iran-as-trumps-sanctions-close-in/?sh=60fa3bd3c90f.
35. 'Trump: Germany is Totally Controlled by Russia', BBC News, 11 July 2018, https://www.bbc.com/news/av/world-europe-44793764.
36. Susan B. Glasser, 'How Trump Made War on Angela Merkel and Europe', *New Yorker*, 17 December 2018, https://www.newyorker.com/magazine/2018/12/24/how-trump-made-war-on-angela-merkel-and-europe.
37. David J. Lynch, Josh Dawsey and Damian Paletta, 'Trump Imposes Steel and Aluminum Tariffs on the E.U., Canada and Mexico', *Washington Post*, 31 May 2018, https://www.washingtonpost.com/business/economy/trump-imposes-steel-and-aluminum-tariffs-on-the-european-union-canada-and-mexico/2018/05/31/891bb452-64d3-11e8-a69c-b944de66d9e7_story.html; Peter Navarro, 'Why Economic Security Is National Security', Trump White House Archives, 10 December 2018, https://trumpwhitehouse.archives.gov/articles/economic-security.
38. Andre Barbe and David Riker, 'The Effects of Offshoring on U.S. Workers: A Review of the Literature', *United States International Trade Commission Journal of International Commerce and Economics* (June 2018), p. 3, https://www.usitc.gov/publications/332/journals/offshoring_and_labor_final.pdf.
39. Lulu Garcia-Navarro, 'A Steelworkers Union on Trump's Tariffs', NPR, 10 June 2018, https://www.npr.org/2018/06/10/618648606/a-steelworkers-union-on-trumps-tariffs.
40. Senator Ben Sasse, Twitter, 31 May 2018, https://twitter.com/SenSasse/status/1002210624372379650.

41. 'DS548: United States – Certain Measures on Steel and Aluminum Products', World Trade Organization, 20 January 2022, https://www.wto.org/english/tratop_e/dispu_e/cases_e/ds548_e.htm.
42. Natalie Sherman and Jonathan Josephs, 'WTO Says Trump's US Steel Tariffs Broke Global Trade Rules', BBC News, 9 December 2022, https://www.bbc.com/news/business-63920063.
43. Jeff Mason, 'Trump Lashes Germany over Gas Pipeline Deal, Calls It Russia's "Captive"', Reuters, 11 July 2018, https://www.reuters.com/article/us-nato-summit-pipeline/trump-lashes-germany-over-gas-pipeline-deal-calls-it-russias-captive-idUSKBN1K10VI.
44. 'Order Activating Suspended Denial Order Relating to Zhongxing Telecommunications Equipment Corporation and ZTE Kangxun Telecommunications LTD', US Department of Commerce Bureau of Industry and Security, 15 April 2018, https://www.commerce.gov/sites/default/files/zte_denial_order.pdf; Adam Jourdan and Cate Cadell, 'U.S. Strike on China's ZTE Another Blow for Qualcomm', Reuters, 17 April 2018, https://www.reuters.com/article/us-china-zte-qualcomm-analysis/u-s-strike-on-chinas-zte-another-blow-for-qualcomm-idUSKBN1HO0XT.
45. Sara Salinas, 'Six Top US Intelligence Chiefs Caution Against Buying Huawei Phones', CNBC, 15 February 2018, https://www.cnbc.com/2018/02/13/chinas-hauwei-top-us-intelligence-chiefs-caution-americans-away.html.
46. Julia Horowitz, 'Huawei CFO Meng Wanzhou Arrested in Canada, Faces Extradition to the United States', CNN Business, 6 December 2018, https://www.cnn.com/2018/12/05/tech/huawei-cfo-arrested-canada/index.html.
47. Jacob Kastrenakes, 'US Lifts Trade Ban on ZTE in Controversial Deal with Chinese Phone Maker', *The Verge*, 13 June 2018, https://www.theverge.com/2018/7/13/17565450/zte-trade-ban-lifted-us-commerce-department-trump.
48. Ibid.
49. Michelle Kosinski, Schams Elwazer and Stephen Collinson, 'Cables from UK's Ambassador to the US Blast Trump as "Inept," "Incompetent"', CNN Politics, 8 July 2019, https://www.cnn.com/2019/07/06/politics/uk-ambassador-cables-donald-trump/index.html.
50. Jacob Kastrenakes, 'Trump Signs Bill Banning Government Use of Huawei and ZTE Tech', *The Verge*, 13 August 2018, https://www.theverge.com/2018/8/13/17686310/huawei-zte-us-government-contractor-ban-trump.
51. Richard Wike et al., 'Trump's International Ratings Remain Low, Especially Among Key Allies', Pew Research Center, 1 October 2018, https://www.pewresearch.org/global/2018/10/01/trumps-international-ratings-remain-low-especially-among-key-allies.
52. Moira Warburton, 'Key Events in Huawei CFO Meng Wanzhou's Extradition Case', Reuters, 24 September 2021, https://www.reuters.com/technology/key-events-huawei-cfo-meng-wanzhous-extradition-case-2021-08-11.
53. Nik Martin and Roman Goncharenko, 'Siemens to Step Up Investment in Russia', *DW,* 16 February 2019, https://www.dw.com/en/siemens-to-hike-russia-investment-despite-crimea-scandal/a-47548791.

CHAPTER 10: 5G BECOMES A GLOBALIZATION LIGHTNING ROD

1. 'Key Statistics and Trends in International Trade 2019', United Nations, 2020, https://unctad.org/publication/key-statistics-and-trends-international-trade-2019.
2. 'DAX 30 Index – 27 Year Historical Chart', Macrotrends, https://www.macrotrends.net/2595/dax-30-index-germany-historical-chart-data; Graeme Wearden, 'FTSE 100 Posts 12% Gain for 2019 After Strong Year for Market – As It Happened', *Guardian*, 31 December 2019, https://www.theguardian.com/business/live/2019/dec/31/global-markets-rally-shares-ftse-100-pound-oil-markets-business-live.
3. Xixi Hong, 'Italy Changes Track: From the Belt and Road to (Re)Alignment with Washington', Istituto Affari Internazionali, 20 December 2021, https://www.iai.it/en/pubblicazioni/italy-changes-track-belt-and-road-realignment-washington.
4. Giselda Vagnoni, 'Italy Endorses China's Belt and Road Plan in First for a G7 Nation', Reuters, 23 March 2019, https://www.reuters.com/article/us-italy-china-president/italy-endorses-chinas-belt-and-road-plan-in-first-for-a-g7-nation-idUSKCN1R40DV.
5. Arjun Kharpal, 'Huawei Tops $100 Billion Revenue for First Time Despite Political Headwinds', CNBC, 28 March 2019, https://www.cnbc.com/2019/03/29/huawei-earnings-full-year-2018.html#:~:text=Huawei's%20revenue%20grew%2019.5%20percent,(%24107.13%20billion)%20last%20year.
6. Jon Russell, 'Lenovo has Completed the $2.91 Billion Acquisition of Motorola from Google', *TechCrunch*, 30 October 2014, https://techcrunch.com/2014/10/30/lenovo-has-completed-the-2-91-billion-acquisition-of-motorola-from-google.
7. Chuin-Wei Yap, 'State Support Helped Fuel Huawei's Global Rise', *Wall Street Journal*, 25 December 2019, https://www.wsj.com/articles/state-support-helped-fuel-huaweis-global-rise-11577280736.
8. Catalin Cimpanu, 'Building China's Comac C919 Airplane Involved a Lot of Hacking, Report Says', ZD Net, 14 October 2019, https://www.zdnet.com/article/building-chinas-comac-c919-airplane-involved-a-lot-of-hacking-report-says.
9. Indictment, *United States of America vs. Zhang Zhang Gu et al*, United States District Court, Southern District of California, June 2017, https://www.justice.gov/opa/press-release/file/1106491/download.
10. Imogen Saunders, 'Artificial Islands and Territory in International Law', Vanderbilt University, https://cdn.vanderbilt.edu/vu-wp0/wp-content/uploads/sites/78/2019/07/12052304/Imogen-Saunders.pdf, p. 648.
11. 'Yang Jiechi Gives Interview to State Media on the So-Called Award by the Arbitral Tribunal for the South China Sea Arbitration', Ministry of Foreign Affairs of the People's Republic of China, https://www.fmprc.gov.cn/eng/wjdt_665385/zyjh_665391/201607/t20160715_678561.html.
12. Serena Seyfort, 'Explainer: What Are China's "Artificial Islands" and Why Are There Concerns About Them', 9 News, 26 November 2021, https://www.9news.com.au/world/what-are-chinas-artificial-islands-in-the-south-china-sea-and-why-are-there-concerns-about-them/3f0d47ab-1b3a-4a8a-bfc6-7350c5267308.
13. 'Berlin Stops Chinese Firm Buying Stake in 50Hertz', *DW*, 27 July 2018, https://www.dw.com/en/berlin-beats-chinese-firm-to-buy-stake-in-50hertz-power-company/a-44848676.

14. Axel Vogelmann and Markus Käppler, 'Germany's Foreign Direct Investment Regime: Further Changes Ahead', Akin Gump, 16 December 2019, https://www.akingump.com/en/news-insights/germany-s-foreign-direct-investment-regime-further-changes-ahead.html.
15. 'UK PM Theresa May to Ban Huawei from Providing "Core" Parts of Britain's 5G Network', *South China Morning Post*, 24 April 2019, https://www.scmp.com/news/world/europe/article/3007406/uk-pm-theresa-may-ban-huawei-providing-core-parts-britains-5g.
16. Tucker Higgins, 'Trump declares National Emergency over Threats Against US Technology Amid Campaign Against Huawei', CNBC, 15 May 2019, https://www.cnbc.com/2019/05/15/trump-signs-executive-order-declaring-national-emergency-over-threats-against-us-technology.html.
17. 'Recommendations: Commission Recommendation (EU) 2019/534 of 26 March 2019', *Official Journal of the European Union,* 29 March 2019, https://eur-lex.europa.eu/legal-content/EN/TXT/PDF/?uri=CELEX:32019H0534&from=ES.
18. Isabel Oakeshott, 'Britain's Man in the US Says Trump is "Inept": Leaked Secret Cables from Ambassador Say the President is "Uniquely Dysfunctional and His Career Could End in Disgrace"', *Daily Mail*, 7 July 2019, https://www.dailymail.co.uk/news/article-7220335/Britains-man-says-Trump-inept-Cables-ambassador-say-dysfunctional.html.
19. 'Executive Order on Addressing the Threat Posed by TikTok', Trump White House Archives, 6 August 2020, https://trumpwhitehouse.archives.gov/presidential-actions/executive-order-addressing-threat-posed-tiktok.
20. Annabelle Dickson and Laurens Cerulus, 'Boris Johnson Allows Huawei to Build Parts of UK 5G Network', Politico, 28 January 2020, https://www.politico.eu/article/boris-johnson-allows-huawei-to-build-parts-of-uk-5g-network.
21. Amanda Macias, 'Pelosi Warns US Allies: "Don't Go Near Huawei"', CNBC, 14 February 2020, https://www.cnbc.com/2020/02/14/pelosi-warns-us-allies-dont-go-near-huawei.html.
22. Ma Si, 'Huawei Secures 91 5G Commercial Contracts Around the World', *China Daily*, 20 February 2020, https://www.chinadaily.com.cn/a/202002/20/WS5e4e7c2aa3101282172791 4c.html.
23. 'Special Report: Global Warming of 1.5°C', Intergovernmental Panel on Climate Change, 2018, https://www.ipcc.ch/sr15.
24. 'Finland Has an Excellent Opportunity to Rebuild Itself in Line With the Principles of Sustainable Development', Finnish Government, Marin Government Programme, https://julkaisut.valtioneuvosto.fi/bitstream/handle/10024/161935/VN_2019_33.pdf?sequence=1&isAllowed=y.
25. Lloyd Doggett, 'Timeline of Trump's Coronavirus Responses', 2 March 2022, https://doggett.house.gov/media/blog-post/timeline-trumps-coronavirus-responses.
26. Chad P. Brown, 'China Bought None of the Extra $200 Billion of US Exports in Trump's Trade Deal', PIIE, 19 July 2022, https://www.piie.com/blogs/realtime-economic-issues-watch/china-bought-none-extra-200-billion-us-exports-trumps-trade.
27. Andrew Green, 'Li Wenliang', *Lancet,* 18 February 2020, https://www.thelancet.com/journals/lancet/article/PIIS0140-6736(20)30382-2/fulltext.

28. 'The Facts Regarding Taiwan's Email to Alert WHO to Possible Danger of COVID-19', Taiwan Centers for Disease Control, 11 April 2020, https://www.cdc.gov.tw/En/Bulletin/Detail/PAD-lbwDHeN_bLa-viBOuw?typeid=158.
29. Rosel Jackson Stern, 'Brexit Day Events: What is Happening in the UK on 31 January?', *Guardian*, 31 January 2020, https://www.theguardian.com/politics/2020/jan/31/brexit-day-events-what-is-happening-in-the-uk-on-31-january.
30. Rem Rieder, 'Trump's Statements About the Coronavirus', Fact Check, 18 March 2020, https://www.factcheck.org/2020/03/trumps-statements-about-the-coronavirus.
31. 'Täglicher Lagebericht des RKI zur Coronavirus-Krankheit-2019 (COVID-19)', Robert-Koch-Institut, 4 March 2020, https://www.rki.de/DE/Content/InfAZ/N/Neuartiges_Coronavirus/Situationsberichte/2020-03-04-de.pdf?__blob=publicationFile.
32. Angela Merkel, 'An Address to the Nation by Federal Chancellor Merkel', Bundesregierung, https://www.bundesregierung.de/breg-en/service/archive/statement-chancellor-1732302.
33. 'Coronavirus Disease (COVID-19) Pandemic', World Health Organization, https://www.who.int/europe/emergencies/situations/covid-19#:~:text=This%20led%20WHO%20to%20declare,pandemic%20on%2011%20March%202020.
34. Ghazi M. Magableh, 'Supply Chains and the COVID-19 Pandemic: A Comprehensive Framework', *European Management Review*, 18, no. 3 (8 February 2021), https://www.ncbi.nlm.nih.gov/pmc/articles/PMC8014293.
35. 'Export Controls and Export Bans over the Course of the Covid-19 Pandemic', World Trade Organization, 29 April 2020, https://www.wto.org/english/tratop_e/covid19_e/bdi_covid19_e.pdf.
36. 'Germany Bans Export of Medical Protection Gear Due to Coronavirus', Reuters, 4 March 2020, https://www.reuters.com/article/health-coronavirus-germany-exports/germany-bans-export-of-medical-protection-gear-due-to-coronavirus-idUSL8N2AX3D9.
37. Elisabeth Braw, 'The EU Is Abandoning Italy in Its Hour of Need', *Foreign Policy*, 14 March 2020, https://foreignpolicy.com/2020/03/14/coronavirus-eu-abandoning-italy-china-aid.
38. Michael Peel et al., 'China Ramps Up Coronavirus Help to Europe', *Financial Times*, 18 March 2020, https://www.ft.com/content/186a9260-693a-11ea-800d-da70cff6e4d3; David Hutt, 'Coronavirus: Czechs Facing Up to COVID-19 Crisis by Making Masks Mandatory', *Euronews*, 24 March 2020, https://www.euronews.com/2020/03/24/coronavirus-czechs-facing-up-to-covid-19-crisis-by-making-masks-mandatory.
39. Laurens Cerulus, 'Huawei Joins China's Big Tech Donation Spree in Europe', Politico Europe, 25 March 2020, https://www.politico.eu/article/huawei-joins-chinas-big-tech-donation-spree-in-europe.
40. Peel et al., 'China Ramps Up Coronavirus Help to Europe'.
41. Michael Wayland, 'Commerce Secretary Says House Needs to Pass CHIPS Act Immediately to Ease Semiconductor Shortage', CNBC, 29 November 2021, https://www.cnbc.com/2021/11/29/commerce-secretary-says-us-house-needs-to-pass-chips-act-immediately-to-ease-semiconductor-shortage.html.
42. 'Russia to Close Borders Starting on March 30', Reuters, 28 March 2020, https://www.reuters.com/article/uk-health-coronavirus-russia-borders/russia-to-close-borders-starting-on-march-30-idUKKBN21F0LI.

43. Oliver Dowden, 'Digital, Culture, Media and Sport Secretary's Statement on Telecoms', Government of the United Kingdom, 14 July 2020, https://www.gov.uk/government/speeches/digital-culture-media-and-sport-secretarys-statement-on-telecoms.
44. Ibid.
45. 'This Week in Coronavirus: July 31 to August 6', KFF, 7 August 2020, https://www.kff.org/policy-watch/this-week-in-coronavirus-july-31-to-august-6.
46. Laura Silver, Kat Devlin and Christine Huang, 'Unfavorable Views of China Reach Historic Highs in Many Countries', Pew Research Center, 6 October 2020, https://www.pewresearch.org/global/2020/10/06/unfavorable-views-of-china-reach-historic-highs-in-many-countries.
47. 'Domstol stoppar Huawei-förbud – 5g-auktion skjuts upp', *Computer Sweden*, 11 September 2020, https://computersweden.idg.se/2.2683/1.742440/5g-domstol-stoppar-huawei-forbud.

CHAPTER 11: GLOBALIZATION BECOMES A WEAPON AS XI HITS BACK

1. Paul Karp and Helen Davidson, 'China Bristles at Australia's Call for Investigation into Coronavirus Origin', *Guardian*, 29 April 2020, https://www.theguardian.com/world/2020/apr/29/australia-defends-plan-to-investigate-china-over-covid-19-outbreak-as-row-deepens.
2. Zaheena Rasheed, Joseph Stepansky and Farah Najjar, 'Confirmed Coronavirus Recoveries Hit 1m Worldwide: Live Updates', Al Jazeera, 30 April 2020, https://web.archive.org/web/20200501092342/https://www.aljazeera.com/news/2020/04/cities-face-100-million-poor-coronavirus-pandemic-200429233138520.html.
3. Colin Packham, 'Australia Says World Needs to Know Origins of COVID-19', Reuters, 25 September 2020, https://www.reuters.com/article/us-health-coronavirus-australia-china/australia-says-world-needs-to-know-origins-of-covid-19-idUSKCN26H00T.
4. Lily Kuo, 'Australia Called "Gum Stuck to China's Shoe" by State Media In Coronavirus Investigation Stoush', *Guardian*, 28 April 2020, https://www.theguardian.com/world/2020/apr/28/australia-called-gum-stuck-to-chinas-shoe-by-state-media-in-coronavirus-investigation-stoush.
5. Andrius Sytas, 'Lithuania to Support "Those fighting For Freedom" in Taiwan', Reuters, 9 November 2020, https://www.reuters.com/article/us-lithuania-china/lithuania-to-support-those-fighting-for-freedom-in-taiwan-idUSKBN27P1PQ.
6. Jonathan Kearsley, Eryk Bagshaw and Anthony Galloway, '"If You Make China the Enemy, China Will Be the Enemy": Beijing's Fresh Threat to Australia', *Sydney Morning Herald*, 18 November 2020, https://www.smh.com.au/world/asia/if-you-make-china-the-enemy-china-will-be-the-enemy-beijing-s-fresh-threat-to-australia-20201118-p56fqs.html.
7. Ibid.
8. Wine Australia, *Export Market Guide – China*, updated 19 January 2022, https://www.wineaustralia.com/selling/export-market-guide-china.
9. David Uren, 'How Australia Withstood China's Campaign of Economic Warfare', *The Strategist,* 7 February 2023, https://www.aspistrategist.org.au/how-australia-withstood-chinas-campaign-of-economic-warfare.

10. Philip Ball, 'The Lightning-fast Quest for COVID Vaccines – And What It Means for Other Diseases', *Nature*, 18 December 2020, https://www.nature.com/articles/d41586-020-03626-1.
11. 'Cumulative Confirmed COVID-19 Cases and Deaths, World', Our World in Data, https://ourworldindata.org/grapher/cumulative-deaths-and-cases-covid-19.
12. Elizabeth Shim, 'China Puts Sweden on Notice following Huawei, ZTE decision', UPI, 21 October 2020, https://www.upi.com/Top_News/World-News/2020/10/21/China-puts-Sweden-on-notice-following-Huawei-ZTE-decision/8691603284419.
13. 'Borje E. Ekholm', Bloomberg, https://www.bloomberg.com/profile/person/4768459; 'Alibaba Group – Statistics & Facts', Statista, https://www.statista.com/topics/2187/alibaba-group.
14. 'Ericsson Chief Worried About "Impact" of Sweden's Ban on Huawei', *The Local*, 5 January 2021, https://www.thelocal.se/20210105/ericsson-chief-worried-about-impact-of-swedens-ban-on-huawei.
15. Ibid.
16. 'Davos 2021 – Special Address by Xi Jinping, President of the People's Republic of China', World Economic Forum, 25 January 2021, https://www.weforum.org/events/the-davos-agenda-2021/sessions/special-address-by-g20-head-of-state-government-67e386f2d5; 'Explore the Davos Agenda', World Economic Forum, 2021, https://www.weforum.org/events/the-davos-agenda-2021/cochairs.
17. 'President Xi Jinping's Message to the Davos Agenda in Full', World Economic Forum, 17 January 2022, https://www.weforum.org/agenda/2022/01/address-chinese-president-xi-jinping-2022-world-economic-forum-virtual-session.
18. 'China Approves Sinovac Biotech COVID-19 Vaccine for General Public Use', Reuters, 6 February 2021, https://www.reuters.com/article/us-health-coronavirus-vaccine-sinovac/china-approves-sinovac-biotech-covid-19-vaccine-for-general-public-use-idUSKBN2A60AY; 'Antibodies from Sinovac's COVID-19 Shot Fade After About 6 Months, Booster Helps – Study', Reuters, 12 August 2021, https://www.reuters.com/business/healthcare-pharmaceuticals/antibodies-sinovacs-covid-19-shot-fade-after-about-6-months-booster-helps-study-2021-07-26.
19. Daniel Markuson, 'How to Use a VPN in China in 2023', Nord VPN, 8 January 2023, https://nordvpn.com/blog/vpn-for-china/#:~:text=In%20China%2C%20VPN%20traffic%20can,to%20restrict%20the%20free%20internet.
20. Yaqiu Wang, 'In China, the "Great Firewall" Is Changing a Generation', Politico, 1 September 2020, https://www.politico.com/news/magazine/2020/09/01/china-great-firewall-generation-405385.
21. 'Trade Dispute with China Puts Australian Wine Industry in a Precarious Position', *Wine Magazine*, https://www.winemag.com/2022/03/10/china-australia-wine-tariffs.
22. Tim McDonald, 'China and Taiwan Face Off in Pineapple War', BBC News, 19 March 2021, https://www.bbc.com/news/business-56353963.
23. Tsai Ing-wen (@iingwen), Twitter, 26 February 2021, https://twitter.com/iingwen/status/1365253680606289921?ref_src=twsrc%5Etfw%7Ctwcamp%5Etweetembed%7Ctwterm%5E1365253680606289921%7Ctwgr%5Efb6ef1b44a2683b97f87610c2a24861c0c2e36a4%7Ctwcon%5Es1_&ref_url=https%3A%2F%2Fwww.bbc.com%2Fnews%2Fbusiness-56353963.
24. McDonald, 'China and Taiwan Face Off in Pineapple War'.

25. Keoni Everington, 'Taiwanese Buy Entire Year's Worth of Pineapple Exports to China in 4 days', *Taiwan News*, 3 March 2021, https://www.taiwannews.com.tw/en/news/4140768.
26. Darren J. Lim and Victor Ferguson, 'Chinese Economic Coercion during the THAAD Dispute', 28 December 2019, https://theasanforum.org/chinese-economic-coercion-during-the-thaad-dispute.
27. Dan Collyns, '"It's Terrifying": Can Anyone Stop China's Vast Armada of Fishing Boats?', *Guardian*, 25 August 2020, https://www.theguardian.com/environment/2020/aug/25/can-anyone-stop-china-vast-armada-of-fishing-boats-galapagos-ecuador; 'Military and Security Developments Involving the People's Republic of China 2020', US Department of Defense, 2020, https://media.defense.gov/2020/Sep/01/2002488689/-1/-1/1/2020-DOD-CHINA-MILITARY-POWER-REPORT-FINAL.PDF.
28. Ibid.
29. 'Remarks by President Biden in Address to a Joint Session of Congress', White House, press release, 28 April 2021, https://www.whitehouse.gov/briefing-room/speeches-remarks/2021/04/29/remarks-by-president-biden-in-address-to-a-joint-session-of-congress.
30. Jon Hilsenrath, Anthony DeBarros and Kara Dapena, 'The Messy Unwinding of the New World Order – in Charts', *Wall Street Journal*, 3 November 2022, https://www.wsj.com/story/the-messy-unwinding-of-the-new-world-order-b43d7e45.
31. Ericsson, 'Second Quarter report 2021', 16 July 2021, https://www.ericsson.com/4a0a68/assets/local/investors/documents/financial-reports-and-filings/interim-reports-archive/2021/6month21-en.pdf.
32. Supantha Mukherjee, 'Nokia Wins First 5G Radio Contract in China, Ericsson Loses Ground', Reuters, 19 July 2021, https://www.reuters.com/technology/nokia-wins-first-5g-radio-contract-china-2021-07-19.
33. 'Finland's New Telecoms Law "Leaves Room for Nokia in China"', *Global Times*, 8 December 2020, https://www.globaltimes.cn/page/202012/1209308.shtml.
34. 'H&M's China Sales Hit as Boycott Bites', Reuters, 2 July 2021, https://www.reuters.com/business/retail-consumer/hms-china-sales-hit-boycott-bites-2021-07-02.
35. Anna Ringstrom, 'H&M Returns to Profit, China Sales Hit by Boycott', Reuters, 1 July 2021, https://www.reuters.com/business/retail-consumer/hm-swings-back-profit-june-sales-jump-restrictions-ease-2021-07-01.
36. Stephanie Nebehay, 'U.N. says it has credible reports that China holds million Uighurs in secret camps', Reuters, 10 August 2018, https://www.reuters.com/article/us-china-rights-un/u-n-says-it-has-credible-reports-that-china-holds-million-uighurs-in-secret-camps-idUSKBN1KV1SU.
37. 'H&M's China Sales Hit as Boycott Bites', Reuters.
38. Ibid.
39. Ibid.; 'Responsibility', Burberry, June 2017, https://www.burberryplc.com/content/dam/burberry/corporate/Investors/Results_Reports/2017/CRPack-July2017/Corporate%20Responsibility%20Investor%20Pack%20FY%2016-17%20%20FINAL.pdf.downloadasset.pdf; 'Nike Become a Pioneer Member', Better Cotton, 4 April 2014, https://bettercotton.org/nike-become-pioneer-member.
40. Patrick Wintour, 'US and Canada Follow EU and UK in Sanctioning Chinese Officials over Xinjiang', *Guardian*, 22 March 2021, https://www.theguardian.

com/world/2021/mar/22/china-responds-to-eu-uk-sanctions-over-uighurs-human-rights.

41. 'How Are Leading Companies Managing Today's Political Risks? 2021 Survey and Report', Oxford Analytica, https://www.readkong.com/page/how-are-leading-companies-managing-today-s-political-risks-4346441.
42. Ibid.
43. 'Taiwan to Open De-Facto Embassy in Lithuania Under Own Name, Prompting Rebuke from China', *Euronews*, 20 July 2021, https://www.euronews.com/2021/07/20/taiwan-to-open-de-facto-embassy-in-lithuania-under-own-name-prompting-rebuke-from-china.
44. Ibid.
45. Max Seddon, 'Calvey's Arrest Sends Chill Through Russia's Foreign Investors', *Financial Times*, 19 February 2019, https://www.ft.com/content/fc2f021a-32ae-11e9-bd3a-8b2a211d90d5.
46. Max Seddon and Henry Foy, 'Michael Calvey Trial Set to Conclude as Russian Court Delivers Verdict', *Financial Times*, 2 August 2021, https://www.ft.com/content/032789e0-675e-4693-a0c1-8e19e94a3dcb.
47. Lev Sergeev and Alexander Marrow, 'Russia Hands U.S. Investor Calvey 5.5-year Suspended Sentence', Reuters, 7 August 2021, https://www.reuters.com/business/russia-hands-us-investor-calvey-55-year-suspended-sentence-2021-08-06.
48. Helen Davidson, 'China Recalls Lithuania Ambassador in Taiwan Diplomatic Office Row', *Guardian*, 10 August 2021, https://www.theguardian.com/world/2021/aug/10/china-recalls-lithuania-ambassador-taiwan-diplomatic-office-row-beijing-tension-taipei.
49. Pratik Jakhar, 'Whatever Happened to the South China Sea Ruling?', *The Interpreter*, 12 July 2021, https://www.lowyinstitute.org/the-interpreter/whatever-happened-south-china-sea-ruling.
50. Jamaine Punzalan, 'Duterte Calls Philippine Arbitral Victory vs China a Piece of "Paper" That Led to Nothing', ABS-CBN News, 6 May 2021, https://news.abs-cbn.com/news/05/06/21/duterte-china-arbitral-ruling-west-philippine-sea.
51. 'Yahoo Pulls Out of China Amid "Challenging" Environment', NBC News, 2 November 2021, https://www.nbcnews.com/business/business-news/yahoo-pulls-china-challenging-environment-rcna4306#:~:text=Yahoo%20said%20Tuesday%20said%20it,1; Sam Maiyaki, 'LinkedIn is Leaving China!', LinkedIn, 16 October 2021, https://www.linkedin.com/pulse/linkedin-leaving-china-sam-maiyaki.
52. 'China Condemns Opening of Taiwan Office in Lithuania as "Egregious Act"', *Guardian*, 19 November 2021, https://www.theguardian.com/world/2021/nov/19/china-condemns-opening-of-taiwan-office-in-lithuania-as-egregious-act; Davidson, 'China Recalls Lithuania Ambassador in Taiwan Diplomatic Office Row'.
53. Andrius Sytas, 'Lithuania Says Chinese Customs is Blocking Its Exports', Reuters, 3 December 2021, https://www.reuters.com/article/china-lithuania-trade/lithuania-says-chinese-customs-is-blocking-its-exports-idUSKBN2II0Y7.
54. Niklas Becker, 'Deutsche Firmen vom Konflikt zwischen China und Litauen betroffen', Germany Trade & Invest, 14 January 2022, https://www.gtai.de/de/trade/litauen/wirtschaftsumfeld/deutsche-firmen-vom-konflikt-zwischen-china-und-litauen-betroffen-779206.

55. Tobias Kaiser, 'Autozulieferer zwischen den Fronten – Litauens Streit mit China trifft deutsche Firmen', *Die Welt*, 23 December 2021, https://www.welt.de/wirtschaft/article235849914/China-Warum-deutsche-Firmen-unter-der-Blockade-gegen-Litauen-leiden.html.
56. Joe Miller, Guy Chazan and Andy Bounds, 'German Business Hits Out at China After Lithuania Trade Row Snares Exports', *Financial Times*, 17 December 2021, https://www.ft.com/content/15119be1-3d57-4769-8f82-ff8cb36a668b.
57. Pickard, 'Trade Dispute with China Puts Australian Wine Industry in a Precarious Position'.
58. Marti Flacks and Madeleine Songy, 'The Uyghur Forced Labor Prevention Act Goes into Effect', Center for Strategic and International Studies, 27 June 2022, https://www.csis.org/analysis/uyghur-forced-labor-prevention-act-goes-effect#:~:text=In%20December%202021%2C%20Congress%20overwhelmingly,the%20Senate%20by%20unanimous%20consent.
59. Daniel Michaels and Drew Hinshaw, 'EU Hits Back at China Over Trade Limits, Taking Lithuania Fight Global', *Wall Street Journal*, 27 January 2022, https://www.wsj.com/articles/eu-takes-china-to-wto-over-lithuania-trade-restrictions-11643271938?mod=article_inline.
60. Kathryn L. Clune and Marcia Pulcherio, 'EU Challenges China's Anti-Suit Injunctions at the WTO', Crowell, 20 December 2022, https://www.crowell.com/NewsEvents/AlertsNewsletters/all/EU-Challenges-Chinas-Anti-Suit-Injunctions-at-the-WTO.
61. Ibid.
62. 'Addition of Entities and Revision of Entries on the Entity List; and the Addition of Entity to the Military End-user (MEU) List', Federal Register, 26 November 2021, https://www.federalregister.gov/documents/2021/11/26/2021-25808/addition-of-entities-and-revision-of-entries-on-the-entity-list-and-addition-of-entity-to-the.
63. 'US Congress Passes Import Ban on Chinese Uyghur Region', BBC News, 17 December 2021, https://www.bbc.com/news/world-us-canada-59692826; Victor Cha, 'The Biden Boycott of the 2022 Beijing Winter Olympics', CSIS, 18 January 2022, https://www.csis.org/analysis/biden-boycott-2022-beijing-winter-olympics; 'Foreign Ministry Spokesperson Zhao Lijian's Regular Press Conference on December 6, 2021', Ministry of Foreign Affairs of the People's Republic of China, 6 December 2021, https://www.fmprc.gov.cn/mfa_eng/xwfw_665399/s2510_665401/202112/t20211206_10463087.html.
64. 'The Administration's Approach to the People's Republic of China: Speech by Secretary of State Antony J. Blinken', US Department of State, 26 May 2022, https://www.state.gov/the-administrations-approach-to-the-peoples-republic-of-china.
65. 'Huawei Appeals Sweden's Ban on Company for Selling 5G Gear', Reuters, 1 October 2021, https://www.reuters.com/business/media-telecom/huawei-appeals-swedens-ban-company-selling-5g-gear-2021-10-01.
66. Laurens Cerulus, 'Huawei Seeks EU Court Involvement in Swedish Ban', Politico, 6 October 2021, https://www.politico.eu/article/huawei-sweden-china-5g-court-case-european-union.
67. Arjun Kharpal, 'Huawei Posts First-Ever Yearly Revenue Decline as U.S. Sanctions Continue to Bite, But Profit Surges', CNBC, 28 March 2022, https://www.cnbc.com/2022/03/28/huawei-annual-results-2021-revenue-declines-but-profit-surges.html.

CHAPTER 12: RUSSIA INVADES UKRAINE

1. 'Shell and Four European Energy Companies Sign Financing Agreements with Nord Stream 2 AG for Pipeline Project', Shell, press release, 24 April 2017, https://www.shell.com/media/news-and-media-releases/_jcr_content/root/main/section/simple_1285915735/call_to_action_11159_1763820656/links/item0.stream/1665756540207/b383bbb00394d07dbed72bfca43df3333ed13f81/2017-press-releases.pdf, p. 40.
2. Ibid.
3. Gernot Heller and Alissa de Carbonnel, 'Germany Threatens Retaliation If U.S. Sanctions Harm Its Firms', Reuters, 16 June 2017, https://www.reuters.com/article/us-usa-russia-sanctions-germany-idUSKBN197156.
4. Holly Ellyatt, 'US Greenlights Sanctions on Mega Russia – EU Gas Pipeline, But It's Probably Too Late', CNBC, 18 December 2019, https://www.cnbc.com/2019/12/18/us-sanctions-on-nord-stream-2-pipeline.html.
5. 'US-Botschafter Grenell schreibt Drohbriefe an deutsche Firmen', *Spiegel*, 13 January 2019, https://www.spiegel.de/politik/deutschland/richard-grenell-us-botschafter-schreibt-drohbriefe-an-deutsche-firmen-a-1247785.html.
6. Senator Ted Cruz, 'Sens. Cruz, Johnson Put Company Installing Putin's Pipeline on Formal Legal Notice', press release, 18 December 2019, https://www.cruz.senate.gov/newsroom/press-releases/sens-cruz-johnson-put-company-installing-putin-and-146s-pipeline-on-formal-legal-notice.
7. 'Nord Stream 2: Trump Approves Sanctions on Russia Gas Pipeline', BBC News, 21 December 2019, https://www.bbc.com/news/world-europe-50875935.
8. Elisabeth Braw, 'Biden Isn't Selling Out on Nord Stream 2. He's Protecting U.S. Firms', *Foreign Policy*, 29 July 2021, https://foreignpolicy.com/2021/07/29/biden-nord-stream-2-insurance-sanctions-protecting-us-firms.
9. Jennifer Jacobs and Jennifer Epstein, 'Biden Says He Waived Nord Stream Sanctions Because It's Finished', Bloomberg, 25 May 2021, https://www.bloomberg.com/news/articles/2021-05-25/biden-says-he-waived-nord-stream-sanctions-because-it-s-finished.
10. 'Klare Mehrheit für Fertigstellung von Nord Stream 2', Ost-Ausschuss der Deutschen Wirtschaft, 20 May 2021, https://www.ost-ausschuss.de/de/PM%20Umfrage%20Forsa%20NS2.
11. Joe Wallace, 'Natural-Gas Prices Jump as Germany Pauses Certification of Russian Pipeline', *Wall Street Journal*, 16 November 2021, https://www.wsj.com/articles/natural-gas-prices-jump-as-germany-pauses-certification-of-russian-pipeline-11637069393.
12. 'U.S. Intelligence Sees Russian Plan for Possible Ukraine Invasion', *New York Times*, 4 December 2021, https://www.nytimes.com/2021/12/04/us/politics/russia-ukraine-biden.html.
13. Christina Wilkie and Amanda Macias, 'U.S. intelligence Agencies Point to Potential Russian Invasion of Ukraine Within a Month's Time', CNBC, 14 January 2022, https://www.cnbc.com/2022/01/14/russia-could-invade-ukraine-within-next-month-us-intelligence.html.
14. Shane Harris et al., 'Biden Says U.S. Has Not Verified a Pullback of Russian Troops from Ukraine's Border, Despite Moscow's Claims', *Washington Post*, 15 February 2022, https://www.washingtonpost.com/world/2022/02/15/ukraine-russia-nato-putin-germany.

15. Elisabeth Braw, 'Russia Can Win in Ukraine Without Firing a Shot', *Foreign Policy*, 28 January 2022, https://foreignpolicy.com/2022/01/28/russia-ukraine-insurance-black-sea-economy-war.
16. Elisabeth Braw, 'Russia's "Greyzone" Aggression is Already Harming Ukraine', *Financial Times,* 9 December 2021, https://www.ft.com/content/1a4efd5e-99c5-4d42-addb-7217c0a76676.
17. 'Pressekonferenz von Bundeskanzler Scholz und Präsident Putin zum Besuch des Bundeskanzlers in der Russischen Föderation am 15. Februar 2022', Die Bundesregierung, press release, 15 February 2022, https://www.bundesregierung.de/breg-de/suche/pressekonferenz-von-bundeskanzler-scholz-und-praesident-putin-zum-besuch-des-bundeskanzlers-in-der-russischen-foederation-am-15-februar-2022-2005530.
18. Ibid.
19. 'UK Scraps Rich Foreign Investor Visa Scheme', BBC News, 17 February 2022, https://www.bbc.com/news/uk-politics-60410844.
20. 'US Sends First Shipment of Military Aid to Ukraine Amid Standoff With Russia', *Euronews*, 22 January 2022, https://www.euronews.com/2022/01/22/us-sends-first-shipment-of-military-aid-to-ukraine-amid-standoff-with-russia.
21. 'Sanction Measures Following Russia's Recognition of the "Independence" of the "Donetsk People's Republic" and the "Luhansk People's Republic" and the Ratification of Treaties With the Two "Republics" (Statement by Foreign Minister HAYASHI Yoshimasa)', Ministry of Foreign Affairs of Japan, press release, 24 February 2022, https://www.mofa.go.jp/press/release/press4e_003085.html.
22. 'Russia – Ukraine Crisis: Zelenskyy's Address in Full', Al Jazeera, 24 February 2022, https://www.aljazeera.com/news/2022/2/24/russia-ukraine-crisis-president-zelenskky-speech-in-full.
23. '"No Other Option": Excerpts of Putin's Speech Declaring War', Al Jazeera, 24 February 2022, https://www.aljazeera.com/news/2022/2/24/putins-speech-declaring-war-on-ukraine-translated-excerpts.
24. '18 People Killed in Ukraine's Odessa in Missile Attack – Regional Authorities', Reuters, 24 February 2022, https://www.reuters.com/world/europe/18-people-killed-ukraines-odessa-missile-attack-regional-authorities-2022-02-24.
25. Bofit Viikkokatsaus, 'Russia Was Finland's Sixth-Largest Export Market in 2021', Bank of Finland for Emerging Economies, 4 March 2022, https://www.bofit.fi/en/monitoring/weekly/2022/vw202209_3.
26. 'Press Briefing by Press Secretary Jen Psaki and Deputy National Security Advisor for International Economics and Deputy NEC Director Daleep Singh, February 24, 2022', White House, press release, 24 February 2022, https://www.whitehouse.gov/briefing-room/press-briefings/2022/02/24/press-briefing-by-press-secretary-jen-psaki-and-deputy-national-security-advisor-for-international-economics-and-deputy-nec-director-daleep-singh-february-24-2022.
27. 'U.S. Treasury Targets Belarusian Support for Russian Invasion of Ukraine', US Department of the Treasury, press release, 24 February 2022, https://home.treasury.gov/news/press-releases/jy0607.
28. 'Foreign Secretary Imposes UK's Most Punishing Sanctions to Inflict Maximum and Lasting Pain on Russia', UK Foreign, Commonwealth & Development Office, press release, 24 February 2022, https://www.gov.uk/government/news/foreign-secretary-imposes-uks-most-punishing-sanctions-to-inflict-maximum-and-lasting-pain-on-russia.

29. 'EU Restrictive Measures Against Russia', EASA, https://www.easa.europa.eu/en/the-agency/faqs/eu-restrictive-measures-against-russia#:~:text=These%20amending%20acts%20were%20published,territory%20of%20the%20European%20Union; 'Russia's Military Aggression Against Ukraine: EU Imposes Sanctions Against President Putin and Foreign Minister Lavrov and Adopts Wide Ranging Individual and Economic Sanctions', Council of the European Union, 25 February 2022, https://www.consilium.europa.eu/en/press/press-releases/2022/02/25/russia-s-military-aggression-against-ukraine-eu-imposes-sanctions-against-president-putin-and-foreign-minister-lavrov-and-adopts-wide-ranging-individual-and-economic-sanctions.
30. 'EU Sanctions on Russian Aviation – Immediate EU Lessor Action Required', Dentons, 4 March 2022, https://www.dentons.com/en/insights/articles/2022/march/4/eu-sanctions-on-russian-aviation; Jamie Freed, Alexander Cornwell and Tim Hepher, 'Hundreds of Russia Plane Leases to Be Axed After Western Sanctions', Reuters, 28 February 2022, https://www.reuters.com/business/aerospace-defense/hundreds-russia-plane-leases-be-axed-after-eu-sanctions-2022-02-28.
31. 'Ukraine Conflict: What Is Swift and Why Is Banning Russia So Significant?', BBC News, 4 March 2022, https://www.bbc.com/news/business-60521822.
32. 'Joint Statement on Further Restrictive Economic Measures', White House, press release, 26 February 2022, https://www.whitehouse.gov/briefing-room/statements-releases/2022/02/26/joint-statement-on-further-restrictive-economic-measures.
33. Elisabeth Braw, 'What If Moscow Cancels Airline Overflight Rights?', Defense One, 24 January 2022, https://www.defenseone.com/ideas/2022/01/what-if-moscow-cancels-airline-overflight-rights/361103.
34. Ibid.
35. 'Russian Flights Bans Hit Airlines from 36 Countries – Aviation Authority', Reuters, 28 February 2022, https://www.reuters.com/business/aerospace-defense/russia-imposes-sweeping-flight-bans-airlines-36-countries-2022-02-28.
36. 'Policy Statement by Olaf Scholz, Chancellor of the Federal Republic of Germany and Member of the German Bundestag, 27 February 2022 in Berlin', Die Bundesregierug, 27 February 2022, https://www.bundesregierung.de/breg-en/news/policy-statement-by-olaf-scholz-chancellor-of-the-federal-republic-of-germany-and-member-of-the-german-bundestag-27-february-2022-in-berlin-2008378.
37. Georgi Kantchev, 'The Five-Year Engineering Feat Germany Pulled Off in Months', *Wall Street Journal*, 8 December 2022, https://www.wsj.com/articles/natural-gas-terminal-engineering-feat-germany-11670513353.
38. Richard Lough, 'French Minister Declares Economic "War" on Russia, and Then Beats a Retreat', Reuters, 1 March 2022, https://www.reuters.com/world/france-declares-economic-war-against-russia-2022-03-01.
39. Stephanie Kelly and Jessica Resnick-ault, 'One Password Allowed Hackers to Disrupt Colonial Pipeline, CEO Tells Senators', Reuters, 9 June 2021, https://www.reuters.com/business/colonial-pipeline-ceo-tells-senate-cyber-defenses-were-compromised-ahead-hack-2021-06-08.
40. Davide Basso, 'Le Maire Backtracks After Talking of "Economic and Financial War" Against Russia', Euractiv, 2 March 2022, https://www.euractiv.com/section/politics/short_news/le-maire-backtracks-after-talking-of-economic-and-financial-war-against-russia.

41. 'Russia Moves Towards Nationalising Assets of Firms That Leave – Ruling Party', Reuters, 9 March 2022, https://www.reuters.com/business/russia-approves-first-step-towards-nationalising-assets-firms-that-leave-ruling-2022-03-09.
42. 'Statement by Secretary of Defense Lloyd J. Austin III on Security Assistance for Ukraine', 16 March 2022, U.S. Department of Defense, https://www.defense.gov/News/Releases/Release/Article/2968561/statement-by-secretary-of-defense-lloyd-j-austin-iii-on-security-assistance-for; '$800 Million in Additional Security Assistance for Ukraine', U.S. Department of Defense, 13 April 2022, https://www.defense.gov/News/Releases/Release/Article/2999113/800-million-in-additional-security-assistance-for-ukraine.
43. 'Estonia's Aid to Ukraine', Republic of Estonia, Ministry of Foreign Affairs, https://vm.ee/en/estonias-aid-ukraine#:~:text=Defence%20assistance%20%E2%80%93%20%E2%82%AC400%20million,in%20Ukraine%20on%2022%20February.
44. 'Australia to Gift 20 Bushmasters to Government of Ukraine', Australian Government, Defence, 8 April 2022, https://www.minister.defence.gov.au/statements/2022-04-08/australia-gift-20-bushmasters-government-ukraine.
45. Alan Posener, 'Brutale Verweigerung', *Die Zeit*, 10 April 2022, https://www.zeit.de/politik/deutschland/2022-04/waffenlieferungen-ukraine-christine-lambrecht-bundesregierung.
46. 'Ukraine "Retakes Whole Kyiv Region" as Russia Looks East', Al Jazeera, 3 April 2022, https://www.aljazeera.com/news/2022/4/3/ukraine-retakes-whole-kyiv-region-as-russian-troops-pull-back.
47. 'Russian Law Creates New Hurdle for Foreign Plane Lessors', Reuters, 14 March 2022, https://www.reuters.com/world/putin-signs-law-registering-leased-planes-airlines-property-tass-2022-03-14.
48. Jamie Freed, Alexander Cornwell and Tim Hepher, 'Hundreds of Russia Plane Leases to Be Axed After Western Sanctions', Reuters, 28 February 2022, https://www.reuters.com/business/aerospace-defense/hundreds-russia-plane-leases-be-axed-after-eu-sanctions-2022-02-28.
49. Chris Isidore and Chris Liakos, 'Russia Moves to Seize Hundreds of Planes from Foreign Owners', CNN, 17 March 2022, https://www.cnn.com/2022/03/16/business/russia-aircraft-seizure/index.html.
50. 'Sakhalin-1 Oil and Gas Project', NS Energy, https://www.nsenergybusiness.com/projects/sakhalin-1-oil-and-gas-project.
51. 'Shell Intends to Exit Equity Partnerships Held with Gazprom Entities', Shell Global, 28 February 2022, https://www.shell.com/media/news-and-media-releases/2022/shell-intends-to-exit-equity-partnerships-held-with-gazprom-entities.html.
52. James Sillars, 'BP Slumps to $20.4bn Loss as It Books Cost of Russian Exit But Oil and Gas Profits Soar', Sky News, https://news.sky.com/story/bp-slumps-to-20-4bn-loss-as-it-books-cost-of-russia-oil-and-gas-exit-12604485.
53. 'Updated Unilever Statement on the War in Ukraine', Unilever, 8 March 2022, https://www.unilever.com/news/news-search/2022/updated-unilever-statement-on-the-war-in-ukraine.
54. Florian Kolf, 'Unternehmer übernimmt Russland-Geschäft von Obi – für rund zehn Euro', *Handelsblatt*, 15 August 2022, https://www.handelsblatt.com/unternehmen/handel-konsumgueter/baumarktkette-unternehmer-uebernimmt-russland-geschaeft-von-obi-fuer-rund-zehn-euro/28601090.html.

55. Irina Ivanova and Kate Gibson, 'These are the Companies That Have Pulled Out of Russia Since Its Invasion of Ukraine', CBS News, 11 March 2022, https://www.cbsnews.com/news/russia-ukraine-corporations-pull-out-invasion.
56. 'McDonald's to Exit from Russia', McDonald's, press release, 16 May 2022, https://corporate.mcdonalds.com/corpmcd/our-stories/article/mcd-exit-russia.html.
57. 'Exclusive: Heir to McDonald's Russia Craves Success But Big Mac a "Big Loss"', Reuters, 21 June 2022, https://www.reuters.com/business/retail-consumer/exclusive-heir-mcdonalds-russia-craves-success-big-mac-big-loss-2022-06-21.
58. 'Stora Enso Divests Its Sawmills and Forest Operations in Russia', Stora Enso, 25 April 2022, https://www.storaenso.com/en/newsroom/regulatory-and-investor-releases/2022/4/stora-enso-divests-its-sawmills-and-forest-operations-in-russia?prid=e46f473b871fc220.
59. Elisabeth Braw, 'How Corporate Boycotts Could Backfire', *Foreign Policy*, 28 March 2022, https://foreignpolicy.com/2022/03/28/russia-sanctions-ukraine-corporate-boycotts-could-backfire.
60. 'U.S. Treasury Sanctions Russia's Defense-Industrial Base, the Russian Duma and Its Members, and Sberbank CEO', U.S. Department of the Treasury, press release, 24 March 2022, https://home.treasury.gov/news/press-releases/jy0677.
61. Scilla Alecci, 'Russian Bankers Shuffled Personal Wealth Offshore Long Before Latest Sanctions, Pandora Papers Show', ICIJ, 11 April 2022, https://www.icij.org/investigations/pandora-papers/russian-bankers-wealth-sanctions-offshore.
62. Nik Martin and Roman Goncharenko, 'Siemens to Step Up Investment in Russia', *DW*, 16 February 2019, https://www.dw.com/en/siemens-to-hike-russia-investment-despite-crimea-scandal/a-47548791.
63. Mark Faithfull, 'Fast Retailing Defiant as It Keeps Russian Uniqlo Stores Open', *Forbes*, 8 March 2022, https://www.forbes.com/sites/markfaithfull/2022/03/08/fast-retailing-defiant-as-it-keeps–russian-uniqlo-stores-open/?sh=607fddca36a0.
64. Anonymous Operations (@AnonOpsSE), Twitter, 18 March 2022, https://twitter.com/AnonOpsSE/status/1504919224405442568.
65. DrJackBrown (@DrGJackBrown), Twitter, 21 March 2022, https://twitter.com/DrGJackBrown/status/1505789458431426563.
66. Juan Jose Del Rio (@partymola), Twitter, 8 March 2022, https://twitter.com/partymola/status/1501329541951856640.
67. Leila Abboud, 'Nestlé Justifies Staying In Russia as Criticism Mounts', *Financial Times*, 21 March 2022, https://www.ft.com/content/1484606c-3e8f-494e-9e88-528a79aeeeaa.
68. Megan Cerullo, 'Uniqlo Bows to Public Pressure to Close Stores in Russia', CBS News, 10 March 2022, https://www.cbsnews.com/news/russia-ukraine-uniqlo-closes-stores; 'Update on Ukraine and Russia', Nestlé, press release, https://www.nestle.com/ask-nestle/our-company/answers/update-russia-ukraine.
69. 'Rysslands angrepp mot Ukraina ledde till att majoriteten av finländarna nu är för ett medlemskap i Nato', EVA, 22 March 2022, https://www.eva.fi/en/blog/2022/03/22/rysslands-angrepp-mot-ukraina-ledde-till-att-majoriteten-av-finlandarna-nu-ar-for-ett-medlemskap-i-nato.
70. 'Varannan svensk vill gå med i Nato', *SVT*, 20 April 2022, https://www.svt.se/nyheter/inrikes/nastan-halften-av-svenskarna-vill-ga-med-i-nato.

71. 'På tisdag blev det klart: Riksdagen vill ansöka om Natomedlemskap för Finland', *YLE*, 17 May 2022, https://svenska.yle.fi/a/7-10016587.
72. 'Regeringen fattade beslut om att Sverige ska ansöka om medlemskap i Nato', Sweden Abroad, 17 May 2022, https://www.swedenabroad.se/de/botschaften/finland-helsingfors/current/news/regeringen-fattade-beslut-om-att-sverige-ska-ans%C3%B6ka-om-medlemskap-i-nato/#:~:text=Regeringen%20fattade%20beslut%20om%20att%20Sverige%20ska%20ans%C3%B6ka%20om%20medlemskap%20i%20Nato,-17%20Mai%202022&text=Regeringen%20i%20Sverige%20fattade%20m%C3%A5ndagen,ans%C3%B6ka%20om%20medlemskap%20i%20Nato.
73. 'Jährliche Wartungsarbeiten der Nord Stream-Pipeline werden im Juli 2022 statt finden', Nord Stream, press release, https://www.nord-stream.com/de/presse-info/pressemitteilungen/jaehrliche-wartungsarbeiten-der-nord-stream-pipeline-werden-im-juli-2022-stattfinden-524.
74. Benjamin Fredrich, 'Unfriedliche Demo', *Katapult MV*, 25 September 2022, https://katapult-mv.de/artikel/unfriedliche-demo.
75. Naida Hakirevic Prevljak, 'Germany to Transform Rostock, Lubmin Into Energy Ports of the Future', Offshore Energy, 19 September 2022, https://www.offshore-energy.biz/germany-to-transform-rostock-lubmin-into-energy-ports-of-the-future.
76. 'FSRU Arrives in German Port of Lubmin to Start LNG Imports', *Maritime Executive,* 16 December 2022, https://www.maritime-executive.com/article/fsru-arrives-in-germany-port-of-lubmin-to-start-lng-imports.

CHAPTER 13: GEN Z OPENS A SECOND FRONT

1. Sandra Laville and Jonathan Watts, 'Across the Globe, Millions Join Biggest Climate Protest Ever', *Guardian*, 21 September 2019, https://www.theguardian.com/environment/2019/sep/21/across-the-globe-millions-join-biggest-climate-protest-ever.
2. Damian Carrington, '"Our Leaders Are Like Children", School Strike Founder Tells Climate Summit', *Guardian*, 4 December 2018, https://www.theguardian.com/environment/2018/dec/04/leaders-like-children-school-strike-founder-greta-thunberg-tells-un-climate-summit.
3. John Sutter, 'COP24 Climate Talks End In Agreement – Barely', CNN, 16 December 2018, https://www.cnn.com/2018/12/15/health/cop24-climate-change-talks-agreement/index.html.
4. Bill Chappell, 'Greta Thunberg is the "Time" Person of the Year for 2019', NPR, 11 December 2019, https://www.npr.org/2019/12/11/787026271/greta-thunberg-is-time-magazine-s-person-of-the-year-for-2019#:~:text=Greta%20Thunberg%2C%20the%20activist%20who,the%20magazine's%2092%2Dyear%20history.
5. James Workman, '"Our House is on Fire." 16-Year-Old Greta Thunberg Wants Action', World Economic Forum, 25 January 2019, https://www.weforum.org/agenda/2019/01/our-house-is-on-fire-16-year-old-greta-thunberg-speaks-truth-to-power.
6. 'Greta Thunberg Warns We Must Switch to a Vegan Diet or "We Are F***Ed"', *Vegan Food & Living*, 28 May 2021, https://www.veganfoodandliving.com/news/greta-thunberg-warns-we-must-switch-to-vegan-diet.

7. Lisa Feria, 'Gen Z is Leading a Generational Shift in Plant-Based Food Purchasing', *Supermarket News*, 27 September 2022, https://www.supermarketnews.com/health-wellness/gen-z-leading-generational-shift-plant-based-food-purchasing.
8. 'Annual 2021 Global Climate Report', National Centers for Environmental Information, 11 September 2023, https://www.ncei.noaa.gov/access/monitoring/monthly-report/global/202113#:~:text=The%20year%20culminated%20as%20the,ten%20warmest%20years%20on%20record.
9. Michael Standaert, 'China's First Climate Striker Warned: Give It Up or You Can't Go Back to School', *Guardian*, 19 July 2020, https://www.theguardian.com/world/2020/jul/20/chinas-first-climate-striker-cant-return-to-school.
10. Sina Alonso Garcia, '"Schämt euch": Ritter Sport liefert weiter nach Russland – Fans rufen zu Boykott auf', *BW24*, 18 August 2022, https://www.bw24.de/wirtschaft/boykott-aufruf-fans-schaemt-euch-ritter-sport-schokolade-lieferung-russland-zr-91441286.html.
11. Ibid.
12. 'Ukraine-Krieg: Von Unternehmen wird Haltung gefordert', Bitkom, 12 April 2022, https://www.bitkom.org/Presse/Presseinformation/Ukraine-Krieg-Von-Unternehmen-wird-Haltung-gefordert.
13. Wesley Case, 'Americans Overwhelmingly Want Companies to Take Action Against Russia Over Ukraine Invasion', Morning Consult, 28 February 2022, https://morningconsult.com/2022/02/28/russia-ukraine-invasion-companies-take-action.
14. 'Debatt: Bojkotta rysslandsstöttande företag', *Lundagård*, 19 April 2022, https://www.lundagard.se/2022/04/19/debatt-bojkotta-rysslandsstottande-foretag.
15. Laura Silver, Kat Devlin and Christine Huang, 'Most Americans Support Tough Stance Toward China on Human Rights, Economic Issues', Pew Research Center, 4 March 2021, https://www.pewresearch.org/global/2021/03/04/most-americans-support-tough-stance-toward-china-on-human-rights-economic-issues; 'Umfrage: Große Mehrheit der Deutschen für härteren Kurs gegenüber China', *RND*, 29 August 2021, https://www.rnd.de/politik/umfrage-grosse-mehrheit-der-deutschen-fuer-haerteren-kurs-gegenueber-china-RMDNJ4XTZE-7MYKXM2XZKPUPCIA.html.
16. Mike Proulx, 'A Post-Truth Climate is Shaping Gen Z's Consumer Behaviors', Forrester, 14 January 2021, https://www.forrester.com/report/a-post-truth-climate-is-shaping-gen-zs-consumer-behaviors/RES164315?objectid=RES164315.
17. Chris Taylor, 'Boycott Nation: How Americans are Boycotting Companies Now', Reuters, 30 June 2022, https://www.reuters.com/markets/us/boycott-nation-how-americans-are-boycotting-companies-now-2022-06-29.
18. 'Versace Apologises After T-Shirt Angers China', BBC News, 12 August 2019, https://www.bbc.com/news/business-49315317; Lucy Handley, 'Versace, Givenchy and Coach Say Sorry Over Chinese T-shirt Anger', CNBC, 12 August 2019, https://www.cnbc.com/2019/08/12/versace-givenchy-and-coach-say-sorry-over-chinese-t-shirt-anger.html.
19. 'Coach, Givenchy Join Versace in Apologizing to Chinese Consumers Amid T-shirt Outcry', CNN Style, 13 August 2019, https://www.cnn.com/style/article/coach-givenchy-versace-t-shirt-controversy/index.html.
20. 'Versace Apologises After T-Shirt Angers China', BBC News.
21. 'Coach respects and supports China's sovereignty and territorial integrity. In May 2018, we found a serious inaccuracy in the design of a few T-shirts. We imme-

diately pulled those products from all channels globally. We also reviewed our entire assortment to ensure compliance, and have strengthened our internal product development process to avoid the occurrence of a similar issue in the future. We are fully aware of the severity of their error and deeply regret it. We have also taken immediate action to review and correct relevant website content. Coach is dedicated to long-term development in China, and we respect the feelings of the Chinese people. We will continue to strive to provide exceptional products and service to Chinese customers.' Coach (@Coach), Twitter, 12 August 2019, https://twitter.com/Coach/status/1160767914951225344.

22. 'LVMH Annual Results 2019', LVMH, 28 January 2020, https://r.lvmh-static.com/uploads/2020/01/lvmh-fy-2019-va.pdf.
23. 'Chinese Demand Carrefour Boycott for Tibet Support', Reuters, 15 April 2008, https://www.reuters.com/article/us-china-tibet-carrefour/chinese-demand-carrefour-boycott-for-tibet-support-idUSPEK24412820080415.
24. Viking Bohman and Hillevi Pårup, 'Purchasing with the Party: Chinese Consumer Boycotts of Foreign Companies, 2008–2021', Swedish National China Centre, 2022, https://kinacentrum.se/wp-content/uploads/2022/07/purchasing-with-the-party-chinese-consumer-boycotts-of-foreign-companies-20082021-3.pdf.
25. Ibid., p. 5.
26. Ibid., p. 7.
27. Ibid., p. 2.
28. Sam Wilkin, '2022 Political Risk Survey Report', WTW, 31 March 2022, https://www.wtwco.com/en-US/Insights/2022/03/2022-political-risk-survey-report, p. 10.
29. Gavin Bade, 'Fast Fashion Giant With Ties to China Tries to Shake Forced Labour Claims', Politico, 5 June 2023, https://www.politico.com/news/2023/06/05/shein-china-forced-labor-claims-lobbying-fast-fashion-00100065.
30. Kristian Skårdalsmo et al., 'Mehl tar selvkritikk – nå vil Frp legge saken død', *NRK*, 7 February 2023, https://www.nrk.no/norge/tiktok-avklaring-tok-fire-maneder_-slik-har-mehl-svart-stortinget-1.16287750.
31. 'SHEIN Eyes Europe, Testing the Waters With Physical Stores', *Dao Insights*, 6 September 2022, https://daoinsights.com/news/shein-eyes-europe-testing-the-waters-with-physical-stores.
32. Sara Lebow, 'What Were the Most Downloaded Social Media Apps in 2022?', Insider Intelligence, 14 February 2023, https://www.insiderintelligence.com/content/what-were-most-downloaded-social-media-apps-2022.
33. Christian Paz, 'Inside the Lonely and Surprisingly Earnest World of Political TikTok', *Vox*, 3 February 2023, https://www.vox.com/policy-and-politics/23581198/tiktok-ban-campaign-politics-jeff-jackson-katie-porte.
34. David Ingram, 'Biden Signs TikTok Ban for Government Devices, Setting Up a Chaotic 2023 for the App', NBC News, 30 December 2022, https://www.nbcnews.com/tech/tech-news/tiktok-ban-biden-government-college-state-federal-security-privacy-rcna63724.
35. Amanda Aronczyk, 'A Look at the Fallout of TikTok Ban in India', NPR, 15 January 2021, https://www.npr.org/2021/01/15/957371287/a-look-at-the-fallout-of-tiktok-ban-in-india.
36. Laura Silver et al., 'How Young Adults Want Their Country to Engage With the World', Pew Research Center, 8 March 2023, https://www.pewresearch.org/global/2023/03/08/how-young-adults-want-their-country-to-engage-with-the-world.

37. Philip Blenkinsop, 'EU Proposes Banning Products Made With Forced Labour', Reuters, 14 September 2022, https://www.reuters.com/markets/europe/eu-proposes-banning-products-made-with-forced-labour-2022-09-14.
38. Foo Yun Chee, 'Top EU bodies, Citing Security, Ban TikTok on Staff Phones', Reuters, 24 February 2023, https://www.reuters.com/technology/eu-commission-staff-told-remove-tiktok-phones-eu-industry-chief-says-2023-02-23.

CHAPTER 14: FRIENDSHORING SETS SAIL

1. 'China Bans 35 Taiwanese Food Exporters in Warning Ahead of Pelosi Visit', Reuters, 2 August 2022, https://www.reuters.com/world/china/china-bans-35-taiwanese-food-exporters-warning-ahead-pelosi-visit-2022-08-02.
2. 'China Says U.S. Politicians Who "Play with Fire" on Taiwan Will Pay', Reuters, 2 August 2022, https://www.reuters.com/world/china/china-says-us-politicians-who-play-with-fire-taiwan-will-pay-2022-08-02.
3. Lily Kuo et al., 'Nancy Pelosi Departs Taiwan, Ending Contentious Visit That Angered China', *Washington Post*, 3 August 2022, https://www.washingtonpost.com/world/2022/08/02/nancy-pelosi-taiwan-visit.
4. Kevin Casas-Zamora, 'Notes on Costa Rica's Switch from Taipei to Beijing', Brookings Institution, 6 November 2009, https://www.brookings.edu/on-the-record/notes-on-costa-ricas-switch-from-taipei-to-beijing.
5. Xavier Vavasseur, 'US DoD's 2021 China Military Power Report: PLAN is the Largest Navy in the World', *Naval News*, 5 November 2021, https://www.navalnews.com/naval-news/2021/11/us-dods-2021-china-military-power-report-plan-is-the-largest-navy-in-the-world.
6. Huang Tzu-ti, 'Pomelo Farmers in Taiwan Stunned by China Ban', *Taiwan News*, 3 August 2022, https://www.taiwannews.com.tw/en/news/4615370.
7. Luc Olinga, 'Tim Cook and Apple Make a Move That Could Annoy China', *The Street*, 26 September 2022, https://www.thestreet.com/technology/apple-makes-a-bold-move-that-could-annoy-china.
8. Vallery, 'When Did Apple Start Production of iPhones in China?', China Merchants Holdings (International) Company Limited, 19 March 2022, https://www.cmhi.com.hk/when-did-apple-start-production-of-iphones-in-china.
9. Pete Sweeney, 'Apple's Ugly China Deal Mostly Bought Time', Reuters, 8 December 2021, https://www.reuters.com/breakingviews/apples-ugly-china-deal-mostly-bought-time-2021-12-08; Jack Nicas et al., 'Censorship, Surveillance and Profits: A Hard Bargain for Apple in China', *New York Times*, 17 May 2021, https://www.nytimes.com/2021/05/17/technology/apple-china-censorship-data.html.
10. Ashley Capoot, 'Apple Will Reportedly Begin Producing Some MacBooks in Vietnam in 2023 as It Shifts from China', CNBC, 20 December 2022, https://www.cnbc.com/2022/12/20/apple-will-reportedly-begin-producing-some-macbooks-in-vietnam-in-2023.html.
11. Jie Ye-eun, 'Samsung, LG Shift Away from China Toward India as Production Base', *Korea Herald*, 9 February 2023, https://www.koreaherald.com/view.php?ud=20230209000664.
12. Efe Udin, 'Google to Move the Pixel Production Line to Vietnam', Gizchina, 2 September 2022, https://www.gizchina.com/2022/09/02/google-to-move-the-pixel-production-line-to-vietnam.

13. Sissi Cao, 'Intel CEO Pat Gelsinger Says Chip Making Will Shift from Asia to the West Amid Rising Tensions', *Observer*, 25 October 2022, https://observer.com/2022/10/intel-ceo-pat-gelsinger-predicts-chip-industry-geopolitical-tension.
14. Kenichi Yamada, 'South Korean Companies Shift Production Out of China', Nikkei Asia, 22 June 2019, https://asia.nikkei.com/Business/Business-trends/South-Korean-companies-shift-production-out-of-China.
15. Luna Sun, 'Chinese Solar Firms Ramping Up Investment in Southeast Asia to Evade US, European Trade Tensions', *South China Morning Post*, 29 July 2022, https://www.scmp.com/economy/china-economy/article/3186923/chinese-solar-firms-ramping-investment-southeast-asia-evade.
16. Thomas Harloff, 'Tavares: E-Autos aus Indien für Europa', *Auto Motor Sport*, 9 December 2022, https://www.auto-motor-und-sport.de/verkehr/produktionsstopp-stellantis-teil-rueckzug-china.
17. Peter Campbell et al., 'Carmakers Quietly Cut Ties with China in Supply Chain Shake-up', *Financial Times*, 27 December 2022, https://www.ft.com/content/d88955d4-2bc8-476e-9cdb-882ca3c3b10d.
18. 'AmCham Shanghai Releases 2022 China Business Report', AmCham Shanghai, 27 October 2022, https://www.amcham-shanghai.org/en/article/amcham-shanghai-releases-2022-china-business-report.
19. Dan Strumpf, 'From McDonald's to Ralph Lauren, U.S. Companies are Planning China Expansions', *Wall Street Journal*, 27 February 2023, https://www.wsj.com/articles/from-mcdonalds-to-ralph-lauren-u-s-companies-are-planning-china-expansions-c1a33969; Thomas Hale et al., 'Starbucks Braced for Price War in China as Rivals Pile Into Coffee Market', *Financial Times*, 22 March 2023, https://www.ft.com/content/92b2faa0-f4c3-43fd-bbb3-46c60db5d51a.
20. Lazar Backovic et al., 'In China verkauft BYD jetzt mehr Autos als Volkswagen', *Handelsblatt*, 19 April 2023, https://www.handelsblatt.com/unternehmen/industrie/vw-in-china-verkauft-byd-jetzt-mehr-autos-als-volkswagen/29098304.html.
21. 'Schwere Zeiten stehen bevor – Geschäftsvertrauen deutscher Unternehmen in China auf historischem Tiefstand', AHK Greater China, press release, 15 December 2022, https://china.ahk.de/de/news/news-details/rocky-roads-ahead-business-confidence-of-german-companies-in-china-reached-a-historic-low.
22. Elisabeth Braw, 'Companies are Fleeing China for Friendlier Shores', *Foreign Policy*, 2 August 2022, https://foreignpolicy.com/2022/08/02/companies-fleeing-china-friendshoring-supply-chains.
23. Jim Pickard and George Parker, 'UK plc is Cutting Ties to China, Says CBI boss', *Financial Times*, 29 July 2022, https://www.ft.com/content/cd93dd29-7069-4e2e-baa8-7081b385c0c6.
24. 'Schwere Zeiten stehen bevor', AHK Greater China.
25. 'China's Xi Secures Third Term as Head of Communist Party', *DW*, 23 October 2022, https://www.dw.com/en/chinas-xi-secures-third-term-as-head-of-communist-party/a-63529214.
26. 'Transcript: President Xi Jinping's report to China's 2022 party congress', Nikkei, 18 October 2022, https://asia.nikkei.com/Politics/China-s-party-congress/Transcript-President-Xi-Jinping-s-report-to-China-s-2022-party-congress.
27. Ana Swanson, 'Biden Administration Clamps Down on China's Access to Chip Technology', *New York Times*, 7 October 2022, https://www.nytimes.com/2022/10/07/business/economy/biden-chip-technology.html#:~:text=Perhaps%20most%20

significant%2C%20the%20Biden,U.S.%20technology%2C%20software%20 or%20machinery.

28. 'Biden Administration Imposes Sweeping Tech Restrictions on China', *Guardian*, 7 October 2022, https://www.theguardian.com/us-news/2022/oct/07/biden-administration-tech-restrictions-china.
29. Ken Koyanagi and Ryosuke Hanada, 'Tata to Enter Chipmaking in India: Chairman Natarajan Chandrasekaran', Nikkei Asia, 9 December 2022, https://asia.nikkei.com/Business/Tech/Semiconductors/Tata-to-enter-chipmaking-in-India-Chairman-Natarajan-Chandrasekaran?del_type=1&pub_date=20221208190000&seq_num=2.
30. Kif Leswing, 'Tim Cook says Apple Will Use Chips Built in the U.S. at Arizona Factory', CNBC, 6 December 2022, https://www.cnbc.com/2022/12/06/tim-cook-says-apple-will-use-chips-built-in-the-us-at-arizona-factory.html.
31. 'Taiwan Says "Fab 4" Chip Group Held First Senior Officials Meeting', Reuters, 25 February 2023, https://www.reuters.com/technology/taiwan-says-fab-4-chip-group-held-first-senior-officials-meeting-2023-02-25/.
32. Tyler Buchanan, 'Intel's "Ohio One" Mega Chip Factory is Bigger Than You Think', Axios, 24 January 2023, https://www.axios.com/local/columbus/2023/01/24/intel-ohio-one-chip-factory-stats-size-wendys.
33. 'Intel Announces Next US Site with Landmark Investment in Ohio', Intel Newsroom, 21 January 2022, https://www.intel.com/content/www/us/en/newsroom/news/intel-announces-next-us-site-landmark-investment-ohio.html#gs.t6s6na.
34. 'Who is Adolfo Urso, the New Minister of Giorgia Meloni's Government', Agenzia Nova, 21 October 2022, https://www.agenzianova.com/en/news/chi-e-adolfo-urso-nuovo-ministro-del-governo-di-giorgia-meloni.
35. Daniel Michaels, 'EU Sues China in WTO Over Trade Retaliation on Lithuania', *Wall Street Journal*, 7 December 2022, https://www.wsj.com/articles/eu-files-complaint-in-wto-over-chinas-trade-retaliation-on-lithuania-11670402333; 'EU Challenges China's Anti-Suit Injunction at the WTO', Crowell & Moring LLP, 20 December 2022, https://www.crowell.com/NewsEvents/AlertsNewsletters/all/EU-Challenges-Chinas-Anti-Suit-Injunctions-at-the-WTO#:~:text=The%20European%20Union%20has%20filed,in%20any%20non%2DChinese%20court.
36. 'Alibaba Group – Statistics & Facts', Statista, https://www.statista.com/topics/2187/alibaba-group/#topicOverview.
37. Anshuman Daga, 'Timeline: Key Events Behind Suspension of Ant Group's $37 billion IPO', Reuters, 4 November 2020, https://www.reuters.com/article/uk-ant-group-ipo-suspension-events/timeline-key-events-behind-suspension-of-ant-groups-37-billion-ipo-idUKKBN27K1A0.
38. Bien Perez, 'China's E-Commerce Crackdown: Timeline of Beijing's Actions to Bring Tech Giants In Line With National Policy', *South China Morning Post,* 22 November 2021, https://www.scmp.com/tech/policy/article/3156719/chinas-e-commerce-crackdown-timeline-beijings-actions-bring-tech-giants.
39. Ibid.
40. Derek Saul, 'Elusive Chinese Billionaire Jack Ma Living in Tokyo, Report Says', *Forbes*, 29 November 2022, https://www.forbes.com/sites/dereksaul/2022/11/29/elusive-chinese-billionaire-jack-ma-living-in-tokyo-report-says/?sh=3e1cb8cd2e7f.

41. Jan Dörner, 'China-Reise: Zwei Erfolge hat Kanzler Scholz errungen', *Berliner Morgenpost*, 4 November 2022, https://www.morgenpost.de/politik/article 236824185/olaf-scholz-china-xi-jinping-russland-ukraine-krieg.html.
42. 'Ukraine: Civilian Casualty Update 26 December 2022', United Nations Office of the High Commissioner for Human Rights, press release, 27 December 2022, https://www.ohchr.org/en/news/2022/12/ukraine-civilian-casualty-update-26-december-2022.
43. Christina Lamb, 'Ukraine's War Secret: How Many of Their Troops Have Died?', *The Times*, 25 February 2023, https://www.thetimes.co.uk/article/ukraine-war-how-many-died-true-death-toll-2023-6f8t83k06; 'Ukraine War: US Estimates 200,000 Military Casualties on All Sides', BBC News, 10 November 2022, https://www.bbc.com/news/world-europe-63580372.
44. 'Infographic – Refugees from Ukraine in the EU', European Council, https://www.consilium.europa.eu/en/infographics/ukraine-refugees-eu.
45. Oscar Arce et al., 'One Year Since Russia's Invasion of Ukraine – The Effects on Euro Area Inflation', European Central Bank Blog, 24 February 2023, https://www.ecb.europa.eu/press/blog/date/2023/html/ecb.blog20230224~3b75362af3.en.html.
46. Ben Knight, 'Scholz Defends Decision to Send Battle Tanks to Ukraine', *DW*, 25 January 2023, https://www.dw.com/en/german-chancellor-olaf-scholz-defends-decision-to-send-battle-tanks-to-ukraine/a-64509633.
47. 'President Xi Jinping Holds Talks with European Council President Charles Michel', Foreign Ministry of Foreign Affairs of the People's Republic of China, 1 December 2022, https://webcache.googleusercontent.com/search?q=cache:2B871tCZb_oJ:https://www.fmprc.gov.cn/eng/zxxx_662805/202212/t20221201_10983932.html&cd=1&hl=en&ct=clnk&gl=us.
48. Chen Aizhu and Jeslyn Lerh, 'China Boosts Imports of Fuel Oil Blended from Russian Barrels', Reuters, 3 February 2023, https://www.reuters.com/business/energy/china-boosts-imports-fuel-oil-blended-russian-barrels-2023-02-03.
49. 'Chinese Cars, Phones Gain Ground in Russia's Sanctions-Hit Economy', Nikkei Asia, 28 February 2023, https://asia.nikkei.com/Politics/Ukraine-war/Chinese-cars-phones-gain-ground-in-Russia-s-sanctions-hit-economy.
50. Ian Talley and Anthony De Barros, 'China Aids Russia's War in Ukraine, Trade Data Shows', *Wall Street Journal*, 4 February 2023, https://www.wsj.com/articles/china-aids-russias-war-in-ukraine-trade-data-shows-11675466360.
51. Levent Kenez, 'Turkey's Exports to Russia Continue to Rise Amid Declining Trade with Other Countries', Nordic Monitor, 5 July 2023, https://nordicmon itor.com/2023/07/turkeys-exports-to-russia-continue-to-rise-amid-declining-trade-with-other-countries.
52. Aftab Ahmed and Swati Bhat, 'Exclusive: India, Russia Suspend Negotiations to Settle Trade in Rupees', Reuters, 4 May 2023, https://www.reuters.com/markets/currencies/india-russia-suspend-negotiations-settle-trade-rupees-sources-2023-05-04.
53. Alexandra Prokopenko, 'How Sanctions Have Changed Russian Economic Policy', Carnegie Endowment for International Peace, 9 May 2023, https://carn egieendowment.org/politika/89708.
54. 'Factbox: Companies Count the Cost of Ditching Russia', Reuters, 3 November 2022, https://www.reuters.com/markets/europe/companies-count-cost-ditching-russia-2022-11-03.

55. 'Political Risk Insurance', Chubb, https://www.chubb.com/us-en/business-insurance/political-risk.html#:~:text=Political%20risk%20insurance%20is%20designed,Selective%20discrimination; 2023 Political Risk Survey Report, WTW, 18 April 2023, https://www.wtwco.com/en-us/insights/2023/04/2023-political-risk-survey-report#:~:text=the%20industrial%20sector.-,The%20proportion%20who%20reported%20purchasing%20political%20risk%20insurance%20nearly%20trebled,followed%20by%20decoupling%20with%20China.
56. 'China Average Yearly Wages', Trading Economics, https://tradingeconomics.com/china/wages.
57. 'Das Lieferkettengesetz', Bundesministerium für wirtschaftliche Zusammenarbeit und Entwicklung, press release, July 2021, https://www.bmz.de/de/themen/lieferkettengesetz.
58. 'Dell Looks to Phase Out China-Made Chips by 2024', 5 January 2023, Reuters, https://www.reuters.com/technology/dell-looks-phase-out-chinese-chips-by-2024-nikkei-2023-01-05; Koki Izumi, 'Panasonic Moving Some Air Conditioner Output from China to Japan', Nikkei Asia, 23 June 2023, https://asia.nikkei.com/Business/Electronics/Panasonic-moving-some-air-conditioner-output-from-China-to-Japan.
59. Lisa Unbehaun, 'Sonderbefragung: Mittelstand verlagert Lieferketten nach Europa', DZ Bank, 29 March 2023, https://www.dzbank.de/content/dzbank/de/home/die-dz-bank/presse/pressemitteilungen/2022/sonderbefragung-mittelstandverlagertlieferkettennacheuropa.html.
60. Craig Kafura, 'Americans Favor "Friendshoring" Approach for Supply Chains', Chicago Council on Global Affairs, 30 November 2022, https://globalaffairs.org/research/public-opinion-survey/americans-favor-friendshoring-approach-supply-chains.
61. Matthew Smith, 'International Survey: Globalisation is Still Seen as a Force for Good in the World', YouGov, 17 November 2016, https://today.yougov.com/topics/politics/articles-reports/2016/11/17/international-survey.
62. 'World Opinion on Globalization and International Trade in 2021', Ipsos, August 2021, https://www.ipsos.com/sites/default/files/ct/news/documents/2021-08/World%20Opinion%20on%20Globalization%20and%20International%20Trade%20in%202021%20-%20Report.pdf.
63. Shirley Li, 'How Hollywood Sold Out to China', *Atlantic,* 10 September 2021, https://www.theatlantic.com/culture/archive/2021/09/how-hollywood-sold-out-to-china/620021.
64. Shelby Rose and Jessie Yeung, 'Tencent-backed "Top Gun" Cuts Taiwan Flag from Tom Cruise's Jacket', CNN, 22 July 2019, https://www.cnn.com/2019/07/22/media/top-gun-flags-intl-hnk/index.html.
65. Kylie Madry, 'Toymaker Mattel Expands Mexican Plant in "Nearshoring" Push', Reuters, 1 April 2022, https://www.reuters.com/business/retail-consumer/toymaker-mattel-expands-mexican-plant-nearshoring-push-2022-04-01.
66. Aylin Dülger, 'China ist für uns unverzichtbar', *Tagesschau*, 7 January 2023, https://www.tagesschau.de/wirtschaft/unternehmen/mittelstand-lieferketten-regionale-abheangigkeit-europa-asien-nordamerika-101.html.
67. Ralph Jennings, 'Taiwan Tells Start-Ups to Shun Mainland China and Go to Japan Instead, Amid Supply-Chain Decoupling', *South China Morning Post,* 6 February 2023, https://www.scmp.com/economy/china-economy/

article/3209255/taiwan-tells-start-ups-shun-mainland-china-and-go-japan-instead-amid-supply-chain-decoupling.

68. Eri Sugiura, 'China No Longer Viable as World's Factory, Says Kyocera', *Financial Times*, 20 February 2023, https://www.ft.com/content/e21b6f97-3bbb-4223-9916-9f4ac5024953.
69. 'India Part of Friendshoring Strategy, Says Janet Yellen', *Indian Express,* 26 February 2023, https://indianexpress.com/article/cities/bangalore/us-treasury-secretary-janet-yellen-india-friendshoring-plan-tech-supply-chains-8466707.
70. Wang Yi, 'Transfer of a Few Factories Will Not Alter China's Core Place in Global Supply Chain', *Global Times*, 21 February 2023, https://www.globaltimes.cn/page/202302/1285954.shtml.
71. Justin Badlam et al., 'The CHIPS and Science Act: Here's What's In It', McKinsey & Company, 4 October 2022, https://www.mckinsey.com/industries/public-and-social-sector/our-insights/the-chips-and-science-act-heres-whats-in-it.
72. 'Building a Clean Energy Economy: A Guidebook to the Inflation Reduction Act's Investments in Clean Energy and Climate Action', White House, January 2023, https://www.whitehouse.gov/wp-content/uploads/2022/12/Inflation-Reduction-Act-Guidebook.pdf.
73. Emma Newburger, 'Schumer – Manchin Reconciliation Bill has $369 Billion to Fight Climate Change – Here are the Details', CNBC, 28 July 2022, https://www.cnbc.com/2022/07/27/inflation-reduction-act-climate-change-provisions.html#:~:text=The%20legislation%2C%20called%20the%20%E2%80%9CInflation,a%20summary%20of%20the%20deal.
74. Nora Eckert, 'Shift to EVs Triggers Biggest Auto-Factory Building Boom in Decades', *Wall Street Journal*, 1 January 2023, https://www.wsj.com/articles/shift-to-evs-triggers-biggest-auto-factory-building-boom-in-decades-11672503095?st=6zsclgtrev57pl0.
75. Peter Campbell, 'VW to Build $2bn Electric Vehicle Plant in South Carolina', *Financial Times*, 3 February 2023, https://www.ft.com/content/f5623da1-5c31-4090-8c0a-f36e52ea395e; 'Ford Taps Michigan for New LFP Battery Plant; New Battery Chemistry Offers Customers Value, Durability, Fast Charging, Creates 2,500 More New American Jobs', Ford, press release, 13 February 2023, https://media.ford.com/content/fordmedia/fna/us/en/news/2023/02/13/ford-taps-michigan-for-new-lfp-battery-plant–new-battery-chemis.html.
76. Richard Milne et al., 'VW Puts European Battery Plant on Hold as It Seeks €10bn from US', *Financial Times*, 8 March 2023, https://www.ft.com/content/6ac390f5-df35-4e39-a572-2c01a12f666a.
77. Tom Howarth, 'Here's a Glimpse of the EU Response to the Inflation Reduction Act', GreenBiz, 6 February 2023, https://www.greenbiz.com/article/heres-glimpse-eu-response-inflation-reduction-act; Gerald Traufetter, 'Was Robert Habeck von Joe Biden will – und was er vielleicht bekommt', *Spiegel*, 8 February 2023, https://www.spiegel.de/wirtschaft/soziales/mission-in-washington-was-robert-habeck-von-joe-biden-will-und-was-er-vielleicht-bekommt-a-60e4c62d-08a4-4100-9c87-ea8cddd0feca.
78. 'Faustian Bargain: Europe's Answers to the IRA', Allianz, 7 February 2023, https://www.allianz.com/en/economic_research/publications/specials_fmo/inflation-reduction-act.html.
79. Frank Tang, 'China Sets New Bank Risk Rules to Prevent Financial Crisis', *South China Morning Post*, 30 October 2021, https://www.scmp.com/news/article/3154286/china-sets-new-bank-risk-rules-prevent-financial-crisis.

80. Laura He, 'China is Still the Ultimate Prize That Western Banks Can't Resist', CNN, 14 January 2022, https://www.cnn.com/2022/01/14/investing/china-western-banks-mic-intl-hnk/index.html.
81. Cathy Chan et al., 'Bankers are Abandoning Hong Kong as Beijing and Covid Remake the City', Bloomberg, 6 March 2022, https://www.bloomberg.com/news/features/2022-03-06/bankers-are-abandoning-hong-kong-as-beijing-and-covid-remake-the-city#xj4y7vzkg.
82. Nicola Davis, 'Why Did China Relax Its Covid Policy – and Should We Be Worried?', *Guardian,* 29 December 2022, https://www.theguardian.com/world/2022/dec/29/why-did-china-relax-its-covid-policy-and-should-we-be-worried.
83. Cathy Chan, 'Wall Street's Biggest Banks Face a Harsh Reality Check in China', Bloomberg, 17 May 2023, https://www.bloomberg.com/news/articles/2023-05-16/wall-street-rethink-goldman-morgan-stanley-china-ambitions-in-doubt.
84. Casey Hall, 'China's International Schools Hit by Exodus of Teachers Dejected by COVID Curbs', Reuters, 20 May 2022, https://www.reuters.com/world/china/chinas-international-schools-hit-by-exodus-teachers-dejected-by-covid-curbs-2022-05-20.
85. 'World Economic Forum Annual Meeting', World Economic Forum, January 2023, https://www.weforum.org/events/world-economic-forum-annual-meeting-2023.
86. 'Lubmin: Politik-Prominenz bei Eröffnung von LNG-Terminal', NDR, 14 January 2023, https://www.ardmediathek.de/video/nordmagazin/lubmin-politik-prominenz-bei-eroeffnung-von-lng-terminal/ndr-mecklenburg-vorpommern/Y3JpZDovL25kci5kZS84NTU3NDMwOS1hZjJlLTQzYTktOTJmYi05ZjdlNTU5N2FiNGE.
87. Ibid.
88. Shruti Menon, 'Ukraine Crisis: Who is Buying Russian Oil and Gas?', BBC News, 23 May 2023, https://www.bbc.com/news/world-asia-india-60783874.
89. Tsvetana Paraskova, 'Germany Welcomes First LNG Carrier At New Wilhelmshaven Terminal', *Oil Price*, 3 January 2023, https://oilprice.com/Energy/Natural-Gas/Germany-Welcomes-First-LNG-Carrier-At-New-Wilhelmshaven-Terminal.html.
90. Edward Donnelly, 'LNG fever: European Firms Sign Mega-Contracts as US Shale Gas Imports Boom', *Investigate Europe,* 9 January 2023, https://www.investigate-europe.eu/en/2023/lng-fever-mega-contracts-shale-gas-imports-us.
91. Monica Miller, 'US – China Trade Hits Record High Despite Rising Tensions', BBC News, 8 February 2023, https://www.bbc.com/news/business-64563855.
92. Ibid.
93. 'Inside Information: Nokian Tyres plc to Sell Its Operations in Russia', Nokian Tyres Plc, 28 October 2022, https://www.nokiantyres.com/company/news-article/inside-information-nokian-tyres-plc-to-sell-its-operations-in-russia.
94. Oliver Barnes, 'Tobacco Group Philip Morris Admits It May Never Sell Its Russian Business', *Financial Times*, 22 February 2023, https://www.ft.com/content/656714b0-2e93-467b-92d6-a2d834bc0e2b.
95. Polina Ivanova and Anastasia Stognei, 'Western Groups Leaving Russia Face Obligatory Donation to Moscow', *Financial Times*, 27 March 2023, https://www.ft.com/content/77368014-1397-4a08-901d-1f996e66d627.

96. Presidential Address to Federal Assembly, President of Russia, 21 February 2023, http://en.kremlin.ru/events/president/news/70565.
97. Vladimir Isachenkov, 'Russia's Security Chief Blasts West, Dangles Nuclear Threats', Associated Press, 23 March 2023, https://apnews.com/article/medvedev-nuclear-putin-arrest-warrant-germany-ukraine-6dcde92e06f41a7c5cb7386f7939df33.
98. 'Statement on Media Reports Regarding BP's Exit from Russia', BP, 2 December 2022, https://www.bp.com/en/global/corporate/news-and-insights/press-releases/statement-on-media-reports-regarding-bps-exit-from-russia.html.
99. Patricia Nilsson and Anastasia Stognei, 'VW's Plans to Pull Out of Russia at Risk After Assets in Country are Frozen', *Financial Times*, 20 March 2023, https://www.ft.com/content/7ecb9822-d6d0-4186-9dad-4943fbde31a4.
100. Ivanova and Stognei, 'Western Groups Leaving Russia Face Obligatory Donation to Moscow'.
101. The Eagles, 'Hotel California', https://genius.com/Eagles-hotel-california-lyrics.
102. Edward White and Kana Inagaki, 'China Starts "Surgical" Retaliation Against Foreign Companies After US-led Tech Blockade', *Financial Times*, 16 April 2023, https://www.ft.com/content/fc2038d2-3e25-4a3f-b8ca-0ceb5532a1f3?shareType=nongift.
103. 'Factbox: Venezuela's Nationalizations under Chavez', Reuters, 8 October 2012, https://www.reuters.com/article/us-venezuela-election-nationalizations/factbox-venezuelas-nationalizations-under-chavez-idUSBRE89701X20121008.
104. 'China's "Men in Black" Step Up Scrutiny of Foreign Corporate Sleuths', *Financial Times*, 2 May 2023, https://www.ft.com/content/8c21b86d-66de-4c69-8c8d-a0ef270ae3e3.
105. Jamie Gaida et al., 'The Global Race for Future Power', ASPI, 2023, https://ad-aspi.s3.ap-southeast-2.amazonaws.com/2023-03/ASPIs%20Critical%20Technology%20Tracker_0.pdf?VersionId=ndm5v4DRMfpLvu.x69Bi_VUdMVLp07jw, p. 8.
106. Joe Miller, 'Volkswagen and China: The Risks of Relying on Authoritarian States', *Financial Times*, 16 March 2022, https://www.ft.com/content/7fe10b69-bc19-4aff-9b46-e0233e00c638.
107. Iris Ouyang, 'Volkswagen Aims to Fill China's Electric Car Industry Talent Void with New Academy in Hainan', *South China Morning Post*, 10 April 2023, https://www.scmp.com/business/companies/article/3216547/volkswagen-aims-fill-chinas-electric-car-industry-talent-void-new-academy-hainan; Patricia Nilsson et al., 'VW Talks to Huawei to Boost Flagging EV Presence in China', *Financial Times*, 17 May 2023, https://www.ft.com/content/aec66be2-34c7-4e07-abbb-d9dbb510b732.
108. Victoria Waldersee and Jan Schwartz, 'Volkswagen Under Fire Over Xinjiang Plant After China Chief Visit', Reuters, 28 February 2023, https://www.reuters.com/business/autos-transportation/volkswagen-china-chief-visits-xinjiang-plant-sees-no-sign-forced-labour-2023-02-28.
109. Carla Mozée, '"I Can't Get My Money Out": Billionaire Investor Mark Mobius Says China is Restricting Flows of Capital Out of the Country', *Business Insider*, 3 March 2023, https://markets.businessinsider.com/news/stocks/mark-mobius-china-investing-capital-restricting-outflows-markets-strategy-jinping-2023-3.
110. 'Lithuania's Population Increases by 54,000 Due to Ukrainian Refugee Influx', *BNS*, 16 January 2023, https://www.lrt.lt/en/news-in-english/19/

1867505/lithuania-s-population-increases-by-54-000-due-to-ukrainian-refugee-influx.

111. Ben Knight, 'Scholz Defends Decision to Send Battle Tanks to Ukraine', *DW*, 25 January 2023, https://www.dw.com/en/german-chancellor-olaf-scholz-defends-decision-to-send-battle-tanks-to-ukraine/a-64509633.
112. 'Which Countries are Supplying Tanks to Ukraine?', Al Jazeera, 25 January 2023, https://www.aljazeera.com/news/2023/1/25/which-countries-are-supplying-tanks-to-ukraine.
113. 'Sweden to Send Infantry Fighting Vehicles to Ukraine', Reuters, 19 January 2023, https://www.reuters.com/world/europe/sweden-send-infantry-fighting-vehicles-ukraine-2023-01-19.
114. Jeff Masters, '2022: Earth's 5th- or 6th-Warmest Year on Record', Yale Climate Connections, 12 January 2023, https://yaleclimateconnections.org/2023/01/2022-was-one-of-earths-six-warmest-years-on-record.
115. Kenneth Markowitz, Alex Harrison and Chris Treanor, 'COP 27: Political Progress But Transformative Climate Actions Remain Elusive', Reuters, 20 December 2022, https://www.reuters.com/legal/legalindustry/cop-27-political-progress-transformative-climate-actions-remain-elusive-2022-12-20.
116. 'China Approves Biggest Expansion in New Coal Power Plants Since 2015, Report Finds', *Guardian*, 27 February 2023, https://www.theguardian.com/world/2023/feb/27/china-approves-biggest-expansion-in-new-coal-power-plants-since-2015-report-finds.
117. 'January 2023 Global Climate Report', National Oceanic and Atmospheric Administration National Centers for Environmental Information, 2023, https://www.ncei.noaa.gov/access/monitoring/monthly-report/global/202301.
118. Jacob Poushter et al., 'Climate Change Remains Top Global Threat Across 19-Country Survey', Pew Research Center, 31 August 2022, https://www.pewresearch.org/global/2022/08/31/climate-change-remains-top-global-threat-across-19-country-survey.
119. Jason Mitchell, 'China's Stranglehold of the Rare Earths Supply Chain Will Last Another Decade', *Mining Technology*, 26 April 2022, https://www.mining-technology.com/analysis/china-rare-earths-dominance-mining.
120. Daniel J. Cordier, 'Rare Earths', US Geological Survey, January 2022, https://pubs.usgs.gov/periodicals/mcs2022/mcs2022-rare-earths.pdf.
121. Jeff Mason et al., 'United States, EU Agree to Start Talks On Critical Minerals Amid Trade Tensions', Reuters, 10 March 2023, https://www.reuters.com/markets/commodities/amid-trade-dispute-us-eu-seek-minerals-agreement-talks-subsidies-2023-03-10.
122. 'Speech by President von der Leyen on EU – China relations to the Mercator Institute for China Studies and the European Policy Centre', European Commission, 30 March 2023, https://ec.europa.eu/commission/presscorner/detail/en/speech_23_2063.
123. Suzanne Lynch, 'European Commission Signals Game Over for China Investment Deal', Politico, 6 April 2023, https://www.politico.eu/article/european-commission-ursula-von-der-leyen-signal-game-over-china-investment-deal-cai.
124. Sam Fleming et al., 'China's Envoy Warns EU of "Peril" from Following US on Trade Curbs', *Financial Times*, 30 March 2023, https://www.ft.com/content/2d7f355a-4f43-4e12-bd0b-0cac5a99aeac.

CHAPTER 15: GOODBYE GLOBALIZATION

1. Jens Stoltenberg, 'Speech by NATO Secretary General Jens Stoltenberg at the Annual Conference of the Confederation of Norwegian Enterprises', NATO, 6 January 2023, https://www.nato.int/cps/en/natohq/opinions_210445.htm.
2. Kathrin Hille, 'China Warns of Potential Conflict with US Over Containment Strategy', *Financial Times*, 7 March 2023, https://www.ft.com/content/dc3ee895-4ae9-4c1f-9dfd-49261220ef1f.
3. 'Chinese Minister Warns of Conflict Unless US Changes Course', Associated Press, 8 March 2023, https://apnews.com/article/china-congress-2023-qin-us-1938a701c0d7a2114a18226962de4879.
4. Mohamed Younis, 'Americans Continue to View China as the U.S.'s Greatest Enemy', Gallup, 6 March 2023, https://news.gallup.com/poll/471494/americans-continue-view-china-greatest-enemy.aspx.
5. Megan Brenan, 'Record-Low 15% of Americans View China Favorably', Gallup, 7 March 2023, https://news.gallup.com/poll/471551/record-low-americans-view-china-favorably.aspx?utm_source=substack&utm_medium=email.
6. Cheng Ting-Fang, 'TSMC Founder Morris Chang Says Globalization "Almost Dead" ', Nikkei Asia, 7 December 2022, https://asia.nikkei.com/Spotlight/Most-read-in-2022/TSMC-founder-Morris-Chang-says-globalization-almost-dead.
7. Kai Biermann, 'Bundesregierung will Komponenten von Huawei und ZTE verbieten', *Zeit Online*, 6 March 2023, https://www.zeit.de/politik/deutschland/2023-03/5g-ausbau-bundesregierung-verbot-huawei.
8. 'Senate Passes "Inflation Reduction Act" Reconciliation Bill', PWC, August 2022, https://www.pwc.com/us/en/services/tax/library/senate-passes-inflation-reduction-act-reconciliation-bill.html.
9. President Biden (@POTUS), Twitter, 31 January 2023, https://twitter.com/POTUS/status/1620458134773833729.
10. Petr Pavel (@prezidentpavel), Twitter, 30 January 2023, https://twitter.com/general_pavel/status/1620072512532127750.
11. Eunice Yoon (@onlyyoontv), '#China Communist Party paper warns @elonmusk against pushing #COVID19 lab leak theory. @globaltimesnews posts on social media "Elon Musk, are you breaking the pot of China?" ("Breaking the pot after eating" is Chinese "biting the hand that feeds you.")', https://mp.weixin.qq.com/s/Hi9Lu4qgPmyAx4vYeTDb6g';' Twitter, 28 February 2023, https://twitter.com/onlyyoontv/status/1630444499213357058.
12. Vidya Ramakrishnan, 'Dow Jones Pauses; Tesla's, Apple's China Exposure on Watch; What Big Investment Firms Say About 2023 Market', *Investors*, 30 November 2022, https://www.investors.com/market-trend/stock-market-today/dow-jones-pauses-what-big-investment-firms-say-about-2023-stock-market-teslas-apples-china-exposure-on-watch.
13. Emma Farge, 'U.N. body Rejects Debate on China's Treatment of Uyghur Muslims in Blow to West', Reuters, 6 October 2022, https://www.reuters.com/world/china/un-body-rejects-historic-debate-chinas-human-rights-record-2022-10-06.
14. Anna Nishino, 'Japan, U.S. to Take Aim at "Geographic Concentrations" in Chip Production', Nikkei Asia, 27 May 2023, https://asia.nikkei.com/Spotlight/Supply-Chain/Japan-U.S.-to-take-aim-at-geographic-concentrations-in-chip-production.

15. 'New Zealand: Trade Statistics', globalEDGE, https://globaledge.msu.edu/countries/new-zealand/tradestats.
16. Sankalp Phartiyal and Saritha Rai, 'Tim Cook to Open First Apple Stores in India in Pivot Beyond China', Bloomberg, 11 April 2023, https://www.bloomberg.com/news/articles/2023-04-11/cook-to-open-first-apple-stores-in-india-in-pivot-beyond-china#xj4y7vzkg.
17. Julieta Pelcastre, 'China to Increase Bolivian Lithium Extraction', *Dialogo Americas*, 17 May 2023, https://dialogo-americas.com/articles/china-to-increase-bolivian-lithium-extraction.
18. 'Bolivia's YLB Signs Lithium Agreements with Russian and Chinese Companies', *Mining Technology*, 30 June 2023, https://www.mining-technology.com/news/ylb-lithium-russian-chinese.
19. Daniel Ramos, 'Bolivia Picks Chinese Partner for $2.3 billion Lithium Projects', Reuters, 6 February 2019, https://www.reuters.com/article/us-bolivia-lithium-china/bolivia-picks-chinese-partner-for-2-3-billion-lithium-projects-idUSKCN1PV2F7.
20. Richard Martin, 'Bolivia Vies to Join Lithium Producers Club After Years of Disappointment', S&P Global Market Intelligence, 11 July 2022, https://www.spglobal.com/marketintelligence/en/news-insights/latest-news-headlines/bolivia-vies-to-join-lithium-producers-club-after-years-of-disappointment-71065165.
21. 'Factbox: Companies Respond to China's Curbs on Gallium and Germanium Exports', Reuters, 6 July 2023, https://www.reuters.com/markets/commodities/companies-respond-chinas-curbs-gallium-germanium-exports-2023-07-06.
22. 'The Potentially Large Effects of Artificial Intelligence on Economic Growth', Goldman Sachs, 26 March 2023, https://www.key4biz.it/wp-content/uploads/2023/03/Global-Economics-Analyst_-The-Potentially-Large-Effects-of-Artificial-Intelligence-on-Economic-Growth-Briggs_Kodnani.pdf, p. 1.
23. Ibid., p. 7.
24. Hardika Singh and David Uberti, '"War for Talent" at Mines Could Drive Up Cost of Energy Transition', *Wall Street Journal*, 8 June 2023, https://www.wsj.com/articles/war-for-talent-at-mines-could-drive-up-cost-of-energy-transition-30b927eb; 'So entgegnet Tesla in Deutschland dem Fachkräfte-Mangel', *Ecomento*, 9 March 2023, https://ecomento.de/2023/03/09/so-entgegnet-tesla-in-deutschland-dem-fachkraefte-mangel-bericht.
25. 'How Have Countries' Alignments Changed in the Past Five Years?', Willis Towers Watson, https://willistowerswatson.turtl.co/story/political-risk-index-winter-2022-2023-gated/page/3/9.
26. Ibid.
27. Parisa Hafezi et al., 'Iran and Saudi Arabia Agree to Resume Ties in Talks Brokered by China', Reuters, 10 March 2023, https://www.reuters.com/world/middle-east/iran-saudi-arabia-agree-resume-ties-re-open-embassies-iranian-state-media-2023-03-10.
28. Andrew England and Najmeh Bozorgmehr, 'Iran's Finance Minister Highlights Surge in Investment from Russia', *Financial Times*, 23 March 2023, https://www.ft.com/content/c43f7f85-87c3-49f6-85cb-446d1de2bfc6.
29. Antoinette Radford and Frank Gardner, 'Putin Arrest Warrant Issued Over War Crime Allegations', BBC News, 18 March 2023, https://www.bbc.com/news/world-europe-64992727.

30. 'President Xi Jinping Holds Talks with Russian President Vladimir Putin', Ministry of Foreign Affairs of the People's Republic of China, 22 March 2023, https://www.mfa.gov.cn/eng/zxxx_662805/202303/t20230322_11046184.html.
31. 'Westliche Firmen ersetzen: Putin bietet chinesischen Unternehmen Hife an', *Die Presse*, 21 March 2023, https://www.diepresse.com/6266047/westliche-firmen-ersetzen-putin-bietet-chinesischen-unternehmen-hilfe-an.
32. Stefan Boscia and Sebastian Whale, 'Stay Silent on Human Rights to Strike Deals, Gulf States Tell UK', Politico, 12 March 2023, https://www.politico.eu/article/uk-trade-deal-human-rights-uae-minister-thani-bin-ahmed-al-zeyoudi-gulf-cooperation-council.
33. Jim Pickard and George Parker, 'UK plc is Cutting Ties to China, Says CBI boss', *Financial Times*, 29 July 2022, https://www.ft.com/content/cd93dd29-7069-4e2e-baa8-7081b385c0c6.
34. 'Major Foreign Holders of United States Treasury Securities as of April 2023', Statista, https://www.statista.com/statistics/246420/major-foreign-holders-of-us-treasury-debt.
35. Ryan McMorrow et al., 'Chinese Tech Groups Suffer as Foreign Investors Take Flight', *Financial Times*, 12 June 2023, https://www.ft.com/content/7d6c3c8a-97dc-4b98-8421-f881f185661e.
36. Rosa Prince, 'Rishi Sunak Talks Tough on China – But Defense Plan May Not Satisfy Hawks', Politico, 13 March 2023, https://www.politico.eu/article/rishi-sunak-talks-tough-china-uk-defense-strategy-update-tory-hawks.
37. Elisabeth Braw, 'China is Practicing How to Sever Taiwan's Internet', *Foreign Policy*, 21 February 2023, https://foreignpolicy.com/2023/02/21/matsu-islands-internet-cables-china-taiwan.
38. 'Russia Lists World Wildlife Fund, Others as Foreign Agents', AP, 10 March 2023, https://apnews.com/article/russia-world-wildlife-fund-foreign-agents-86b8c97fd44f992264b34de3f7de949e.
39. 'Federal Minister Habeck on China', Federal Ministry for Economic Affairs and Climate Action, 24 May 2022, https://www.bmwk.de/Redaktion/EN/Pressemitteilungen/2022/05/20220524-federal-minister-habeck-on-china.html.
40. Quoted in Jeffry A. Frieden, *Global Capitalism: Its Fall and Rise in the Twentieth Century, and Its Stumbles in the Twenty-first*, New York: W. W. Norton (reissue edn), 2020, p. 189.
41. 'Share of Energy Imported from Russia 34 Per Cent of Total Energy Consumption in 2021', Statistics Finland, 31 December 2021, https://www.stat.fi/en/publication/cl1xmekvw1pp80buvn1cznxmy.
42. Jari Tanner, 'Finland Gets Floating LNG Terminal to Replace Russian Gas', Associated Press, 28 December 2022, https://apnews.com/article/politics-finland-estonia-lithuania-russia-government-0f0df06ec66a5ee7e87f0a9194328613.
43. Joanna Plucinska, 'EU to Propose New Rules, Support for Certain Green Industries – Document', Reuters, 3 March 2023, https://www.reuters.com/business/sustainable-business/eu-propose-new-rules-support-certain-green-industries-document-2023-03-03.
44. Federica di Sario, 'Commission Releases Net-Zero Industry Act', Politico, 16 March 2023, https://www.politico.eu/article/commission-releases-net-zero-industry-act.
45. 'Climate Change 2023 Synthesis Report Summary for Policymakers', Intergovernmental Panel on Climate Change, 2023, https://www.ipcc.ch/report/ar6/syr/downloads/report/IPCC_AR6_SYR_SPM.pdf.

46. Michael Götschenberg and Hoger Schmidt, 'Spuren führen in die Ukraine', *Tagesschau*, 7 March 2023, https://www.tagesschau.de/investigativ/nord-stream-explosion-101.html; 'Intelligence Suggests Pro-Ukrainian Group Sabotaged Pipelines, U.S. Officials Say', *New York Times*, 7 March 2023, https://www.nytimes.com/2023/03/07/us/politics/nord-stream-pipeline-sabotage-ukraine.html; J. Mueller-Töwe et al., 'Russian Tracks', t-online, 26 March 2023, https://www.t-online.de/nachrichten/deutschland/aussenpolitik/id_100149758/nord-stream-russia-may-have-operated-a-submarine-before-the-explosions.html?utm_source=POLITICO.EU&utm_campaign=059a5ed001-EMAIL_CAMPAIGN_2023_03_27_04_14&utm_medium=email&utm_term=0_10959edeb5-059a5ed001-%5BLIST_EMAIL_ID%5D.
47. Thomas Hale et al., 'US Businesses Shy About Attendance at China's Davos', *Financial Times*, 23 March 2023, https://www.ft.com/content/a4478d7f-3486-4ff0-b6aa-fb8d2e79ed07.
48. Jada Jones, 'TikTok Bans Explained: Everything You Need to Know', ZDNET, 9 June 2023, https://www.zdnet.com/article/tiktok-bans-explained-everything-you-need-to-know; Robert Wright and Ian Johnston, 'UK Parliament Bans TikTok from Official Devices', *Financial Times*, 23 March 2023, https://www.ft.com/content/219d7a0e-651c-42a7-a317-3b3e065ec309; Foo Yun Chee, 'European Parliament Latest EU body to Ban TikTok from Staff Phones', Reuters, 28 February 2023, https://www.reuters.com/technology/european-parliament-ban-tiktok-staff-phones-eu-official-says-2023-02-28.
49. 'Kremlin Tells Officials to Stop Using iPhones – Kommersant Newspaper', Reuters, 20 March 2023, https://www.reuters.com/world/europe/kremlin-tells-officials-stop-using-iphones-kommersant-newspaper-2023-03-20.
50. 'TikTok CEO Tells Congress: "150 million Americans Love Our App"', BBC News, 23 March 2023, https://www.bbc.com/news/av/world-us-canada-65059021.
51. Florence Bonnet et al., 'Working from Home: Estimating the Worldwide Potential', CEPR, 11 May 2020, https://cepr.org/voxeu/columns/working-home-estimating-worldwide-potential.
52. Jack Flynn, '25 Trending Remote Work Statistics [2023]: Facts, Trends, and Projections', Zippia, 13 June 2023, https://www.zippia.com/advice/remote-work-statistics/#:~:text=According%20to%20our%20research%3A,prefer%20to%20be%20fully%20remote.
53. 'Ukraine Support Tracker', Kiel Institute for the World Economy, https://www.ifw-kiel.de/topics/war-against-ukraine/ukraine-support-tracker. This includes aid pledged as part of the EU's collective packages.
54. 'Infographic – Refugees from Ukraine in the EU', European Council of the European Union, updated 21 April 2023, https://www.consilium.europa.eu/en/infographics/ukraine-refugees-eu.
55. Lili Bayer, 'NATO Skirts Final Call on Ukraine Membership, Leaving Unity-Testing Fight for Later', Politico, 9 July 2023, https://www.politico.eu/article/nato-skirts-final-call-on-ukraine-membership-leaving-unity-testing-fight-for-later.
56. 'Finland Joins NATO as 31st Ally', NATO Press release, 4 April 2023, https://www.nato.int/cps/en/natohq/news_213448.htm.
57. Anne Kauranen and Essi Lehto, 'Finland's PM Marin Concedes Defeat as Right-Wing NCP Wins Election', Reuters, 2 April 2023, https://www.reuters.com/

world/europe/finlands-marin-faces-tough-re-election-bid-national-election-2023-04-01/.

58. Lorne Cook, 'Turkey and Sweden Fail to End Their NATO Membership Standoff. Their Leaders Will Try Again on Monday', Associated Press, 6 July 2023, https://apnews.com/article/nato-membership-turkey-sweden-hungary-9bdf70de90ac0fb6e0ba1c8cc72f9f10.
59. Simon Kaminski, 'Deutliche Mehrheit der Deutschen für Wiedereinführung der Wehrpflicht', *Augsburger Allgemeine*, 9 March 2023, https://www.augsburger-allgemeine.de/politik/bundeswehr-umfrage-deutliche-mehrheit-der-deutschen-fuer-wiedereinfuehrung-der-wehrpflicht-id65790966.html.
60. Sam LaGrone, 'Pentagon: Chinese Navy to Expand to 400 Ships by 2025, Growth Focused on Surface Combatants', *USNI News*, 29 November 2022, https://news.usni.org/2022/11/29/pentagon-chinese-navy-to-expand-to-400-ships-by-2025-growth-focused-on-surface-combatants.
61. Adam Lucente, 'Iran's Membership in Shanghai Cooperation Organization Further Aligns It with Russia, China', Al-Monitor, 6 July 2023, https://www.al-monitor.com/originals/2023/07/irans-membership-shanghai-cooperation-organization-further-aligns-it-russia-china.
62. 'Last Week the Planet's Hottest on Record', Al Jazeera, 10 July 2023, https://www.aljazeera.com/news/2023/7/10/last-week-the-planets-hottest-on-record.
63. 'Russia Arrests US Journalist Evan Gershkovich on Spying Charge', BBC News, 30 March 2023, https://www.bbc.co.uk/news/world-europe-65121885.
64. 'Statement from Press Secretary Karine Jean-Pierre on Evan Gershkovich', White House, 30 March 2023, https://www.whitehouse.gov/briefing-room/statements-releases/2023/03/30/statement-from-press-secretary-karine-jean-pierre-on-evan-gershkovich.
65. Laurie Chen, 'China Approves Wide-Ranging Expansion of Counter-Espionage Law', Reuters, 26 April 2023, https://www.reuters.com/world/asia-pacific/china-passes-revised-counter-espionage-law-state-media-2023-04-26.
66. Karishma Vaswani and Lionel Lim, 'iPhone maker Foxconn to Switch to Cars as US – China Ties Sour', BBC News, 16 June 2023, https://www.bbc.com/news/business-65886658.
67. 'Zelenskiy Visits Snake Island to Mark 500 Days of Ukraine War', Reuters, 8 July 2023, https://www.reuters.com/world/europe/ukraines-zelenskiy-visits-symbolic-snake-island-mark-500-days-war-2023-07-08.
68. 'Ukraine War Reaches 500 Days, UN Laments 9,000 Civilians Killed', Al Jazeera, 8 July 2023, https://www.aljazeera.com/news/2023/7/8/more-than-9000-civilians-killed-as-ukraine-war-hits-500-days-un.
69. 'NATO Secretary General Welcomes Türkiye's Decision to Forward Sweden Accession Protocols to Parliament', NATO, 10 July 2023, https://www.nato.int/cps/en/natohq/news_217015.htm.
70. 'G7 Joint Declaration of Support for Ukraine: 12 July 2023', UK Government Prime Minister's Office, https://assets.publishing.service.gov.uk/government/uploads/system/uploads/attachment_data/file/1169579/Joint_Declaration_of_Support_for_Ukraine.pdf.
71. Sabine Siebold et al., 'NATO Summit Declaration Says "Ukraine's Future is in NATO"', Reuters, 11 July 2023, https://www.reuters.com/world/europe/nato-summit-declaration-says-ukraines-future-is-nato-2023-07-11.

72. 'Intelligence and Security Committee of Parliament: China', Intelligence and Security Committee of Parliament, 13 July 2023, https://isc.independent.gov.uk/wp-content/uploads/2023/07/ISC-China.pdf, pp. 2–3.
73. 'Philippines Allows Barbie Film With Blurred South China Sea Map', Al Jazeera, 12 July 2023, https://www.aljazeera.com/news/2023/7/12/philippines-allows-barbie-film-with-blurred-south-china-sea-map; Alexander Smith, 'Did "Barbie" Cross the Line? How a "Child-Like" Map Stirred a South China Sea Dispute', NBC News, 7 July 2023, https://www.nbcnews.com/news/world/warner-bros-defends-barbie-banned-vietnam-south-china-sea-map-rcna93013.
74. 'Federal Government Strategy on China', Die Bundesregierung, 13 July 2023, https://www.auswaertiges-amt.de/blob/2608580/317313df4795e104f1ea3263d41860d8/china-strategie-en-data.pdf, pp. 5–6.
75. Ibid., p. 4.
76. Yuchen Li in Taipei and Wesley Rahn, 'Germany's New China Strategy: What Beijing Thinks', *DW*, 14 July 2023, https://www.dw.com/en/germanys-new-china-strategy-what-beijing-thinks/a-66236415.
77. Henning Peitsmeier, 'Mehr Erlangen, weniger Chengdu', *Frankfurter Allgemeine Zeitung*, 13 July 2023, https://www.faz.net/aktuell/wirtschaft/unternehmen/siemens-investiert-eine-milliarde-euro-in-deutschland-weniger-china-19031509.html.
78. 'China Blasts US for Forcing It to Accept South China Sea Ruling', Reuters, 12 July 2023, https://www.reuters.com/world/asia-pacific/china-says-it-does-not-accept-philippines-2016-south-china-sea-arbitration-win-2023-07-12.
79. Alexander Marquardt, 'Vladimir Putin: Prime Minister, Action Man, Crooner', ABC News, 13 December 2010, https://abcnews.go.com/International/vladimir-putin-sings-blueberry-hill-charity/story?id=12381482; 'Vladimir Putin Sings "Blueberry Hill"', Channel 4 News, 11 December 2010, https://www.youtube.com/watch?v=TbkGkr0iceI.

BIBLIOGRAPHICAL ESSAY

The retreat of post-Cold War globalization is history in the making. Future historians, economists and sociologists will have an extraordinarily rich field from which to select research topics.

While this round of globalization has been the most intense yet, it was preceded by other rounds, though none of them were as comprehensive as this round. Sven Beckert's *Empire of Cotton: A Global History* (London: Vintage, 2015) chronicles the commodity's remarkable global expansion, a process that involved ingenious arrangements that allowed cotton to be efficiently picked, shipped, processed and woven long before the arrival of the telephone. Jonathan Fenby's *The Penguin History of Modern China: The Fall and Rise of a Great Power, 1850 to the Present* (London: Penguin, 2019) is a classic that unsurprisingly also covers pre-Communist China's lively participation in globe-spanning trade.

Time and again, globe-spanning commerce has been undone by war. Geoffrey Parker's *Global Crisis: War, Climate Change and Catastrophe in the Seventeenth Century* (New Haven and London: Yale University Press, 2013) is an extraordinarily comprehensive account of such a period. The post-World War II world's lasting achievement has been to make war unacceptable in a great many countries – countries that had spent centuries fighting wars against each other, in one combination or another. Yes, there have been post-World War II conflicts conducted by democratic, industrialized powers (including Vietnam, Iraq and Afghanistan), but they remain highly controversial. And even though the Cold War featured a massive and tense military standoff between NATO and the Warsaw Pact, citizens of Western Europe and other Western countries could live and conduct commerce in the knowledge that their countries would never go to war against one another. Oona Hathaway and Scott Shapiro's *The Internationalists: How a Radical Plan to Outlaw War Remade the World* (New York: Simon & Schuster, 2017) chronicles the plan that helped make war unacceptable among self-respecting nations – at least in theory.

It's remarkable how little the wars in Iraq and Afghanistan affected post-Cold War globalization. One might, in fact, argue that the main way in which these two wars launched by the United States manifested themselves in the West was through large migrant waves to Europe. The two wars remain a crucial and often painful memory of war in our time. George Packer's *The Assassins' Gate: America in Iraq* (New York: Weidenfeld & Nicolson, 2013) is a tour de force of reporting, and Michael Hastings' *The Operators* (New York: Penguin, 2011) – which focuses on General Stanley McChrystal – provides an inside perspective of the war in Afghanistan. Stefano Pontecorvo, an Italian diplomat who served as NATO's top civilian in Afghanistan until the end of the chaotic evacuation in August 2021, gives a vivid account of the evacuation – and the dysfunction of the Afghan government – in *L'ultimo aereo da Kabul* (Milan: Piemme, 2022). (Reading the book in Italian – it hasn't been translated into English – was a good way for me to improve my knowledge of Italian *passato remoto* verb forms.)

The early, turbulent post-Cold War years in Europe are beautifully chronicled, from completely different perspectives, by Geert Mak and David Remnick. Mak's travelogue *In Europe: Travels Through the Twentieth Century* (trans. Sam Garrett, London: Vintage, 2008) has become a classic, and Remnick's *Resurrection: The Struggle for a New Russia* (London: Vintage, 1998) offers masterful reporting on nineties Russia. Remnick's book is also a reflection of the hopefulness of those years, with the author concluding that Russia had made peace with its role in the world. In *The Revenge of Geography: What the Map Tells Us about Coming Conflicts and the Battle Against Fate* (London: Random House, 2012), Robert Kaplan brings a contrasting – what some might call pessimistic – perspective.

Shipping is perhaps the most fundamentally globalized part of globalization, but because it's out of sight, it's also out of mind. That's a pity, because every consumer – that is, every one of us – should understand the extremely complex and often dangerous maritime operations that get us the goods we need for our daily lives. Without shipping, there would be no globalization. Even as the world moves away from globalization and towards regionalization, we'll continue to require legions of seafarers on countless merchant vessels. Rose George's *Deep Sea and Foreign Going: Inside Shipping, the Invisible Industry that Brings You 90% of Everything* (London: Granta, 2014) is a gripping in-depth account that sees George accompany seafarers as they steward all manner of goods with skill and bravery. In *The Outlaw Ocean: Crime and Survival in the Last Untamed Frontier* (Oxford: Bodley Head, 2019), Ian Urbina reports about an equally borderless business: fishing. John Darwin's *Unlocking the World: Port Cities and Globalization in the Age of Steam, 1830–1930* (London: Allen Lane, 2020) offers a more academic account of the rise of port cities – many of which owe their lasting prominence to shipping.

Goodbye Globalization is a first-hand account of events that are in large part taking place in front of us, which means I have consulted an enormous amount of news reporting – a sometimes exasperating exercise since events have taken new twists and turns on a daily basis. There have been books suggesting the world ought to deglobalize, which is rather different from it happening. In *Zivilisiert den Kapitalismus: Grenzen der Freiheit* (Civilize Capitalism: Limits of Freedom; Rheda Wiedenbrück: Bertelsmann-Club, 1998), Marion Dönhoff delivers a powerful plea for a gentler capitalism, and perhaps gentler capitalism could have been the answer – had geopolitics not begun rearing its head again. I look forward to seeing future books about the rise and fall of globalization from a Russian or Chinese perspective. My favourite account so far of post-Cold War globalization is Jeffry Frieden's *Global Capitalism* (New York: W. W. Norton (reissue edn), 2020).

But even though Frieden anticipated some of the tensions now appearing, globalization has tumbled much more dramatically than seemed possible even when *Global Capitalism* was published in 2020.

The best literary guides to today's global turbulence are, though, to be found in history. As Jim Mattis, the legendary Marine Corps general, points out in *Call Sign Chaos* (New York: Random House, 2019), 'history lights the often dark path ahead; even if it's a dim light, it's better than none'. No writer has portrayed the delights of a free and prosperous country, and its sudden tumbling into war, better than Stefan Zweig in his moving *Die Welt von gestern* (The World of Yesterday; Frankfurt am Main: Bermann-Fischer, 1942). The Austrian novelist describes the well-ordered life in Austria, where everyone goes about his or her life in a preordained sort of way, and where people are by and large content. They are, in fact, so content that they don't realize how fragile their society – and indeed the coexistence of countries – is. When they do, it's too late. That's not to say that a new world war is imminent, or even likely. But history does indeed light the path ahead, even if it's a dim light.

INDEX